OXFORD READINGS

DEMONSTR

Also published in this series

The Concept of Evidence, edited by Peter Achinstein
The Philosophy of Artificial Intelligence, edited by Margaret A. Boden
Perceptual Knowledge, edited by Jonathan Dancy
The Philosophy of Law, edited by Ronald M. Dworkin
Theories of Ethics, edited by Philippa Foot
The Philosophy of History, edited by Patrick Gardiner
The Philosophy of Mind, edited by Jonathan Glover
Scientific Revolutions, edited by Ian Hacking
Hegel, edited by Michael Inwood
The Philosophy of Linguistics, edited by Jerrold J. Katz
Reference and Modality, edited by Leonard Linsky
The Philosophy of Religion, edited by Basil Mitchell
The Concept of God, edited by Thomas V. Morris
A Priori Knowledge, edited by Paul K. Moser
The Theory of Meaning, edited by G. H. R. Parkinson
The Philosophy of Education, edited by R. S. Peters
Political Philosophy, edited by Anthony Quinton
Practical Reasoning, edited by Joseph Raz
The Philosophy of Social Explanation, edited by Alan Ryan
Propositions and Attitudes, edited by Nathan Salmon and Scott Soames
Consequentialism and its Critics, edited by Samuel Scheffler
The Philosophy of Language, edited by J. R. Searle
Semantic Syntax, edited by Pieter A. M. Seuren
Applied Ethics, edited by Peter Singer
Philosophical Logic, edited by P. F. Strawson
Locke on Human Understanding, edited by I. C. Tipton
Free Will, edited by Gary Watson
The Philosophy of Action, edited by Alan R. White
Liebniz: Metaphysics and Philosophy of Science,
edited by R. S. Woolhouse

Other volumes are in preparation

DEMONSTRATIVES

edited by

PALLE YOURGRAU

OXFORD UNIVERSITY PRESS
1990

Oxford University Press, Walton Street, Oxford OX2 6DP

Oxford New York Toronto
Delhi Bombay Calcutta Madras Karachi
Petaling Jaya Singapore Hong Kong Tokyo
Nairobi Dar es Salaam Cape Town
Melbourne Auckland
and associated companies in
Berlin Ibadan

Oxford is a trade mark of Oxford University Press

Published in the United States
by Oxford University Press, New York

British Library Cataloguing in Publication Data
Yourgrau, Palle
Demonstratives.—(Oxford readings in philosophy).
1. Philosophy of language
I. Title
401
ISBN 0–19–824869–5
ISBN 0–19–824868–7 (pbk)

Library of Congress Cataloging in Publication Data
Demonstratives / edited by Palle Yourgrau.
p. cm.—(Oxford readings in philosophy)
Includes bibliographical references.
1. Language and logic. 2. Metaphysics. 3. Languages—Philosophy.
I. Yougrau, Palle. II. Series.
BC37.D42 1990 160–dc20 89–27448
ISBN 0–19–824869–5
ISBN 0–19–824868–7 (pbk.)

Set by Cambrian Typesetters, Frimley, Surrey
Printed in Great Britain by Biddles Ltd, Guildford and King's Lynn

CONTENTS

Introduction
by Palle Yourgrau   1

PART I FREGE AND DEMONSTRATIVES

1. Dthat
   David Kaplan   11

2. Thoughts on Demonstratives
   David Kaplan   34

3. Frege on Demonstratives
   John Perry   50

4. Understanding Demonstratives
   Gareth Evans   71

5. The Path Back to Frege
   Palle Yourgrau   97

PART II THE FIRST PERSON

6. The First Person
   G. E. M. Anscombe   135

7. Descartes's *Cogito*
   Jerrold J. Katz   154

PART III THOUGHT AND TOUCH

8. Thought and Touch: A Note on Aristotle's *De Anima*
   Stanley Rosen   185

9. Mathematical Intuition
   Charles Parsons   195

10. Form and Content
    Michael Friedman   215

PART IV REALITY AND THE PRESENT

11. Omniscience and Immutability
    Norman Kretzmann   235

12. Time, Reality, and Relativity
   Lawrence Sklar   247

13. A Remark about the Relationship between Relativity Theory
   and Idealistic Philosophy
   Kurt Gödel   261

   Notes on the Contributors   267

   Select Bibliography   269

   Index   273

INTRODUCTION

PALLE YOURGRAU

When I use 'I' I refer to myself, while when you use the very same term, you pick out someone else. This phenomenon of context-sensitivity, or *indexicality*, is common to all so-called demonstratives, not just 'I' but also 'now', 'this', 'here', and (more controversially) 'actual'. Clearly, for example, 'now', said at noon, refers to noon, said at midnight, to midnight. This feature of demonstratives stands in sharp contrast to descriptive phrases, such as 'the author of *The Odyssey*', which refers to Homer, no matter who utters it. Proper names, in turn, like 'Homer', have seemed to many to resemble more closely descriptive phrases in not being slavishly dependent on their context of use to determine a unique referent. Beyond the context-dependence of demonstratives, however, we can also recognize a feature these terms seem to share with proper names, rather then with definite descriptions, namely their apparent *lack of descriptive content*. To refer to myself as 'I' seems no more to describe myself than when I call myself by my own name. Further, demonstratives seem to presuppose or imply a more *direct* or *immediate association* with their referents than do descriptions. You have to be here, in New York, for example, to refer to New York as 'here', to be current, to refer to the present time as 'now', and to be me, to pick out me as 'I'.

Given this characterization of demonstratives, with their distinctive context-sensitivity, lack of descriptive content, and cognitive–situational immediacy, why should philosophers with no professional interest in the semantic be concerned with such peculiar referential devices? The answer is that for various demonstratives the correct analysis of their use raises issues at the very centre of the traditional concerns of philosophy. The correct account of 'I', for example, should shed light on the cogency of the *cogito*, and hence illuminate such issues as the Cartesian conception of the self, of self-knowledge, and, indeed, of knowledge in general. Similarly, a proper account of the elusive term, 'now', should help determine whether each 'now' marks a moment in the passage of time, or whether the latter is a mere illusion. And, in the case of 'actual', there is a curious tension

I wish to thank Jerrold Katz for his excellent comments on an earlier version of this Introduction.

between the reasonable inclination to take 'the actual world' as a non-relative specification of the unique possible world that in fact obtains, and the embarrassing difficulty one has in defending such 'modal chauvinism' against those, like David Lewis, who maintain the indexicality of actuality, i.e. the doctrine that each possible world is merely actual *relative* to itself. Further, the truth about 'actual' may well help shed some light on the so-called 'many-worlds' interpretation of quantum-mechanics. Clearly, then, the phenomenon of indexicality is by no means only a matter for linguistics and the philosophy of language, but raises fundamental questions about the perennial philosophy, from ontology to epistemology to philosophy of mind.

The present collection of essays, then, though it contains an extended section on Frege and Demonstrative Reference, is not semantic in focus, but attempts, rather, to acquaint the reader with the full richness of the phenomenon of indexicality, which, in the end, concerns the most general features of Perspective and Reality. It has been my intention, in selecting these essays, to turn our attention 'back to the phenomena', and to show, by example, the surprising, and even dramatic, consequences for our world-view that follow from the attitude we adopt towards the various indexical devices our language presents us with. Do demonstratives, one wants to know, represent the shortest distance between thought and object, or is this impression itself the product of a distorted point of view? Do these terms offer a perspective on reality denied to purely descriptive devices, which seem, in turn, not to point to the world from the privileged position of some singular vantage point, but rather to offer a view *sub specie aeternitatis*? To go further still, do they represent not just a special view of reality, but a special reality?

Consider first the innocent-seeming demonstrative, 'now'. Does it really contain the clue to the phenomenon of time, which eluded Parmenides and amazed Plato? Is not time rather a matter for Einstein and physics than for Frege and semantics? The great logician, Kurt Gödel, for one, seems to have found these issues inseparable, for when offering 'A Remark about the Relationship between Relativity Theory and Idealistic Philosophy' (see Chapter 13), he says succinctly that: 'The existence of an objective lapse of time, however, means (or, at least, is equivalent to the fact) that reality consists of an infinity of layers of "the now" which come into existence successively.'[1] He goes on to argue,

---

[1] For philosophical discussion of Gödel's enigmatic paper see H. Stein, 'On the Paradoxical Time-Structures of Kurt Gödel', *Philosophy of Science*, 37 (1970), 589–601, and P. Yourgrau, 'The Universe and Kurt Gödel' (unpublished). For a more formal treatment see D. Malament, ' "Time-Travel" in the Gödel Universe', *Proceedings of the Philosophy of Science Association*, 2 (1984), 91–100.

however, that the objectivity of the perspective of 'the now' has already been shown by Einstein's Special Theory of Relativity, which establishes the relativity of simultaneity and hence of 'the now', to be an illusion. For good measure, Gödel goes on to employ General Relativity to construct new cosmological models in which there could occur 'temporal loops' permitting 'time-travel', establishing, even more dramatically, by Gödel's account, that the existence of an objective succession of times is, as Parmenides and Kant suspected, merely 'ideal'. This account of Gödel's, denying as it does any ontological privilege to the present, to what is happening *now*, is, of course, only as sound as its use of the Theory of Relativity, but Lawrence Sklar, in his essay included in this volume as Chapter 12, 'Time, Reality, and Relativity', argues that the special status of the present cannot be so straightforwardly dismissed in Special Relativity, due to the fact that this theory itself, for Sklar, depends on epistemological assumptions about 'the given' that, if unchecked, would lead to a verificationist slide with no easy stopping-place; and Sklar finds no easy or natural way to check this epistemological slide.

One might feel uneasy, in any case, in basing one's metaphysical pronouncements about 'the now', in defence of Kant and Parmenides, on what is after all an empirical theory, like Relativity. Elsewhere, indeed, D. H. Mellor, in *Real Time*,[2] has anchored his own critique of 'the now' (which he, unlike Gödel, sees as irrelevant to 'real' time) on the *semantic* account of demonstratives like 'now' offered by John Perry, in 'Frege on Demonstratives'. The latter appears as Chapter 3 in this volume, and will be addressed shortly. For now, we can ask what the consequences are if we take for granted that what is now happening does enjoy an ontological privilege over what has already faded into the past. Norman Kretzmann, in 'Omniscience and Immutability', Chapter 11 in this volume and our final contribution on 'the now', takes seriously the absence of any distinction to the present from the point of view of a divine consciousness, which, to many Christian theologians, has seemed to represent, and only to represent, the immutable perspective of eternity. Concluding, then, that God cannot, literally, tell what time it is *now*, Kretzmann notes the inconsistency this gives rise to, assuming God's omniscience.[3] Lest one conclude too hastily, however, that this is a problem inherent in the very idea of God, it should be pointed out that from another theological point of view, that of Aristotle, in Book 12 of the *Metaphysics*, Kretzmann's

[2] Cambridge, 1981.
[3] Kretzmann has since revised his position. See his 'Eternity' (with Eleanor Stump), *Journal of Philosophy*, 78: 8 (Aug. 1981), 429–58, repr. in T. V. Morris (ed.), *The Concept of God*, Oxford Readings in Philosophy (Oxford, 1987), where he argues that God's 'eternity' is not incompatible with his having a relationship with the world of time.

problem would hardly arise, since the 'Unmoved Mover' is represented as all-knowing only of what is most worthy of knowing—the eternal verities—and, in fact, as taking notice of human-being not at all. In fact, it was a characteristic of Plato's and Aristotle's philosophies to see the human point of view, and not the divine, as the bridge between the temporal and the eternal.

What is necessary, then, is to be able to find our position in nature, to place ourselves in the scheme of things. In thus asking one of the oldest of philosophical questions, 'Who am I?', one finds oneself once again employing a 'demonstrative', 'I', in this case the one that puts me into contact with myself. The question of the importance of the view 'from here', i.e. of the world as I see it, has been investigated recently by Colin McGinn, in *The Subjective View*,[4] while the relationship of such a conception of the world to the neutral, 'objective', conception—*The View From Nowhere*[5]—is treated at length in Thomas Nagel's new study. Once again, however, the question arises whether the crucial demonstrative, here, 'I', is, as Descartes believed, a potential source of deep metaphysical insights, or whether its 'grammatical' peculiarities are a mere invitation to ontological invention. In her contribution to this collection, 'The First Person', Chapter 6, G. E. M. Anscombe offers a deflationary view of the Cartesian 'I'. Casting a sober, semantical, eye on the allures of the first person, Anscombe concludes that Descartes has been insufficiently attentive to the actual linguistic context in which this seemingly referential device finds its natural home. Noting that 'I' seems to be guaranteed a reference, and that it appears immune from somehow picking out the 'wrong' object, Anscombe concludes, following a line of reasoning familiar from Wittgenstein, that if one can't get it wrong here, then one also can't get it right, and so, appearances notwithstanding, 'I' turns out not to be a referring term at all. Jerrold Katz, however, though agreeing with Anscombe to adopt a purely semantical point of view, reaches entirely different conclusions in his contribution on 'Descartes's *Cogito*'[6] in Chapter 7. By his lights, the *cogito* represents a far-reaching semantic insight. What is necessary, however, according to Katz, in order to appreciate this insight, is to broaden our own logico-semantic horizons, so that we do not mistake a genuine intuition of Descartes's, that is struggling for the appropriate semantic realization, for a mere inability of Descartes to recognize the limitations of the vernacular. If Katz is right,

---

[4] Oxford, 1983.
[5] New York, 1986.
[6] Katz's chapter is drawn from his full-length study of the *cogito*, *Cogitations* (New York, 1986).

Descartes has something to teach us, not just about 'I', but also about our ability to 'grasp' ourselves, in thought.

What is it, however, to 'grasp' an object 'intellectually'? Does the mind always impose a general, descriptive, condition that reality may, once and for all, either satisfy or fail to, or can thought really reach out like a hand, as demonstratives would suggest, and 'touch reality'? In his selection, 'Thought and Touch: A Note on Aristotle's *De Anima*', Chapter 8, Stanley Rosen offers some (Platonic) reflections on Aristotle's account of how the mind gets its most immediate contact with reality.[7] According to Rosen, Aristotle's preoccupation with the metaphor of touch led him astray, and, in particular, gave rise to grave problems in regard to self-knowledge (the hand cannot grasp itself). More impressed with Plato's image of sight (a kind of intellectual action-at-a-distance which does not impose its own form upon its object), Rosen is suspicious both of Aristotle's identification of thought with its object and with Descartes's optimism about the mind's transparency to itself. The question, indeed, whether the degree of intimacy reflects the strength of the mind's knowledge of its objects, continues in our own century to disturb the most systematic thinkers. Does acquaintance (to use the term Bertrand Russell introduced) offer the most direct and complete knowledge between mind and object, or, rather, does such a view represent a mere confusion between experience, or 'enjoyment', and the structured account of a complex whole that is required of genuine knowledge? In his distinguished philosophical career, Moritz Schlick, caught at the crossroads between Einstein, Russell, and Wittgenstein, found himself torn between these extreme positions. Michael Friedman, in his selection, 'Form and Content',[8] Chapter 10, traces the dialectic, with which Schlick struggled but failed to resolve, between the doctrines of knowledge as mathematical–structural, as in the paradigm of theoretical physics, and the contrary paradigm of the immediacy of the given of first-person experience.

The richness of the 'dialectic' that Friedman has uncovered, however, has become increasingly attenuated as this century has progressed, since one side, the doctrine of 'acquaintance', has, since its heyday with Russell, suffered a considerable decline, so that, even in as serious and perceptive a study as Mark Sainsbury's *Bertrand Russell*,[9] the very idea of acquaintance is dismissed with a minimum of ceremony. One of the few thinkers to persist in maintaining the existence, and importance, of a kind

[7] For more of his Platonic reflections on this theme, see Rosen's collection of essays, *The Quarrel Between Philosophy and Poetry* (New York, 1988), from which the present chapter is reproduced.
[8] I have taken the liberty of so renaming Friedman's 'Critical Notice: Moritz Schlick, *Philosophical Papers*', in the present volume. [9] London, 1979.

of non-descriptive, quasi-perceptive, mode of access to reality was in fact Gödel, who combined his Platonism with a doctrine of 'intellectual intuition' of mathematical form. Charles Parsons, in his contribution to this volume on 'Mathematical Intuition', Chapter 9, has provided an elaborate analysis and defence of the kind of doctrine that Gödel seems to have been recommending, though from a perspective more Kantian than Platonic.[10]

This doctrine of a special 'intuition' which would enable us to gain insight into mathematical reality would appear to have been precisely what Frege, though as much a 'Platonist' as Gödel, was trying to avoid in his own logic and mathematical epistemology (leaving aside the question of geometry). Indeed, one of the goals of Frege's logistic 'reduction' of arithmetic to logic was to cut through Kant's epistemological difficulties and still maintain the existence of mathematical objects, which, reinterpreted now as purely logical in nature, required, for their intellectual apprehension, no other 'faculty' than the logical (whatever that may turn out to be). In developing a logico-semantic framework in which to think about numbers, moreover, Frege felt he had come up with a *Begriffsschrift* that was so powerful, and so universal in scope, that it could serve as the appropriate vehicle for all 'scientific', i.e. objective, investigation of reality, whether mathematical or otherwise. The 'semantic' theory this developed into (more strictly a theory of pure *thought* than one of *language*), was organized around the basic notion of truth, of which logic was supposed to provide the basic 'laws' (of truth-preservation, in inference), and of the basic vehicle of truth, which he called: *the thought*. Here Frege made a powerful 'transcendental' assumption, in the spirit of Kant. Just as Kant had asserted, in *The Groundwork of the Metaphysics of Morals*, that if ethics is not to be a mere illusion, something must be capable of being literally good, good in itself, without qualification (namely, the will), Frege assumed, as he made fully explicit in 'The Thought', that logic, and indeed rational thought as such, requires a truth-bearer that can be literally true, true in itself, and so true without qualification in terms of context ('here', 'now', 'for me', etc.). Thoughts that might, on the surface, appear to be contextually dependent in their

---

[10] Parsons extends, and modifies, his position in 'Intuition in Constructive Mathematics', in J. Butterfield (ed.), *Language, Mind and Logic* (Cambridge, 1986), 211–29. For a discussion of Gödel's crucial passages on intuition from a Wittgensteinian perspective, see W. Tait, 'Truth and Proof: The Platonism of Mathematics', *Synthèse*, 69 (1986), 341–70. Indeed, Gödel and Wittgenstein would seem to offer 2 very different perspectives on the correct analysis of intuition and (mathematical) reality. Hao Wang has contrasted these 2 points of view in various places in his writings on Gödel, but most succinctly and explicitly in 'Gödel and Wittgenstein', *Logic, Philosophy of Science, and Epistemology*, Proceedings of the 11th International Wittgenstein Symposium, Aug. 1986 (Vienna, 1987), 83–90.

truth-values are, for Frege, merely the result of incomplete specifications of what are in reality complete thoughts.

Frege's basic semantic framework, then, would seem to be constitutionally incapable of recognizing demonstratives—whose very essence resides in their context-sensitivity—as more than semantic epiphenomena. This is either good news or bad, depending on how seriously one takes demonstratives. David Kaplan, who takes demonstratives very seriously indeed, has argued, in a series of influential writings, that these referential devices demand a semantical framework alternative to the Fregean.[11] In his first contribution 'Dthat', which appears as Chapter 1, he argues that semantics has need, in addition to descriptive, Fregean thoughts, of Russellian, 'singular' thoughts (which incorporate the referent itself, and not just a conceptual representative). Kaplan draws an analogy between (*a*) non-descriptive demonstratives and (*b*) proper names and definite descriptions, in their 'referential' use (as this has been defined by Keith Donnellan), and introduces, for good measure, an artificially constructed operator, 'dthat', to make certain that something does indeed function, if only by stipulation, *vis-à-vis* singular thought, the way he has urged (by description) demonstratives already do. In his second contribution, 'Thoughts on Demonstratives', he traces out some crucial logical and epistemological consequences of his new approach.

John Perry goes even further than Kaplan in his critique of Frege and urges, in his contribution, 'Frege on Demonstratives', in Chapter 3, that Frege demands too much from his notion of 'sense'—that the variety of tasks required of Fregean sense simply cannot all be satisfied by a single theoretical device. In the course of his study Perry develops further a theme introduced by Kaplan (especially in 'Demonstratives') that one should not conflate epistemological issues with the pure semantical analysis of demonstratives. Indeed, the themes addressed earlier in this Introduction, concerning the cognitive modalities of intuition and acquaintance, are dramatically and deliberately absent from Kaplan's and Perry's semantics; Kaplan, after taking pains to reintroduce 'Russellian', singular thought in 'Demonstratives', takes equal pains to upbraid Russell for introducing (what is for Kaplan) the semantically irrelevant doctrine of acquaintance.

Frege has not only met with detractors, however, and in his contribution to the present volume, 'Understanding Demonstratives', Chapter 4,

---

[11] For his fullest statement, see his MS, 'Demonstratives', Draft 2 (UCLA, 1977), long an unpublished classic, now in J. Almog, *et al.* (eds.), *Themes from Kaplan* (New York, 1989) 481–563. Another seminal thinker here is H.-N. Castañeda. See e.g. his ' "He": A Study in the Logic of Self-Consciousness', *Ratio*, 8 (1966), 130–57.

Gareth Evans mounts a vigorous defence of Frege's account of demonstrative reference. In the course of investigating the 'cognitive dynamics' of keeping track of an object over time, Evans argues both that Perry's own account of demonstratives is internally unstable and that Frege's semantic machinery has been so well designed that it is already well suited to take on the problem of demonstratives. In my own contribution to this collection, 'The Path Back to Frege',[12] Chapter 5, though agreeing that the force of Frege's insights has been seriously underestimated, I have argued, as against Evans, that demonstratives do bring to light an ingredient missing from Frege's semantics even on its own terms. I have urged, however, that this missing ingredient—a non-descriptive mode of 'cognitive access'—can be smoothly integrated into the rest of Frege's theory when this is seen in the proper light, and that it also offers the best hope both of supporting Gödel's suspicions about mathematical intuition and of confuting his doubts concerning our intuition of the passage of time.

Demonstratives, then, as I hope even this brief sketch has made apparent, offer a bracing challenge to philosophers of every stripe, Fregeans and non-Fregeans, inflationists and deflationists, those influenced by Wittgenstein and those more strongly affected by Gödel. Windows on to reality, or mere painted glass, these little words repay richly the attention of systematic investigation. The reader who finds the time to contemplate them will discover here rich and disturbing implications.

[12] I have responded more directly to the Kaplan–Perry critique of Frege, in 'Frege, Perry, and Demonstratives', *Canadian Journal of Philosophy* (1982), 725–52.

PART I

FREGE AND DEMONSTRATIVES

1

DTHAT

DAVID KAPLAN

Donnellan, in 'Reference and Definite Descriptions' says, 'Using a definite description referentially a speaker may say something true even though the description correctly applies to nothing.'[1] His example—taken from Linsky[2]—has someone saying of a spinster:

Her husband is kind to her.

after having had Mr Jones—actually the spinster's brother—misintroduced as the spinster's husband. And—to fill it out—having noticed Jones's solicitous attention to his sister. The speaker used the non-denoting description 'Her husband' to refer to Mr Jones. And so, what he said was true.

There are a lot of entities associated with the utterance of 'Her husband is kind to her' which are commonly said to have been said: tokens, types, sentences, propositions, statements, etc. The something-true-said, Donnellan calls a *statement*.

This chapter appeared originally in its present form in P. Cole (ed.), *Syntax and Semantics* (New York: Academic Press, 1978), ix. 221–43, with the following warning: 'This paper was prepared for and read at the 1970 Stanford Workshop on Grammar and Semantics. Peter Cole has persuaded me—against my better judgement—that it has aged long enough to be digestible. The paper has not been revised other than to remove the subtitle comment "[Stream of Consciousness Draft: Errors, confusions, and disorganizations are not to be taken seriously]." ' That injunction must still be strictly obeyed. Some parts of this ramble are straightened out in the excessive refinements of "Bob and Carol and Ted and Alice" which appeared in the proceedings for which this was destined: J. Hintikka, J. Moravcsik, and P. Suppes (eds.), *Approaches to Natural Language* (Dordrecht, 1973). A more direct presentation of the resulting theory along with some of its applications is to be found in "Demonstratives" (mimeo, Los Angeles: Dept. of Philosophy, 1977). An intermediate progress report occurs in "On the Logic of Demonstratives", *The Journal of Philosophical Logic*, 8 (1979), 81–98; reprinted in N. Salmon and S. Soames (eds.), *Propositions and Attitudes* (New York: Oxford University Press, 1988).
'DTHAT' is pronounced as a single syllable.'

[1] K. S. Donnellan, 'Reference and Definite Descriptions', *Philosophical Review*, 75 (1966), 298.
[2] L. Linksy, 'Reference and Referents', in C. Caton (ed.), *Philosophy and Ordinary Language* (Urbana, 1963).

On the other hand, 'If . . . the speaker has just met the lady and, noticing her cheerfulness and radiant good health, made his remark from his conviction that these attributes are always the result of having good husbands, he would be using the definite description attributively.'[3]

After pointing out that 'in general, whether or not a definite description is used referentially or attributively is a function of the speaker's intentions in a particular case',[4] he mentions that according to Russell's theory of descriptions, the use of *the* φ might be thought of as involving reference 'in a very weak sense . . . to *whatever* is the one and only one φ, if there is any such'.[5] Donnellan then concludes:

Now this is something we might well say about the attributive use of definite descriptions . . . But this lack of particularity is absent from the referential use of definite descriptions precisely because the description is here merely a device for getting one's audience to pick out or think of the thing to be spoken about, a device which may serve its function even if the description is incorrect. More importantly, perhaps, in the referential use as opposed to the attributive, there is a right thing to be picked out by the audience, and its being the right thing is not simply a function of its fitting the description.[6]

Donnellan develops his theory by adducing a series of quite plausible examples to help him answer certain theoretical questions, e.g. are there sentences in which the contained definite description can only be used referentially (or only attributively)?, can reference fail when a definite description is used referentially?, etc.

In my own reading and rereading of Donnellan's article I always find it both fascinating and maddening. Fascinating, because the fundamental distinction so clearly reflects an accurate insight into language use, and maddening, because, first, the examples seem to me to alternate between at least two clearly discriminable concepts of *referential use*; second, the notion of *having someone in mind* is not analysed but used; and third, the connections with the developed body of knowledge concerning intensional logics—their syntax and semantics—are not explicitly made, so we cannot immediately see what Donnellan and intensional logic have to offer each other, if anything.

As one of the body developers, I find this last snub especially inexcusable. This is not a divergent perception for those of my ilk. Hintikka remarks (plaintively?), 'The only thing I miss in Donnellan's excellent paper is a clear realization that the distinction he is talking about is only operative in contexts governed by propositional attitudes or other modal terms.'[7]

---

[3] Donnellan, 'Reference and Definite Descriptions', p. 299.
[4] Ibid. 297.   [5] Ibid. 303.   [6] Ibid.
[7] J. Hintikka, 'Individual, Possible Worlds, and Epistemic Logic', *Noûs*, 1 (1967), 47.

Hintikka's remark is at first surprising, since none of Donnellan's examples seems to have this form. But the remark falls into place when we recognize that Donnellan is concerned essentially with a given speaker who is *asserting* something, *asking* something, or *commanding* something. And thus if we pull back and focus our attention on the sentence *describing* the speech act:

John asserted that Mary's husband is kind to her.

the intensional operator appears.

Probably Hintikka wanted to argue that the sentence:

Her husband is kind to her.

is not itself ambiguous in the way that, say:

Every boy kissed a girl.

is. The fact that an ambiguous sentence is produced by embedding φ in some sentential context (for example, an intensional or temporal operator) should not be construed to indicate an ambiguity in φ. For were it so, (almost?) all sentences would be ambiguous.

Donnellan's distinction is a contribution to the redevelopment of an old and commonsensical theory about language which—at least in the philosophical literature—has rather been in a decline during the ascendency of semantics over epistemology of the 1930s, 1940s, and 1950s. The common-sense theory is one that Russell wrestled with in *The Principles of Mathematics*[8] but seemed to reject in 'On Denoting'.[9] This theory asserts roughly that the correct analysis of a typical speech act, for example:

John is tall.

distinguishes *who* is being talked about, i.e. the individual under consideration—here, John—from *how* he is being characterized—here, as tall.

Russell's analysis of the proposition expressed by

John is tall.

provides it with two components: the property expressed by the predicate is tall, and the individual John. That's right, John himself, right there, trapped in a proposition.

During the Golden Age of Pure Semantics we were developing a nice

[8] B. Russell, *The Principles of Mathematics* (Cambridge, 1903).
[9] B. Russell, 'On Denoting', *Mind*, 14 (1905), 479–93.

homogeneous theory, with language, meanings, and entities of the world each properly segregated and related one to another in rather smooth and comfortable ways. This development probably came to its peak in Carnap's *Meaning and Necessity*.[10] Each *designator* has both an intension and an extension. Sentences have truth-values as extensions and propositions as intensions, predicates have classes as extensions and properties as intensions, terms have individuals as extensions and *individual concepts* as intensions, and so on. The intension of a compound is a function of the intensions of the parts and similarly the extension (except when intensional operators appear). There is great beauty and power in this theory.

But there remained some nagging doubts: proper names, demonstratives, and quantification into intensional contexts.

Proper names may be a practical convenience in our mundane transactions, but they are a theoretician's nightmare. They are like bicycles. Everyone easily learns to ride, but no one can correctly explain how he does it. Completely new theories have been proposed within the last few years, in spite of the fact that the subject has received intense attention throughout this century, and in some portions of Tibet people have had proper names for even longer than that.

The main difficulty has to do, I believe, with the special intimate relationship between a proper name and its bearer. Russell said that in contrast with a common noun, like 'unicorn', a proper name *means* what it names. And if it names nothing, it means nothing. In the case of 'unicorn' we have a meaning, perhaps better a *descriptive meaning*, which we make use of in looking for such things. But in the case of the name 'Moravcsik' there is just Moravcsik. There is no basis on which to ask whether Moravcsik exists. Such a question is—for Russell—meaningless. But people persist in asking this question. Maybe not this very question, but analogous ones like:

Does Santa Claus exist?

There were other apparent difficulties in Russell's theory. The astronomical discovery that Hesperus was identical with Phosphorus became a triviality. The sentence expressing it expressed the same proposition as 'Hesperus is identical with Hesperus.' Furthermore, although the bearer of a given proper name is the be-all and end-all of the name's semantic relata, almost every proper name has dozens of bearers.

And then there are the unforgivable distortions of the minimal descriptive content of proper names. We all know of butchers named

[10] R. Carnap, *Meaning and Necessity* (Chicago, 1947).

'Baker' and dogs named 'Sir Walter'. The ultimate in such perversity occurs in titles of the top administrative officers at UCLA. We have four vice-chancellors at UCLA, one of whom has the title 'The Vice-Chancellor'.

All in all, proper names are a mess and if it weren't for the problem of how to get the kids to come in for dinner, I'd be inclined to just junk them.

At any rate, the attempt during the Golden Age was to whip proper names into line. In fact into the line of common nouns. People do ask:

Does Santa Claus exist?

So that must mean something like:

Does a unicorn exist?

They do ask:

Is Hesperus identical with Phosphorus?

So that must mean something like:

Are bachelors identical with college graduates?

Thus was waged a war of attrition against proper names. Many were unmasked as disguised descriptions, e.g. 'Aristotle' means *the student of Plato and teacher of Alexander who . . .*—not an unreasonable proposal.

However, some of these exposés did seem a bit oppressive, e.g. Russell's suggestion that:

Scott is Sir Walter.

really means:

The person named 'Scott' is the person named 'Sir Walter'.

followed by his nonchalant remark: 'This is a way in which names are frequently used in practice, and there will, as a rule, be nothing in the phraseology to show whether they are being used in this way or as names.'[11] But at least they isolated the few real trouble-makers—who turned out not to be our good old proper names at all but a handful of determined outside demonstratives: 'this', 'that', etc.

In summary, the technique was first to expose a proper name as a disguised description (sometimes on tenuous and unreliable evidence) and then ruthlessly to eliminate it.

[11] B. Russell, *Introduction to Mathematical Philosophy* (London, 1920), 174.

We thus reduce the exciting uncertainties of:

Socrates is a man.

to the banality of:

All men are mortal.

The demonstratives were still there, but they were so gross they could be ignored.

Lately, under the pressure of the new interest in singular propositions generated by intensional logic, the verities of the Golden Age are breaking down. Once logicians became interested in formalizing a logic of necessity, belief, knowledge, assertion, etc., traditional syntactical ways quickly led to formulas like

John asserted that x is a spy.

with free 'x' and then with 'x' bound to an anterior operator. Under what circumstances does a given individual, taken as value of 'x', satisfy this formula? Answer: If the appropriate singular proposition was the content of John's assertive utterance.

It seems that in at least certain speech acts, what I am trying to express can't quite be put into words. It is that proposition of Russell's with John trapped in it.

The property of being tall is exactly expressed by 'is tall', and the concept of the unique spy who is shorter than all other spies is exactly expressed by 'the shortest spy'; but no expression exactly expresses John. An expression may express a concept or property that, in reality, only John satisfies. There are many such distinct concepts; none of which is John himself.

I would like to distinguish between the kind of propositions which were considered by Aristotle (*all S is P*, *some S is not-P*, etc.) and the kind of proposition considered by the early Russell. I call the former *general propositions* and the latter *singular propositions*. Suppose, just for definiteness, that we fix attention on sentences of simple subject–predicate form. The following are examples:

(1) A spy is suspicious.
(2) Every spy is suspicious.
(3) The spy is suspicious.
(4) John is suspicious.

Now let us think of the proposition associated with each sentence as having two components. Corresponding to the predicate we have the property of being suspicious; and corresponding to the subject we have either what Russell in 1903 called a *denoting concept* or an individual. Let us take the proposition to be the ordered couple of these two components.

Again, to fix ideas, let us provide a possible-world style of interpretation for these notions. We think of each total or complete possible state of affairs as a possible world. The possible worlds are each constituents through time and may in fact overlap at certain times. For example, a possible world may agree with the actual world up to the time at which some individual made a particular decision; the possible world may then represent an outcome of a decision other than the one actually taken. (In science fiction, such cases are called *alternate time lines*.)

Within this framework we can attempt to represent a number of the semantic notions in question. We might represent the property of *being suspicious* by that function P which assigns to each possible world w and each time t the set of all those individuals of w which, in w, are suspicious at t. We might represent the denoting concepts expressed by the denoting phrases 'A spy', 'Every spy', and 'The spy' as, say, the ordered couples: $\langle$'A', $S\rangle$, $\langle$'Every', $S\rangle$, $\langle$'The', $S\rangle$ where S is the property (represented as above) of *being a spy*.[12] The fact that the logical words 'A', 'Every', and 'The' are just carried along reflects our treatment of them as *syncategorematic*, i.e. as having no independent meaning but as indicators of how to combine the meaning-bearing parts (here 'spy' and the predicate) in determining the meaning of the whole. For (1), (2), and (3) the corresponding propositions are now represented by:

(5) $\langle$ $\langle$'A', $S\rangle$, $P\rangle$
(6) $\langle$ $\langle$'Every', $S\rangle$, $P\rangle$
(7) $\langle$ $\langle$'The', $S\rangle$, $P\rangle$

It should be clear that each of (5)–(7) will determine a function which assigns to each possible world w and time t a truth-value. And in fact the truth-value so assigned to any w and t will be exactly the truth-value in w at t of the corresponding sentence. For example: (6) determines that function which assigns truth to a given w and t if and only if every member of $S(w,t)$ is a member of $P(w,t)$. Notice that the function so determined by (6) also correctly assigns to each w and t the truth-value in w at t of (2). (For the purpose of (7), let us take * to be a 'truth-value' which is assigned to w and t when $S(w,t)$ contains other than a single member.)

The proposition corresponding to (4) would be:

(8) $\langle$John, $P\rangle$

---

[12] Both 'denoting concept' and 'denoting phrase' are Russell's terms used in Russell's way.

not ⟨'John', *P*⟩ mind you, but ⟨John, *P*⟩. And (8) will determine that
function *F* which assigns Truth to *w* and *t* if and only if John is a member
of *P(w,t)*. If John is an individual of *w* at the time *t* (i.e. John exists in *w*
and is alive at *t*) but is not a member of *P(w,t)*, then *F(w,t)* is falsehood;
and if John is not an individual of *w* at the time *t*, then *F(w,t)* is *.

This brief excursion into possible-world semantics is only to fix ideas in
a simple way within that framework (I will later make further use of the
framework) and is not put forward as an ideal (in any sense: generaliz-
ability, elegance, etc.) representation of the semantic notions of property,
proposition, denoting concept, etc. My main motivation is to present a
representation which will clearly distinguish singular and general propositions.

It would, of course, have been possible to supply a representation of the
proposition expressed by (4) which is, in a sense, formally equivalent to
(8) and which blurs the distinction I wish to emphasize. I do it now lest
anyone think that the possibility is a relevant refutation of my later
remarks. Let us clearly depart from Russell by associating a denoting
concept:

(9) ⟨'Proper Name', *J*⟩

where *J* is what we might call *John's essence*, the property of *being John*,
namely, that function which assigns to each possible world *w* and time *t*
the set {John} if John is an individual of *w* and is alive in *w* at *t* and the
empty set otherwise. The analogue to (8) is now

(10) ⟨ ⟨'Proper Name', *J*⟩, *P*⟩

It will be noted that we have now treated the proper name 'John' rather
like the definite description 'The John', in which the proper name plays
the role of a common noun. Accordingly the function from possible
worlds and times to truth values which is determined by (10) is identical
with that determined by:

(11) ⟨ ⟨'The', *J*⟩, *P*⟩

There are certainly other representations of these propositions which
ally various subgroups. In fact, once any formal structure is established,
the production of isomorphic structures satisfying specified 'internal'
conditions is largely a matter of logical ingenuity of the 'pure' kind.[13]

[13] An e.g. is the possibility of producing set theoretical representations of the system of
natural numbers which make all even numbers alike in certain set theoretical features (distinct
from such numerical features as divisibility by 2) and all odd numbers alike in other set
theoretical features, or which provide simple and elegant definitions (i.e. representations) of
certain basic numerical operations and relations such as *less than* or *plus*, etc.

To return to the point, I have represented propositions in a way which emphasizes the singular–general distinction, because I want to revive a view of language alternate to that of the Golden Age. The view of the Golden Age is, I believe, undoubtedly correct for a large portion of language behaviour, in particular communication by means of general propositions. But the alternate view accounts for a portion of language behaviour not accommodated by the view of the Golden Age.

The alternate view is: *that some or all of the denoting phrases used in an utterance should not be considered part of the content of what is said but should rather be thought of as contextual factors which help us interpret the actual physical utterance as having a certain content.* The most typical of such contextual factors is the fact that the speaker's utterance is to be taken as an utterance of some specific language, say, English. When I utter 'yes' in English and *no* in Knoh, you must know I am speaking Knoh to know I have said *no*. It is no *part* of what I have said that I am speaking Knoh, though Knoh being a complete tongue, I could add that by uttering 'I am speaking English.' Such an utterance is of doubtful utility in itself; but, fortunately, there are other means by which this fact can be ascertained by my auditor, e.g. by my general physical appearance, or, if I am not a native Knoh, by my pointing to Knoh on a celestial globe. A homelier example has a haberdasher utter to a banker, 'I am out of cheques.' Whether the utterance takes place in the store or at the bank will help the banker determine what the haberdasher has said. In either case it is no *part* of what was said that the haberdasher used 'cheques' to mean bank cheques rather than suits with a chequered pattern. Of course the haberdasher could go on, if he desired, so to comment on his past performance, but that would be to say something else. Still closer to home is my wife's utterance: 'It's up to you to punish Jordan for what happened today.' It is by means of various subtle contextual clues that I understand her to be charging me to administer discipline to our son and not to be calling on me to act where the United Nations has failed. Again, should I exhibit momentary confusion she might, by a comment, a gesture, or simply some more discourse on the relevant naughtiness, assist me in properly decoding her first utterance so that I could understand what she was, in fact, saying. There are other ways—more controversial than the intentional resolution of the reference of a proper name among the many persons so dubbed—in which contextual factors determine the content of an utterance containing a proper name; but I am reserving all but the most blatantly obvious remarks for later.

Now let us narrow our attention to utterances containing *singular denoting phrases* (i.e. denoting phrases which purport to stand for a unique individual, such as 'the spy', 'John', '$\sqrt{2}$', etc.).[14]

How can contextual factors determine that part of the content of an utterance which corresponds to a singular denoting phrase? Two ways have already been mentioned: by determining what language is being spoken and by determining which of the many persons so dubbed a proper name stands for. But the most striking way in which such contextual factors enter is in connection with *demonstratives*: 'this', 'this spy', 'that book', etc. In at least some typical uses of these phrases, it is required that the utterance be accompanied by a *demonstration*—paradigmatically, a pointing—which indicates the object for which the phrase stands.[15] I will speak of a *demonstrative* use of a singular denoting phrase when the speaker intends that the object for which the phrase stands be designated by an associated demonstration.[16]

Now we can add another example of a subject–predicate sentence to those of (1)–(4):

> (12) He [the speaker points at John] is suspicious.

I am adopting the convention of enclosing a description of the relevant demonstration in square brackets immediately following each denoting phrase which is used demonstratively.[17]

---

[14] It's not too easy to single our such phrases without the help of some theory about logical form or some semantical theory. I suppose what I am after is what linguists call syntactical criteria. But I have had difficulty in finding one which will not let in phrases like 'a spy'. Another difficulty is concerned with phrases like 'John's brother' which seem to vary in their uniqueness suppositions. 'John's brother is the man in dark glasses' carries, for me, the supposition that John has just one brother; whereas 'The man in dark glasses is John's brother' does not. In fact the latter seems the most natural formulation when suppositions about the number of John's brothers are completely absent, since both 'The man in dark glasses is one of John's brothers' and 'The man in dark glasses is a brother of John' suppose, for me, that John has more than one brother.

[15] The question whether all uses of demonstratives are accompanied by demonstrations depends on a number of factors, some empirical, some stipulative, and some in the twilight zone of theoretical ingenuity. The stipulative question is whether we use 'demonstrative' to describe certain phrases which might also be described by enumeration or some such syntactical device, e.g. all phrases beginning with either 'this' or 'that' and followed by a common noun phrase; or whether we use 'demonstrative' to describe a certain characteristic *use* of such phrases. In the latter case it may be stipulatively true that an utterance containing a demonstrative must be accompanied by a demonstration. In the former case, the question turns both on how people in fact speak and on how clever our theoretician is in producing recherché demonstrations to account for apparent counter-examples.

[16] This formulation probably needs sharpening. Don't take it as a definition.

[17] It should not be supposed that my practice indicates any confidence as to the nature and structure of what I call *demonstrations* or the proper form for a *demonstration–description* to take. Indeed, these are difficult and important questions which arise repeatedly in what follows.

What shall we take as the proposition corresponding to (12) (which I also call the *content* of the *utterance* (12))? In line with our programme of studying contextual factors which are not *part* of what is said but whose role is rather to help us interpret the utterance as *having* a certain content, we shall take the component of the proposition which corresponds to the demonstrative to be the individual demonstrated. Thus the varying *forms* which such a demonstration can take are not reflected in the content of the utterance (i.e. the proposition). The demonstration 'gives us' the element of the proposition corresponding to the demonstrative. But *how* the demonstration gives that individual to us is here treated as irrelevant to the content of the utterance; just as the different *ways* by which I might have come to understand which Jordan was relevant to my wife's utterance, or the different *ways* by which one might come to understand that a speaker is speaking Knoh rather than English, do not alter the content of those utterances. Thus, for example, the utterances (in English):

(13) He [the speaker points at John, as John stands on the demonstration platform nude, clean shaven, and bathed in light] is suspicious.

(14) He [the speaker points at John, as John lurks in shadows wearing a trench-coat, bearded, with his hat pulled down over his face] is suspicious.

are taken, along with other refinements of (12), as expressing the same proposition, namely:

(15) ⟨John, *P*⟩.

It should immediately be apparent that we are in store for some delightful anomalies. Erroneous beliefs may lead a speaker to put on a demonstration which does not demonstrate what he thinks it does, with the result that he will be under a misapprehension as to *what* he has said. Utterances of identity sentences containing one or more demonstratives may express necessary propositions, though neither the speaker nor his auditors are aware of it. In fact, we get extreme cases in which linguistic competence is simply insufficient to determine completely the content of what is said. Of course this was already established by the case of the Knoh–English translation problem, but the situation is more dramatic using the demonstratives.

The present treatment is not inevitable. An alternative is to incorporate the demonstration in the proposition. We would argue as follows: Frege's *sense and denotation* distinction[18] can be extended to all kinds of indicative devices. In each case we have the object indicated (the 'denotation') and the manner of indication (the 'sense'). It is interesting to note that (at least in Feigl's translation) Frege wrote of 'the sense (connotation, meaning) of the sign in which is contained the *manner and context* of presentation of the denotation of the sign'.[19] I think it reasonable to interpret Frege as saying that the sense of a sign is what is grasped by the linguistically competent auditor, and it seems natural to generalize and say that it is the 'sense' of the demonstration that is grasped by the competent auditor of utterances containing demonstratives. Thus we see how the drawn-out English utterance:

(16) That [the speaker points at Phosphorus in early morning] is the same planet as that [the speaker points at Hesperus in the early evening].

could be both informative and true.

Let us call the preceding a *Fregean treatment of demonstratives*. It is worth developing (which means primarily working on the ontology (metaphysics?) of demonstrations and the semantics of demonstration descriptions) but, I believe, will ultimately be unsatisfactory. For now I'll just outline some of the reasons. The demonstrative use of demonstratives plays an important role in language learning, in general, in the learning and use of proper names, in our misty use of *de re* modalities, in our better grounded use of what Quine calls the *relational* senses of epistemic verbs (i.e. the senses of those intensional verbs that permit quantification in).[20] And, in general, I believe that we can sharpen our epistemological insights in a number of areas by taking account of what I call the demonstrative use of expression. Such uses are far more widespread than one imagined.

I earlier called the Fregean treatment of demonstratives 'unsatisfactory'. I would be more cautious in saying that it was wrong. (However I do think an empirical argument from linguistic behaviour could be developed to show that it is wrong. I take Donnellan's study of the phenomenology of what he calls referential use to be an excellent start in that direction.) What I am confident of is that if we force all phenomena that suggest a special *demonstrative* use of language, along with what I regard as a

---

[18] G. Frege, 'Ueber Sinn und Bedeutung', *Zeitschrift für Philosophie und philosophische Kritik*, trans. (by Feigl) in H. Feigl and W. Sellars (eds.), *Readings in Philosophical Analysis* (New York, 1949). Also trans. (by Black) in P. Geach and M. Black. (eds.), *Translations from the Writings of Gottlob Frege*, (Oxford, 1966).   [19] Ibid., emphasis added.
[20] W. V. Quine, 'Quantifiers and Propositional Attitudes', *Journal of Philosophy*, 53 (1956), 177–87.

corresponding feature—a special *singular* form of proposition—into the Fregean mould of linguistic elements with a sense and a denotation, the sense being the element which appears in the proposition (thus leaving us with only general propositions), then important insights will be lost. I don't deny that on a phenomenon-by-phenomenon basis we can (in some sense) keep stretching Frege's brilliant insights to cover. With a little ingenuity I think we *can* do that. But we shouldn't.

Now let me offer a slightly different and somewhat a priori justification for studying the phenomena of demonstrative uses of expressions and singular propositions. I leave aside the question whether we have correctly analysed any actual linguistic behaviour, whether concerned with the so-called demonstrative *phrases* or otherwise.

Having explained so clearly and precisely what such a use of language would amount to, in terms of a possible-world semantics, I can simply resolve so to use the word 'that' in the future. At a minimum I could introduce the *new* word 'dthat' for the demonstrative use of 'that'. Couldn't I? I can, and I will. In fact I do.

I like this intentional (i.e. stipulative) way of looking at the use of 'dthat' because I believe that in many cases where there are competing Fregean and demonstrative analyses of some utterances or class of utterances the matter can be resolved simply by the intentions of the speaker (appropriately conveyed to the auditor?). Thus in the ease of proper names (to which I will return below) I might simply resolve to use them demonstratively (i.e. as demonstrating the individual whom they are a name *of* in the nomenclature of an earlier paper[21]) on certain occasions and in a Fregean way[22] on other occasions. Of course, one who did not have a clear understanding of the alternatives might have difficulty in characterizing his own use, but once we have explored each choice there is nothing to prevent us from choosing either, 'unnatural' though the choice may be.

It should probably be noted that despite the accessibility of the semantics of 'dthat' our *grasp* of the singular propositions so expressed is, in John Perry's apt phrase, a bit of *knowledge by description* as compared

---

[21] D. Kaplan, 'Quantifying In', *Synthèse*, 19 (1968), 178–214. I will attempt later to press the case that this use of proper names, which involves no waving of hands or fixing of glance, may be assimilated to the more traditional forms of demonstrative use.

[22] 'In the case of genuinely proper names like "Aristotle" opinions as regards their sense may diverge. As such may, e.g., be suggested: Plato's disciple and the teacher of Alexander the Great. Whoever accepts this sense will interpret the meaning of the statement "Aristotle was born in Stagira" differently from one who interpreted the sense of "Aristotle" as the Stagirite teacher of Alexander the Great' (from Feigl's translation of Frege's 'Ueber Sinn und Bedeutung').

with our rather more direct acquaintance with the general propositions expressed by non-demonstrative utterances.

Armed with 'dthat' we can now explore and possibly even extend the frontiers of demonstrations.

When we considered the Fregean analysis of demonstrations, we attempted to establish parallels between demonstrations and descriptions.[23] In so far as this aspect of the Fregean programme is successful, it suggests the possibility of a demonstrative analysis of descriptions. *If pointing can be taken as a form of describing, why not take describing as a form of pointing?* Note that our demonstrative analysis of demonstrations need not, indeed should not, deny or even ignore the fact that demonstrations have both a sense and a demonstratum. It is just that according to the demonstrative analysis the sense of the demonstration does not appear in the proposition. Instead the sense is used only to fix the demonstratum which itself appears directly in the proposition. I propose now to do the same for descriptions. Instead of taking the sense of the description as the subject of the proposition, we use the sense only to fix the denotation which we then take directly as the subject component of the proposition. I now take the utterance of the description as a demonstration and describe it with the usual quotation devices, thus:

(17) Dthat ['the spy'] is suspicious.

For fixity of ideas, let us suppose, what is surely false, that in fact, actuality, and reality there is one and only one spy, and John is he. We might express this so:

(18) 'the spy' denotes John.[24]

In the light of (18), (17) expresses:

(19) $\langle$John, $P\rangle$

(also known as '(8)' and '(15)').

Recollecting and collecting we have:

(3) The spy is suspicious.

(4) John is suspicious.

(7) $\langle$ $\langle$'The', $S\rangle$, $P\rangle$

(12) He [the speaker points at John] is suspicious.

---

[23] A third kind of indicative device is the picture. Consideration of pictures, which to me lie somewhere between pointing and describing, may help drive home the parallels—in terms of the distinction between the object indicated and the manner of indication—between description, depiction, and demonstration.

[24] That all utterances are in English is a general and implicit assumption except where it is explicitly called into question.

or as we might now write (12):

   (20) Dhe [the speaker points at John] is suspicious.[25]

Earlier we said that an utterance of (3) expresses (7), and only an utterance of (12) [i.e. (20)] or possibly (4) expresses (19). I have already suggested that an utterance of (4) may sometimes be taken in a Fregean way to express something like (7), and now I want to point out that for want of 'dthat' some speakers may be driven to utter (3) when they intend what is expressed by (17).

If an utterance of (3) may indeed sometimes express (19), then Donnellan was essentially correct in describing his referential and attributive uses of definite descriptions as a 'duality of function'. And it might even be correct to describe this duality as an *ambiguity* in the sentence type (3). I should note right here that my demonstrative use is not quite Donnellan's referential use—a deviation that I will expatiate on below—but it is close enough for present purposes.

The ambiguity in question here is of a rather special kind. For under no circumstances could the choice of disambiguation for an utterance of (3) affect the truth-value. Still there are two distinct propositions involved, and even two distinct functions from possible worlds and times to truth-values, determined by the two propositions.

Before continuing with the ambiguity in (3), it would be well to interject some remarks on sentence types and sentence tokens (of which utterances are one kind) especially as they relate to demonstratives.

Sentence types vary considerably in the degree to which they contain implicit and explicit references to features of the context of utterance. The references I have in mind here are those that affect the truth-value of the sentence type on a particular occasion of utterance. At one extreme stand what Quine (in *Word and Object*) called *eternal sentences*: those in which the feature linguists call *tense* does not really reflect a perspective from some point in time, which contain no *indexicals* such as 'now', 'here', 'I', etc., and whose component names and definite descriptions are not understood to require contextual determination as did the 'Jordan' of our earlier example. Quine describes such sentences as 'those whose truth value stays fixed through time and from speaker to speaker'.[26] But I prefer my own vaguer formulation: *those sentences which do not express a perspective from within space-time.* Quine and I would both count 'In 1970 American women exceed American men in wealth' as eternal; he would

---

[25] 'Dhe' is really a combination of the demonstrative with a common noun phrase. It stands for 'dthat male'. More on such combinations later.

[26] W. V. Quine, *Word and Object* (Cambridge, Mass., 1960), 193.

(presumably) also count 'The UCLA football team always has, does, and will continue to outclass the Stanford football team' as eternal. I would not.

Truth-values are awarded directly to eternal sentences without any relativization to time, place, etc.[27] But for the fugitive sentence no stable truth-value can be awarded. Let us consider first tensed sentences, e.g.:

> (21) American men will come to exceed American women in intelligence.

Without disputing the facts, if (21) were true at one time, it would fail to be true at some later time. (Since one doesn't come to exceed what one already exceeds.)

Now let's dredge up the possible worlds. We associated with (21) a function which assigns to each possible world and time a truth-value. Such a function seems to represent, for reasons which have been much discussed, at least part of the meaning of (21) or part of what we grasp when we understand (21).[28] There is another kind of 'content' associated with a fugitive sentence like (21), namely, the content of a particular utterance of (21). In a sense, any particular utterance (token) of a fugitive sentence (type) is an *eternalization* of the fugitive sentence. The relativization to time is fixed by the time of utterance. We can associate with each utterance of a fugitive sentence the same kind of function from possible worlds to truth-values that we associate directly with eternal sentences.

Before becoming completely lost in vague nomenclature, let me make some stipulations. I will call the function which assigns to a time and a possible world the truth-value of a given fugitive sentence (type) at that time in that world the *meaning* of the given sentence. The meaning of a sentence is what a person who is linguistically competent grasps, it is common to all utterances of the sentence, and it is one of the components which goes into determining the *content* of any particular utterance of the sentence. The *content* of an utterance is that function which assigns to each possible world the truth-value which the utterance would take if it

---

[27] There are, of course, 2 hidden relativizations involved even for eternal sentences. One is to a *language*, i.e. an association of meanings with words. The Knoh–English example was meant to dramatize this relativization. The other is to a possible world. There is always the implicit reference to the actual world when we use just the expression 'true'. If the analogy between moments of time and possible worlds holds—as some philosophers think—then maybe we should begin our classification of sentences not with explicitly dated eternal sentences like 'in 1970 . . .' but with 'perfect' sentences like 'In the possible world Charlie in 1970 . . .'.

[28] Rather than talking directly of these functions, I should really talk of entities like ⟨ ⟨'The', S⟩, P⟩ and only derivatively of the functions. I will do so in the next draft.

were evaluated with respect to that world. There is some unfortunate slack in the preceding characterizations, which I will try to reduce.[29]

Let ϕ be a fugitive sentence like (21); let ϕ be the meaning of ϕ, let W be the set of possible worlds; let T be the set of times (I assume that all possible worlds have the same temporal structure and, in fact, the very same times, i.e. a given time in one world has a unique counterpart in all others); let U be the set of possible utterances; for $u\varepsilon U$ let $S(u)$ be the sentence uttered in u; let $T(u)$ be the time of u (when only $S(u)$ and $T(u)$ are relevant; we might identify u with $\langle S(u), T(u) \rangle$ and let u be the content of u. The relation between the meaning of a sentence (whose only fugitive aspect is its temporality) and the content of one of its possible utterances can now be concisely expressed as follows:

(22) $\Lambda u\varepsilon U \Lambda w\varepsilon W(\bar{u}(w) = \overline{S(u)} \ (T(u),w) \ )$

or, identifying u with $\langle S(u),T(u) \rangle$:

(23) $\Lambda w\varepsilon W \Lambda t\varepsilon T(\ \overline{\langle \phi,t \rangle} \ (w) = \phi(t,w) \ )$

To put it another way, an utterance of ϕ fixes a time, and the content of the utterance takes account of the truth value of ϕ in all possible worlds but *only at that time*.

From (22) and (23) it would appear that the notions of meaning and content are interdefinable. Therefore, since we already have begun developing the theory of meaning for fugitive sentences (see especially the work of Montague),[30] why devote any special attention to the theory of content? Is it not simply a subtheory of a definitional extension of the theory of meaning? I think not. But the reasons go beyond simple examples like (21) and take us, hopefully, back to the main track of this paper. It is worth looking more deeply into the structure of utterances than a *simple* definition of that notion within the theory of meaning would suggest. (I stress *simple* because I have not yet really investigated sophisticated definitions.)

First we have problems about the counterfactual status of possible utterances: are utterances *in* worlds, are they assumed to occur in worlds in which their content is being evaluated, or are they extra-worldly, with their content evaluated independent of their occurrence? Consider the infamous 'I am here now', or perhaps more simply:

(24) An utterance is occurring.

---

[29] This is aside from the inadequacy mentioned in the previous footnote, which continues to bother me.

[30] The most relevant works are 'Pragmatics' (1968) and 'Pragmatics and Intensional Logic' (1970), both reprinted in R. Montague, *Formal Philosophy* (New Haven, 1974).

Is the meaning of (24) to assign to a time and world the truth-value which an utterance of (24) *would* take *were* it to occur in that world at that time? Or does it assign simply the truth-value of (24) in that world at that time? Presumably the latter. But this is to assume that utterances come complete, with the value of all of their contextually determined features filled in (otherwise the utterance alone—without being set in a world—would not have a content). I do not want to make this assumption since I am particularly interested in the *way* in which a demonstration, for example, picks out its demonstratum.

And now we are back to the ambiguity in (3). I would like to count my *verbal* demonstration, as in (17), as part of the sentence type. Then it seems that an utterance of such a sentence either must include a world, or else, what is more plausible, must be in a world. I guess what I want to say, what I should have said, is that an utterance has to occur *somewhere*, in some world, and the world in which it occurs is a crucial factor in determing what the content is. This really says something about how (I think) I want to treat (possible) demonstrations. I want the same (possible) demonstrations (e.g. ['the spy']) to determine different demonstrata in different worlds (or possibly even at different times in the same world). Now I see why I was so taken with the Fregean treatment of demonstrations. We should be able to represent demonstrations as something like functions from worlds, times, etc., to demonstrata. Thus, *just like the meaning of a definite description!* The difference lies in how the content of a particular utterance is computed.

I realize that the foregoing is mildly inconsistent, but let us push on. Let u be an utterance of (17) in w at t, and let u' be an utterance of (3) in w at t. Let's not worry, for now, about the possibility of a clash of utterances. If we look at the content of u and the content of u' we will see that they differ—though they will always agree in w. The content of u is like what I earlier called a singular proposition (except that I should have fixed the time), whereas the content of u' is like what I earlier called a general proposition. For the content of u to assign truth to a given world w', the individual who must be suspicious in w' at t is not the denotation of 'the spy' in w' at t, but rather the denotation of 'the spy' in w at t. The *relevant individual* is determined in the world in which the utterance takes place, and then that same individual is checked for suspicion in all other worlds, whereas for the content of u', we determine a (possibly) new relevant individual in each world.[31]

---

[31] I am still bothered by the notion of an utterance at t in w, where there is no utterance at t in w.

What is especially interesting is that these two contents must agree in the world *w*, the world in which the utterance took place.

Now note that the verbal form of (3) might have been adopted by one who lacked 'dthat' to express what is expressed by (17). We seem to have here a kind of *de dicto–de re* ambiguity in the verbal form of (3) and without benefit of any intensional operator. No question of an utterer's intentions has been brought into play. *There is no question of an analysis in terms of scope, since there is no operator.* The two sentence types (3) and (17) are such that when uttered in the same context they have different contents but always the same truth-value where uttered. Donnellan vindicated! (Contrary to my own earlier expectations.)

I am beginning to suspect that I bungled things even worse than I thought in talking about meanings, contents, etc. The meaning of a sentence type should probably be a function from utterances to *contents* rather than from something like utterances to truth-values. If this correction were made then we could properly say that (13) and (17) differ in meaning.

It would also give a more satisfactory analysis of a sentence type like:

(25) Dthat ['the morning star'] is identical with dthat ['the evening star'].

Although (25) expresses a true content on some possible occasions of use and a false content on others, it is not simply contingent, since on all possible occasions its content is either necessary or impossible. (I am assuming that distinct individuals don't merge.) Even one who grasped the meaning of (25) would not of course know its truth-value simply on witnessing an utterance. Thus we answer the question how an utterance of an identity sentence can be informative though *necessary!*

Another example on the question of necessity. Suppose I now utter:

(26) I am more than thirty-six years old.

What I have said is true. Is it necessary? This may be arguable. (*Could* I be younger than I am at this very same time?) But the fact that the sentence, if uttered at an earlier time or by another person, could express something false is certainly irrelevant. The point is: simply to look at the spectrum of *truth-values* of different utterances of (25) and (26) and not at the spectrum of *contents* of different utterances of (25) and (26) is to miss something interesting and important.

I earlier said that my demonstrative use is not quite Donnellan's referential use, and I want now to return to that point. When a speaker uses an expression demonstratively he *usually* has in mind—so to speak—

an intended demonstratum, and the demonstration is thus *teleological*. Donnellan and I disagree on how to bring the intended demonstratum into the picture. To put it crudely, Donnellan believes that for most purposes we should take the demonstratum to be the intended demonstratum. I believe that these are different notions that may well involve different objects.

From my point of view the situation is interesting precisely because we have a case here in which a person can fail to say what he intended to say, and the failure is not a linguistic error (such as using the wrong word) but a factual one. It seems to me that such a situation can arise only in the demonstrative mode.

Suppose that without turning and looking I point to the place on my wall which has long been occupied by a picture of Rudolf Carnap and I say:

(27) Dthat [I point as above] is a picture of one of the greatest philosophers of the twentieth century.

But unbeknownst to me, someone has replaced my picture of Carnap with one of Spiro Agnew. I think it would simply be wrong to argue an 'ambiguity' in the demonstration, so great that it can be bent to my intended demonstratum. I have said of a picture of Spiro Agnew that it pictures one of the greatest philosophers of the twentieth century. And my speech and demonstration suggest no other natural interpretation to the linguistically competent public observer.

Still, it would be perhaps equally wrong not to pursue the notion of the intended demonstratum. Let me give three reasons for that pursuit:

1. The notion is epistemologically interesting in itself.

2. It may well happen—as Donnellan has pointed out—that we succeed in communicating what we intended to say in spite of our failure to say it. (E.g. the mischievous fellow who switched pictures on me would understand full well what I was intending to say.)

3. There are situations where the demonstration is sufficiently ill-structured in itself so that we would regularly take account of the intended demonstratum as, *within limits*, a legitimate disambiguating or vagueness-removing device.

I have two kinds of examples for this third point. First, there are the cases of vague demonstrations by a casual wave of the hand. I suppose that ordinarily we would allow that a demonstration had been successful if the intended object were *roughly* where the speaker pointed. That is, we would not bring out surveying equipment to help determine the content of the speaker's assertion; much more relevant is what he intended to point at. Second, whenever I point at something, from the surveyor's point of view I point at many things. When I point at my son (and say 'I love dthat'), I may also be pointing at a book he is holding, his jacket, a button on his jacket, his skin, his heart, and his dog standing beside him—from the surveyor's point of view. *My* point is that if I intended to point at my son and it is true that I love him, then what I said is true. And the fact that I do not love his jacket does not make it equally false. There are, of course, limits to what can be accomplished by intentions (even the best of them). No matter how hard I intend Carnap's picture, in the earlier described case, I do not think it reasonable to call the content of my utterance true.

Another example where I would simply distinguish the content asserted and the content intended is in the use of 'I'.[32] A person might utter:

(2) I am a general.

intending—that is 'having in mind'—de Gaulle, and being under the delusion that he himself was de Gaulle. But the linguistic constraints on the possible demonstrata of 'I' will not allow anyone other than de Gaulle so to demonstrate de Gaulle, no matter how hard they try.

All this familiarity with demonstratives has led me to believe that I was mistaken in 'Quantifying In' in thinking that the most fundamental cases of what I might now describe as a person having a propositional attitude (believing, asserting, etc.) towards a singular proposition required that the person be *en rapport* with the subject of the proposition. It is now clear that I can assert *of* the first child to be born in the twenty-first century that *he* will be bald, simply by assertively uttering,

(29) Dthat ['the first child to be born in the twenty-first century'] will be bald.

I do not now see how the requirement of being *en rapport* with the subject of a singular proposition fits in. Are there two kinds of singular propositions? Or are there just two different ways to know them?

Exciting future episodes

1. Making sense out of the foregoing.
2. Showing how nicely (3) and (17) illustrate an early point about the

---

[32] 'I' is, of course, a demonstrative; as opposed, e.g., to 'the person who is uttering this utterance', which contains only the demonstrative 'this utterance'. Let us compare utterances of: (i) I am exhausted; (ii) The person who is uttering this utterance is exhausted. Both are uttered by s on the same occasion (!). To find the truth-value of the content of (ii) in w' we must first locate the same utterance in w' (if it exists there at all) and see who, if anyone, is uttering it. Since s could well be exhausted silently in w', the two contents are not the same.

possibility of incorporating contextual factors (here, a demonstration) as part of the content of the utterance. Another example compares uses of 'the person at whom I am pointing' as demonstration and as subject.

3. Justifying calling (17) a *de re* form by showing how it can be used to explicate the notion of modality *de re* without depending on scope.

4. Extending the demonstrative notion to *in*definite descriptions to see if it is possible so to explicate the ± specific idea. (It isn't.)

5. Improving (by starting all over) the analysis of the relation between Montague's treatment of indexicals and my treatment of demonstratives.

6. Showing how the treatment of proper names in the Kripke–Kaplan–Donnellan way (if there is such) is akin (?) to demonstratives.

7. Discussing the role of common noun phrases in connection with demonstratives, as in:

(30) Dthat coat [the speaker points at a boy wearing a coat] is dirty.

8. Quine's contention that the content of any utterance can also be expressed by an eternal sentence. Is it true?

9. Much more to say about the phenomenology of intending to demonstrate x, and also about the truth conditions of 'y intends to demonstrate x'.

10. Demonstratives, dubbings, definitions, and other forms of language learning. Common nouns: what they mean and how we learn it. This section will include such pontifications as the following:

It is a mistake to believe that normal communication takes place through the encoding and decoding of general propositions, by means of our grasp of *meanings*. It is a more serious mistake, because more pernicious, to believe that other aspects of communication can be accounted for by a vague reference to 'contextual features' of the utterance. Indeed, we first learn the meanings of almost all parts of our language by means quite different from those of the formal definitions studied in metamathematics; and the means used for first teaching the meanings of words, rather than withering away, are regularly and perhaps even essentially employed thereafter in all forms of communication.

BIBLIOGRAPHIC POSTSCRIPT

This paper was written (if that is the right word for it) in early 1970. Since that time I have written (really written, and even published) several papers in which the ideas of the present work are expounded and developed. These works are:

'On the Logic of Demonstratives', *The Journal of Philosophical Logic*, 8 (1979), 81–98; reprinted in N. Salmon and S. Soames (eds.), *Propositions and Attitudes* (New York: Oxford University Press, 1988).
'Demonstratives: An Essay on the Semantics, Logic, Metaphysics, and Epistem-

ology of Demonstratives and other Indexicals', in J. Almog, J. Perry, and H. K. Wettstein (eds.), *Themes from Kaplan* (New York: Oxford University Press, 1989), 481–563.

'Afterthoughts' in J. Almog, J. Perry, and H. K. Wettstein (eds.), *Themes from Kaplan* (New York: Oxford University Press, 1989), 565–614.

And to some extent:

'Bob and Carol and Ted and Alice' in J. Hintikka *et al.* (eds.), *Approaches to Natural Language* (Dordrecht: Reidel, 1973), 490–518.

'Opacity', in L. Hahn (ed.), *The Philosophy of W. V. Quine*, The Library of Living Philosophers (Open Court, 1986), La Salle, Ill.: 229–89. See especially section 7.

2

THOUGHTS ON DEMONSTRATIVES

DAVID KAPLAN

Logic

In this chapter, I propose to outline briefly a few results of my investigations into the theory of demonstratives: words and phrases whose *in*tension is determined by the contexts of their use. Familiar examples of demonstratives are the nouns 'I', 'you', 'here', 'now', 'that', and the adjectives 'actual' and 'present'. It is, of course, clear that the *ex*tension of 'I' is determined by the context—if you and I both say 'I' we refer to different persons. But I would now claim that the intension is also so determined. The intension of an 'eternal' term (like 'The Queen of England in 1973') has generally been taken to be represented by a function which assigns to each possible world the Queen of England in 1973 of that world. Such functions would have been called *individual concepts* by Carnap. It has been thought by some—myself among others— that by analogy, the intension of 'I' could be represented by a function from speakers to individuals (in fact, the identity function). And similarly, that the intensions of 'here' and 'now' would be represented by (identity) functions on places and times. The role of contextual factors in determining the extension (with respect to such factors) of a demonstrative was thought of as analogous to that of a possible world in determining the extension of 'The Queen of England in 1973' (with respect to that possible world). Thus an enlarged view of an intension was derived. The intension of an expression was to be represented by a function from certain factors to the extension of the expression (with respect to those factors). Originally such factors were simply possible worlds, but as it was noticed that the so-called tense operators exhibited a

---

This chapter has been put together for this volume by the author from selections from 2 of his essays. The first section is from 'On the Logic of Demonstratives', *Journal of Philosophical Logic*, 8 (1979), 81–98 (repr. in N. Salmon and S. Soames *Propositions and Attitudes*, Oxford Readings in Philosophy (New York, 1989); the second section is drawn from 'Demonstratives: An Essay on the Semantics, Logic, Metaphysics, and Epistemology of Demonstratives and other Indexicals', in J. Almog, J. Perry, and H.K. Wettstein (eds.), *Themes from Kaplan* (New York, 1989) 481–563.

structure highly analogous to that of the modal operators, the factors with respect to which an extension was to be determined were enlarged to include moments of time. When it was noticed that contextual factors were required to determine the extension of sentences containing demonstratives, a still more general notion was developed and called an 'index'. The extension of an expression was to be determined with respect to an index. The intension of an expression was that function which assigned to every index, the extension at that index. Here is a typical passage.

The above example supplies us with a statement whose truth-value is not constant but varies as a function of $i \varepsilon I$. This situation is easily appreciated in the context of time-dependent statements; that is, in the case where I represents the instants of time. Obviously the same statement can be true at one moment and false at another. For more general situations one must not think of the $i \varepsilon I$ as anything as simple as instants of time or even possible worlds. In general we will have

$$i = (w,t,p,a, \ldots)$$

where the index i has many co-ordinates: for example, w is a *world*, t is a *time*, $p = (x,y,z)$ is a three-dimensional) *position* in the world, a is an *agent*, etc. All these co-ordinates can be varied, possibly independently, and thus affect the truth-values of statements which have indirect reference to these coordinates. From the Advice of a prominent logician.)

A sentence ϕ was taken to be logically true if true at every index (in every 'structure'), and $\Box\phi$ was taken to be true at a given index (in a given structure) just in case ϕ was true at every index (in that structure). Thus the familiar principle of modal generalization: if $\models\phi$, then $\models\Box\phi$, is validated.

This view, in its treatment of demonstratives, now seems to me to have been technically wrong (though perhaps correctable by minor modification) and, more importantly, conceptually misguided.

Consider the sentence

(1) I am here now.

It is obvious that for many choices of index—i.e. for many quadruples (w, x, p, t) where w is a possible world, x is a person, p is a place, and t is a time—(1) will be false. In fact, (1) is true only with respect to those indices $\langle w, x, p, t \rangle$ which are such that in the world w, x is located at p at the time t. Thus (1) fares about on a par with

(2) David Kaplan is in Los Angeles on 21 April 1973.

(2) is contingent, and so is (1).

But here we have missed something essential to our understanding of demonstratives. Intuitively, (1) is deeply, and in some sense universally, true. One need only understand the meaning of (1) to know that it cannot be uttered falsely. No such guarantees apply to (2). A *Logic of Demonstratives* which does not reflect this intuitive difference between (1) and (2) has bypassed something essential to the logic of demonstratives.

Here is a proposed correction. Let the class of indices be narrowed to include only the *proper* ones—namely, those $\langle w, x, p, t \rangle$ such that in the world w, x *is* located at p at the time t. Such a move may have been intended originally since improper indices are like impossible worlds; no such contexts *could* exist and thus there is no interest in evaluating the extensions of expressions with respect to them. Our reform has the consequence that (1) comes out, correctly, to be logically true. Now consider

(3) □ I am here now.

Since the contained sentence (namely (1)) is true at every proper index, (3) also is true at every proper index and thus also is logically true. (As would be expected by the aforementioned principle of modal generalization.)

But (3) should not be *logically* true, since it is false. It is certainly *not* necessary that I be here now. But for several contingencies, I would be working in my garden now, or even writing this in a location outside of Los Angeles.

Perhaps enough has now been said to indicate that there are difficulties in the attempt to assimilate the role of a *context* in a logic of demonstratives to that of a *possible world* in the familiar modal logics or a *moment of time* in the familiar tense logics.

I believe that the source of the difficulty lies in a conceptual confusion between two kinds of meaning. Ramifying Frege's distinction between sense and denotation, I would add two varieties of sense: content and character. The content of an expression is always taken *with respect to* a given context of use. Thus when I say

(4) I was insulted yesterday.

a specific content—*what I said*—is expressed. Your utterance of the same sentence, or mine on another day, would not express the same content. What is important to note is that it is not just the truth-value that may change; what is said is itself different. Speaking today, my utterance of (4) will have a content roughly equivalent to that which

(5) David Kaplan is insulted on 20 April 1973.

would have been spoken by you or anyone at any time. Since (5) contains no demonstratives, its content is the same with respect to all contexts. This content is what Carnap called an 'intension' and what, I believe, has been referred to as a 'proposition'. So my theory is that different contexts for (4) produce not just different truth-values, but different propositions.

Turning now to character, I call that component of the sense of an expression which determines how the content is determined by the context, the 'character' of an expression. Just as contents (or intensions) can be represented by functions from possible worlds to extensions, so characters can be represented by functions from contexts to contents. The character of 'I' would then be represented by *the function (or rule, if you prefer) which assigns to each context that content which is represented by the constant function from possible worlds to the agent of the context*. The latter function has been called an 'individual concept'. Note that the character of 'I' is represented by a function from contexts to individual *concepts*, not from contexts to individuals. It was the idea that a function from contexts to individuals could represent the intension of 'I' which led to the difficulties discussed earlier.

Now what is it that a competent speaker of English knows about the word 'I'? Is it the content with respect to some particular occasion of use? No. It is the character of 'I': the rule italicized above. Competent speakers recognize that the proper use of 'I' is—loosely speaking—to refer to the speaker. Thus, that component of sense which I call 'character' is best identified with what might naturally be called 'meaning'.

To return, for a moment, to (1). The character (meaning) of (1) determines each of the following:

(a) In different contexts, an utterance of (1) expresses different contents (propositions).

(b) In most (if not all) contexts, an utterance of (1) expresses a contingent proposition.

(c) In all contexts, an utterance of (1) expresses a true proposition (i.e. a proposition which is true at the world of the context).

On the basis of (c), we might claim that (1) is analytic (i.e. it is true solely in virtue of its meaning). Although as we see from (b), (1) rarely or never expresses a necessary proposition. This separation of analyticity and necessity is made possible—even, I hope, plausible—by distinguishing the kinds of entities of which 'is analytic' and 'is necessary' are properly predicated: characters (meanings) are analytic, contents (propositions) are necessary.

The distinction between character and content was unlikely to be noticed before demonstratives came under consideration, because demonstrative-free expressions have a constant character, i.e. they express the same content in every context. Thus, character becomes an uninteresting complication in the theory.

Though I have spoken above of contents of utterance, my primary theoretical notion of *content with respect to a context* does not require that the agent of the context utter the expression in question. I believe that there are good reasons for taking this more general notion as fundamental.

I believe that my distinction between character and content can be used to throw light on Kripke's distinction between the a priori and the necessary. Although my distinction lies more purely within logic and semantics, and Kripke's distinction is of a more general epistemic metaphysical character[1], both seem to me to be of the same *structure*. (I leave this remark in a rather cryptic state.)

The distinction between content and character and the related analysis of demonstratives have certainly been foreshadowed in the literature (though they are original-with-me, in the sense that I did not consciously extract them from prior sources). But to my knowledge they have not previously been cultivated to meet the standards for logical and semantical theories which currently prevail. In particular, Strawson's distinction between the significance (meaningfulness) of a sentence and the statement (proposition) which is expressed in a given use is clearly related.[2] Strawson recognizes that such sentences as 'The *present* King of France is *now* bald' may express different propositions in different utterances, and he identifies the meaningfulness of the sentence with its potential for expressing a true or false proposition in some possible utterance. Though he does not explicitly discuss *the* meaning of the sentence, it is clear that he would not identify such a meaning with any of the propositions expressed by particular utterances. Unfortunately Strawson seems to regard the fact that sentences containing demonstratives can be used to express different propositions as immunizing such sentences against treatment by 'the logician'.

In order to convince myself that it is possible to carry out a consistent analysis of the semantics of demonstratives along the above lines, I have attempted to carry through the programme for a version of first order predicate logic. If my views are correct, the introduction of demonstratives into intensional logics will require more extensive reformulation than was thought to be the case.

---

[1] S. Kripke, 'Naming and Necessity', in Donald Davidson and Gilbert Harman (eds.), *Semantics of Natural Language* (Dordrecht: Reidel, 1972), 253–355; Addenda, pp. 763–9.

[2] P. Strawson, *Introduction to Logical Theory* (New York: John Wiley & Sons, 1952).

Epistemology

How do content and character serve as objects of thought?[3] Let us state Frege's problem

(FP) How can (an occurrence of) $[\alpha = \beta]$ (in a given context), if true, differ in cognitive significance from (an occurrence of) $[\alpha = \alpha]$ (in the same context)?

In (FP) α, β are arbitrary singular terms. (In future formulations, I will omit the parentheticals as understood.) When α and β are demonstrative free, Frege explained the difference in terms of his notion of sense. A notion which, his writings generally suggest, should be identified with our *content*. But it is clear that Frege's problem can be reinstituted in a form in which resort to contents will not explain differences in 'cognitive significance'. We need only ask,

(FPD) How can $[\text{dthat}[\alpha] = \text{dthat}[\beta]]$ if true, differ in cognitive significance from $[\text{dthat}[\alpha] = [\text{dthat}[\alpha]]$?

Since, as we shall show, for any term γ,

$[\gamma = \text{dthat}[\gamma]]$ is analytic

the sentence pair in (FP) will differ in cognitive significance if and only if the sentence pair in (FPD) differ similarly. [There are a few assumptions built in here, but they are O.K.] Note, however, that the *content* of $[\text{dthat}[\alpha]]$ and the *content* of $[\text{dthat}[\beta]]$ are the same whenever $[\alpha = \beta]$ is true. Thus the difference in cognitive significance between the sentence pair in (FPD) cannot be accounted for in terms of content.

If Frege's solution to (FP) was correct, then α and β have different contents. From this it follows that $[\text{dthat}[\alpha]]$ and $[\text{dthat}[\beta]]$ have different characters. [It doesn't really, because of the identification of contents with intensions, but let it pass.] Is character, then, the object of thought?

If you and I both say to ourselves,

(B) 'I am getting bored'

have we thought the same thing? We could not have, because what you thought was true while what I thought was false.

What we must do is disentangle two epistemological notions: *the objects of thought* (what Frege called 'Thoughts') and the *cognitive significance of*

---

[3] This section has benefited from the opportunity to read, and discuss with him, John Perry's paper 'Frege on Demonstratives', which first appeared in *Philosophical Review*, 86 (Oct. 1977), 474–97, and appears now as ch. 3 in this volume.

an object of thought. As has been noted above, a character may be likened to a manner of presentation of a content. This suggests that we identify objects of thought with contents and the cognitive significance of such objects with characters.

Principle I: Objects of thought (Thoughts) = Contents

Principle II: Cognitive significance of a Thought = Character

According to this view, the thoughts associated with [dthat[α] = dthat[β]] and [dthat[α]] = dthat[α]] are the same, but the thought (not the denotation, mind you, but the *thought*) is *presented* differently.

It is important to see that we have not *simply* generalized Frege's theory, providing a higher order Fregean sense for each name of a regular Fregean sense.[4] In Frege's theory, a given manner of presentation presents the same object to all mankind.[5] But for us, a given manner of presentation—a character—what we both said to ourselves when we both said (B)—will, in general, present different objects (of thought) to different persons (and even different Thoughts to the same person at different times).

How then can we claim that we have captured the idea of cognitive significance? To break the link between cognitive significance and universal Fregean senses and at the same time forge the link between cognitive significance and character we must come to see the *context-sensitivity* (dare I call it ego-orientation?) of cognitive states.

Let us try a Putnam-like experiment. We raise two identical twins, Castor and Pollux, under qualitatively identical conditions, qualitatively identical stimuli, etc. If necessary, we may monitor their brain states and make small corrections in their brain structures if they begin drifting apart. They respond to all cognitive stimuli in identical fashion.[6] Have we not been successful in achieving the same cognitive (i.e. psychological) state? Of course we have, what more could one ask! But wait, they believe different things. Each sincerely says,

---

[4] According to Church, such higher order Fregean senses are already called for by Frege's theory.

[5] See his remarks in 'On Sense and Nominatum' regarding the 'common treasure of thoughts which is transmitted from generation to generation' and remarks there and in 'The Thought' in connection with tensed sentences, that 'Only a sentence supplemented by a time-indication and complete in every respect expresses a thought.'

[6] Perhaps it should be mentioned here, to forestall an objection, that neither uses a proper name for the other or for himself—only 'my brother' and 'I'—and that raising them required a lot of environmental work to maintain the necessary symmetries, or, alternatively, a lot of work with the brain state machine. If proper names are present, and each uses a different name for himself (or, for the other), they will never achieve the same *total* cognitive state since one will sincerely say, 'I am Castor' and the other will not. They may still achieve the same cognitive state in its relevant part.

My brother was born before I was

and the beliefs they thereby express conflict. In this, Castor speaks the truth, while Pollux speaks falsely. This does not reflect on the identity of their cognitive states, for, as Putnam has emphasized, circumstances alone do not determine extension (here, the truth-value) from cognitive state. In so far as distinct persons can be in the same cognitive state, Castor and Pollux are.

> Corollary I: It is an almost inevitable consequence of the fact that two persons are in the same cognitive state, that they will disagree in their attitudes towards some object of thought.

The corollary applies equally well to the same person at different times, and to the same person at the same time in different circumstances.[7] In general, the corollary applies to any individuals x, y, in different contexts.

My aim was to argue that the cognitive significance of a word or phrase was to be identified with its character, the way the content is presented to us. In discussing the twins, I tried to show that persons could be in the same total cognitive state and still, as we would say, believe different things. This doesn't prove that the cognitive content of, say, a single sentence or even a word is to be identified with its character, but it strongly suggests it.

Let me try a different line of argument. We agree that a given content may be presented under various characters and that consequently we may hold a propositional attitude towards a given *content* under one character but not under another. (For example, on 27 March of this year, having lost track of the date, I may continue to hope to be finished by this 26 March, without hoping to be finished by yesterday.) Now instead of arguing that character is what we would ordinarily call cognitive significance, let me just ask why we should be interested in the character under which we hold our various attitudes. Why should we be interested in that special kind of significance that is sensitive to the use of indexicals; 'I', 'here', 'now', 'that', and the like? John Perry, in his stimulating and insightful paper 'Frege on Demonstratives' asks and answers this question. [Perry uses 'thought' where I would use 'object of thought' or 'content', he uses 'apprehend' for 'believe' but *note that other psychological verbs would yield analogous cases*. I have taken a few liberties in substituting my own terminology for Perry's and have added the emphasis.]

---

[7] The corollary would also apply to the same person at the same time in the same circumstances but in different places, if such could be.

Why should we care under what character someone apprehends a thought, so long as he does? I can only sketch the barest suggestion of an answer here. *We use the manner of presentation, the character, to individuate psychological states, in explaining and predicting action.* It is the manner of presentation, the character and not the thought apprehended, that is tied to human action. When you and I have beliefs under the common character of 'A bear is about to attack me', we behave similarly. We both roll up in a ball and try to be as still as possible. Different thoughts apprehended, same character, same behavior. When you and I both apprehend that I am about to be attacked by a bear, we behave differently. I roll up in a ball, you run to get help. Same thought apprehended, different characters, different behaviors.[8]

Perry's examples can be easily multiplied. My hope to be finished by a certain time is sensitive to how the content corresponding to the time is presented, as 'yesterday' or as 'this 26 March'. If I see, reflected in a window, the image of a man whose pants appear to be on fire, my behaviour is sensitive to whether I think, 'His pants are on fire', or 'My pants are on fire', though the object of thought may be the same.

So long as Frege confined his attention to indexical free expressions, and given his theory of proper names, it is not surprising that he did not distinguish objects of thought (content) from cognitive significance (character), for that is the realm of *fixed* character and thus, as already remarked, there is a natural identification of character with content. Frege does, however, discuss indexicals in two places. The first passage, in which he discusses 'yesterday' and 'today' I have already discussed. Everything he says there is essentially correct. (He does not go far enough.) The second passage has provoked few endorsements and much scepticism. It too, I believe, is susceptible of an interpretation which makes it essentially correct. I quote it in full.

Now everyone is presented to himself in a particular and primitive way, in which he is presented to no one else. So, when Dr. Lauben thinks that he has been wounded, he will probably take as a basis this primitive way in which he is presented to himself. And only Dr. Lauben himself can grasp thoughts determined in this way. But now he may want to communicate with others. He cannot communicate a thought which he alone can grasp. Therefore, if he now says 'I have been wounded', he must use the 'I' in a sense that can be grasped by others, perhaps in the sense of 'he who is speaking to you at this moment', by doing which he makes the associated conditions of his utterance serve for the expression of his thought.[9]

What is the particular and primitive way in which Dr Lauben is presented to himself? What cognitive content presents Dr Lauben to himself, but presents him to nobody else? Thoughts determined this way can be grasped by Dr Lauben, but no one else can grasp *that* thought

---

[8] Perry, 'Frege on Demonstratives', p. 494.

[9] G. Frege, 'The Thought: A Logical Inquiry', *Mind*, 65 (1956), p. 298.

determined in *that* way. The answer, I believe, is, simply, that Dr Lauben is presented to himself under the character of 'I'.

A sloppy thinker might succumb to the temptation to slide from an acknowledgement of the privileged *perspective* we each have on ourselves—only I can refer to me as 'I'—to the conclusions: first, that this perspective necessarily yields a privileged *picture* of what is seen (referred to), and second, that this picture is what is intended when one makes use of the privileged perspective (by saying 'I'). These conclusions, even if correct, are not forced upon us. The character of 'I' provides the acknowledged privileged perspective, whereas the analysis of the content of particular occurrences of 'I' provides for (and needs) no privileged pictures. There may be metaphysical, epistemological, or ethical reasons why I (so conceived) am especially *important* to myself. (Compare: why *now* is an especially important time to me. It too is presented in a particular and primitive way, and this moment cannot be presented at any other time in the same way.)[10] But the phenomenon noted by Frege—that everyone is presented to himself in a particular and primitive way—can be fully accounted for using only our semantical theory.

Furthermore, regarding the first conclusion, I sincerely doubt that there is, for each of us on each occasion of the use of 'I', a particular, primitive, and incommunicable Fregean self-concept which we tacitly express to ourselves. And regarding the second conclusion: even if Castor were sufficiently narcissistic to associate such self-concepts with his every use of 'I', his twin Pollux, whose mental life is qualitatively identical with Castor's, would associate the *same* self-concept with *his* every (matching) use of 'I'.[11] The second conclusion would lead to the absurd result that when Castor and Pollux each say 'I', they do not thereby distinguish themselves from one another. (An even more astonishing result is possible. Suppose that due to a bit of self-deception the self-concept held in common by Castor and Pollux fits neither of them. The second conclusion then leads irresistibly to the possibility that when Castor and Pollux each say 'I' they each refer to a third party!)

The perceptive reader will have noticed that the conclusions of the sloppy thinker regarding the pure indexical 'I' are not unlike those of the Fregean regarding true demonstratives. The sloppy thinker has adopted a *demonstrative theory of indexicals*: 'I' is synonymous with 'this person'

[10] At other times, earlier and later, we can know it only externally, by description as it were. But now we are directly acquainted with it. (I believe I owe this point to John Perry.)

[11] Unless, of course, the self-concept involved a bit of direct reference. In which case (when direct reference is admitted) there seems no need for the whole theory of Fregean self-concepts. Unless, of course, direct reference is limited to items of direct acquaintance, of which more below.

[along with an appropriate *subjective* demonstration], 'now' with 'this
time', 'here' with 'this place' [each associated with some demonstration],
etc. Like the Fregean, the sloppy thinker errs in believing that the sense of
the demonstration is the sense of the indexical, but the sloppy thinker
commits an additional error in believing that such senses are in any way
necessarily associated with uses of pure indexicals. The slide from
privileged perspective to privileged picture is the sloppy thinker's original
sin. Only one who is located in the exact centre of the Sahara Desert is
entitled to refer to that place as 'here', but aside from that, the place may
present no distinguishing features.[12]

The sloppy thinker's conclusions may have another source. Failure to
distinguish between the cognitive significance of a thought and the
thought itself seems to have led some to believe that the elements of an
object of thought must each be directly accessible to the mind. From this it
follows that if a singular proposition is an object of thought, the thinker
must somehow be immediately acquainted with each of the individuals
involved. But, as we have seen, the situation is rather different from this.
Singular propositions may be presented to us under characters which
neither imply nor presuppose any special form of acquaintance with the
individuals of the singular propositions. The psychological states, perhaps
even the epistemological situations, of Castor and Pollux are alike, yet
they assert distinct singular propositions when they each say 'My brother
was born before me'. Had they lived at different times they might still
have been situated alike epistemologically while asserting distinct singular
propositions in saying 'It is quiet here now'. A kidnapped heiress, locked

---

[12] So far, we have limited our attention to the 3 sentences of the quotation from Frege. How
are we to account for the second part of Frege's remarks?

Suppose Dr Lauben wants to communicate his thought without disturbing its cognitive
content. (Think of trying to tell a colour-blind person that the green light should be replaced.
You would have to find another way of communicating what you wanted to get across.) He
can't communicate *that* thought with *that* significance, so, he himself would have to attach a
non-standard significance to 'I'. Here is a suggestion. He points at his auditor and uses the
demonstrative 'you'. If we neglect fine differences in perspective, the demonstration will have
the same character for all present and it certainly will have the same demonstratum for all
present, therefore the demonstrative will have the same *character and content* for all present.
The indexical 'now' will have the same character and content for all present. Thus 'the person
who is speaking to you [points] now' will have a common character and content for all those
present. Unfortunately the content is not that of 'I' as Dr Lauben standardly uses it. He needs a
demonstrative like 'dthat' to convert the description to a term with a fixed content. He chooses
the demonstrative 'he', with a relative clause construction to make clear his intention. Now, if
Dr Lauben uses 'I' with the non-standard meaning usually attached to 'he who is speaking to
you [points] now' he will have found a way to communicate his original thought in a form whose
cognitive significance is common to all. Very clever, Dr Lauben.

[Perhaps it is poor pedagogy to join this fanciful interpretation of the second part of the
passage with the serious interpretation of the first part.]

in the trunk of a car, knowing neither the time nor where she is, may think 'It is quiet here now' and the indexicals will remain directly referential.[13]

Corollary II: Ignorance of the referent does not defeat the directly referential character of indexicals.

From this it follows that a special form of knowledge of an object is neither required nor presupposed in order that a person may entertain as object of thought a singular proposition involving that object.

There is nothing inaccessible to the mind about the semantics of direct reference, even when the reference is to that which we know only by description. What allows us to take various propositional attitudes towards singular propositions is not the form of our acquaintance with the objects but is rather our ability to manipulate the conceptual apparatus of direct reference.[14]

The foregoing remarks are aimed at refuting *Direct Acquaintance Theories of direct reference*. According to such theories, the question whether an utterance expresses a singular proposition turns, in the first instance, on the speaker's *knowledge of the referent* rather than on the *form of the reference*. If the speaker lacks the appropriate form of acquaintance with the referent, the utterance cannot express a singular proposition, and any apparently directly referring expressions used must be abbreviations or disguises for something like Fregean descriptions. Perhaps the Direct Acquaintance theorist thought that only a theory like his could permit singular propositions while still providing a solution for Frege's problem. If we could *directly* refer to a given object in non-equivalent ways (e.g., as 'dthat[Hes]' and 'dthat[Phos]'), we could not— so he thought—explain the difference in cognitive significance between the appropriate instances of $[\alpha = \alpha]$ and $[\alpha = \beta]$. Hence, the objects susceptible to direct reference must not permit such reference in inequivalent ways. These objects must, in a certain sense, be wholly local and completely given so that for any two *directly* coreferential terms α and β, $[\alpha = \beta]$ will be uniformative to anyone appropriately situated, epistemologically, to be able to use these terms.[15] I hope that my discussion of the two kinds of meaning—content and character—will have

[13] Can the heiress plead that she could not have believed a singular proposition involving the place p since when thinking 'here' she didn't *know* she was at p, that she was, in fact, unacquainted with the place p? No! Ignorance of the referent is no excuse.

[14] This makes it sound as if an exact and conscious mastery of semantics is prerequisite to having a singular proposition as object of thought. I will try to find a better way to express the point in a succeeding draft.

[15] For some consequences of this view with regard to the interpretation of demonstratives see 'Bob and Carol and Ted and Alice,' appendix VII in J. Hintikka *et al.* (eds.), *Approaches to Natural Language* (Dordrecht: Reidel, 1973), 490–518.

shown the Direct Acquaintance theorist that his views are not the inevitable consequence of the admission of directly referential terms. From the point of view of a lover of direct reference this is good, since the Direct Acquaintance theorist admits direct reference in a portion of language so narrow that it is used only by philosophers.[16]

I have said nothing to dispute the epistemology of the Direct Acquaintance theorist, nothing to deny that there exists his special kind of object with which one can have his special kind of acquaintance. I have only denied the relevance of these epistemological claims to the semantics of direct reference. If we sweep aside metaphysical and epistemological pseudo-explanations of what are essentially semantical phenomena, the result can only be healthy for all three disciplines.

Before going on to further examples of the tendency to confuse metaphysical and epistemological matters with phenomena of the semantics of direct reference, I want to raise briefly the problem of *cognitive dynamics*. Suppose that yesterday you said, and believed it, 'It is a nice day today.' What does it mean to say, today, that you have retained *that* belief? It seems unsatisfactory just to believe the same content under any old character—where is the *retention*?[17] You *can't* believe that content under the same character. Is there some obvious standard adjustment to make to the character, for example, replacing *today* with *yesterday*? If so, then a person like Rip van Winkle, who loses track of time, can't retain any such beliefs. This seems strange. Can we only *retain*

---

[16] There is an obvious connection between the fix in which the Direct Acquaintance theorist finds himself, and *Kripke's problem*: how can [α = β] be informative if α and β differ in neither denotation nor sense (nor, as I shall suggest is the case for proper names, character)?

[17] The sort of case I have in mind is this. I first think, 'His pants are on fire.' I later realize, 'I am he' and thus come to think 'My pants are on fire.' Still later, I decide that I was wrong in thinking 'I am he' and conclude 'His pants were on fire.' If, in fact, I *am* he, have I *retained* my belief that my pants are on fire simply because I believe the same content, though under a different character? (I also deny that content under the former, but for change of tense, character.) When I first thought 'My pants are on fire', a certain singular proposition, call it 'Eek', was the object of thought. At the later stage, both Eek and its negation are believed by me. In this sense, I still believe what I believed before, namely Eek. But this does not capture my sense of *retaining a belief*: a sense that I associate with saying that some people have a very rigid cognitive structure whereas others are very flexible. It is tempting to say that cognitive dynamics is concerned not with retention and change in what is believed, but with retention and change in the characters under which our beliefs are held. I think that this is basically correct. But it is not obvious to me what relation between a character under which a belief is held at one time and the set of characters under which beliefs are held at a later time would constitute retaining the original belief. Where indexicals are involved, for the reasons given below, we cannot simply require that the very same character still appear at the later time. Thus the problem of cognitive dynamics can be put like this: what does it mean to say of an individual who at one time sincerely asserted a sentence containing indexicals that at some later time he has (or has not) *changed his mind* with respect to his assertion? What sentence or sentences must he be willing to assert at the later time?

beliefs presented under a fixed character? This issue has obvious and important connections with Lauben's problem in trying to communicate the thought he *expresses* with 'I have been wounded.' Under what character must his auditor believe Lauben's thought in order for Lauben's communication to have been successful? It is important to note that if Lauben said 'I am wounded' in the usual meaning of 'I', there is no one else who can report what he said, using *indirect* discourse, and convey the cognitive significance (to Lauben) of what he said. This has interesting consequences for the inevitability of so-called *de re* constructions in indirect discourse languages which contain indexicals. (I use 'indirect discourse' as a general term for the analogous form of all psychological verbs.)

A prime example of the confusion of direct reference phenomena with metaphysical and epistemological ideas was first vigorously called to our attention by Saul Kripke in *Naming and Necessity*. I wish to parallel his remarks disconnecting the a priori and the necessary.

The form of a prioricity that I will discuss is that of logical truth (in the logic of demonstratives). We saw very early that a truth of the logic of demonstratives, like 'I am here now', need not be necessary. There are many such cases of logical truths which are not necessary. If α is any singular term, then

$$\alpha = \text{dthat}[\alpha]$$

is a logical truth. But

$$\square \, (\alpha = \text{dthat}[\alpha])$$

is generally false. We can, of course, also easily produce the opposite effect.

$$\square \, (\text{dthat}[\alpha] = \text{dthat}[\beta])$$

may be true, although

$$\text{dthat}[\alpha] = \text{dthat}[\beta]$$

is not logically true, and is even logically equivalent to the contingency,

$$\alpha = \beta.$$

(I call ϕ and ψ logically equivalent when $[\phi \leftrightarrow \psi]$ is logically true.) These cases are reminiscent of Kripke's case of the terms, 'one meter' and 'the length of bar x'. But where Kripke focuses on the special epistemological situation of one who is present at the dubbing, the descriptive meaning associated with our directly referential term dthat[α] is carried in the semantics of the language.[18]

How can something be both logically true, and thus *certain*, and *contingent* at the same time? In the case of indexicals the answer is easy to see.

> E. Corollary III: The bearers of logical truth and of contingency are different entities. It is the character (or, the sentence, if you prefer) that is logically true, producing a true content in every context. But it is the content (the proposition, if you will) that is contingent or necessary.

As can readily be seen, the modal logic of demonstratives is a rich and interesting thing.

It is easy to be taken in by the effortless (but fallacious) move from certainty (logical truth) to necessity. In his important article 'Three Grades of Modal Involvement',[19] Quine expresses his scepticism of the first grade of modal involvement: the sentence predicate and all it stands for, and his distate for the second grade of modal involvement: disguising the predicate as an operator 'It is necessary that'. But he suggests that no new metaphysical undesirables are admitted until the third grade of modal involvement: quantification across the necessity operator into an open sentence.

I must protest. That first step let in some metaphysical undesirables, falsehoods. All logical truths are analytic, but they can go false when you back them up to '□'.

One other notorious example of a logical truth which is not necessary,

> I exist.

One can quickly verify that, in every context, this character yields a true proposition—but rarely a necessary one. It seems likely to me that it was a

---

[18] A case of a seemingly different kind is that of the logical equivalence between an arbitrary sentence φ and the result of prefixing either or both of the indexical operators, 'it is actually the case that' (symbolized '*A*') and 'it is now the case that' (symbolized '*N*'). The biconditional [(φ ⟷ *AN*φ)] is logically true, but prefixing either '□' or its temporal counterpart can lead to falsehood. It is interesting to note, in this case, that the parallel between modal and temporal modifications of sentences carries over to indexicals. The foregoing claims are verified by the formal system. Note that the formal system is constructed in accordance with Carnap's proposal that the intension of an expression be that function which assigns to each circumstance, the extension of the expression with respect to that circumstance. This has commonly been thought to insure that logically equivalent expressions have the same intension (Church's Alternative 2 among principles of individuation for the notion of sense) and that logically true sentences express the (unique) necessary proposition. Homework Problem: What went wrong here?

[19] *Proceedings of the XI International Congress of Philosophy*, 14 (Brussels, 1953) 65–81; repr. in W. V. Quine, *The Ways of Paradox* (New York, 1966).

conflict between the feelings of contingency and of certainty associated
with this sentence that has led to such painstaking examination of its
'proofs'. It is just a truth of logic!

Dana Scott has remedied one lacuna in this analysis. What of the
premiss

> I think

and the connective

> Therefore   ?

His discovery was that the premiss is incomplete, and that the last five
words

> up the logic of demonstratives

has been lost in an early manuscript version.[20]

---

[20] Again, it is probably a pedagogical mistake to mix this playful paragraph with the
preceding serious one.

3

FREGE ON DEMONSTRATIVES[1]

JOHN PERRY

In 'The Thought', Frege briefly discusses sentences containing such demonstratives as 'today', 'here', and 'yesterday', and then turns to certain questions that he says are raised by the occurrence of 'I' in sentences (T 24–6). He is led to say that, when one thinks about oneself, one grasps thoughts that others cannot grasp, that cannot be communicated. Nothing could be more out of the spirit of Frege's account of sense and thought than an incommunicable, private thought. Demonstratives seem to have posed a severe difficulty for Frege's philosophy of language, to which his doctrine of incommunicable senses was a reaction.

In the first part of this chapter, I explain the problem demonstratives pose for Frege, and explore three ways he might have dealt with it. I argue that none of these ways provides Frege with a solution to his problem consistent with his philosophy of language. The first two are plausible as solutions, but contradict his identification of the sense expressed by a sentence with a thought. The third preserves the identification, but is implausible. In the second part, I suggest that Frege was led to his doctrine of incommunicable senses as a result of some appreciation of the difficulties his account of demonstratives faces, for these come quickly to the surface when we think about 'I'. I argue that incommunicable senses won't help. I end by trying to identify the central problem with Frege's approach, and sketching an alternative.

This chapter appeared originally in *Philosophical Review*, 86 (Oct. 1977), 474–97. Reprinted by permission of the Editor and the author.

[1] The following abbreviations are used for works cited in the text. 'T' for G. Frege, 'The Thought: A Logical Inquiry', repr. in P. F. Strawson, *Philosophical Logic* (Oxford, 1967), 17–38. This trans., by A. M. and M. Quinton, appeared originally in *Mind*, 65 (1956), 289–311. The original, 'Der Gedanke. Eine logische Untersuchung', appeared in *Beiträge zur Philosophie des deutschen Idealismus*, 1 (1918), 58–77. 'SR' for Frege 'On Sense and Reference', in M. Black and P. Geach (eds.), *Translations from the Philosophical Writings of Gottlob Frege* (Oxford, 1960), trans. M. Black. The original, 'Über Sinn und Bedeutung', appeared in *Zeitschrift für Philosophie und philosophische Kritik*, 50 (1892), 25–50. 'CT' for 'Compound Thoughts', in E. D. Klemke (ed.), *Essays on Frege*, trans. R. H. Stoothoff (Urbana, Ill., 1968). The original, 'Gedankenfuge', appeared in *Beitrage zur philosophie des deutschen Idealismus*, 3 (1923), 36–51. 'F' for M. Dummett, *Frege* (London, 1973).

I

Before explaining the problem posed by demonstratives, certain points about Frege's philosophy of languages need to be made.

In 'On Sense and Reference', Frege introduces the notion of sense, in terms of the cognitive value of sentences. He then goes on to make two key identifications. First, he identifies the sense of a sentence with the thought it expresses. Then, he identifies the thought expressed by a sentence, and so the sense it has, with the indirect reference of the sentence in the scope of a cognitive verb.

The phrases 'the sense of a sentence', 'the thought expressed by a sentence', and 'the indirect reference of a sentence', are not mere synonyms. They have different senses, though, if Frege's account is correct, they have the same reference. In particular, each is associated, as Frege introduces it, with a separate criterion of difference.

Sense In the beginning of 'On Sense and Reference', Frege introduces the notion of sense as a way of accounting for the difference in cognitive value of the senses of '$a = a$' and '$a = b$', even when both are true, and so made up of coreferential expressions (SR 56–8). So a criterion of difference for sense is,

> If S and S' have differing cognitive value, then S and S' have different senses.

Dummett's explanation of sense will help us to convert this to something more helpful. He emphasizes that sense is linked to understanding and truth. The sense of an expression is 'what we know when we understand it', and what we know when we understand it is something like an ideal procedure for determining its reference (F 293, 589 ff.). In the case of a sentence, whose reference is a truth-value, the sense is what we know when, roughly, we know what would have to be done—whether or not this is humanly possible—to determine whether or not it is true.

What Frege seems to have in mind at the beginning of 'On Sense and Reference', then, is a situation in which some person A who understands both '$a = a$' and '$a = b$', accepts the first while rejecting, or being unsure about, the second. The assumption seems to be, that if A associated just the same ideal procedures with both sentences, he would accept the second if he accepted the first. So he must not associate the same ideal procedures with both sentences, and so, since he understands them, their senses differ. So we have:

> If A understands S and S', and accepts S as true while not accepting S', then S and S' have different senses.

This criterion of difference allows that sentences might have different senses, though provably or necessarily equivalent. A complex true mathematical equation might be provably equivalent to '2 + 3 = 5', and yet a perfectly competent speaker might accept the latter and reject the former, having made an error in calculation. To know an ideal procedure for determining reference is not necessarily to have carried it out, or even to be able to.

Thought   'Thought' is not just a term introduced by Frege as another way of saying 'sense of a sentence'. The notion derived from Frege's untangling of the jumbled notion of a judgement, into act, thought, and truth-value. The thought is, first and foremost, 'that for which the question of truth arises' (T 20–2). This is clearly intended to be a criterion of difference for thoughts:

If S is true and S' is not, S and S' express different thoughts.

Indirect reference   Consider a report of a belief: 'Copernicus believed that the planetary orbits are circles.' On Frege's analysis, this is relational. 'Believed that' stands for a relation, which is asserted to hold between Copernicus and whatever it is that 'the planetary orbits are circles' refers to as it occurs in this sentence. Standing alone, 'the planetary orbits are circles' would refer to the False, but here it clearly does not have that ordinary reference. If it did, the substitution of any false sentence at all should preserve truth of the whole report (SR 66–7). The notion of the indirect reference of 'the planteary orbits are circles', is just whatever it is that this sentence has as reference here. (The phrase is first used in connection with indirect discourse [SR 59].) Now if '$a R b$' is true, and 'a R c' is not, b is not c. So we have a clear criterion of difference:

If 'A believes S' is true, and 'A believes S'' is not, then, S and S' do not have the same indirect reference.

So we have three separable criteria of difference. But Frege, as noted, identifies the sense of S, the thought expressed by S, and the indirect reference of S. So we are led to a further principle:

S and S' have different senses, if and only if they express different thoughts, and if and only if they have different indirect references.

Sense completers   Frege takes the structure of language as a suggestive guide to the structure of senses and objects. Just as he views the sentence,

Two plus two equals four.

as the result of combining the complete

Two

with the incomplete

( ) plus two equals four

so he sees the sense of 'two plus two equals four' as determined by the sense of 'two' and the sense of '( ) plus two equals four'. The sense of the latter is incomplete; the sense of the former completes it, to yield the complete sense of 'Two plus two equals four.'

'( ) plus two equals four' could also be made into a sentence by writing 'something' in the blank; similarly the sense of '( ) plus two equals four' can be completed with the sense of 'something'. The sense of 'something', however, unlike the sense of 'two', is itself also incomplete. Where 'two' refers to an object, 'something' refers to a concept. Two appropriately related incomplete senses can combine to form a complete sense; two complete senses cannot combine at all (CT 538).

Thus the class of *sense completers* for a given incomplete sense is hybrid, containing both complete and incomplete senses. But the term will be useful in what follows.

Sense had and sense expressed The structure of language is not always a sure guide to the structure of senses. Not everything we count as a sentence has a complete sense. Consider (1),

(1) Russia and Canada quarrelled when Nemtsanov defected.

'Russia and Canada quarrelled', as it occurs as a clause in (1), does not have a complete sense (SR 71; T 37). It refers to a concept of times and thus must have an incomplete sense. 'When Nemtsanov defected' refers to a time; the sentence is true if the time referred to falls under the concept referred to. Thus the sense of 'when Nemtsanov defected' is a sense completer for the sense of 'Russia and Canada quarrelled'.

So the sense of the sentence 'Russia and Canada quarrelled' is not a thought. Not any sentence, but only a sentence 'complete in every respect' expresss a thought (T 37).

Now 'Russia and Canada quarrelled' could be used, without a dependent clause, to express a thought. If it appeared alone, we might take it to express, *on that occasion*, the sense of.

At some time or other, Russia and Canada quarrelled.

In another setting, for example after the question, 'What happened when

Nemtsanov defected?', the sentence would express the sense of (1). So we must, even before considering demonstratives, distinguish between the sense a sentence *has* on each occasion of use and the senses it *expresses* on various occasions of use. For an 'eternal' sentence, one that really is 'complete in every respect', the two will be the same; for a sentence like 'Russia and Canada quarrelled', the sense *had* is incomplete; the sense *expressed* on a given occasion will be the result of completing that sense, with some sense completer available from the context of utterance. It is clearly only the sense expressed on such occasions, that Frege wants to identify with a thought.

The problem posed by demonstratives　We are now in a position to see why demonstratives pose a problem for Frege.

I begin by quoting the passage in 'The Thought' in which Frege discusses demonstratives in general.

> Often . . . the mere wording, which can be grasped by writing or the gramophone, does not suffice for the expression of the thought . . . If a time indication is needed by the present tense [as opposed to cases in which it is used to express timelessness, as in the statement of mathematical laws] one must know when the sentence was uttered to apprehend the thought correctly. Therefore, the time of utterance is part of the expression of the thought. If someone wants to say the same today as he expressed yesterday using the word 'today', he must replace this word with 'yesterday'. Although the thought is the same its verbal expression must be different so that the sense, which would otherwise be affected by the differing times of utterance, is readjusted. The case is the same with words like 'here' and 'there'. In all such cases the mere wording, as it is given in writing, is not the complete expression of the thought, but the knowledge of certain accompanying conditions of utterance, which are used as means of expressing the thought, are needed for its correct apprehension. The pointing of fingers, hand movements, glances may belong here too. The same utterance containing the word 'I' will express different thoughts in the mouths of different men, of which some may be true, others false. (T 24)

Consider (2),

(2) Russia and Canada quarrelled today.

The sentence 'Russia and Canada quarrelled' has in (2), as in (1), only an incomplete sense. So presumably 'today' in (2) must somehow do what 'when Nemtsanov defected' does in (1), and supply us with a completing sense. But it does not seem to do this at all.

If I uttered (2) on 1 August, I expressed something true, on 2 August, something false. If 'today' had the same sense on 1 August as on 2 August, then (2) in its entirety must have had the same sense on both occasions. If so, the sense of (2) must be incomplete, for if it were complete, its truth-value could not change.

So, if 'today' provides a completing sense on both days, its sense must change just at midnight. But what we know when we understand how to use 'today' doesn't seem to change from day to day.

When we understand a word like 'today', what we seem to know is a rule taking us from an occasion of utterance to a certain object. 'Today' takes us to the very day of utterance, 'yesterday' to the day before the day of utterance, 'I' to the speaker, and so forth. I shall call this the *role* of the demonstrative. I take a context to be a set of features of an actual utterance, certainly including time, place, and speaker, but probably also more. Just what a context must include is a difficult question, to be answered only after detailed study of various demonstratives. The object a demonstrative takes us to in a given context, I shall call its value in that context or on that occasion of use. Clearly, we must grant 'today' a role, the same on both occasions of use. And we must, as clearly, give it different values on the two occasions.

Any reasonable account has to recognize that demonstratives have roles. The role of a demonstrative does not seem reducible to other notions available from Frege's philosophy. Senses do not carry us from context to references, but directly to references, the same on each occasion of use. One might suppose that 'yesterday' could be thought to have just the sense of 'the day before'. But,

(3) Russia and Canada quarrelled the day before.

does not have the same sense as (4).

(4) Russia and Canada quarrelled today.

If I ask on 5 August, 'Did Russia and Canada quarrel on 2 August?', (3) would imply that they quarrelled on 1 August, (4) that they quarrelled on 4 August. If (3) were uttered when no day had already been mentioned, it would not express anything complete, but simply give rise to the question, 'before what?' An utterance of (4) would still be fully in order.

Frege recognizes that demonstratives have roles, or at least that the context of utterance is crucial when dealing with demonstratives. He does not talk about the sense of 'today' or 'I' so he also seems to have recognized that the role of a demonstrative is not just a sense, as he has explained senses.

But Frege clearly thinks that, given knowledge of the accompanying conditions of utterance, we can get from an utterance of a sentence like (2) or (4) to a thought. He must have thought, then, that the demonstrative provides us not simply with an object—its value on the occasion of utterance—but with a *completing sense*. This is puzzling.

Neither the unchanging role of 'today', nor its changing value, provides us with a completing sense. A day is not a sense, but a reference corresponding to indefinitely many senses (SR 71). There is no route back from reference to sense. So how do we get from the incomplete sense of 'Russia and Canada quarrelled', the demonstrative 'today', and the context to a thought? This is the problem demonstratives pose for Frege.

I shall first describe two options Frege might have taken, which would have excused him from the necessity of finding a completing sense. I shall argue that Frege did not take these options, and could not, given his identification of sense expressed and thought.

Sense as roles?   Let $S(d)$ be a sentence containing a demonstrative d. Without the demonstrative, we have something, $S(\ )$, that has an incomplete sense, and so refers to a concept. This may actually still be a sentence, as when we remove 'today' from (2), or it may look more like it should, as when we remove the 'I' from 'I am wounded.'

The following scheme gives us a rule for getting from a particular context, to a truth-value, for any such sentence $S(d)$.

$S(d)$ is true when uttered in context c, if and only if the value of d in c falls under the concept referred to by $S(\ )$.[2]

Such a rule is the *role of $S(d)$*. It is just an extension of the notion of the role of a demonstrative. Roles take us from contexts to objects. In the case of a sentence, the object is a truth-value.

Thus (4) is true as uttered on 2 August, if and only if 1 August is a day that falls under the concept referred to by 'Russia and Canada quarrelled'. 'I am ill' as uttered by Lauben is true if and only if Lauben falls under the concept referred to by '( ) is ill'.

The role of a sentence containing a demonstrative is clearly analogous in many ways to the sense of a sentence not containing a demonstrative. The role is a procedure for determining truth-value, just as the sense is. The difference is that the role is a procedure which starts from a context.

This analogy suggests an option, which Frege might have taken. He might have identified the sense expressed by a sentence containing a demonstrative with its role. This would amount to a generalization of the notion of sense. On this view, an incomplete sense, like that of 'Russia and Canada quarrelled', could be completed in two ways. A sense

---

[2] Here and elsewhere I assume, for the sake of simplicity of exposition, that we are considering sentences containing no more than one demonstrative. Given the notion of a sequence of objects, there would be no difficulties in extending various suggestions and options for the general case. In some of the examples I use, additional demonstratives are really needed. 'Lauben is wounded', for example, still needs a time indication.

completer, such as the sense of 'when Nemtsanov defected', gives us a complete sense of the old sort. A demonstrative, like 'today', yields a sense of the new sort, a role. No complete sense of the old sort is involved at all in the utterance of a sentence containing a demonstrative, so no completing sense need be found.

But this cannot have been Frege's view. For it is clear that he thinks a thought has been expressed in the utterance of a sentence containing a demonstrative. The role of the sentence cannot be identified with the thought, for a sentence could express the same role on different occasions while having different truth-values. So by the criteria of difference for thoughts, roles are not thoughts. By the identification of the sense expressed by a sentence and the thought expressed, roles are not the senses expressed by a sentence.

Thoughts as information? We can put the problem this way. (2), as uttered on 1 August, with the role of 'today' fully mastered, seems to yield just this information:

(*i*) an incomplete sense, that of 'Russia and Canada quarrelled';
(*ii*) an object, the day 1 August 1976.

(*i*) and (*ii*) do not uniquely determine a thought, but only an equivalence class of thoughts. Belonging to this equivalence class will be just those thoughts obtainable by completing the sense of 'Russia and Canada quarrelled' with a sense completer which determines, as reference, 1 August 1976. I shall call thoughts related in this manner *informationally equivalent*.[3]

The second option I shall discuss is introducing a new notion of a thought, corresponding to such a class of informationally equivalent thoughts. Since the information (*i*) and (*ii*) is sufficient to identify such a class, without identifying any one of its members, this would explain how we can get from (*i*) to (*ii*) to a thought, without needing a completing sense.

On this view, an utterance of $S(d)$ in context c, and $S'(d')$ in context c', will express the same thought if the (incomplete) senses of $S(\ )$ and $S'(\ )$ are the same, and if the value of d in c is the same as the value of d' in c'. Thus (2), uttered on 1 August, and (4), uttered on 2 August, would express the same thought. Dummett interprets in this way (F 384) Frege's remark,

---

[3] This notion is taken from A. W. Burks, 'Icon, Index, and Symbol', *Philosophy and Phenomenological Research*, 9 (1949), 685. In this pioneering and illuminating work on demonstratives, Burks emphasizes the ineliminability of demonstratives.

If someone wants to say the same today as he expressed yesterday using the word 'today', he must replace this with 'yesterday'. Although the thought is the same its verbal expression must be different.

But this cannot have been Frege's view. This criterion actually introduces a new kind of thought, corresponding to informationally equivalent classes of thoughts of the old kind. The thought expressed by Lauben, when he says 'I am wounded' to Leo Peter, cannot be identified with the thought expressed by any non-demonstrative completion of the same incomplete sense in which the singular term refers to Lauben, such as

> The man born on 13 September 1875 in N.N. is wounded.
> The only doctor who lives in the house next door to Rudolf Lingens is wounded.

These express different thoughts, so the thought Lauben expresses with 'I am wounded' cannot be identified with *the* thought they both express; there just isn't any such thought. There is no more reason to identify it with the one than with the other, or with any other such thought. Nor can thoughts of this new type be identified with classes of thoughts of the old, for in different possible circumstances the pair, Dr Lauben and the incomplete sense of '( ) am ill', would correspond to different sets of Fregean thoughts. If Lauben had moved, the two Fregean thoughts in question would not be informationally equivalent. We have here a radically new kind of thought, of which Frege would not have approved, even if he had seen its necessity. We have in effect made the value of the demonstrative a part of the thought. But Frege insists that only senses can be parts of senses.

Dummett remarks,

It is, of course, quite unnecessary to suppose that a thought expressible by the utterance on a particular occasion of a sentence containing a token reflexive expression can also be expressed by some 'eternal' sentence containing no such expressions. (F 384)

But it is not only unnecessary, but impossible, on this account, that the thought should be expressed by an eternal sentence. It is not the right kind of thought for an eternal sentence to express.

Second, and closely related, this notion of a thought would violate the criteria of difference.

Suppose I am viewing the harbour from downtown Oakland; the bow and stern of the aircraft carrier *Enterprise* are visible, though its middle is obscured by a large building. The name '*Enterprise*' is clearly visible on the bow, so when I tell a visitor, 'This is the *Enterprise*', pointing towards the bow, this is readily accepted. When I say, pointing to the stern clearly several city blocks from the bow, 'That is the *Enterprise*', however, she refuses to believe me. By the criterion of difference, a different sense was expressed the first time than the second. On the present suggested criterion of identity for thoughts, the same thought was expressed; the incomplete sense was the same in both cases, and the value of the demonstratives was the *Enterprise* in both cases. To adopt this notion of a thought, Frege would have to give up the identification of sense expressed and thought expressed.

This is, of course, simply a variation on Frege's own Morning Star example. Suppose I point to Venus in the morning, and again in the evening, saying 'That's the Morning Star.' My listener may accept what I say the first time, and continue to think I was right, while rejecting what I say the second time. Here the *same* sentence has a different cognitive value at different times—for my listener has not changed her mind. The sentence does not have different cognitive values because the words have undergone a change of meaning, but because the sentence alone does not express the complete sense. Some supplementation is needed; here the gestures towards Venus provide it. But just what supplementation do they provide? If the supplementation were merely taken to be Venus itself— which is what the present proposals amount to—then the sense of the sentence would have been supplemented in the same way on both occasions. But then we would have the same sense expressed on both occasions, in violation of the criterion of difference for senses.

Frege does not explicitly mention the demonstratives 'this' and 'that'. So it is worth pointing out that examples can be constructed using demonstratives he does mention. For example, I might accept what you say at 11.50 p.m. when you utter 'Russia and Canada quarrelled today', but disbelieve you at 12.15 a.m. when you utter 'Russia and Canada quarrelled yesterday', having lost track of time.

Of course, Frege may have meant to introduce such a new notion of a thought at this point. That he does not explain it, counts against this interpretation. And what he goes on to say, in the next paragraph, seems to make it totally implausible. There he discusses proper names, and arrives at a point where he has all the materials for this notion of a thought in his hand, so to speak, and yet passes up the opportunity to mould them into the new notion. He describes a situation in which two men express different thoughts with the sentence 'Gustav Lauben has been wounded', one knowing him as the unique man born a certain day, the other as the unique doctor living in a certain house. He recognizes that these different thoughts are systematically equivalent:

The different thoughts which thus result from the same sentence correspond in their truth-value, of course; that is to say, if one is true then all are true, and if one is false then all are false.

But he insists,

Nevertheless their distinctness must be recognized.

His reason here is clearly a complex example he has just constructed, in which sentences expressing such informationally equivalent thoughts have different cognitive value:

It is possible that Herbert Garner takes the sense of the sentence 'Dr. Lauben has been wounded' to be true while, misled by false information, taking the sense of 'Gustav Lauben has been wounded' to be false. Under the assumptions given these thoughts are therefore different. (T 25)

If demonstratives had driven Frege, three paragraphs before this, to the introduction of a class of thoughts, corresponding to a class of informationally equivalent thoughts of the old sort, I think he would have employed it, or at least mentioned it, here.

Senses, considered to be roles, cannot be thoughts. Thoughts, considered as information, cannot be senses. If Frege is to keep his identification of sense expressed by a sentence, with thought expressed by a sentence, he must find, somewhere, a completing sense.

Demonstratives as providing a completing sense   How can we extract from a demonstrative an appropriate completing sense? Such a sense, it seems, would have to be intimately related to the sense of a unique description of the value of the demonstrative in the context of utterance. But where does such a description come from? 'Today' seems to get us only to a day. And a day does not provide a particular description of itself.

In the case of proper names, Frege supposes that different persons attach different senses to the same proper name. To find the sense a person identifies with a given proper name, we presumably look at his beliefs. If he associates the sense of description *D* with Gustav Lauben, he should believe,

Gustav Lauben is *D*.

Perhaps, with demonstratives too, Frege supposes that speakers and listeners, in grasping the thought, provide the demonstrative with an appropriate sense. To understand a demonstrative, is to be able to supply a sense for it on each occasion, which determines as reference the value the demonstrative has on that occasion.[4] This is, I think, as near as we are likely to come to what Frege had in mind.

[4] This interpretation was suggested to me by Dagfinn Føllesdal.

There is a problem here, with no analog in the case of proper names. One can attach the same sense to a proper name, once and for all. But, since the demonstrative takes a different value on different occasions, different senses must be supplied. So the demonstrative could not be regarded as an abbreviation, or something like an abbreviation, for some appropriate description.

But still, can we not say that, for each person, the sense of the demonstrative 'today' for that person on a given day is just the sense of one of the descriptions D (or some combination of all the descriptions) such that on that day be believes,

Today is D.

One objection to this is that we seem to be explaining the senses of sentences containing demonstratives in terms of beliefs whose natural expressions contain demonstratives. But there are three more serious problems.

The first problem might be called the *irrelevancy of belief*.[5] The sense I associate with my use of a demonstrative does not determine the thought expressed by a sentence containing that demonstrative.

Suppose I believe that today is 14 October 1976. From that it does not follow that, when I utter

Today is sunny and bright.

I express the thought

The fourteenth of October is sunny and bright.

For suppose today is really the fifteenth, cloudy, and dull. Then what I have said is wrong, whatever the weather was like on the fourteenth.

The second problem we might call the *non-necessity of belief*. I can express a thought with 'Today is sunny and bright'—that is, say something for which the question of truth arises—whether or not I associate any correct sense at all with 'today'. I may have no idea at all what day it is, and not be able, without recourse to 'today' or other demonstratives, to say anything about today at all that does not describe dozens of other days equally well.

---

[5] In the 3 problems that follow, and the balance of this chapter, I am much in debt to a series of very illuminating papers by H.-N. Castañeda. The fullest statement of his view is in 'Indicators and Quasi-Indicators', *American Philosophical Quarterly*, 4 (1967), 85–100. See also ' "He": A Study in the Logic of Self-Consciousness', *Ratio*, 8 (1966), 130–57, and 'On the Logic of Attributions of Self-Knowledge to Others', *Journal of Philosophy*, 65 (1968), 439–56. All the e.g.s of what I later call 'self-locating knowledge' are adaptations from Castañeda, and the difficulties they raise for Frege's account are related to points Castañeda has made.

Both these problems are illustrated by Rip Van Winkle. When he awakes on 20 October 1823, and says with conviction,

Today is 20 October 1803.

the fact that he is sure he is right doesn't make him right, as it would if the thought expressed were determined by the sense he associated with 'today'. And, what is really the same point from a different angle, he doesn't fail to be wrong, as would be the case if 'today' had to be associated with a completing sense which determined the value of 'today' as reference, before the question of truth arose for sentences in which it occurs.

To state my third objection, the *non-sufficiency of belief*, I shall shift to an example using the demonstrative 'I'. I do so because the objection is clearest with respect to this demonstrative, and because some awareness of this problem might help explain how consideration of 'I' led Frege to incommunicable senses.

Let us imagine David Hume, alone in his study, on a particular afternoon in 1775, thinking to himself, 'I wrote the *Treatise*.' Can anyone *else* apprehend the thought he apprehended by thinking this? First note that what he thinks is true. So no one could apprehend the same thought, unless they apprehended a true thought. Now suppose Heimson is a bit crazy, and thinks himself to be David Hume. Alone in his study, he says to himself, 'I wrote the *Treatise*.' However much his inner life may, at that moment, resemble Hume's on that afternoon in 1775, the fact remains: Hume was right, Heimson is wrong. Heimson cannot think the very thought to himself that Hume thought to himself, by using the very same sentence.

Now suppose Frege's general account of demonstratives is right. Then it seems that, by using the very same sense that Hume supplied for 'I', Heimson should be able to think the same thought, without using 'I', that Hume did using 'I'. He will just have to find a true sentence, which expresses the very thought Hume was thinking, when he thought to himself, 'I wrote the *Treatise*.' But there just does not seem to be such a thought.

Suppose Heimson thinks to himself, 'The author of the *Inquiries* wrote the *Treatise*.' This is true, for the sense used to complete the sense of '( ) wrote the *Treatise*' determines Hume not Heimson as reference. But it seems clear that Hume could acknowledge 'I wrote the *Treatise*' as true, while rejecting 'The author of the *Inquiries* wrote the *Treatise*.' He might have forgotten that he wrote the *Inquiries*; perhaps Hume had episodes of forgetfulness in 1775. But then the thought Heimson thinks, and the one

Hume apprehended, are not the same after all, by the identification of thoughts with senses, and the criterion of difference for senses.

One might suppose that, while there is no particular sentence of this sort that must have had, for Hume, the same cognitive value as 'I wrote the *Treatise*', there must be some such sentence or other that would have had the same cognitive value for him.

But I see no reason to suppose this is so. For now we have reached just the point where the first objection takes hold. There is no reason to believe we are on each occasion each equipped with some non-demonstrative equivalent of the demonstratives we use and understand. This goes for 'I' as well as 'today'. After all, as I am imagining Heimson, he does not have any correct demonstrative free description of himself at hand. Every correct demonstrative free description he is willing to apply to himself refers to Hume instead. I'm not at all sure that I have one for myself.

To keep the identification between thought and sense intact, Frege must provide us with a completing sense. But then his account of demonstratives becomes implausible.

II

Frege follows his general discussion of demonstratives by saying that 'I' gives rise to certain questions. He then makes the point, with the examples concerning Dr Lauben discussed above, that various persons might associate various senses with the same proper name, if the person were presented to them in various ways. This discussion seems intended to prepare the way for the startling claim about thoughts about ourselves,

Now everyone is presented to himself in a particular and primitive way, in which he is presented to no-one else. So, when Dr. Lauben thinks that he has been wounded, he will probably take as a basis this primitive way in which he is presented to himself. And only Dr. Lauben himself can grasp thoughts determined in this way. But now he may want to communicate with others. He cannot communicate a thought which he alone can grasp. Therefore, if he now says 'I have been wounded', he must use the 'I' in a sense which can be grasped by others, perhaps in the sense of 'he is speaking to you at this moment', by doing which he makes the associated conditions of his utterance serve for the expression of his thought. (T 25–6)

Frege's doctrine appears to be this. When I use 'I' to communicate, it works like other demonstratives, and perhaps could even be replaced by some phrase which included only other demonstratives. The sense would be completed in whatever way is appropriate for sentences containing these demonstratives. When I use 'I' to think about myself, however, it has an incommunicable sense.

This is not quite right, for Frege would not have thought it necessary, in order to think about myself, to use language at all. It is at this point that Frege makes his famous remark, about how the battle with language makes his task difficult, in that he can only give his readers the thought he wants them to examine dressed up in linguistic form.

Nevertheless, it seems clear that Frege thinks there are senses, for each of us, that determine us as reference, which are incommunicable, and which would be the natural sense to associate with 'I' if it did happen to be used, not merely to communicate with others, but think about oneself.

I suggest this doctrine about 'I' is a reaction to the problems just mentioned, the third in particular. I am not at all certain that this is so. Philosophers have come to hold somewhat similar views about the self, beliefs about oneself, and 'I', without thinking as rigorously as Frege did about these matters. Perhaps Frege had adopted some such view independently of his thinking about demonstratives, and simply wished to show he could accommodate it. It seems to me more likely, however, that Frege was led to this view by his own philosophical work, in particular by some realization of the problems I have discussed for his general account, as they apply particularly to 'I'. All three problems turned on the failure to find a suitable description for the value of the demonstrative, whose sense would complete the sense of the sentence in just the right way. If the sense we are looking for is private and incommunicable, it is no wonder the search was in vain.

But the appeal to private and incommunicable senses cannot, I think, be a satisfactory resolution of the problem.

In the first place, I see no reason to believe that 'everyone is presented to himself in a particular and primitive way'. Or at least, no reason to accept this, with such a reading that it leads to incommunicable senses.

Suppose M is the private and incommunicable sense, which is to serve as the sense of 'I' when I think about myself. M cannot be a complex sense, resulting from the compounding of simpler, generally accessible senses. For it seems clear that it is sufficient, to grasp the result of such compounding, that one grasp the senses compounded. So M will have to be, as Frege says, primitive.

A sense corresponds to an aspect or mode of presentation (SR 57, 58). There are, I hope, ways in which I am presented to myself that I am presented to no one else, and aspects of me that I am aware of that no one else is aware of. But this is not sufficient for Frege's purposes.

Suppose that only I am aware of the scratchiness of a certain fountain pen. Still, 'thing which is scratchy' does not uniquely pick out this pen; this pen may not be the only one which falls under the concept this phrase stands for, though perhaps the only one of which I am aware. Similarly, just because there is some aspect, such that only I am aware that I have it, and M is the sense corresponding to that aspect, it does not follow that M determines as reference a concept that only I fall under, or that *the M* (by which I mean the result of combining the sense of 'the' with M), is a sense which determines just me as reference, and can appropriately be associated with my utterances of 'I'.

What is needed is a primitive aspect of me, which is not simply one that only I am aware of myself as having, but that I alone have. While there are doubtless complex aspects that only I have, and primitive aspects that only I am aware of myself as having, I see no reason to believe there are primitive aspects that only I have. Even if there were, if they were incommunicable, I should have no way of knowing there were, since I hardly ask others if they happened to have *mine*. So I shouldn't know that *the M* determined me as reference. But I do know that I am thinking about me, when I use the word 'I' in thinking to myself.

My second point in opposition to incommunicable senses is that the third objection does not merely apply to 'I', but to at least one other demonstrative, 'now'. However one may feel about one's private and unique aspects, Frege's doctrine must appear less plausible when it is seen that it must be extended to other demonstratives.

Suppose the department meeting is scheduled for noon, 15 September 1976. Then only at that time could we say something true with (5).

(5) The meeting starts now.

Now consider any of the informationally equivalent thoughts we might have had the day before, for example (6).

(6) The meeting starts at noon, 15 September 1976.

It seems that one could accept this the day before, and continue to accept it right through the meeting, without ever accepting (5), and even rejecting it firmly precisely at noon, simply by completely losing track of time. So (5) and (6) express different senses, and so different thoughts. And it seems this would be true, no matter what non-demonstrative informational equivalent we came up with instead of (6). So with 'now', as with 'I', it is not sufficient to grasp the thought expressed with a demonstrative, to grasp an informational equivalent with a complete sense. Frege will have to have, for each time, a primitive and particular way in which it is presented to us at that time, which gives rise to thoughts accessible to us at that time, and expressible, at it, with 'now'. This strikes me as very implausible. An appeal to incommunicable senses won't serve to patch up Frege's treatment.

I will conclude by sketching an alternative treatment of these problems. I try to show just how these recent examples motivate a break between sense and thought, and how, once that break is made, senses can be treated as roles, thoughts as information, and the other examples we have discussed handled.

III

Consider some of the things Hume might have thought to himself,

> I am David Hume.
> This is Edinburgh.
> It is now 1775.

We would say of Hume, when he thought such things, that he knew *who* he was, *where* he was, and *when* it was. I shall call these self-locating beliefs. The objections, posed in the last section to Frege's account of demonstratives, may be put in the following way: having a self-locating belief does not consist in believing a Fregean thought.

We can see that having such beliefs *could* not consist *wholly* in believing Fregean thoughts. Consider Frege's timeless realm of generally accessible thoughts. If Hume's knowing he was Hume consisted in his believing certain true thoughts in this realm, then it would seem that anyone else could know that *he* was Hume, just by believing those same thoughts. But only Hume can know, or even truly believe, that he is Hume. Analogous remarks apply to his knowing where he was, and when it was.

Either there are some thoughts only Hume can apprehend, and his believing he is Hume consists in believing those thoughts, or self-locating knowledge does not consist wholly in believing some true subset of the Fregean thoughts. Frege chose the first option; let's see what happens when we choose the second.

We accept that there is no thought only Hume can apprehend. Yet only he can know he is Hume. It must not just be the thought that he thinks, but the way that he thinks it, that sets him apart from the rest of us. Only Hume can think a true thought, by saying to himself,

> I am Hume.

Self-locating knowledge, then, requires not just the grasping of certain thoughts, but the grasping of them via the senses of certain sentences containing demonstratives.

To embed firmly in our minds the importance that thinking a thought via one sense rather than another can have, let us consider another example. An amnesiac, Rudolf Lingens, is lost in the Stanford library. He reads a number of things in the library, including a biography of himself, and a detailed account of the library in which he is lost. He believes any Fregean thought you think might help him. He still won't know who he is, and where he is, no matter how much knowledge he piles up, until that moment when he is ready to say,

> *This* place is aisle five, floor six, of Main Library, Stanford.
> *I* am Rudolf Lingens.

If self-locating knowledge consists not merely in believing certain thoughts, but believing them by apprehending certain senses, then senses cannot be thoughts. Otherwise it would make no sense to say that Hume and Heimson can apprehend all the same thoughts, but Hume can do so by apprehending different senses.

Let us then see how things begin to resolve themselves when this identification is given up. Let us speak of *entertaining* a sense, and apprehending a thought. So different thoughts may be apprehended, in different contexts, by entertaining the same sense (without supposing that it is an incomplete sense, somehow supplemented by a sense completer in the context), and the same thought, by entertaining different senses.

By breaking the connection between senses and thoughts, we give up any reason not to take the options closed to Frege. We can take the sense of a sentence containing a demonstrative to be a role, rather than a Fregean complete sense, and thoughts to be the new sort, individuated by object and incomplete sense, rather than Fregean thoughts. Though senses considered as roles, and thoughts considered as information, cannot be identified, each does its job in a way that meshes with the other. To have a thought we need an object and an incomplete sense. The demonstrative in context gives us the one, the rest of the sentence the other. The role of the entire sentence will lead us to Truth by leading us to a true thought, that is just in case the object falls under the concept determined as reference by the incomplete sense.[6]

Let us see how some of the examples we have discussed are handled.

[6] The notions of the role of a sentence, and of a thought as information, are similar to the concepts of *character* and *context* in D. Kaplan's 'Demonstratives' (mimeo, Los Angeles; UCLA Depart. of Philosophy, 1977). This is no accident, as my approach to these matters was formed, basically, as a result of trying to extract from this work of Kaplan's, and Kaplan himself, answers to questions posed by Castañeda's work. One should not assume that Kaplan would agree with my criticisms of Frege, my treatment of self-locating knowledge, or the philosophical motivation I develop for distinguishing between sense and thought.

We must suppose that both Hume and Heimson can entertain the same senses, and think the same thoughts. The difference between them is that they do not apprehend the same thoughts when they entertain the same senses. When Heimson entertains the sense of 'I am the author of the *Treatise*' he apprehends the thought consisting of Heimson and the sense of '( ) is the author of the *Treatise*'. This thought is false. When Hume entertains the same sense, he apprehends the thought consisting of Hume and the sense of '( ) is the author of the *Treatise*', which is true. Hume is right, Heimson is crazy.

Similarly, only at twelve noon can someone think the thought consisting of noon and the sense of 'The meeting starts at ( )' by entertaining the sense of 'the meeting starts now'.

Why should we have a special category of self-locating knowledge? Why should we care how someone apprehends a thought, so long as he does? I can only sketch the barest suggestion of an answer here. We use senses to individuate psychological states, in explaining and predicting action. It is the sense entertained, and not the thought apprehended, that is tied to human action. When you and I entertain the sense of 'A bear is about to attack me', we behave similarly. We both roll up in a ball and try to be as still as possible. Different thoughts apprehended, same sense entertained, same behaviour. When you and I both apprehend the thought that I am about to be attacked by a bear, we behave differently. I roll up in a ball, you run to get help. Same thought apprehended, different sense entertained, different behaviour. Again, when you believe that the meeting begins on a given day at noon by entertaining, the day before, the sense of 'the meeting begins tomorrow at noon', you are idle. Apprehending the same thought the next day, by entertaining the sense of 'the meeting begins now', you jump up from your chair and run down the hall.

What of the indirect reference? Is the indirect reference of a sentence containing a demonstrative in the scope of such a cognitive verb the sense or the thought?

It seems, a priori, that the 'believes that' construction (to pick a particular verb) could work either way. That is,

A believes that S

might be designed to tell us the sense A entertains, or the thought A apprehends. The first seems a little more efficient. If we know the sense entertained, we can compute the thought apprehended, given the believer's context.

Nevertheless, it is surely the thought apprehended that is the indirect reference of a sentence containing a demonstrative in the scope of 'believes'. Consider (7), (8), and (9),

(7) I believe that Russia and Canada quarrelled today.

(8) Mary believed that Russia and Canada quarrelled today.

(9) Mary believed that Russia and Canada quarrelled yesterday.

Suppose Mary utters (7) on 1 August, and I want to report the next day on what she believed. If I want to report the sense entertained, I should use (8). But this gives the wrong result. Clearly I would use (9). To get from the sentence embedded in (9) to the thought Mary apprehended, we take the value of the demonstrative in the context of the belief reporter, not in the context of the believer.

It has been suggested that we try to use the sense entertained by the believer in reporting his belief, whenever possible. What we have just said does not conflict with this. The point is simply that the function of thought identification dominates the function of sense identification, and when we use demonstratives there is almost always a conflict.

There will be no conflict when one is dealing with eternal sentences, or when one is reporting one's own current beliefs. The need for distinguishing sense from thought will not be forced to our attention, so long as we concentrate on such cases.

Let us now consider the Morning Star example.

Mary says, 'I believe that is the Morning Star' in the morning while pointing at Venus, and 'I believe that is not the Morning Star' at night while pointing at Venus. It seems that Mary, though believing falsely, has not changed her mind, and does not believe a contradiction.

As long as we think of thoughts as senses it will seem that anyone who understands the relevant sentences will not believe both a thought and its negation. So long as we think of senses as thoughts, we shall think that anyone who accepts a sense at one time, and its negation at another, must have changed her mind. The correct principle is simply that no thoughtful person will accept a sense and its negation in the same context, since just by understanding the language she should realize that she would thereby believe both a thought and its negation.

We should take 'believing a contradiction', in the sense in which thoughtful people don't do it, to mean accepting senses of the forms S and not-S, relative to the same context of utterance. Mary doesn't do this; she accepts S in the morning, not-S in the evening. Has she then changed her mind? This must mean coming to disbelieve a thought once believed. We shouldn't take it to mean coming to reject a sense once accepted. I can reject 'Today is sunny and bright' today, though I accepted it yesterday, without changing my mind about anything. So Mary hasn't changed her mind, either.

What she does do, is believe a thought and its negation. (Here we take the negation of a thought consisting of a certain object and incomplete sense, to be the thought consisting of the same object, and the negation of the incomplete sense.) I am inclined to think that only the habit of identifying sense and thought makes this seem implausible.

I have tried to suggest how, using the concepts of sense, thought, and indirect reference in a way compatible with the way Frege introduced them, but incompatible with his identification, sentences containing demonstratives can be handled. I do not mean to imply that Frege could have simply made these alterations, while leaving the rest of his system intact. The idea of individuating thoughts by objects, or sequences of objects, would be particularly out of place in his system. The identification of thought with complete sense was not impulsive, but the result of pressure from many directions. I do not claim to have traced the problems that come to surface with demonstratives back to their ultimate origins in Frege's system.

IV

I have argued that Frege's identification of senses of sentences with thoughts leads to grave problems when sentences containing demonstratives are considered. The utterance of such a sentence in a context seems to yield only an incomplete sense and an object, not a complete sense of the sort a Fregean thought is supposed to be. He probably supposed that context supplies not just an object, but somehow a completing sense. There seems no place for such a sense to be found, save in the mind of the person who apprehends the thought expressed by the sentence. But, to understand such a sentence, it is neither necessary nor sufficient to have grasped, and associated with the value of the demonstrative, any such sense. Frege's appeal to incommunicable senses in the case of 'I', is probably an implausible attempt to deal with these problems. What is needed is to give up the identification of sense expressed with thought expressed. This would allow us to see the sense as a procedure for determining reference from a context, and the thought as identified by the incomplete sense and the value of the demonstrative. The identification of the thought with the indirect reference of the sentence in the scope of a cognitive verb need not be given up.

4

UNDERSTANDING DEMONSTRATIVES

GARETH EVANS

It has recently been claimed that the use of demonstrative or indexical expressions like 'today', 'yesterday', 'here', 'I', 'you', 'this', etc. resists incorporation into a Fregean theory of meaning.[1] I have two reasons for attempting to show that this claim is not true. First, the reasoning seems to me to rest upon a common view of Frege's notions of sense and reference which is neither attractive nor required by the text, and second, because I believe that a Fregean approach to demonstrative expressions is essentially correct.

The argument which is supposed to show that demonstratives provide an insuperable problem for Frege runs like this. Consider the sentence:

(1) Today is fine.

as uttered upon a particular day, d. Now, the concept expression '(ξ) is fine' has (on that occasion) a sense, but if the whole sentence is to have (on that occasion) a sense—express a Fregean thought—the expression 'today' must have (on that occasion) a sense as well as a referent, namely d. Now, the expression-type, 'today', certainly has a meaning, which does not vary from occasion to occasion, which Kaplan[2] calls its character and

An early version of this chapter appeared in H. Parret and J. Bouveresse (eds.), *Meaning and Understanding*, (Berlin: W. de Gruyter, 1981). The present chapter rests on an idea of John McDowell's. Quite a few years ago, and more recently in 'On the Sense and Reference of a Proper Name' (*Mind*, 86 (1977), 159–85), he argued that it was possible to ascribe Fregean sense to singular terms which I describe in this paper as 'Russellian'. The present chapter is an attempt to apply this basic idea of McDowell's to demonstratives, though in the course of doing so I develop it in ways for which he must not be held responsible, particularly by tying sense to a way of *thinking of* a reference. Reading through Frege's works, I became convinced that the position McDowell argued for as a possibility is one to which he is in fact committed. (For similar views of McDowell's, see 'Truth-value Gaps' in *Logic, Methodology and Philosophy of Science*, vi (Amsterdam, 1982).) In my interpretation of Frege I am much indebted to Dummett, whose writings I follow closely. I somehow seem to end up at a quite different place.

This chapter reprinted from G. Evans, 'Understanding Demonstratives', in *Collected Papers* (Oxford, 1985), 291–321. © Antonia Phillips 1985. Reprinted by permission of Oxford University Press.

[1] J. Perry, 'Frege on Demonstratives', *Philosophical Review* 86 (1977), 474–97. This paper appears as ch. 3 in the present volume.
[2] D. Kaplan, 'Demonstratives' (mimeo, Los Angeles: UCLA Depart. of Philosophy, 1977).

Perry calls its role. But that cannot by itself provide a completing sense, if for no other reason than that a 'thought' which is a function of these unchanging senses could no more be assigned a truth-value than can the sentence-type 'Today is fine.' But, equally, the referent, d, cannot be regarded as providing a completing sense. So:

Neither the unchanging role of 'today' (its constant meaning) nor its changing value, provides us with a completing sense. A day is not a sense but a reference corresponding to indefinitely many different senses. So how do we get from the incomplete sense of '(ξ) is fine', the demonstrative 'today', and the context to a thought? This is the problem demonstratives pose for Frege.[3]

Obviously, if a Fregean approach to this utterance is to be sustained, the demonstrative in context must have a sense, and a different sense in different contexts. To this, Perry replies:

How can we extract from a demonstrative an appropriate completing sense? Such a sense, it seems, would have to be intimately related to the sense of a unique description of the value of the demonstrative in the context of utterance. But where does such a description come from? 'Today' seems only to get us to a day.[4]

Perry then goes on to show rather convincingly that no unique description can serve the purpose, for no thought about a day expressible with the use of a definite description true of that day is the same as the thought expressed with the use of a demonstrative; one can always take different epistemic attitudes towards them if one does not know that the day in question satisfies the description.

As far as I can make out, this is the main case against a Fregean approach to demonstrative expressions, and it rests, quite plainly, upon the view that a Fregean sense of any singular term must be either the sense of a definite description or 'intimately related' to such a sense. This assumption is quite unwarranted, and, when this is realized, the case collapses. In order to establish this, I need to explain what I take to be essential to Frege's notion of sense.

I

I am attracted by the following, very abstract, account of the interrelations between Fregean concepts of sense and reference—an account which owes considerably to Michael Dummett.[5]

The heart of a semantic theory for a language constructed on Fregean lines will be a *theory of reference*: a theory which assigns to each

---

[3] Perry, 'Frege on Demonstratives', p. 480. (I have changed the example.)
[4] Ibid. 485.
[5] M. Dummett, *Frege: Philosophy of Language* (London, 1973), chs. 5–7, 12.

meaningful expression of the language something that can be regarded as that expression's reference or semantic value. Such a theory will proceed by discerning structure in the complex expressions of the language, and assigning references to those expressions upon the basis of assignments of references to their parts. A Fregean theory of references will observe the principle of compositionality: the reference of a complex expression is a function of the reference of its parts. Frege himself advocated a theory of reference according to which the references, or semantic values, of sentences and singular terms are truth-values and objects, respectively, but neither of these choices is required by the adoption of the general conception. The only fixed point is this: an understanding of the language must be capable of being regarded as involving knowledge of the semantic values of expressions. In the case of sentences this knowledge can be regarded as more or less explicit, but, for subsentential expressions, knowledge of their semantic values will simply be a logical construction out of the knowledge of the semantic values of the sentences in which they occur.

Before you object that one can understand a sentence without knowing its truth-value, I hasten to remind you that the references of expressions can be thought of, or identified, in many different ways. One is thinking of the value True both when one thinks of it as the value True, and as the value of the thought that snow is white, though one may not know that one is thinking of the same thing. Similarly, the function which is the semantic value of the concept expression '(ξ) is bald' can either be thought of as the function which yields truth given as inputs the objects . . . (here follows a list of the bald men) or as the function which yields truth given any object if and only if that object is bald. Frege's idea was that, to understand an expression, one must not merely think of the reference that it is the reference, but that one must, in so thinking, think of the reference *in a particular way*. The way in which one must think of the reference of an expression in order to understand it is that expression's *sense*. No substantial, or positive theory of the notion of a way of thinking of something is presupposed by this conception of sense. If the intuitive notion needs to be supplemented, we can appeal to the general idea of an account of what makes it the case that a thought is about the object which it is about; two people will then be thinking of an object in the same way if and only if the account of what makes the one person's thought about that object is the same as the account of what makes the other person's thought about that object.[6]

---

[6] I should explain the main point of departure from Dummett's account of Frege's views. Dummett is impressed, to my mind overly impressed, by the fact that one can understand a

Although a theory of meaning for a language must give the senses of expressions, we are not to think of the theory of sense as a separate tier, additional to and independent of the theory of reference. If sense is a way of thinking of reference, we should not expect to be given the sense of an expression save in the course of being given the reference of that expression. Rather than look for a theory quite independent of the theory of reference, we must take one formulation of the theory of reference—the formulation of the theory which identifies the references of expressions in the way in which one must identify them in order to understand the language—and make it *serve as* a theory of sense. Thus, the clauses:

(2) The reference of 'Hesperus' = Hesperus.
(3) The reference of 'Hesperus' = Phosphorus.

are equivalent as clauses in the theory of reference, but only (2) can occur in a theory of reference which is to serve as a theory of sense, for it alone identifies the reference of the name in a way which *shows*, or *displays*, its sense. The use of the *Tractatus* metaphor to make this point is due to Dummett:

Indeed, even when Frege is purporting to give the sense of a word or symbol, what he actually *states* is what the reference said: and, for anyone who has not clearly grasped the relation between sense and reference, this fact makes his hold on the notion of sense precarious. The sense of an expression is the mode of presentation of the referent: in saying what the reference is, we have to choose a particular way of saying this . . . In a case in which we are concerned to convey, or stipulate, the sense of the expression, we shall choose that means of stating what the referent is which displays the sense: we might here borrow a famous pair of terms from the *Tractatus*, and say that, for Frege, we *say* what the referent of a word is, and thereby *show* what its sense is.[7]

sentence without knowing its truth-value. To take account of this, he regards sense, not as a way of thinking of reference, but as a way of *determining* reference—possibly by means which only a being with superior powers is capable of employing. To think of the sense of a singular term as a procedure for recognizing an object as the referent generates just the idea of sense as independent of the existence of a referent which is resisted in this chapter.

[7] Dummett, *Frege*, p. 227. This passage of Dummett's seems to me to contain the answer to those who argue, like Wallace (see 'Logical Form, Meaning, Translation', in F. Guenther and M. Guenther-Reutter (eds.), *Meaning and Translation* (London, 1977), 45–58, that Davidsonian theories of meaning are inadequate because they do not state the meanings of sentences. The similarity between a Davidsonian conception of the theory of meaning as a theory of truth, and a Fregean conception of a theory of sense as a theory of reference should be particularly striking. Davidson lightens the ontological load, but the general idea is the same. I should explain that I am ignoring in this brief presentation the distinction between 'model–theoretic' and 'truth–theoretic' approaches to semantics—a Fregean theory of reference, with its ontological weight, should really be regarded as exemplifying the former approach. I have tried to explain the relation between these approaches in 'Semantic Structure and Logical Form', in G. Evans and J. H. McDowell (eds.), *Truth and Meaning* (Oxford, 1976).

As I have already said, Frege quite generally regarded the referent of a singular term as its semantic value. Therefore, on the present conception, the sense of a singular term is a way of thinking about a particular object: something that obviously could not exist if that object did not exist to be thought about. If we take seriously Frege's metaphor of sense as a mode of presentation of reference, we shall not expect to be provided with specifications of sense save by means of specifications of reference, and therefore, if we remember Frege's equation of the reference of a singular term with its referent, we apparently discover at the heart of Frege's semantical system singular terms whose sense depends upon their having a referent—singular terms we more typically regard as Russellian than Fregean. But what makes a Fregean recognition of Russellian singular terms so much more sophisticated than Russell's own is that it allows such terms to have a sense as well as a reference. Russell himself did not grasp this possibility:

> For the name itself is merely a means of pointing to the thing . . . so that, if one thing has two names, you make exactly the same assertion whichever of the two names you use, provided that they really are names and not truncated descriptions.[8]

The semantic difference between two such Russellian terms which have the same referent can be acknowledged, with all the benefits which Frege derived from that acknowledgement. The theory of reference will state their references like this:

(4) The reference of 'a' = a.
(5) The reference of 'b' = b.

These clauses *show* the different senses which the two terms possess, but at the same time they could not truly be stated if the terms had no referent.[9]

Attractive though this possibility may be, various things that Frege explicitly says seem to rule it out as an interpretation of his views. Frege says in several places that empty singular terms may have a sense, and, what would be a consequential inconsistency with the conception outlined, he also says that sentences containing empty singular terms may have a sense (express a thought) even though they have no reference (no truth-value). How can we attribute to Frege the view that sense is a mode of presentation of reference, is a way of thinking of reference, when he

[8] B. Russell, *Lectures on Logical Atomism*, ed. D. Pears (London, 1972), 103.
[9] The significance of clauses like (4) and (5) as providing a formal recognition of the possibility of ascribing Fregean sense to Russellian singular terms is first elaborated in J. McDowell, 'On the Sense and Reference of a Proper Name', *Mind* 86 (1977), 159–85.

seems to say things explicitly inconsistent with it? However, before abandoning this interpretation of Frege's ideas, which does incorporate much that Frege says, and which takes into account his willingness to apply the distinction between sense and reference to linguistic expressions quite generally, we should examine carefully what Frege actually says about empty singular terms. For, though he does say that they, and sentences containing them, may have a sense, other things that he says in the same connection make it clear that this is far less the unequivocal rejection of the conception I have outlined than it might at first appear.

In the first place, it is clear that Frege regarded empty singular terms as *defective*, in the same way, and indeed for the same reason, as he regarded vague concept expressions as defective. His picture of the functioning of atomic sentences required them to be composed of expressions of two kinds: one (or more) which signified an object, and one which signified a function which mapped objects (or n-tuples of objects) on to truth-values. If any expression in an atomic sentence failed to refer to an entity of an appropriate kind, the possibility would be open that no further truth-value would be determined for the sentence, and it is clear that Frege regarded this as a defect in a sentence of a quite fundamental kind—which he was quite right to do.[10] With this picture in mind, Frege was simply prepared to insist that concept expressions must be precise; there is no concession that vague concept expressions may nevertheless have a sense of a kind appropriate for concept expressions, or that a sentence which has no truth-value on account of vagueness may nevertheless express a thought. He did not make quite the same uncompromising statements about empty singular terms, despite the fact that the motivation is precisely the same— indeed Frege frequently treats the two cases together—because of his willingness to regard empty singular terms as *fictional* (or *mythical*). Instead of simply saying: 'Proper names must have a reference', he says: 'Myth and fiction aside, proper names must have a reference', or 'For scientific purposes, proper names must have a reference.' Frege was well aware that language could be used in fiction, story-telling, and drama, and he appeared to be willing to regard the serious use of an empty singular term as of this kind; he says that the speaker has 'lapsed into the sphere of fiction', without knowing it. The following is one of the many passages in which he takes this line:

> But if my intention is not realized, if I only think I see without really seeing, if on that account the designation 'That lime tree' is empty, then I have gone astray into the sphere of fiction without knowing it or wanting to.[11]

[10] See Dummett, *Frege*, pp. 342–8.
[11] G. Frege, 'The Thought' (trans. by A. and M. Quinton), *Mind*, 65 (1956), 287–311, p. 300. A similar use of the notion of fiction is made on almost all of the occasions on which

So, Frege regarded serious utterances containing empty singular terms as belonging with the fictional use of language, and however much we may deplore this idea, it forces us to turn to Frege's account of fiction for our understanding of his views on empty singular terms. The most extended treatment is in the material for a book on logic which Frege never finished dated around 1897.[12]

Names that fail to fulfil the usual role of a proper name, which is to name something, may be called mock proper names. Although the tale of William Tell is a legend and not history and the name 'William Tell' is a mock proper name, we cannot deny it a sense. But the sense of the sentence 'Willam Tell shot an apple off his son's head' is no more true than is that of the sentence 'William Tell did not shoot an apple off his son's head'. I do not say that this sense is false either, but I characterize it as fictitious.

Instead of speaking of 'fiction' we could speak of 'mock thoughts'. Thus, if the sense of an assertoric sentence is not true, it is either false or fictitious, and it will generally be the latter if it contains a mock proper name. (Footnote: We have an exception where a mock proper name occurs within a clause in indirect speech.) . . . Assertions in fiction are not to be taken seriously: they are only mock assertions. Even the thoughts are not to be taken seriously as in the sciences: they are only mock thoughts. If Schiller's *Don Carlos* were to be regarded as a piece of history, then to a large extent the drama would be false. But a work of fiction is not meant to be taken seriously in this way at all: it's all play.

The logician does not have to bother with mock thoughts, just as a physicist, who sets out to investigate thunder, will not pay any attention to stage-thunder. When we speak of thoughts in what follows we mean thoughts proper, thoughts that are either true or false.[13]

This passage makes it clear that Frege's claim that empty singular terms, and sentences containing them, have a sense, expressed briefly elsewhere, is much more complex and qualified than is usually realized. We might gloss it as follows. Yes: a sentence containing an empty singular term can have a sense, in that it does not necessarily have to be likened to a sentence containing a nonsense-word, but no: it does not *really* have a sense of the kind possessed by ordinary atomic sentences because it does not function properly, it is only *as if* it functions properly. Frege's use of the notion of fiction wrongly directs our attention to just one case in which it is *as if* a singular term refers to something, namely when we are engaged

Frege discusses empty singular terms. See e.g. 'On Sense and Reference' (pp. 62–3), 'Grundgesetze' (p. 167), and the review of Schröder (p. 104), in *Translations from the Philosophical Writings of Gottlob Frege*, trans. and ed. P. T. Geach and M. Black (Oxford, 1970) and many places in *Posthumous Writings*, ed. H. Hermes, F. Kambartel, F. Kaulbach, trans. P. Long, R. White (Oxford, 1979), e.g., 118, 122, 129–30, 191, 225, 232.

[12] 'Logic', in *Posthumous Writings*, pp. 126–51.

[13] *Posthumous Writings*, p. 130. I am grateful to Dagfinn Føllesdal for pointing this passage out to me. I have followed the translation of Peter Long and Roger White, save in retaining the traditional translation of 'Bedeutung' as 'reference'.

in a pretence that it does, but there are others, and if we think of them we will perhaps speak of apparent, rather than mock or pretend, thoughts.

However indefensible Frege's idea of unwitting lapses into fiction may be, and however much his treatment of fiction depends upon a slide from 'mock assertions' to 'mock thoughts', his intention in this passage is clearly to deny that sentences containing empty singular terms really express thoughts, and is therefore one which makes it not at all impossible that he held the conception of the relations between sense and reference which I have outlined. (Indeed, the idea of 'mock', or anyway 'apparent', thoughts indicates a further direction in which Russell's conception of Russellian singular terms needs to be extended if it is to have any plausibility.)

I want to stress that the idea of sense as a mode of presentation of reference is not *by itself* inconsistent with the quite unqualified ascription of sense to empty singular terms. Even if a Fregean went along with Russell and hived off definite descriptions for treatment as quantifiers, he might want to recognize a category of 'descriptive names'—names introduced by means of, and governed by, a 'reference-fixing' stipulation like: 'Let "α" refer to whatever is " φ "—whose sense is thereby guaranteed to be independent of whether or not it has a referent.[14] But for names such as these the equation of reference with referent would have to be given up. One formally adequate possibility would be to take the reference, i.e. the semantic value, of such a name to be a set, determined by the rule:

(6) (x) $(x \; \varepsilon \;$ Reference of 'α' iff φ (x))

with corresponding adjustments to the semantic values of concept expressions. When nothing is φ, the name 'α' has no *referent*, but its *reference* is the empty set.[15]

I have tried to show that on a perfectly possible understanding of Frege's semantic theory he recognized only Russellian singular terms—terms whose customary sense depends upon their having a referent. Although this seems to me to be the correct position, I am aware that

---

[14] The idea of a reference-fixing stipulation is Kripke's, see 'Naming and Necessity', in D. Davidson and G. Harman (eds.), *Semantics of Natural Language* (Dordrecht, 1972), 253–355. I am presuming that φ is incapable of being satisfied by more than one thing. I have discussed the semantics of descriptive names in 'Reference and Contingency', *Monist*, 62 (1979).

[15] Here and elewhere I rely upon the verbal distinction between 'referent' and 'reference' introduced by Dummett, *Frege*, pp. 409 ff. Were we accustomed to Long and White's translation of 'Bedeutung' as 'meaning', the position adopted in the text would have stood out as a possibility more clearly.

many will regard it as highly controversial. It is therefore important to emphasize that the argument of this chapter depends only upon a much weaker claim, namely: that there is at least nothing to prevent Frege recognizing Russellian singular terms: i.e. that there is no difficulty in ascribing to such terms a Fregean sense. Since this claim is the basis of my defence of Frege against Perry's attack, it is as well to work through the argument in detail.

The essential use to which Frege puts the ascription of sense to singular terms is to explain the differing cognitive values of the sentences $A(t)$ and $A(t')$ when t and t' refer to the same thing. (The difference between $t = t$ and $t = t'$ is just a special case of this phenomenon.) Now, to say that two sentences differ in cognitive value is to say that it is possible for anyone who understands them correctly to take coherently different epistemic attitudes towards them—to accept one sentence as true and to reject, or to be unsure about the other sentence.

Suppose now that to ascribe a Fregean sense to a singular term is to say that there is a particular way in which its referent must be thought of (as the referent) if the term is to be understood. If two co-referring Russellian singular terms have different senses, different ways of thinking of their common referent are required in order to understand them. We have linked the idea of a way of thinking of something to an account that may be offered of what makes a subject's thought about its object, and certainly no argument can be based upon this idea alone to the conclusion that senses can be grasped in the absence of a referent.

Now if the assignment of senses to singular terms t and t' is to explain the differing cognitive values of the sentences $A(t)$ and $A(t')$, it must be the case that if the singular terms t and t' have different senses the sentences will have different cognitive values—i.e. it must be possible for anyone who understands the sentences to take different epistemic attitudes towards them. And this will be so, provided the following very plausible principle is true:

(P) If the account of what makes a subject's thought T_1 (about x to the effect that it is F) about x is different from the account of what makes his thought T_2 (about x to the effect that it is F) about x, it is possible for the subject coherently to take, at one and the same time, different epistemic attitudes towards the thoughts he entertains in T_1 and in T_2.

At no point is it necessary for Frege to adopt any substantial theory of what form these accounts must take. In particular it is not necessary for him to suppose that ways of thinking of objects can always be given by giving some definite description uniquely true of the object, or to make any other supposition which would lead to 'existence-independent' senses. It is not necessary, because it is not plausible to suggest that the only kind of account of what makes a subject's thought about an object which is capable of making (P) true is one which relies upon the subject's possessing a unique description of the object.

The initial 'if' in (P) can be strengthened to an 'if and only if' without loss of plausibility and if this strengthening is acceptable Frege is entitled to his equation of the sense of a singular sentence and a thought, when this is understood to be the object of propositional attitudes. An equation can be made between the senses of a singular sentence and a thought only if it is not possible for someone who has understood two singular sentences which agree in sense to take different attitudes to them, but on Frege's view this will not be possible. A difference in attitude would require a difference in the ways the subject thought of the object referred to (by the strengthening of (P)), and this would conflict with the hypothesis of an identity of sense, given that sense is a way of thinking of the referent.

Thus, we see that far from the Fregean sense of a singular term being restricted to the sense of some definite description (and therefore being 'existence-independent'), it is perfectly possible for there to be 'existence-dependent' Fregean senses—the Fregean senses of Russellian singular terms. I have in fact suggested that we should re-examine those passages in which Frege showed himself willing to ascribe sense to empty singular terms, but, in any case I know of no passage in which Frege can be construed as insisting that singular terms *must* have an existence-independent sense. In view of this we can appreciate how wrong-headed it is to consider a Fregean sense as necessarily *intermediary* between thinker and referent, as something which must, from a certain point of view, *get in the way*, or anyway render indirect what might be direct. A way of thinking of an object is no more obliged to get in the way of thinking of an object, or to render thinking of an object indirect, than is a way of dancing liable to get in the way of dancing, or to render dancing somehow indirect.[16] And, finally, we can appreciate how baseless it is to maintain that an extension of a Fregean theory to demonstrative singular terms *must* involve assigning to them the sense of, or anything like the sense of, some definite description. So Perry's argument against Frege collapses.

[16] I have in mind here several remarks of Kaplan's, who advocates 'the semantics of direct reference . . . theories of meaning according to which certain singular terms refer directly without the mediation of a Fregean *Sinn* as meaning' (Kaplan, 'Demonstratives', p. 1). See also Kaplan, 'How to Russell a Frege-Church', *Journal of Philosophy*, 72 (1975), 716–29.

II

Let us return to the problem of demonstratives. We have seen that Perry's demonstration that there can be no 'completing sense' for 'today' is unsound, but something must be said about what such a completing sense might be.

'Today', as uttered on d, has a completing sense, if and only if there is some particular way in which one must think of the referent, d, in order to understand the utterance containing it. And of course there is. Even if d is the first day after my last lecture, I shall not have understood the utterance of (1) if I think of d only as the first day after my last lecture, thereby coming to believe that the utterance is true if and only if the first day after my last lecture is fine, perhaps not realizing that today is the first day after my last lecture. In order to understand (1) I must think of d as the current day, thereby coming to have the thought which I might express in the words: 'What the speaker said is true if and only if it is fine today'.[17] Now, what makes a man's thought about a day when he thinks of it as the current day—as 'today'—is not something which it is incumbent upon Frege to explain. It is indeed a difficult question. I myself would say something like this.

To give an account of how a thought concerns an object is to explain how the subject knows what object is in question. In the case of 'today', the subject, of course, knows which day is in question, but this knowledge at least partly consists in a disposition to judge the thoughts (which depend upon this knowledge) as true or false according to how things observably are upon that day which in no way rests upon his capacity to identify that day as meeting some antecedently given condition, but depends only upon his being alive on that day. There should be no mystery here; we can test very easily whether or not someone, in his interpretation of a sentence, is thinking of the day in the right way by seeing if he is disposed to judge the sentence as true or false according to how things observably are on that day. Similarly, I should want to place in a central position in any account of what makes a man's thought concern a particular place in the way which is required for understanding sentences containing the term 'here', a knowledge of which place is in question which at least partly consists in a disposition to judge that thought as true or false according to how things observably are at that place—a disposition which he can have *vis-à-vis* just one place in the universe in virtue of his occupying it, and which in no way depends upon his capacity to recognize that place as the unique satisfier of some description. If these

---

[17] It is therefore not true that 'today' only gets us to a day.

accounts are on anything like the right lines, it is very easy to understand how these 'ways of thinking' are irreducible to any other, since no other way of knowing which object is in question, certainly no 'descriptive' way, can guarantee the existence of the relevant dispositions.

However, these are speculations which need to be embedded in a general theory of thought if they are to carry conviction. All that a Fregean needs from his opponent is an acknowledgement that those thoughts about a day which we typically express with the use of 'today' do involve a particular way of thinking about a day; if this is granted, he can explain how 'today', in a context, has a 'completing sense'.

Therefore, in order to understand the utterance of (1) made on d, one must have, on d, the thought which one might express in words by:

(7) What the speaker said is true if it is fine *today*.

It seems reasonable to say that such a statement is capable of showing the sense which the sentence has on that occasion. However, there might appear to be a difficulty here. A theory of reference was conceived to be a finite set of principles from which the references of complex expressions, particularly sentences, could be derived. When we think of the principles from which (7) might be derived, we naturally think of the general statement:

(8) For all days d, 'today' as uttered on d refers to d.

But now, this universally quantified principle cannot be thought to show the sense of any particular use of the expression, nor does it appear to issue exclusively in theorems of the form (7), which can. After all,

(9) What the speaker said in uttering 'Today is fine' on my birthday is true if it is fine on my birthday

is equally a consequence of (8), but it apparently does not show the sense which that sentence had on that occasion.

Our interest in theories of reference and of sense is ultimately to understand better the capacity of speakers to speak and understand their language, and, when we remember this interest, the present difficulty will be seen as spurious. Speakers do not literally deduce the truth conditions which sentences have from certain universally quantified principles, whose precise form we must endeavour to establish. Speakers judge the truth conditions of particular sentences, and in so doing they exercise complex and interconnected dispositions in which their understanding of the individual atoms of the language may be taken to consist. We are therefore not required to attribute to speakers the general belief that any token of 'today' refers to the day on which it is uttered—and then wonder what form that belief takes, or how they derive the right kind of judgement of truth conditions from it. We are rather ascribing to speakers a *propensity to form particular beliefs*, of particular tokens of 'today', that they refer to the day of utterance, identified in a particular way, the exercise of which yields thoughts of the form of (7). The inclusion in a theory of reference of a general principle like (8) is a gesture in the direction of identifying the relevant propensity, and it certainly requires supplementation. But this point, though it needs to be borne in mind in interpreting systematic theories of meaning, is irrelevant to a Fregean theory of the sense and reference of 'today'. What matters for that theory is that tokens of 'today' should have a sense as well as a reference, not that the sense of all tokens of the expression should be capable of being shown in a single principle of the theory of reference.

Thus we have found no reason to depart from Frege's view:

> The thought, for example, that this tree is covered with green leaves will surely be false in six months' time. No, for it is not the same thought at all. The words, 'This tree is covered with green leaves' are not sufficient by themselves for the utterance, the time of utterance is involved as well. Without the time indication this gives we have no complete thought, i.e. no thought at all . . . the same words, on account of the variability of language with time, take on another sense, express another thought.[18]

III

In understanding the sentence 'Today is fine', said on d_1, one can be regarded as having a Fregean thought, but is it a thought which one can have on any other day? Frege appears to have thought that it is:

> If someone wants to say the same today as he expressed yesterday using the word 'today', he must replace this word with 'yesterday'.[19]

Frege appears to have held that to have on d_2 just the thought which one has when one thinks 'Today is fine' on d_1, one must think 'Yesterday was fine'. Presumably this means that it is possible for someone reading yesterday's newspaper to understand sentences like:

(10) The Prime Minister is holding a cabinet meeting today.

by realizing that it is true if the Prime Minister held a cabinet meeting the day before. Now, many philosophers, commenting on this passage, have concluded that Frege intended to abandon a notion of 'what is said', or

---

[18] Frege, 'The Thought', pp. 309–102.
[19] Ibid. 296.

'the thought expressed' which was 'psychologically real' in the sense of being the object of propositional attitudes, and was giving expression to the idea that two people would express the same thought provided that they refer to the same object (in whatever way) and say the same thing about it.[20] Such a conception of *what is said*, or *the thought expressed* is so wholly antagonistic to the theory of language ushered in by the distinction between sense and reference, and is otherwise so wholly absent from his work, that it seems to me to be doubtful that the passage has been correctly interpreted. It is clear, for example, that Frege would have been willing to continue the passage:

. . . he must replace this word with 'yesterday', or 'my birthday', or any other expression designating the same day?

Might Frege not have had in mind an idea of a thought the grasp of which, on a later day, requires just as specific a way of thinking of a day as does its grasp on an earlier day—namely as the preceding day? Pursuing this suggestion, we discover that, far from abandoning the 'psychologically real' notion of a thought in favour of a psychologically quite uninteresting equivalence class of thoughts, Frege may well have glimpsed what results when the notion is extended to the sphere of human thinking which depends upon the position human beings have in space and time.

We must agree that, if a subject thinks, on d_1, about d_1, to the effect that it is fine by thinking 'Today is fine', and thinks on d_2, about d_1, to the effect that it is fine, by thinking 'Yesterday was fine', there is some level of description at which he is thinking of the same day in different ways—the account of what makes his thoughts about d_1 in the two cases will not be entirely the same. And it is natural to think that this difference in ways of thinking can be exploited to produce the possibility of differing epistemic attitudes to the thoughts, which would then preclude their being the same thought, if thoughts are intended to be the object of propositional attitudes.

However, the natural suggestion is not correct; there is no headlong collision between Frege's suggestion that grasping the same thought on different days may require different things of us, and the fundamental criterion of difference of thoughts which rests upon the principle that it is not possible coherently to take different attitudes towards the same thought. For that principle, properly stated, precludes the possibility of coherently taking different attitudes towards the same thought *at the same*

---

[20] See e.g. Kaplan, 'Demonstratives', p. 43. Dummett comes close to this in *Frege*, p. 384, although, there, other expressions which can be used to express the same thought are restricted to other *demonstrative* expressions with the same referent.

time. Consider S, who accepted the sentence 'Today is fine' when uttered on d_1, and who rejects the sentence 'Yesterday was fine' when uttered on d_2, perhaps because he has misremembered the weather, or because he has 'lost track of time'. Now, in order to apply the criterion of difference in this situation, we must first make a decision as to what it would be for S to have exactly the same thought on d_2 as he had when he thought on d_1 'Today is fine.' Because its application requires a prior decision on this question, the criterion for difference cannot by any means be the whole story of the identity and distinctness of thoughts, and it is powerless to upset Frege's suggestion. For, either we hold that it is possible to think again the thought entertained on d_1 or we do not. If we hold that it *is* possible, no better account than Frege's can be given of the circumstances under which it is possible. (If this is not obvious, some merits of his account will be given below.) Hence, on this alternative, to think 'Yesterday was fine' *is* to think the same thought again, and so no possibility opens up, on d_2, of coherently assenting to the same thought as one accepted when one judged on d_1 'Today is fine', and of dissenting from the thought 'Yesterday was fine.' To hold, on the other hand, that it is not possible to have on d_2 the very same thought as one had on d_1, while not at all a ridiculous proposal, obviously precludes use of the criterion of difference against Frege's contrary view. Some other consideration must be appealed to.

Frege's idea is that being in the same epistemic state may require different things of us at different times; the changing circumstances force us to change in order to keep hold of a constant reference and a constant thought—we must run to keep still. From this point of view, the acceptance on d_2 of 'Yesterday was fine', given an acceptance on d_1 of 'Today is fine' can manifest the *persistence* of a belief in just the way in which acceptance of different utterances of the same sentence 'The sun sets in the West' can. Are there any considerations which can be advanced in favour of this way of looking at matters?

To answer this question, we must contrast Frege's conception with the opposing conception, according to which the thoughts associated with sentences containing temporal indexicals cannot be grasped at later times. On this atomistic conception, what Frege regards as a persistence of a belief is really a succession of different but related beliefs concerning the same time. It must of course be acknowledged that these patterns, or sequences, of beliefs are very commonly to be met with—that human beings do have a general propensity, on forming one belief in this series, later to have the other beliefs in the series, but this fact by itself does not settle the issue. Admittedly it is not clear what account can be given of this succession of belief on the atomistic conception. One belief cannot give rise to another by any *inference*, since the identity belief that would be required to underwrite the inference is not a thinkable one; no sooner does one arrive in a position to grasp the one side of the identity than one has lost the capacity to grasp the other. But one can be suspicious of the atomistic conception for other, deeper, reasons.

On the atomistic conception, whether there are later elements in the series, and whether or not they concern the same object is quite irrelevant to the subject's capacity to entertain one of the atoms. The atom must be a perfectly coherent unit of thought by itself, even if it is entertained by one who has not the least propensity to form the other members of the series. But this, Frege might well have thought, is wrong. No one can be ascribed at *t* a belief with the content 'It is now ψ', for example, who does not have the propensity as time goes on to form beliefs with the content 'It was ψ just a moment ago', 'It was ψ earlier this morning', 'It was ψ this morning', 'It was ψ yesterday morning', etc., though of course this propensity can be counteracted by new evidence. Frege might be credited with the insight that a capacity to keep track of the passage of time is not an optional addition to, but a precondition of, temporal thought. If this is so, the thought units of the atomist are not coherent, independent thoughts at all, but, so to speak, cross-sections of a persisting belief state which exploits our ability to keep track of a moment as it recedes in time.

The metaphor of 'keeping track of something' originates in connection with another kind of thought about an object, and it provides a useful, if only partial, parallel. Suppose that one is watching a scene in which there are several similar objects moving about fairly rapidly, but not so rapidly as to prevent one's keeping track of one in particular. In such a situation, one can think about one of these objects rather than any other, but any such thought rests upon a skill we possess of keeping track of an object in a visual array over time. Our eyes and our heads move, perhaps we are also obliged to turn or move our bodies, but these changes are required to maintain contact with the same object over time. So, one's thought *at* a time is dependent upon an ability which is necessarily manifested only *over* time. One might begin the period with the belief of an object that it is valuable, and end it with a belief of the same object that it is valuable. Now, a move parallel to the one which Frege made in connection with 'today' and 'yesterday', would be to hold that one belief has persisted over time, despite the local differences which the changing circumstances have imposed upon one. And there is a parallel, opposing atomistic move which would regard the subject as holding a *sequence* of different beliefs over the relevant period of time, altering as the subject's relation to the object altered. And the objection to the atomistic position here is the same as in the earlier case. If the atomistic position were correct, it ought to be possible to have just one of the members of the sequence no matter which others accompanied it, i.e. in the absence of any capacity to keep track of the object. But if that ability is missing, it is not possible for a subject to have a thought about an object in this kind of situation at all. Now Frege himself did not give this parallel, but he did write, after the passage just quoted: 'The case is the same with "here" and "there".' Indeed it is; our ability to think of a place as 'here' is dependent upon our general ability to keep track of places as we move about (which requires, in general, the ability to know when we are moving), so, once again, there could not be thoughts interpretable as 'It's ψ here', if they were not entertained by a subject who had the propensity to entertain, as he moves about, thoughts expressible in the words 'It's ψ there.'

These examples suggest that we have to regard the static notion of 'having hold of an object at t' as essentially an abstraction from the dynamic notion of 'keeping track of an object from t to t''. And the grasp, at t, of a thought of the kind suggested by the passage from Frege, a *dynamic* Fregean thought, requires a subject to possess at t an ability to keep track of a particular object over time. It is not precluded that one should have only a momentary grasp of a dynamic Fregean thought, for it is not precluded that, after an object has engaged with one's capacity to keep track of objects of that kind, one should lose track of it, and with it, the thought. Indeed, it is an aspect of the capacity that the subject will, in general, know when this has happened. The capacities upon which certain kinds of thought rest can only be described in dynamic terms; it does not follow that any exercise of those capacities must be extended over time.

Consequently, the *way of thinking of an object* to which the general Fregean conception of sense directs us is, in the case of a dynamic Fregean thought, a *way of keeping track of an object*. This permits us to say after all that a subject on d_2 is thinking of d_1 *in the same way as* on d_1, despite lower level differences, because the thought episodes on the two days both depend upon the same exercise of a capacity to keep track of a time.[21]

---

[21] Kaplan briefly raises the possibility sketched in this section, under the heading 'cognitive dynamics', but dismisses it: 'Suppose that yesterday you said, and believed it, "It is a nice day today". What does it mean to say, today, that you have retained *that* belief? . . . Is there some obvious standard adjustment to make to the character, for example, replacing *today* with *yesterday*? If so, then a person like Rip van Winkle, who loses track of time, can't retain any such beliefs. This seems strange.' I see no more strangeness in the idea that a man who loses track of time cannot retain beliefs than in the idea that a man who loses track of an object

V

In discussing thoughts expressed with the use of the pronoun 'I' Frege
wrote:

Now, everyone is presented to himself in a particular and primitive way in which he
is presented to no one else.[22]

Replacing Frege's metaphor of 'being presented with an object' with the
notion of 'thinking of' which underlies it, Frege appears to be saying that
each person thinks about himself in a way which is primitive and available
to no one else. Since this way of thinking about oneself would be neither
primitive nor available to anyone else if it exploited one's knowledge that
one uniquely satisfied some description, the passage appears to provide
the clearest possible evidence that Frege did not hold that all ways of
thinking of objects must involve thinking of those objects as uniquely
satisfying some description. It is not unreasonable to suppose, on the
strength of this passage, that Frege had noticed the irreducibility of 'I'-
thoughts to any other kind of thought fifty years before Castañeda made it
part of the philosopher's stock in trade.[23]

However, Perry holds that Frege's conception of a thought was such
that to have an 'I'-thought could not possibly be to have a Fregean
thought. One of his reasons is that Frege held that thoughts are 'generally
accessible'.

We can see that having such beliefs *could* not consist *wholly* in believing Fregean
thoughts. Consider Frege's timeless realm of generally accessible thoughts.[24]

Since it is an immediate consequence of what Frege said about 'I'-
thoughts that they are *not* 'generally accessible', Perry appears to be
arguing that a Fregean approach to 'I'-thoughts must be inadequate by
citing a supposed requirement upon Fregean thoughts—that they be
generally accessible—which Frege appears to have shown himself free of
precisely in what he says about 'I'-thoughts. Presumably Perry would
justify his line of criticism by arguing that the shareability of thoughts was
such a central Fregean doctrine that nothing recognizably Fregean could
exist in its absence:

cannot retain the beliefs about it with which he began. If one has in fact lost track of time
without knowing it, then one could think that one had retained one's beliefs when one has not.
But, since in general thoughts associated with Russellian singular terms are such that the
subject cannot infallibly know that he has one, we should not jib at denying the subject
infallible knowledge of when he has the same one.

[22] Frege, 'The Thought', p. 298.
[23] See H.-N. Castañeda, ' "He": A Study in the Logic of Self-Consciousness', *Ratio*, 8
(1966), 130–57, and in many other papers.
[24] Perry, 'Frege on Demonstratives', p. 492.

Nothing could be more out of the spirit of Frege's account of sense and thought than an incommunicable, private thought.[25]

I do not beleive that this is true. It is true that Frege stresses that it is *possible* for thoughts to be grasped by more than one person; were this not so, neither communication nor disagreement would be possible. But this point requires only that thoughts are not by their very nature precluded from being grasped by more than one person, not that every single thought must be capable of being grasped by more than one person. What *is* absolutely fundamental to Frege's philosophy of language is that thoughts should be *objective*—that the existence of a thought should be independent of its being grasped by anyone, and hence that thoughts are to be distinguished from *ideas* or the contents of a particular consciousness. When Frege stresses that thoughts can be grasped by several people, it is usually to emphasize that it is not like an idea:

A true thought was true before it was grasped by anyone. A thought does not have to be owned by anyone, the same thought can be grasped by several people.[26]

His most extended treatment of the nature of thoughts—'The Thought'— makes it clear that it is the inference from shareability to objectivity which is of paramount importance to Frege, rather than shareability itself. Since an unshareable thought can be perfectly objective—can exist and have a truth-value independently of anyone's entertaining it—there is no clash between what Frege says about 'I'-thoughts and this, undeniably central, aspect of his philosophy. Although Frege does tend to speak without qualification of thoughts as graspable by more than one person, I do not myself see why this should be regarded as an indispensable tenet, rather than a slight overstatement, of his position. Perry certainly does not tell us why he attaches such importance to it.

Perry makes clear that, quite independently of any question of Fregean scholarship, he thinks that fatal objections can be raised to the idea of an unshareable thought. This might seem a bit steep, coming after a criticism of Frege based upon his supposed insistence that all thoughts be 'generally accessible'. However, Perry will explain that the peculiarities of 'I'-thoughts can be accommodated on his system without recognizing unshareable thoughts. On Perry's system, both you and I can grasp the thought you express when you say 'I am hot', only we grasp it *in different ways*. However, I try to show in the next section that this is just a notational variant of Frege's theory.

It is true that Perry has other reasons for saying that an 'I'-thought cannot be a Fregean thought, for he thinks that objection can be raised to

---

[25] Ibid. 474.   [26] *Posthumous Writings*, p. 251.

a Fregean treatment of 'I'-thoughts even if Frege is allowed the 'private senses' to which he so desperately resorted. The argument here contains no surprises, for the difficulties result from the excessively wooden interpretation which Perry places on Frege's notion of 'way of being presented to oneself' as a result of trying to force it into the mould of descriptive identification.[27] He does point out that thoughts about times expressible with 'now' are also irreducible to description, and therefore if Frege's strategy is general:

Frege will have to have, for each time, a primitive and particular way in which it is presented to us at that time, which gives rise to thoughts accessible only at that time, and expressible at it, with 'now'. This strikes me as very implausible.[28]

In fact we have seen that Frege does not appear to hold that such thoughts are only graspable at one time (Section III), but even if we ignore this, I do not see that the approach can be so easily dismissed. What is so absurd about the idea that there are thoughts which one can have only because one occupies a particular position in space, or time, or because one is currently perceiving an object? This is just to say that there are ways of thinking about objects which require one to stand in a specific spatial, temporal, or causal relation to the object, and rather than deserving dismissal as implausible, the point seems to me to be worthy of the greatest respect. And to say that the ways of thinking are primitive is to say that they are not reducible to any other, particularly not to any which exploit knowledge of a description of the object, and this too is a point which Perry should applaud, figuring as it does so extensively in his own work.

Perhaps the implausibility is supposed to lie in the consequence of there being an infinite number of distinct, primitive, and particular ways of thinking of objects—one for each time—but alarm at this idea can only rest upon a confusion. A way of thinking about an object is given by an account of what makes some thinking about that object. In the case of a particular 'I'-thought, for example, I envisage statements of the form

(11) S is thinking of S' at t because $R_1 (S, S', t)$

where R_1 is an as yet unspecified relation which can only be satisfied by a triple of S, S', and t if $S = S'$. In terms of this idea, we can make perfectly good sense of the claim that different people think of different things (i.e. themselves) *in the same way*; we do not hold that precisely the same account can be given of what makes each of their thoughts have the object that it does, but that the same *type* of account can be given—namely in

---

[27] Perry, 'Frege on Demonstratives', p. 491.   [28] Ibid.

terms of the relation R_1. While it would no doubt be implausible to suppose that there are an infinite number of different *types* of account, I see no difficulty whatever in the idea of as many different *particular* accounts as there are times and persons.

V

A Fregean thought of the kind associated with a sentence 'Today is F' said on d can be equated with the ordered pair of the sense which 'Today' has on d and the sense of the concept expression '(ξ) is F', thus:

    (12) ⟨Sense on d of 'today', Sense of '(ξ) is F'⟩.

One grasps the sense of 'today' on d if and only if one thinks of d as the current day—i.e. in virtue of one's satisfying some relational propery $\lambda x(R_2(x, d))$—so we may equivalently equate the Fregean thought with the ordered pair:

    (13) ⟨$\lambda x(R_2(x, d))$, Sense of '(ξ) is F'⟩.

One entertains the object (13) if one thinks of a day in virtue of one's satisfying the first component, to the effect that it is F. If we wished to bring out the way in which any two utterances of (1) are similar, we might, equivalently, equate the thought with the triple:

    (14) ⟨d, $\lambda x \lambda y(R_2(x, y))$, Sense of '($\xi$) is F'⟩;

one entertains (14) if one thinks of the first member, in virtue of oneself and the first member, satisfying the second member, to the effect that it is F. In this construction the second and third components of the sense of an utterance of (1) are always the same, though the sense which 'today' has on d can be equated with neither the first member, nor the second member, taken singly, but only with the pair. Then, when Hume thinks 'I am hot' he entertains:

    (15) ⟨Hume, $\lambda x \lambda y(R_1(x, y))$, Sense of '($\xi$) is hot'⟩,

and when I think that I am hot, I entertain:

    (16) ⟨G.E., $\lambda x \lambda y(R_1(x, y))$, Sense of '($\xi$) is hot'⟩.

We know that Perry thinks that it is necessary to abandon the notion of a Fregean thought when dealing with sentences containing demonstratives, but with what would he replace it? He introduces a notion of thought according to which the sentence $F(t)$ uttered in context c, and the sentence $F(t')$ uttered in c' express the same thought provided the referent of t in c

is the same as the referent of t' in c'. Let us call a thought of this kind a 'P-thought'; a P-thought can be identified with an equivalence class of Fregean thoughts, or alternatively with an ordered pair of an object and a sense of a concept expression ('. . . a thought consisting of a certain object and an incomplete sense . . .').[29] It is the introduction of thoughts of this kind that Perry claims to be his greatest departure from Frege: 'The idea of individuating thoughts by objects or sequences of objects would be particularly out of place in (Frege's) system.'[30] However, for Perry, when we entertain a thought, we do not just stand in a certain relation to a P-thought; we entertain a P-thought *in a certain way*. When Hume thinks 'I am F' and then thinks 'That man is F' (indicating himself in a mirror), he entertains the same P-thought, but in a different way. Perry has a positive proposal about ways of entertaining thoughts, one which links them to the 'roles' of meanings of demonstrative expressions of natural language. I shall come to this aspect of his position in a moment, but what concerns me now is to see whether, the positive characterization apart, Perry is putting forward anything other than a notational variant of Frege's position.

Perry frequently speaks as though P-thoughts are the objects of propositional attitudes; this is, indeed, what their name would suggest. This means, I take it, that a belief ascription asserts a relation between a subject and a P-thought. If this is Perry's intention, then his position is not a notational variant of Frege's, since although Frege can say everything Perry can say (using the equivalence class of Fregean thoughts) the converse is not the case. (This is generally true when the ontology of Theory T_1 is less 'fine-grained' than the ontology of theory T_2.) *Frege, for example, can consistently describe the belief system of a subject S who understands and accepts, in context c, the sentence $F(t)$, and who understands, and neither accepts nor rejects, in context c', the sentence $F(t')$* when t in c refers to what t' in c' refers to. S believes one Fregean thought, and neither believes nor disbelieves another Fregean thought. If belief is simply a relation to a P-thought, this situation cannot be described.[31]

If Perry is to be able to report S's epistemic situation, his belief reports must be more complex than just a simple relational statement between a subject and a P-thought; the way in which the thought is apprehended

---

[29] Perry, 'Frege on Demonstratives', p. 496.   [30] Ibid. 496.

[31] Perry makes life too easy for himself by considering only the case where S rejects $F(t')$ in c'; this he can, and does, describe as S's believing the different P-thought, concerning the object, that it is not F ('Frege on Demonstratives', pp. 495–6). The importance of the case of agnosticism was noticed by Kaplan in 'Quantifying In', in D. Davidson and J. Hintikka (eds.), *Words and Objections* (Dordrecht, 1969), 206–42.

must come in as well. Perry uses locutions like 'By entertaining the sense of "I", S apprehended the thought consisting of Hume and the sense of "(ξ) is hot" ', and so perhaps he has in mind some such construction as:

(17) S apprehends-in-way-w $\langle x$, Sense of '(ξ) is F'$\rangle$.

But surely this is now a notational variant of Frege's approach, at best. Where Frege would write:

(18) S believes $\langle x, w$, Sense of '(ξ) is F'$\rangle$.

Perry will write:

(19) S believes-in-way-w $\langle x$, Sense of '(ξ) is F'$\rangle$.

or 'S believes, by apprehending such-and-such a sense, the thought consisting of x and the sense of "(ξ) is hot".'

So, finally, we can come to examine Perry's positive proposals about the various ways of thinking about objects which are involved in the understanding of sentences containing demonstratives, clear in our minds that they are not opposed, but supplementary to any views of Frege's. If Perry has succeeded in making these ways of thinking clear, if he has explained the various R-relations upon which they depend, all other Fregeans have reason to be grateful. For as I have said, Frege left these ways of thinking of objects quite uncharacterized, and so the nature of the senses of these expressions is unknown, even if their existence is not. Furthermore, it has seemed that such an account must presuppose some of the profoundest philosophy. In the case of 'I' for example, one might think that an account of the relation R_1 which explicates 'self-identification' must incorporate the insights, as well as illuminate the struggles, of Descartes, Kant, and Wittgenstein, and many others. One might have expected an account of self-identification—of the way in which we know, when we think of ourselves, which object is in question—would have to relate it to our special ways of gaining knowledge of ourselves, both mental and physical, both past and present. (At the very least, Hume's realizing that he is Hume must involve appreciating the bearing of the knowledge he can gain in these special ways to the truth-value of very many thoughts that Hume is F.) In this way, the 'immunity to error through misidentification' of these ways of gaining knowledge would be explained.[32] And one might have thought that an explanation of one's capacity to grasp indefinitely many thoughts about oneself which one does

[32] S. Shoemaker, 'Self-Knowledge and Self-Identification', *Journal of Philosophy*, 65 (1968), 555–68.

not know to be true—thoughts about one's remote past, or one's future—could be provided only when the role of conceptions of personal identity in self-identification had been made clear.[33]

Similarly, one might have thought that an account of demonstrative identification, which underlies the thoughts we might express in (certain uses of) sentences like 'This table is round' would have to show how thought can depend upon perception, at least in such a way that we would know what kind of perception can sustain demonstrative identification. Can one demonstratively identify a man when one sees him in a mirror, on a television, in a photograph, in an X-ray? Can one demonstratively identify a man when one hears his footsteps, when one hears him on the telephone, on the radio, on a record? Can one demonstratively identify a city when one perceives only the inside of a room located within it?[34]

Perry's answers to these profound questions have an appealing simplicity. In the case of a 'self-conscious' thought, for example, he writes:

We accept that there is no thought only Hume can apprehend. Yet only he can know that he is Hume. It must not just be the thought that he thinks, but the way that he thinks it, that sets him apart from the rest of us. Only Hume can think a true thought, by saying to himself

I am Hume

Self-locating knowledge, then, requires not just the grasping of certain thoughts, but the grasping of them via the senses of certain sentences containing demonstratives.[35]

By 'entertaining' the meaning or role of the demonstrative 'I', Hume thinks of himself. Similarly, by entertaining the meaning or role of the demonstrative 'here', Hume thinks of a particular place.

Simple though it is, I find that the proposal evades me. The role of a demonstrative was explained as that aspect of the meaning of the expression which was constant from occasion to occasion—presumably a (constant) function from contexts of utterance to objects. So to 'entertain the role' of the demonstrative 'I', for example, would presumably be to have this function in mind in some way. The function is determined by the rule that in any context of utterance the value of the function is the speaker in that context, so I suppose that in a derivative sense one could

---

[33] For 2 papers that help to bring out the profundity of the question, see L. Wittgenstein, 'Notes for a Lecture on Private Experience', *Philosophical Review*, 77 (1968), 275–320, and G. E. M. Anscombe, 'The First Person', in S. Guttenplan (ed.), *Mind and Language* (Oxford, 1975), 45–65 (this paper appears as ch. 6 in this volume).

[34] For a discussion of this latter question, see G. E. Moore, 'Some Judgements of Perception', *Philosophical Papers* (London, 1922), 220–53.

[35] Perry, 'Frege on Demonstratives', p. 492.

be said to have the function in mind, and so to be entertaining the role of the demonstrative, if one had in mind the description 'the person speaking', or 'the person who utters the token of "I" '. Since Perry insists that the meaning of 'I' is not a complete Fregean sense, and that different people entertain precisely the same meaning, perhaps we should think of this as like a description containing a free variable:

(20) The person who utters x and x is a token of 'I'.

But, leaving aside the question of how reference is achieved to a particular token—which is an aspect of the same general problem with which we are concerned—what has the idea in (20) got to do with one's capacity to think of oneself self-consciously? The problem is this. No one can give an account of the constant meaning (= role) of a demonstrative without mentioning some relational *property* (relating an object to a context of utterance) which an object must satisfy if it is to be the referent of the demonstrative in that context of utterance, but the idea of this property plays no part in an explanation of what makes a subject's *thought* about himself, or the place he occupies, or the current time.

It seems clear that we are on the wrong track; these suggestions must be as far from capturing what Perry intended by 'entertaining the role of a demonstrative' as they are from answering the questions with which we began. An alternative interpretation is suggested by Perry's remark: 'Only Hume can think a true thought by *saying to himself* "I am Hume".'[36] Perhaps 'entertaining the sense of "I am Hume" ' is to be understood along the lines of 'mentally uttering "I am Hume" ', or 'saying in one's heart "I am Hume" '. But this would be to suggest that self-conscious thought depends upon the interior exploitation of the conventional meaning of certain public linguistic devices, which is surely neither necessary nor sufficient for it. It could not be suggested that self-conscious thought would be beyond the reach of those who spoke a language which had no first person pronoun, and who had to refer to themselves with their own names, or that one's capacity to think about the place one occupies is dependent upon one's language possessing a device with the meaning of 'here'. These suggestions would surely get things exactly the wrong way round.

Perhaps Perry has no sympathy with these suggestions. Perhaps, contrary to first impressions, he intended by his use of the phrase 'entertaining the sense of' not to characterize, but merely to label these ways of thinking. Perry has adopted a terminology according to which one can grasp the same thought in different ways, and when Perry speaks of

---

[36] Perry, 'Frege on Demonstratives', p. 492; emphasis added.

Hume's grasping the thought ⟨Hume, sense of '(ξ) is Hume'⟩ 'by entertaining the sense of "I am Hume" ', perhaps he means simply Hume's self-consciously thinking that he is Hume—however that is ultimately to be characterized.[37] Whether or not this last suggestion is correct, it seems clear that all good Fregeans must live in hope of a yet profounder philosophy.

[37] This is certainly all I am able to understand by Kaplan's parallel talk of Hume's thinking of himself 'under the character of "I" '. He gives evidence of the intention to be enlightening about 'the particular and primitive way in which each person is presented to himself' ('Demonstratives', p. 65), but I can derive no more enlightenment from the literal meaning of the phrase, 'under the character' than I can from 'entertaining the role', and further elucidation is not to be found.

5

THE PATH BACK TO FREGE

PALLE YOURGRAU

> From the synthesizers and bandwagon performers in the philo-
> sophical profession there have come names for the unified theory:
> 'The Causal Theory of Reference', 'The Historical Explanation
> Theory of Reference'. But these names have no reference; the
> bandwagon is going nowhere.
>
> Gareth Evans, *The Varieties of Reference*

Frege's writings set a standard in the analysis of thought, that light of the
intellect, that has scarcely been met with since. Indeed, I think it is not
altogether unfair to suggest that the high water mark of recent years, Saul
Kripke's 'Naming and Necessity', has done more to illuminate the forceful
new ideas of Kripke than to shed light on the forceful old ideas of Frege.
Moved, then, by the urgent need to find a path back to Frege, I have
drawn up the following Seven Theses on Reference. It is my hope that
their explicitness will help us take our bearings: agree to them, if you will,
but take exception and you are invited to explore the consequences of the
alternatives you have adopted.

I

Thesis I: The Fundamental Task of semantics is to illuminate that
relation between a subject and his world in virtue of which the one is
able to think about, or refer to, the other.

Reference is thus what secures the world as *my* world. Semantics is then
interesting and important only to the extent that the semantic relation of
reference connects with ideas cognitive, epistemic, and doxastic. There is
thus no profit in engaging in endless debates over the 'real' translation of
Frege's 'Bedeutung', and none in establishing some 'technical' ('purely
semantic') notion of reference, free of the contaminations of epistemology
and philosophy of mind.[1] If you want such a notion, I give it to you—but

Adapted by the author for this volume from his paper 'The Path Back to Frege', *Proceedings of
the Aristotelian Society*, NS 87 (1986–7), 169–210. Copyright © Aristotelian Society 1987.
Reprinted by courtesy of the Editor.

[1] Thus G. Evans writes in 'The Causal Theory of Names', in S. Schwartz (ed.), *Naming,
Necessity and Natural Kinds* (Ithaca and London, 1977), 199, 200: 'One could regard the aim of

please leave me reference, in my sense, else I will never be able to understand how the mind makes a home for itself in the world. Whatever your account of that relation, R, that is the bridge between thought and object, whether it be causal, contextual, or 'socialistic', if it provides no intrinsic connection between R and what is within our cognitive, epistemic, reach it will only issue in a kind of 'noumenalization' of reference; that is, our referents—our very own objects-of-thought, our intentional objects (in Brentano's sense)—will simply drop out of the picture of our cognitive lives, like Kant's *noumena* (which forever elude our epistemic grasp).[2] Those like McGinn, therefore, (in 'The Structure of Content')[3] who want to make a clean break between that aspect of meaning that is 'internal' to the speaker and within his ken, and that component out there in the real world, *not determined* by the former (or even intrinsically linked to it), have helped issue in the noumenalization of reference that Fodor's paradoxical 'methodological solipsism',[4] merely recognized. For if the technical, semantic, 'external', referent of McGinn (*et al.*) is nothing-for-me, then the science of what *is* for-me—namely, psychology—had better occupy itself with a more visible referent.

Now, the ingenious reply has sometimes been made that reference does indeed intrinsically connect with belief, thought, and knowledge, but that we

---

this paper [to be] to restore the connection which must exist between strict truth conditions and the beliefs and interests of the users of the sentences if the technical notion of strict truth conditions is to be of interest to us.'

[2] This principle is violated even by neo-Fregeans like Peacocke, who talks about the 'mode of presentation' of a time *as* now, and calls it:[[now]]. But since this mode of presentation determines all times equally, Peacocke hits on the ingenious strategy of 'indexing' it to a particular time, t, to get: [[now$_t$]]. The trouble is that he still has not told us *how* the user of 'now' at t, *grasps* t (i.e. has it within his cognitive-epistemic reach)! (see C. Peacocke, 'Demonstrative Thought and Psychological Explanation', *Synthèse*, 49 (1981), 187–217.) Similar problems arise for 'contextualists', like Howard Wettstein, who insist that it is the context itself (whether or not you grasp it) that determines your referent (see his 'Has Semantics Rested Upon a Mistake?', *Journal of Philosophy*, 83:4 (1986), 185–209). Tyler Burge, in his critique of Frege, still admits that for communication, you must 'note' (i.e. *grasp?*) the context of the speaker: '*Sinning* Against Frege', *Philosophical Review*, 88:3 (1979), 398–433, p. 331. (Of course Burge, here, is simply repeating a point Frege already made in 'The Thought', in E. D. Klemke (ed.), *Essays on Frege*, Urbana, Chicago, and London, 1968) 507–35, p. 516.

[3] A. Woodfield (ed.), *Thought and Object* (Oxford, 1982), 207–58.

[4] See J. Fodor, 'Methodological Solipsism Considered as a Research Strategy in Cognitive Psychology', *Journal of Behavioural and Brain Science*, 3 (1980). I discuss the relation between internalism–externalism in semantics and similar issues in epistemology in 'Information Retrieval and Cognitive Accessibility', *Synthèse* (1986), special issue: *Information—Semantics and Epistemology*, ed. B. Loewer), where I also criticize the excesses of the 'externalistic' approach in both domains. I argue that once an intrinsic break is made between the internal and the external, in semantics and epistemology, the solipsism that we are threatened with is more than merely 'methodological'.

have no necessary grasp of the latter.[5] This is at least better—but in the end it only shifts the burden of anti-Cartesian prejudice from reference on to belief, thought, and desire (and even knowledge, see n. 4). It is indeed commonplace, in our Freudian, Marxist, Skinnerian times to make light of Descartes's conception of the transparency (i.e. intrinsic accessibility) of our own thoughts. Just as Freud and Marx do not so much ask you as tell you what you 'really' believe, Donnellan, Putnam, McGinn, *et al.* do not ask you what your very own thoughts are about, what you are referring to—they look at you (at your historical background, at your physical context, at your social environment) and tell you what you're 'really thinking'. That this approach is bound to refute itself, however, can be seen with a few strokes of the pen. Suppose McGinn, through observing me 'externally', learns what my beliefs and thoughts really are. He thinks to himself, (1) Yourgrau is thinking that *P*. Now, if the Cartesian view of thought is false, there is absolutely no reason why McGinn, too, should be expected to have some privileged, guaranteed access to his own thought. Suppose, therefore, he doesn't. It remains for some outsider, Putnam, who perceives McGinn from a broader, more objective viewpoint, to note what McGinn really thinks. So, Putnam thinks to himself, (2) McGinn thinks thought—(1). But of course exactly the same problem will arise again for *Putnam*, and we will be landed in an infinite regress, whereby (it is possible that) *nobody* will *ever* be able to have access to his own thoughts—i.e. no one will ever be able to find out what he's 'really' thinking! (Note: we are discussing not the *truth* of our thoughts, but their *content*.) There is no profit, therefore, in trying to satisfy the demand that there be an intrinsic link between our referent and our cognitive grasp of this referent by admitting the internal connection between reference and thought, only to bring to bear an anti-Cartesian prejudice that thought and belief are not themselves (somehow) essentially graspable by those who have them.

> Subthesis I: Semantics must face the transcendental question of Kant: what must our world be like if thought about it, reference to it, is to be possible at all?

(Compare this with Wittgenstein: what must pain be like, if thought about it, reference to it, is to be possible?)

---

[5] See Mike Byrd, 'Biro on Kripke's Puzzle' (mimeo, Madison: University of Wisconsin, Dept. of Philosophy, 1983). Byrd objects to Kripke's Principle of Disquotation (that, all else being equal, a speaker's sincere assent to '*P*' means that he believes that *P*) that it represents an outdated Cartesian assumption that we have (some sort of) privileged access to our own beliefs. Belief, for Byrd, seems to be a theoretical entity posited as what is causally operant in guiding my behaviour. I will have more to say, below, on the (out-of-date—but correct, in my view) Cartesianism of Kripke's philosophy.

Strawson (in *Individuals*) was one of the last thinkers clearly to pose Kant's question (which is not to be confused with the empirical question: what does our world happen to be like?). The answer Strawson gave, the Kantian, is of course not the only one possible. Broadly speaking there are three main positions here: (1) that Reality is *somehow* (by 'contemplation'?) itself thinkable, graspable by us (Plato), (2) that while Reality in itself (or as it is) cannot be known, we can know the features we must impose on 'our' world if we are to be at home in it (Kant), and (3) that the very notion of Reality (capturable or not in language) is a mistake, an imposition on nothingness of our own wilful categories of experience (Nietzsche).[6] These thumbnail sketches are of course nearly caricatures—but I think they are close enough to the spirit of the Three Paths to serve our purposes here. It is no accident, then, that when Putnam[7] finally brought himself to face Subthesis I, he recognized Thesis I as well, and realized that as a philosopher of language it behoved him to choose one of these paths. That he chose (his version of) the Kantian way is of less interest here than the fact that he chose a way at all. A clear sign that a philosopher has not yet come to Thesis I and Subthesis I is that he fails to see the true significance of the symmetric-universe, or twin-earth, argument, addressed already by Strawson in *Individuals* (p. 8) and recreated in Putnam's earlier writings.[8]

For many, the failure of (their simplified version of) Frege's theory, that all reference is made possible, and determined, by a descriptive sense (expressible by a definite description), to apply in the event of our world having an epistemically indistinguishable twin (i.e. there being in fact a mirror-universe, symmetric with ours) provides one of the most decisive refutations of the whole Fregean perspective. Thus in as sophisticated and exacting a book as Nathan Salmon's recent *Frege's Puzzle*[9], the symmetric-universe argument is once again invoked to prove, conclusively, that that part of Fregean sense (that Salmon, following Burge,[10] calls Sense$_1$), which reflects our own ('internal', conceptual) grasp of our referent cannot be what determines what our words are really about

---

[6] W. W. Tait seems to adopt (3), which Stanley Rosen calls nihilism (*Nihilism*, New Haven, 1969), when he writes: 'And the assertions that sensations and sensible objects exist are unassailable—so long as we remember that these are assertions in our language and do not think of them as somehow mysteriously transcending our language and serving as justification for our normal form of expression' ('Wittgenstein and the "Skeptical Paradoxes" ', *Journal of Philosophy*, 83: 9 (1986), 475–88, at p. 488.

[7] See his *Reason, Truth and History* (Cambridge, 1981).

[8] 'The Meaning of "Meaning" ', in H. Putnam (ed.), *Philosophical Papers*, ii, *Mind, Language and Reality* (Cambridge, 1975).

[9] Cambridge, Mass. 1986, 66, 67 and *passim*.

[10] Belief *De Rè*, *The Journal of Philosophy*, 69 (1977), 338–62.

('externally speaking'), i.e. our semantic referent (determined by what Salmon calls $Sense_2$). The idea is this. If our universe really is mirror symmetric, then the two halves are descriptively, epistemically indistinguishable, and therefore any $Sense_1$ that determines, say, Putnam, also determines twin-Putnam. But say I'm in *this* half of the universe, looking at Putnam. Then clearly my use of 'Putnam' determines Putnam, not his twin, and therefore no $Sense_1$ can account for this use.

To understand fully what is going on here we must introduce a number of distinctions. There is, to begin with, the fascinating mathematical problem of describing the properties and transformations of symmetrical figures in mathematical space. Hermann Weyl's beautiful book, *Symmetry*, takes on this task. This is then to be distinguished from the metaphysical–cosmological problem of whether our universe could turn out either to be different from a possible mirror-symmetric (looking-glass) world, or to be itself but one of an actual pair of such worlds. The famous Leibniz–Kant controversy about the absolute vs. relational theory of space concerned this very question. Leibniz, of course, denied the possible existence of a universe in principle indiscernible from this one, while Kant introduced the notion of (mirror-symmetric, but yet distinct) incongruous counterparts to try to prove that our actual universe has a non-actual, distinct, possible mirror-symmetric twin, conceptually indistinguishable from it. And this brings us to the third and final question, which is the one relevant to our discussion, namely: if the universe has (or could have) an epistemically indistinguishable twin, would we be in a position to *refer* to (it or) objects within it (without at the same time referring to the looking-glass twin)? If now we look more closely at Kant's answer to (2), we realize that he paid a high price for his insistence on the possibility of a symmetric universe—to wit, the (transcendental) ideality of space. Now, to understand this in turn, we must separate out three senses of 'indiscernible': (1) indiscernible by *any* means—including (non-conceptual) 'intuition', (2) descriptively, or conceptually, indiscernible, and (3) epistemically indiscernible (where you must fill in your favourite theory of knowledge).

We can now try to put the pieces back together to understand Kant's position. Since he claimed that 'intuitions without concepts are blind, and concepts without intuitions are empty' (and thus that knowledge requires both), and since the symmetric universe (whether possible or actual) is (by definition) conceptually indistinguishable from ours, we can have at most a (blind) intuition of (our) space (which, he said, is in fact the mere 'form' of our intuition). And hence, (1) it makes no sense to speak of the *correspondence* of anything real to our word for, or intuition of, space (hence, the transcendental ideality of space), and (2) we cannot be said to *know* (our) space (as distinguished from its epistemic twin). This is not the place to discuss whether this means Kant did not succeed in refuting Leibniz.[11] All that matters here is that we be aware of the distinctness of the question of whether we could *refer* to our world if it had a symmetric twin, and the price Kant paid for the privilege of a positive answer. For our purposes, we must now go back and ask whether $Sense_1$ was to capture (1) our 'intuitive' (i.e. non-conceptual) grasp of objects, or (2) only our distinctively conceptual (i.e. 'descriptive') access, or (3) rather the broader notion of our cognitive–epistemic access to reality (and, correspondingly, in which sense of '$Sense_1$' twin-earth is to be a $sense_1$—indiscernible world). I think we know enough already to see that we can hardly use the symmetric-universe thought experiment to decide (conclusively!) the question of the nature of reference, of the connection of $sense_1$ to $sense_2$. *If*, now, $sense_1$ is used in the second sense (the one Salmon attributes to Frege), and *if* we assume (*contra* Leibniz) that a universe indistinguishable from ours in this sense is possible (and may in fact be actual), then *if* we go on to claim that nevertheless we can refer to (objects in, and) our universe, we can with justice claim that it follows that $sense_1 \neq sense_2$. But note, (1) we have hardly *shown* that $S_1 \neq S_2$, since we have still to *establish* all of our assumptions (about Frege's conception of S_1, about the possible existence of such universes, and our ability to refer in them), which Salmon has not done, and (2) even if we establish our assumptions, depending on how we did it, we may have to pay the Kantian price of the (transcendental) ideality of space (Putnam does (n. 7)—would Salmon?), and/or explain in our theory of reference the connection between S_1 in the first and third conceptions, and S_2. Let us focus on the latter task.

Note first that it has been assumed by Salmon that Frege employed S_1 in the second ('purely descriptive') sense. I will examine, later, the question

---

[11] The relevance of Kant's incongruous counterparts to the question of relational vs. absolute space is still being debated in our relativistic times. See, e.g. L. Sklar, 'Incongruous Counterparts, Intrinsic Features and the Substantiviality of Space', *Journal of Philosophy*, 71 (74), 277–90. As to Kant's own account of the matter, we should note that since for him to be a genuine intentional object, i.e. a referent, *in* the world, required of the cognizer the ability to have epistemic access to it, or (as in Strawson's *Individuals*) to place it in our objective scheme of things, it would seem that (1) we cannot in this sense be said to refer to space at all, i.e. to make it an intentional object (of thought and knowledge), and, more troubling still, (2) it is hard to see how we could even refer to objects *within* our world, if we can only place them in a world which itself we cannot 'place'! We see thus that to extend the bounds of the metaphysically possible gives rise to serious problems in regard even to the issue of local reference and cognitive accessibility—problems that, we will see, will recur with Kripke's notion of rigidly designating something (i.e. the problem of rigid local designation of something from out of a sea of infinitely many possible alternatives).

whether this was Frege's actual view, and whether it ought to have been (consistent with the rest of his theory). In any case, Salmon seems to be claiming that in a descriptively symmetric universe reference need not break down. Now we need to know, (1) what cognitive relation between myself and my referent is left to me in such a looking-glass world, and (2) what are the cognitive–epistemic constraints on reference? In regard to the first question, we either say that all we can possess is a 'blind' Kantian 'intuition', or else we need to elaborate on a new kind of cognitive access to reality. Salmon does not address this question about reference, though he does (briefly) worry about the cognitive constraints on *de re* belief; but I will have a go at it below. As concerns the second, there is on Salmon's part a dramatic silence, for it is a distinctive feature of the adherents of the New Theory of Reference to minimize or dimiss the question of the cognitive–epistemic constraints on reference. For having satisfied himself that S_1 (in the descriptive, second—to his mind, Fregean—sense) does not determine S_2 (i.e. what fixes, semantically, the 'external' referent, 'out there'), he simply never reaches the question of whether S_1 in the first or third sense *does*. It is my contention, however, that it is precisely S_1 in the third sense, what gives me my cognitive access to reality (whether descriptive or otherwise), that determines S_2. Universes S_1 indiscernible in this sense, I would argue, would not permit unique reference. One cannot refer to X if it can in no way be cognitively–epistemically distinguished from Y. And this brings us to the next Thesis.

> Thesis II: There must be some sense in which we must know what we are talking about.

Russell puts this nicely: '. . . it is scarcely conceivable that we can make a judgment or entertain a supposition without knowing what it is we are judging or supposing about.'[12] The New Theory of Reference has had little to do with this principle, finding in it a conflation of semantic with epistemic issues (Kaplan, 'Demonstratives'),[13] or a vague and almost empty condition, easily fulfillable (Kripke, 'Naming and Necessity').[14] Two exceptions to this are a paper I wrote some years ago, 'Frege, Perry, and Demonstratives',[15] and Evans's *The Varieties of Reference*.[16] It is, indeed, a difficult principle to unpack, and requires us to develop the relevant sense of 'knowledge', or 'cognitive access', required by it,[17] but

---

[12] *The Problems of Philosophy* (Oxford, 1912), 58.

[13] Mimeo (Los Angeles: UCLA Dept. of Philosophy, 1977), 66, 69.

[14] In G. Harman and D. Davidson (eds.), *Semantics for Natural Language* (2nd edn., Dordrecht, 1972), 293.

[15] *Canadian Journal of Philosophy*, 12: 4 (1982), 725–52.

[16] Ed. J. McDowell (Oxford, 1982).

[17] I took a stab at this nasty problem in 'Information Retrieval and Cognitive Accessibility'.

something like it must be true, else we cast over our own referents (and hence our thoughts) a mantle of darkness, and thus once again threaten to noumenalize semantics. It in turn leads directly to the following:

Subthesis II: To refer to something I must be able to discriminate it from all ('relevant'?) alternatives.[18]

As Plato says, in the *Theaetetus* (209 a): '[If] . . . I had in my thought one of the common things, none of which you have to any greater extent than anyone else does . . . in such conditions how on earth could it be you that I had in my judgement any more than anyone else? . . . or, as one might say, the remotest peasant in Asia?'[19] This leaves us with the nasty question whether the referent should be discriminated from all alternatives, or only from the 'relevant' ones (which we must of course then go on to elucidate). Since this is a principle about the epistemic constraints on reference, the issue turns on the relevance of the discrimination of relevant alternatives in a more general epistemological setting. Evans seems to follow epistemologists like Dretske,[20] when he endorses the relevant alternative version of Subthesis II in *The Varieties of Reference*. I, on the other hand, have argued at length, in 'Knowledge and Relevant Alternatives',[21] against this aspect of Dretske's epistemology, and am inclined, therefore, to be suspicious of its implementation in semantics. The danger of its rejection in epistemology is the threat of scepticism (which I discuss at the end of that article), and in semantics, it is that we do not (very often) fully succeed in referring after all, or at least not to objects completely determinate in nature. If we now regard a 'completely determinate' object as something determined by a kind of 'function' that once and for all exhaustively divides the universe into two sets of objects—those that satisfy it and those that don't, then we can perhaps see Wittgenstein as adopting Evans's position, on the basis of his suspicions about the *existence* of such functions (even for purely mathematical, or logical, objects), whereas my position seems closer to Frege's. This is a profound debate, and here is not the place to try to settle it. Note, however, that the debate is not over the soundness of Subthesis II, but only over the issue of whether the principle should be circumscribed. But until this principle is clearly acknowledged, we will not be able to gain a deeper insight into which position is the correct one, and why. (One

[18] See 'Frege, Perry, and Demonstratives' and *The Varieties of Reference*.
[19] Trans. J. McDowell (Oxford, 1973).
[20] 'Epistemic Operators', *Journal of Philosophy*, 67 (1970), 1007–23.
[21] *Synthèse*, 55: 2 (1983), special issue: *Justification and Empirical Knowledge*, ed. R. Audi, 175–90.

cannot, in Hegel's sense, 'transcend' (*aufheben*) Frege by going around him—rather we must, like Wittgenstein, meet him on the same path.)

Subthesis II shines some light on the symmetric-universe problem. If we define such universes as non-discriminable, then by this principle it follows that we can refer to neither or both—but not to either, separately. The principle cuts even deeper than this, however. For the notion of rigid designation invented by Kripke, which is supposed, again, to be incompatible with Fregeanism, turns out to be similarly problematic. A rigid designator is a term, a, used in a context, c, such that when used (in c) to talk about something in any other context, c', a still refers to its original referent in c. Kripke then extends the notion of context so that it includes not only time, place, and speaker, but also possible world. Now it follows from Subthesis II that if term a is to be used (in c) successfully to refer, its referent (in c) must be discriminable from all others. That means that although, as Kripke says, I need not be able to recognize a if I met it in c' (just as I can now refer to baby Reagan, although if I were there then I would not have recognized the baby), he cannot escape the burden of showing how I manage locally, in c itself, to discriminate a from all possible Reagan twins in other worlds. (For obviously, for any purely general description of Reagan I can give, it will be equally satisfied by some Reagan twin in one of the infinitely many possible worlds.) What are Kripke's options here? Well, it would suffice if I could refer to the actual world, α (and then perform Plantinga's 'α-transform' on my descriptions producing 'the unique $\varnothing$ in α'). Only the problem simply returns with trying to refer to α. Some have objected at this point that modal co-ordinates are somehow different from space–time co-ordinates, and that my terms automatically succeed in having an α-transform. Evans suggests such a disanalogy between space-and-time and modality in 'Does Tense Logic Rest on a Mistake?',[22] and others have argued to similar effect. But I am suspicious of such claims, and have tried to provide arguments for my misgivings in 'On Time and Actuality: The Dilemma of Privileged Position'.[23] In any case, Subthesis II is a general requirement on reference to anything at all, and so any (alleged) metaphysical–epistemological asymmetries here would simply affect whether or not we could refer to α, not the conditions necessary to refer to it.

Another option open to Kripke would be to adopt Evans's relevant alternatives version of Subthesis II, and insist that the only relevant

[22] G. Evans, *Collected papers* (London, 1985), 343–63. See also P. Van Inwagen, 'Indexicality and Actuality', *Philosophical Review*, 89: 3 (1980), 470, 403–27, and R. Stalnaker, 'Possible Worlds', *Noûs*, 10 (1976) 65–75.
[23] *The British Journal for the Philosophy of Science*, 37 (1986), 405–17.

alternatives to *a* are the other objects in *c*. It is interesting to compare this strategy with Kant's for allowing us to refer to items in our world (which is conceptually indistinguishable from its mirror twin). As I indicated in n. 11, Kant's option has the embarrassing effect that I can 'place' (in my objective scheme of things) an object *in* this world, although I cannot similarly place *this world* itself! (Thus, as Plato mischievously says in the *Theaetetus*, founding knowledge on ignorance.) Something similar would happen if Kripke adopted the amended principle; for it would turn out that I could refer to (hence, 'place') an object located in a modal frame, though I could not tell you in which modal frame it was located. In any event, as noted above, I am inclined to reject the Evans version of the principle, and so could not accept this reliance on it. And that would leave Kripke two final options: either I cannot refer to particular objects at all (or at best to sets of non-discriminable ones), or I can have some alternative method of cognitive–epistemic access to the objects in my own world (other than the merely descriptive, conceptual mode).

Now, unfortunately, Kripke has said very little about such an alternative epistemic tie. You may be tempted to object: haven't I left out Kripke's well-known introduction of causality into semantics? The answer is that (1) I will argue later that to a large extent causality, in Kripke's account, is a wheel that turns nothing in the machine, and (2) in any case, Kripke did not urge causality as a kind of *cognitive–epistemic* tie at all. Rather, he seemed to be urging us to accept a causal connection as relevant to reference when there *was* no cognitive–epistemic tie (as conceived by him in (his conception of) Fregean (i.e. purely descriptive) terms. Further, it can hardly be that we are tied (epistemically or otherwise) to the actual world by *causal* chains—for causal relations connect objects *within* a possible world; they are simply not the kind of thing that can provide the modal link that ties you *to* a world. Kripke, like most members of the New Theory of Reference, simply has not spent much time seeking for modes of cognitive access alternative to the purely descriptive variety whose significance they are at pains to belittle.[24] The most that is usually managed is a moment taken to make fun of Russell's alternative—namely, acquaintance. I will discuss Russell's notion shortly,

---

[24] An interesting exception may be David Kaplan in 'Quantifying In', in L. Linsky (ed.), *Reference and Modality*, (Oxford, 1971), 112–44. The trouble is that (1) Kaplan (as far as I can tell) has since expressed reservations about the epistemic excesses of that essay; (2) it is just not clear if the complex relation, 'Represents', of that essay is intended as an *epistemic* foundation for a semantic relation, or simply as some other kind of foundation for reference; and (3) the complex relation developed in 'Quantifying In' was really intended not so much for reference, as for the peculiar notion of *de re* belief. I believe, however, that the search for the *en rapport* relation necessary for *de re* belief of an object, like the search for the Fountain of Youth, is not likely to end in success. But this is not the place to argue the point.

as well as the general idea of cognitive access to an object. What should be clear by now, however, is:

> Thesis III: Reference is a cognitive relation, supported by a method of cognitive access to an object.

I have been hedging, so far, between requiring for reference a cognitive, or requiring a full epistemic, relation. The reason is that although it is clear that for something to be my referent it must be accessible to my belief- (thought-, knowledge-) world, it is not clear whether it is required that this relation be knowledge, as opposed to some weaker cognitive tie from which I can develop knowledge. We can see the problem if we look closely at Russell's idea that there are two kinds of knowledge: knowledge by description vs. knowledge by acquaintance. For Russell, if I know Reagan as the President, I know some statement of the form: $a = \imath x(Px)$. By his theory of descriptions, this is analysed into: $(\exists x)(y) (Py \equiv y = x . x = a)$. Here the only referring terms are the logically proper predicate, P, and the logically proper name, a, with whose referents I must be acquainted. Acquaintance is the primitive, basic, cognitive relation that connects me with reality, and is thus the foundation for knowledge by description. This is a beautiful theory. The only question is how acquaintance can be a kind of *knowledge*. For, by one famous model of knowledge (developed by Plato[25] and Aristotle) to know something is to know what-it-is—i.e. its (formal) 'definition' or 'analysis', what makes it *it*. A good example would be: knowing that water $= H_2O$. But, as Plato says in the *Theaetetus*, this seems to imply that we can only know something complex, by weaving an account of its 'atoms', and thus leaving the (logical) atoms themselves unknowable. (And how, says Plato (again), can knowledge be based on ignorance?) Moreover, Russell's notion of acquaintance seems more like (direct) experience or perception—and the author of the *Theaetetus* went to great pains to show that while we can, it seems, perceive (logical) atoms, this will not solve our problem, since perception $\neq$ knowledge.[26]

---

[25] See R. Sharvy, '*Euthyphro* 92–116: Analysis and Definition in Plato and Others', *Noûs* (1971), 119–37. Sharvy's study contains some valuable hints on how to read Plato, but I must demur from his concluding suggestion that Plato in the *Theaetetus* countenances a kind of logical atomism like Russell's. For this dialogue precisely shows the paradoxes that ensue if we adopt that position. Indeed, Plato anticipates (the atomistic) Russell and Wittgenstein in pointing out that we cannot even say the 'atoms' exist; and he thus in effect drops the humorous Heideggerian hint that this would mean that the universe of big somethings emerges mysteriously from a lot of little nothings.

[26] For a modern version of the point Plato makes see Schlick's neglected classic, *Form and Content* (1932; repr. in *Philosophical Papers*, ed. H. L. Mulder and B. F. B. van de Velde-Schlick, Dordrecht, 1979): 'Intuition, identification of mind with an object, is not knowledge . . . identification with a thing does not help us to find its order, but prevents us from it.

It seems safer, therefore, to require of reference only cognitive access to the referent, and leave open the question of knowledge. What is clear is that there are a variety of kinds of cognitive access, and that denoting (i.e. uniquely describing) is but one—acquaintance (an immediate, 'direct', non-descriptive connection), or something *like* it, seems to be another. If we take denoting to be the only form of cognitive access, we will be tempted to ignore the question of what *other* cognitive tie must bind speaker to object when denoting is missing. If Thesis III is sound, however, it follows that

> Subthesis III: A causal theory of reference stands in need of a causal theory of knowledge/cognition.

The problem this principle brings with it is that the most sophisticated versions of the causal theory of knowledge impose conditions on the subject far stronger than those of the causal theory of reference. In particular, there is a counterfactual (hence, in a sense, future-oriented) requirement: if I know that P, then, if not-P then I would not have believed that P. But it is no part of the causal theory of reference that had the object at the origin of the causal name chain not been at the origin, we would not have intended to use the name as a name for that (supposed) object. Quite the reverse: in 'Speaking of Nothing'[27] Donnellan even insists that with a vacuous name like 'Santa Claus' the casual–historical theory still applies: we use it as a name, and the fact that the causal name chain ends in a 'block', not in a referent, simply makes the name vacuous. And as is clear from the rest of Donnellan's account, there is no requirement that a speaker be able to tell, of any given name he uses, whether the associated name chain ends in a block or not. Given the insistence, moreover, by Donnellan that there is no reason at all to suppose that speakers can in general fathom whether at the end of some long, historical–causal name chain, lost in the mists of time, there stands a referent, it is unlikely the causal theory of reference could be amended to

Intuition is enjoyment, enjoyment is life, not knowledge' (p. 196). (This last is one of my favourite lines in philosophy.) But, as Michael Friedman points out, in his 'Critical Notice: Moritz Schlick, *Philosophical Papers*', *Philosophy of Science*, 50 (1983), 498–514 (repr. here as ch. 10 under the title 'Form and Content'), Schlick came to realize that this critique of acquaintance leads to a conception of knowledge as something only applicable to structured wholes: but then the theoretical system by which we express the knowledge seems not to be connected anywhere to reality, and we are threatened with idealism (or its cousin, coherence theory). According to Friedman, Schlick never freed himself from this dialectic. To my mind, it still represents a profound challenge to philosophy (see 'Information Retrieval and Cognitive Accessibility'.

[27] In S. P. Schwartz (ed.), *Naming, Necessity, and Natural Kinds* (Ithaca and London, 1977), 216–44.

accommodate the corresponding theory of knowledge. But since the causal connection was supposed to represent that relation, R, that connects speaker with referent, if Thesis III is sound (that R must be cognitive–epistemic), then the fact that the causal semantics of R resists explication by a causal epistemology suffices to refute the causal theory of reference. We see, moreover, that part of the problem with the causal theory of reference is that it, unlike the corresponding theory for knowledge, is purely backward looking—it is an aetiological theory, representing the past of the speaker, while the ability to refer is precisely an *ability*—and hence implies a future capacity.

> Thesis IV: Referring reflects a semantic competence—a complex skill that is learnable as well as losable.

Kripke's new picture of reference grossly violates this principle. To oversimplify considerably, Kripke's lead idea seems to be that we can pick up the use of a name at a bar the way we can pick up the flu there: by being in the right causal context. Thus, acquiring the use of a name is likened, on this account, to catching a disease. That so outlandish a conception of reference has dominated the philosophical scene for so long is a testament to Kripke's considerable powers of persuasion. A truer picture, I would suggest, comes from the very root of the word 'intentionality' (making something an object-of-thought, referring): *intendo arcum in* (I draw a bow at . . .)[28] (an image for directed thought Plato was also fond of). To refer to something is to strike it, wherever in the universe it might be, with the arrow of the mind. The good archer strikes what is, while the bad chases illusions. It is an extraordinary feature of the mind that it can somehow, 'without travelling', reach out and strike at any conceivable corner of reality. What is important for our purposes here, however, is that the ability to refer is a linguistic *capacity*, a competence or skill in getting to objects; it is not something passive, acquired simply by being the *descendant* in a historical name chain. To refer means to have certain future directed capacities—e.g. to reidentify the object.

In neglecting the competence required for referring, Kripke misses two of Wittgenstein's lessons. His discussion of Wittgenstein on 'Moses'[29] is unsatisfactory precisely because one of the points Wittgenstein seems to be making is that one can use a name like 'Moses', and get by in most contexts, without having decided yet how to answer certain crucial hypotheticals ('What would you say if the so-called Moses never did lead

---

[28] See P. T. Geach, 'Intentional Identity', in *Logic Matters* (Berkeley and Los Angeles, 1972), 147.   [29] See 'Naming and Necessity'.

the Jews out of Egypt?', etc.) Kripke misses Wittgenstein's focus on the speaker's unreadiness to settle these questions, and insists on foisting on our (relatively) undetermined speaker a determinate referent—Moses— based rather on the historical–causal *ancestry* of the name the speaker is using. While for Wittgenstein the facts indicate that the speaker has not yet, as it were, ruled on such hypotheticals that we might wish to put to him,[30] Kripke ignores this, focuses on his social environment, and *tells* him whom he is 'really' referring to.

The other lesson not absorbed concerns Wittgenstein's remarks on pain (in *Investigations*). Surely it is one of Wittgenstein's points that to be able to refer to a pain it is not enough simply to have it—i.e. to be, as it were, in its 'environment'. What is required of the competent speaker is the capacity to use the terms for pain (in the present as well as in the future) in the relevant contexts—including future hypotheticals. As a consequence of this account, we can always *lose* this (acquired) capacity; if we can no longer identify pain correctly, etc., then the fact that we once acquired the use of the name does not touch the question of whether we are now competent to use it.

> Subthesis IV: There is no correct principle of 'semantic inertia' (namely the principle that the past acquisition of the ability to refer suffices in and of itself to establish your present referential credentials).

In 'Lost Knowledge'[31] Dretske and I deny that in memory-knowledge there is a principle of 'cognitive inertia'. Here I focus on the related issue of referential, semantic inertia. But the very spirit of the causal theory of reference—that the referent is the causal ancestor of my use of the name—violates this Subthesis, since once someone is my ancestor, this past fact alone suffices to keep him always my ancestor. It may be objected, however, that this criticism only applies to 'pure' causal theories that do not, like Kripke's, bring in the speaker's intention to refer. Let us focus, then, on the very interesting question of the role of intentions in Kripke's account.

Kripke, it will be recalled, insisted that when I acquire the use of a proper name from you, I must intend to refer to whatever you were

---

[30] Again, it is a deep question whether there is such a thing as finally reaching that stage of competence whereby you can 'in principle' settle *all* relevant hypotheticals about the object, and so, once and for all, have a particular, determinate object in mind to refer to.

[31] *Journal of Philosophy*, 80:6 (1983), 356–67. The idea is that there is no correct principle that says: once you learn something (i.e. come to know it) the mere retention of it (in 'storage') as a belief continues to preserve its status as knowledge. (We thus distinguish the belief-acquisition process from the belief-preservation process.)

referring to. A number of questions arise here. What happens after I formed the original intention? Can it dissipate, and the causal tie alone suffice to continue to determine my referent? This is surely unlikely—for then it becomes mysterious why the intention had to be there in the first place. Moreover, counter-examples, within the spirit of the theory, would be easy to supply. For example, if I first learned 'Kripke' from Donnellan, I would intend to co-refer with Donnellan (and so refer to Kripke with his name). But nothing prevents me from later forming the intention to use the name to refer to my pet bulldog. But surely 'Kripke', as I now use it, would no longer refer to Kripke, no matter what my original intentions were. Thus Kripke cannot but hold that for me to continue to use 'Kripke' to refer to him I must somehow preserve my original referential intention. But how do I accomplish this feat? It will come as no surprise to the reader that I will reject any suggestion of a principle of 'intentional inertia'. Unfortunately, Kripke has also insisted that I may well forget from whom I learned the name, so that I may not be able to preserve my intention by saying to myself: I intend to use 'Kripke' to co-refer with Donnellan's use of this name (at the time I first acquired it from him). Could I not use, instead of 'Donnellan', 'the person from whom I learned the name'? Well, for one, these manœuvres must seem to Kripke uncomfortably similar to the description theorist's. More seriously, there is the problem of ambiguity. Suppose I acquired the name 'Einstein' twice—once as it refers to the great physicist, another time as a name for the great Mozart scholar. Clearly, I am now unable to preserve either referential intention simply by using the phrase: 'the person from whom I originally acquired the name'. (Of course, I might be able to get the job done if I could recall some facts about either Einstein—that one of them was a friend of Gödel's, say. But this would strongly clash with Kripke's idea that referring does not require the ability of future reidentification of the referent.)

Beyond these problems of semantic or intentional inertia there lies a further question about the role of intention in his theory. The question is the simple one of why, if the relevant referential intention is present (and continues to be), we need bring in a causal connection at all to secure a referent? If I intend to co-refer with Donnellan with 'Kripke', and he uses it to refer to Kripke, don't I also so refer—whatever the facts may be about my causal ties with Kripke? Thus, isn't the causal nexus in Kripke's own theory a wheel that turns nothing, and so not part of the machine at all? One could, again, insist (as Evans seems to, in 'The Causal Theory of Names')[32] that intention (like other metal concepts) is itself a causal—

---

[32] See 'The Causal Theory of Names', pp. 195–7.

contextual notion—but there is no hint that these are Kripke's intentions. He keeps quite distinct the intentional requirement and the causal sketch, and is even at pains to point out that since his theory adverts to the intention to refer it is not reductionistic (of reference to any other— including causal—notion).

Now, I believe in fact that the tensions I have brought out in Kripke's theory do more to recommend than to harm it. In spite of some strong contrary tendencies, he seems to have developed a point of view that has, in many respects, a courageously Cartesian flavour. It was after all Descartes (in the *Meditations*) who urged that what makes an idle 'idea' in the mind a true–false representation of something is the mental force— will or intention—behind it. Recall, further, that it is in 'Naming and Necessity' that Kripke offers a bold defence of Descartes's view that since pains, but not brain-states, are essentially painful, the two cannot be identical. Indeed not only are Kripke's conclusions on this point, and specific methodology, strongly Cartesian, the modal metaphysics that pervades the essay is also suggestive of the author of the *Meditations* (recall the modal-ontological argument which even seems—eerily—to require the Kripkean semantics of the modal system S-5 to work).[33] One could therefore, I think, with not too much irony, say that 'Naming and Necessity' is a candidate for the title of Descartes's *Seventh Meditation*.[34] It is thus a testament to the extraordinary ability of philosophers to misread each other that the author of the *Seventh Meditation* was invoked by the materialist, reductionist, causal, nominalist Hartry Field (in his 'Tarski's Theory of Truth').[35]

> Thesis V: It is no more true to say that language is a social institution designed for communication (Wittgenstein, Quine, Kripke) than it is to say it is a tool for the expression of an individual's thought (Plato, Descartes, Frege).

There is no profit in insisting only on the social, communicative element in language, as is done so often these days. Indeed if Kripke has in effect accused Frege, who insisted on your knowing what you are talking about, of a kind of 'transcendental deduction' of encyclopaedias (which the speaker can luckily advert to to ensure that there is knowledge somewhere sufficient to determine his referent), we can with some justice accuse Kripke of the 'transcendental deduction of the other speaker'! For on Kripke's excessively socialistic account of reference it would appear lucky for me

---

[33] To gather what I mean by this, see my essay, 'The Dead', *The Journal of Philosophy*, 84:2 (Feb. 1987), 84–101.

[34] Recall our discussion in n. 5 of Byrd's 'Biro on Kripke's Puzzle'.

[35] *Journal of Philosophy*, 69:13 (July 1972), 347–75.

indeed that other speakers are around to complete the job of referring that it seems I cannot manage alone. Of course Kripke himself at least distinguishes between the original 'independent' users of a name, and the later 'dependent' users. But in general, Quine's idea that language is a 'social art' has become the accepted wisdom. And Wittgenstein's name is also often invoked here. But consider: is thinking (and hence, referring), itself, really to be thought of as a social art, like baseball? Does it take two to think (or use language)? (Or perhaps it's three?) If my interlocutor suddenly dies do I have to revert to whistling?

Again, I think it is unlikely anyone would have accepted so strange and counter-intuitive a doctrine unless in the grip of a picture—in this case one commonly associated with Wittgenstein, and developed to excess by the New Theory of Reference. It is easy to see, however, that there can only be a false dichotomy between the use of language as a means of expression of solitary thought, and its social use as a vehicle for communication with others. The reason, in a nutshell, is that all 'solitary' thought is already a form of 'communication' among one's own past, present, and future selves. Thought is a process that takes place in time, and in order for this to be successful there must be a fundamental unity of conception among the various 'selves'. This is the source of Kant's famous thesis of the unity of consciousness, and something like it was already present in Plato. In the *Theaetetus* Plato focuses on counting, and insists that there must be a fundamental unity in that, whatever it is, that does the counting (else, for example, one will never be able to *combine*, in a single thought, the 1 smell, 2 tastes, and 3 sounds into 6 sensations). The self, one might say, is already a community of sorts, and thus even the most solitary reverie is already an exercise in 'communication'. Note, further, how many of Wittgenstein's messages already apply to this conception: if you can communicate with your future self, you can miscommunicate, and you can learn to correct your own mistakes. Again, you must not mistake merely having some future sensation, with the participation of the future self in a common practice (e.g. Plato's counting), shared with the past self. Finally, what matters is the objectivity of the practice (e.g. whether you really did count correctly, over time), not whether your future self believes you did.[36] It should be clear then that,

> Subthesis V: Nothing is gained by avoiding the perspective of Descartes's solitary meditator.

[36] In 'Lost Knowledge' Dretske and I briefly advert to the fact that short-term memory (i.e. one's own short-term memory) cannot be 'proved' to be reliable; it follows that the objectivity of memory knowledge cannot, ultimately, be based on a *social* practice of checking one another's memories. For what good is it to me if you check my memories, if I must in the end rely again on my own memory of this very checking of yours?

There is indeed, however, a dialectical problem here that cuts very deep, and that I believe Wittgenstein was struggling with. On the one hand one must rely on the future to reveal whether one really was using an expression correctly (i.e. as one thought he was), and in general to reveal decisions about linguistic practice that simply could not all be addressed in the present (you simply can't, in the present, consider and decide on all possibilities to which your usage must address itself—cf. our earlier remarks on 'Moses'). On the other hand, life is obviously *lived* in the present, and one must always, therefore, in the present, 'reconstruct' one's whole reality; it is no good relying on having done it in the past—for now one must repurchase this very past itself and make it one's own. (Remember Descartes's suspicion of overly long mathematical proofs, even when each step was achieved—in the past—with certainty.) Yet again I insist: there is no 'principle of inertia' to help us here: past thought does not, unaided and of its own, fulfil the justificatory, definitional and projective duties incumbent on all present thinking. Thus although the *world* may do just fine without my constant attention, my *conception of the world* cannot survive without my unending ministrations. Now, I am not suggesting that Wittgenstein did not have a tendency to minimize the Cartesian side of this dialectic—but I am suggesting that, unlike many of his followers, he did seem to be aware of and to struggle with the dialectic itself. The 'socialistic' theories of reference, with their 'division of linguistic labor', are guilty, I believe, of becoming preoccupied with just one side of this dialectic: that my own use of a term to refer conforms with a social, shared, linguistic practice, and therefore gets its identity from its role in the past and future conduct of this linguistic community. The grains of truth in this conception must be squared with the equally valid point that a speaker must in principle be able to recover his own referent—i.e. 'make it his' (for thinking is not something others can do for you). Otherwise, we will eventually arrive at the possibility that it is not the individual who thinks, at all, but only Society! In fact, just the reverse is the case: even a dialogue is only a genuine *dialogue*, and not mere parallel soliloquies, if the interlocutors are 'of one mind' (thus, in a way all dialogue, even with another, is a form of Plato's 'internal speech' with oneself; there is a sense, therefore, in which we must all carry the world on our own shoulders).

Let us now combine our revival of the Cartesian insights of Kripke with our admonitions about the misuse of causality in the theory of reference, to combat one of the most beguiling images of representation around today, the photograph model.

Thesis VI: Reference is determined by referential intentions; thus any representational device, like a photograph, refers or represents only in virtue of the intentions behind its use.

In opposition to this Thesis, there is the conception (no doubt strongly influenced by Grice's causal theory of perception) of the photograph, together only with its causal genesis, as the very paradigm of a referential–representational structure. The *locus classicus* of this view is no doubt Kaplan's discussion in 'Quantifying In', p. 132:

The genetic character of a picture is determined by the causal chain of events leading to its production. In the case of photographs and portraits we say that the picture is *of* the person who was photographed or who sat for the portrait.

(Of course this only represents part of Kaplan's theory in this essay.) Now, I think that there *is* a notion of *photograph-of*, and that Kaplan has correctly (and succinctly) characterized its causal–genetic character. In some suitable sense, a photograph is *of* the object that plays the appropriate role in the causal genesis of the image on the film. (We must always add that the causal mechanism be 'relevant', lest we end up maintaining that if the Loch Ness monster swims up to our camera and clicks it from behind, the resulting image on the photographic plate, since caused by the monster, is *of* it.) But we must distinguish the relation (1) photograph-of, from (2) picture- (or representation-) of.[37] If I am a photographer it is up to me how to use the photographs I take. Thus, if asked to provide a passport photo for Kaplan, I am free to save time and photograph his identical twin brother, Saul, and let this photo serve, for passport purposes, *as* a representation of David Kaplan. I thus use a *photo-of* Saul as a picture or *representation-of* David. Again, a police officer hunting a criminal is free to use a photo of the criminal's twin brother to represent, to informers, the person he is hunting. (It would surely be crazy to be told that one *couldn't* do this: that since it is simply not a photo-of the criminal it *cannot* be used to represent him in the hunt—if the officer has already (seemingly) used it this way, successfully, what exactly was it he was failing really to do?)

Now it will be observed that when I used the photo-of Saul to represent David I exploited its resemblance to David. But there is nothing essential in this, and I am not suggesting a resemblance theory of representation. I am free to exploit *any* feature of the photograph to serve in my representation of David. I can choose a photograph that resembles him to *inform* you of what he really looks like, or I can use a different photo (that

---

[37] 'Obviously one would not call a picture true unless there were an intention behind it' ('The Thought', 509).

does not in the least resemble him) to represent him and so deceive you into forming the wrong impression of his looks. Or I can use a rare old photo of Lincoln, that scarcely resembles him, to represent Lincoln, and I can sell you this representation for a lot of money—not because it illuminates his looks, and not because it 'really' represents him (for so do $10 paintings of Lincoln), but rather because it is really a *photograph-of* him. In none of these cases is it the visual appearance or the causal genesis of the photo that *makes it* a representation of *x*—this is achieved, rather, by the representor's intentions. We should distinguish the photograph-as-photograph, therefore, from its use as-a-(representational)-picture.

Now, for pictures in general, or paintings, exactly the same considerations hold. It is really quite extraordinary to be told that a portrait is a portrait of the person (i.e. the model) who sat for it! How many paintings of Jesus would that leave us with? Rather, here again, we must distinguish the person the artist intends to represent with the portrait from the immediate (relevant) causal source of its genesis. It is of course open to Kaplan to reply that: (1) intention is itself a causal notion (but this is not the theory he gave, and in any case needs independent motivation), or (2) the person a picture represents must have at *some* point in time, no matter how removed, a causal–aetiological connection with the painting—thus perhaps some ancestor of my ancestors must have met (someone who met) Jesus himself. The trouble with this last ploy is that it simply lacks motivation. The driving force behind the idea that representation is a causal–genetic notion was the *striking connection* between such notions and that of *photograph-of*. Once it is pointed out, however, that the latter (genuinely causal–aetiological) ideas are unfortunately not the very *representational* notions we were looking for, we need some *new* reason to believe that the latter notions are yet capturable by some highly attenuated version of the original causal conception. And such new reasons have not, I believe, been provided.

Well, I have been hammering away for some time now on the dangers of following the New Theory of Reference down paths that lead nowhere. But what of the insights of Krikpe and the others? I want to say here that one genuine insight, against Frege, incorrectly understood, has done more harm than good for the task of comprehending Frege's thought, and has thus in effect hampered progress in semantics. Frege claimed that there is no reference without sense. The examples of senses he offered were usually expressed by definite descriptions. But in 'The Thought' he speaks of a sense of the word 'I' that shows how I am presented to myself, and that is 'primitive and incommunicable'. Is this sense 'descriptive'? Further, although he produces definite descriptions to express the senses of proper names, he includes other proper names in these new descriptions. Must we be able to 'purify' descriptions, in the end, of all proper names (and demonstratives)? He never says. It is simply not clear, therefore, whether Frege's senses were intended to be 'purely descriptive (or conceptual)'. His other views on senses help us, however, to pin down his conception a bit more. Senses, we read in 'The Thought', are eternal, changeless, entities that 'are neither things in the external world nor ideas', but occupy, rather, 'a third realm', and determine (or fail to determine) their referents all on their own, without any help from us. Thought is made possible by somehow attaching ourselves, via our language, to the realm of senses. It would seem to follow, moreover, that senses, since out there in 'the third realm', can always in principle be shared; but his remarks on 'I' are in tension with this. Further, it would seem that no one is ever in a more privileged position to express a sense that anyone else (since we are all in the same position in regard to the 'third realm'); but his remarks on 'I', as well as on 'today' and 'yesterday', at least seem to conflict with this.

Let us focus for a moment on the latter. In 'The Thought' (p. 516) he says: 'If someone wants to say the same today as he expressed yesterday using the word "today", he must replace this word with "yesterday".' This may suggest to you (as it did to Evans)[38] that the sense of the word 'yesterday' is the kind of thing that, when expressed tomorrow, makes the same contribution to some thought, T, as the sense of the word 'today' did, when it was expressed today. This would be to give up, however, Frege's 'third realm' of thoughts—including the idea that senses do their determining of referents all on their own, without depending on who expresses them where and when. Moreover, the text can just as easily be read another way. Suppose there is a classical Fregean thought, T, containing a part, α, which is a sense that determines (once and for all) a particular time, t. Now, what English sentence expresses this thought? It may be that, given the conventions of usage for 'today' (i.e. the rules which tell us how to use the word, in any given context, to get to a sense), if I use this term today, it expresses α, and so contributes to T (say: α is a fine day). Nothing then prevents there being a rule for 'yesterday' that determines that if I use this term tomorrow, it will also express α, and so contribute in the same way to the classical, eternal Fregean thought, T. Which of these interpretations of the text is correct? I am inclined to buy the latter, which does less violence to the rest of Frege's philosophy.

[38] 'Understanding Demonstratives', in H. Parret and J. Bouveresse (eds.) *Meaning and Understanding* (Berlin and New York, 1981), 280–303, which appears as ch. 4 of the present volume.

However, it is apparent that this aspect of his theory is simply not clearly made out.

There is a further problem, however. For on the same page of 'The Thought' he writes: 'If a time indication is needed by the present tense one must know when the sentence was uttered to apprehend the thought correctly. Therefore the time of the utterance is part of the expression of the thought.' This passage seems to do violence to Frege's insistence, in 'On Sense and Reference', that although sense provides a 'path' to the referent, there is no path back from reference to sense. Yet here we are told that by merely exploiting (our knowledge of) a time, t, we can manage to get back to, express, a specific sense, α, (that determines t). Moreover, it is far from clear how we manage to get to that specific sense, α, and it is also not clear just which sense it could be.[39]

There are thus mysteries aplenty in trying to pin down exactly which theory Frege was actually offering us, and in explicating key ideas in that theory. Instead of speaking of 'purely descriptive senses', therefore, I will simply speak of senses (or Frege's senses). And I will say (although, as we have seen, it may be misleading) that to express a sense, s, that determines or is a sense of t, is to describe or denote t, with s.

> Thesis VII: Frege was mistaken that reference requires sense; referring is not the same thing as denoting.

On this rock, many have thought, Frege stumbles. Indeed he does—as on many a rock. But the remarkable thing is that once we repair the damage, the new, improved theory hangs together and is even more flexible and powerful. This is what has not been recognized. Rather, it has been thought that on this rock the whole theory crumbles. What needs to be seen clearly, then, is (1) why Thesis VII is true, (2) whether and how the damage can be repaired, and (3) whether Frege can be yet further improved and can thus speak to the concerns of current semantic theory.

Of the many arguments that have been put forward by Kripke and others to demonstrate Thesis VII, none, I believe, is decisive. I won't belabour the issue here, but refer you to 'Frege, Perry, and Demonstratives' (and to the writings of Dummett and Evans). No matter. The following seems to be a conclusive argument for the Thesis, and moreover one that arises from Frege's theory itself. To refer to something, t, I must express a sense, s, which denotes t. But to 'express' a sense means to 'grasp' it, to (in Strawson's phrase) introduce it into my thought. But how do I manage this? If the only way to introduce something into my thought,

---

[39] For a detailed discussion of these problems, and some suggestions on how to repair Frege's theory, see 'Frege, Perry, and Demonstratives'.

to cognitively 'grasp' it, is to *denote* it, then to express s I must denote it by expressing another sense, s'. But of course the very same problem will arise for s'. We thus have an infinite regress. Is it a vicious regress? It must be, since for any sense, s, in order to grasp it I must first grasp another sense, s'.

It follows that denoting is not the only method of introducing an item into our thought. There must be, to hold Frege's own theory together, a non-descriptive mode of access.[40] To get a clearer picture of what is going on, consider Fig. 5.1. Column [B] represents the eternal, self-contained, determination of objects by senses. Column [A], contrariwise, shows how we gain cognitive access to the items in [B]. The diagram shows that each item is in fact reachable in two ways: by denoting and by some non-descriptive method of access (called here 'grasping'). Two questions arise: (1) can one grasp objects in general (i.e. not just senses)?, and (2) can one refer to an item by grasping it? In regard to the first question, we note that Russell, whose candidate for *grasping* was *being acquainted with*, thought that one could be acquainted with particular objects. Why might one deny this? The answer would depend on how narrowly one construed the relation of *grasping*, but one with Platonistic sympathies might well believe that senses (like the Forms) are somehow intrinsically intuitable by the light of reason, unlike the more solid realm of empirical objects, which shine only by the reflected light of senses (or Forms). To reject this

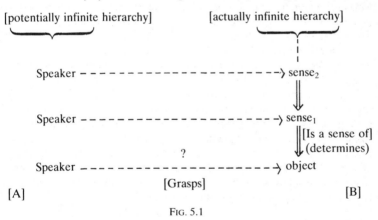

FIG. 5.1

[40] Is this a general feature of Platonistic theories? Well, it is interesting to note that similar conclusions have been drawn about Plato and the Theory of Forms: '. . . the mode of cognition of Forms must be a form of unmediated acquaintance . . .' (R. D. Mohr, *The Platonic Cosmology* (Leiden, 1985), 52). And, Gödel, it will be recalled, combined his Platonism with a belief in intellectual 'intuition'.

view means to hold that one can somehow have cognitive access to, or know, particular objects (which have properties), but not *via* their properties. How could this be possible? Well, properties also have properties, but we can know the originals, and not just via their properties. Why should particular objects be different? But to address these questions would take us too far into pure metaphysics. All that matters here is that there must be a method of cognitive access which is non-descriptive. As for the second question, I can see no good reason to deny that 'grasping' an item (in at least the sense in which you grasp a sense when you express it) suffices to enable you to refer to it. If a sense, for example, is grasped in the 'expressive mode', nothing prevents us from going on to reconsider it (just by grasping) in the 'referential mode' (i.e. from referring to it). Thus we have our Thesis, that not all referring is denoting.

Please note, however, that the non-descriptive mode of access we have uncovered is a genuine *cognitive* mode of access (possibly knowledge; possibly even acquaintance). If it were not, a Platonic riddle would arise: how can that paradigm of intentionality—being able to uniquely describe your referent (to pick it out from among all other objects in the universe) be itself founded on a relation, R, that is cognitively blind? Note further that Frege's theory has now not so much been contradicted, as supplemented and improved. In fact, the 'improvements' are simply a working out of the implications of the theory itself, once it is better understood. It is clear, also, that the theory can now satisfy not only Thesis VII (as can the New Theory of Reference), but as well all the other Theses (unlike the other theory). The task that remains pressing, to get a clearer insight into this new non-descriptive cognitive relation (and to which Russell, like Plato, devoted a lot of time), is (as we saw before) for the most part ignored by the New Theorists. They seem to be so preoccupied with Thesis VII, that, given their narrowly descriptive conception of a cognitive theory of reference, like Frege's, and their suspicions of Russellian acquaintance, they are tempted to give up the general Fregean project (of a cognitive theory of reference) altogether, and thereby forget Theses I–VI. What we should be impressed with, however, is just how smoothly Frege adjusts to the emendations, and how powerful and flexible the resultant theory is.

II

Before discussing just how flexible the new Frege is, however, I want to suggest two further improvements. (These will prove crucial in helping

Frege address some new problems that have only been raised quite recently.) The first concerns the fact that for Frege a sentence is a kind of singular term, and that it refers, if at all, to its truth-value. This strange doctrine, never exactly demonstrated by Frege, was seemingly clinched by an ingenious argument developed by both Gödel and Church. Fortunately, the argument is unsuccessful. I make a case for this in 'Frege on Truth and Reference',[41] and so will not take up space here to rehearse my reasoning. If my article is correct, however, we are free to develop a theory of sentential referents that will (1) fit commodiously into the rest of Frege's theory, and (2) best serve semantics. (As long as we are careful to make these sentential referents—call them 'facts', if you will—logically iso-morphic with the corresponding sentences.) On a plausible reconstruction, these new referents, or facts, would be facts in the (more or less ordinary) sense of that term (i.e. ordered n-tuples of objects and concepts). The resulting theory would now have for a sentence's sense, a *thought*, and for its reference, a *'fact'*. Once again, the theory that emerges from the correction of a mistake on Frege's part fits smoothly into the rest of the system and dramatically increases its power and flexibility.

But again this is not how these results have been received. When Barwise and Perry[42] reached similar conclusions about Frege's (or Church's and Gödel's) truth and reference argument, and responded by developing their own theory of facts (or 'situations'), they treated their results as the key to how to avoid Frege's semantics, and proceeded to try to get the job done with only half of the improved-Fregean theory (i.e. with facts, but not Fregean senses). This is (to put it mildly) a strange response to the new discovery. For if my interpretation of it is correct, it reveals that Frege's only mistake was simply not to see that his own theory could incorporate a whole *new* realm of referents, the sentential referents, and thus could provide *more* tools with which to accomplish the goals of semantics. (Contrast this with the discovery of Russell's Paradox in Frege's set theory and logic, and the difficulty of finding any solution that would preserve the basic lines of his logicist foundations of arithmetic.) But the theory can be made stronger still. We need to look briefly at Frege's analysis of belief, or in general, 'indirect' contexts.

As is well known, Frege argued that in belief contexts, terms refer to what were their ordinary senses. The new referent of a sentential clause,

---

[41] *Notre Dame Journal of Formal Logic*, special issue, *Frege*, 28:1 (Jan. 1987), 132–8.

[42] 'Semantic Innocence and Uncompromising Situations', *Midwest Studies in Philosophy*, vi, *The Foundations of Analytic Philosophy*, ed. P. A. French *et al.* (Minneapolis, 1981), 387–404. Note, also, that their analysis differs from the one I put forward, since they rely on Donnellan's referential–attributive distinction for definite descriptions, while on my account the central problem with the argument lies elsewhere.

then, after 'believes', would be the ordinary thought that sentence would express by itself. Thus, in 'Plato believes Socrates is wise', we get the analysis shown in Fig. 5.2. There are a number of problems that arise with this theory—but note first its marvellous simplicity. Senses, which for (pre-improved) Frege represent our sole cognitive grasp of reality via language, having been exploited by Frege as (1) what determines reference and (2) what gives cognitive significance to our refence to and hence statements about reality, is now used again for (3) the indirect reference of terms in belief contexts. Not only does this represent an admirable conservation of material, it is highly intuitive as well. For is it not plausible that in belief—or in general (to use Russell's term) propositional attitude (i.e. *thought*)—contexts, what is being singled out for our attention (i.e. referred to) is precisely the *thought* (ordinarily) expressed by the dependent clause? In our sample case, we wish to attribute to Plato a belief, and so a thought, and in doing so we produce a sentence: 'Socrates is wise', which (we know) *already* (on its own) *expresses a thought*. It does not take a genius to put these pieces together and thus to arrive at the conclusion that when placed in the belief context, this sentence is about (i.e. refers to) this very thought.

There are a number of problems with this theory, as applied to natural language. We must be careful, however, not to foist on to Frege problems inherent in the coarseness of this language itself—for he, of all thinkers, was at pains to show how imperfectly ordinary language captures the realm of pure thought! But this is exactly what many have done to Frege. Salmon, for example, in *Frege's Puzzle*, p. 126, raises the following (genuine) problem about Frege's analysis of belief contexts in natural

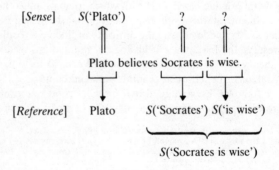

Fig. 5.2

language, and in effect accuses Frege of a deficiency which ought to be attributed not to the professor from Jena, but rather to our mother tongue itself. As Salmon points out, our analysis seems to attribute to Plato a belief about Socrates, in terms of S ('Socrates'). But the latter represents how *we* think of (and are thus able to refer to) Socrates; what reason is there to believe this is how Plato thought of him? To this there are a number of replies: (*a*) people do say things like 'Plato believes Socrates is wise'. If the Fregean analysis of belief contexts is right, then (if Salmon is also right) people are here vastly oversimplifying their picture of Plato's mental life and foisting on him their own mental contents. Fair enough. Why doesn't this show, not that Frege is wrong, but rather that people tend to oversimplify and not realize that they often attribute to others conceptions borrowed from their own heads? Further, (*b*) if this is how natural language works (and why expect otherwise—language evolved for many reasons, but to be a precise vehicle for the elucidation of our conceptual lives seems not to be high on the evolutionary list), even the best-intentioned commentator on Plato will have trouble not committing this intellectual sin; (*c*) we need to know much more about S('Socrates') to be able to decide whether (1) it does not after all capture something central even in Plato's method of access to Socrates, and (2) perhaps S('Socrates'), though anachronistic as attributed to Plato, is more naturally associated with our own language group (circumscribed in some appropriate way); (*d*) finally, given (*c*2), nothing prevents Frege from finessing his theory by giving the following as a 'safer', alternative, reading of belief sentences, when they involve those whose cognitive lives we do not wish, chauvinistically, to assume are sufficiently close cousins to ours to permit our earlier analysis:

$(\exists s)(\exists t)$(Sense(s) and Thought(t) and Plato believes t and $t = $f($s$) and s denotes Socrates).

I do not see, thus, why Frege, too, cannot 'go existential', like some modern theorists, when there is reason to believe caution (in attributing cognitive contents to others) is the wisest counsel. There is not the slightest reason here, moreover, to suggest (as Salmon appears to) that because this renders the fine points of Plato's cognitive life inaccessible (NB *de facto*, not *de jure*) to me (at least if I try to capture it in natural language), this is a *problem* with the theory; quite the opposite, I should think.

Finally, it behoves us to address a nasty problem even with Frege's original analysis of our belief sentence. We specified that the indirect referent of 'Socrates' was S('Socrates') (the 'ordinary' sense of 'Socrates'). But since there is no reference without sense, we must decide on an indirect *sense* for 'Socrates'. But what can this be? Fregeans have gone through nightmares to solve this problem, producing one ingenious failure after another as a candidate for the indirect sense. But we are now in a position to see where they went wrong. For note that the problem only arises if we reject Thesis VII—that reference does not require sense. The solution to our problem lies rather in seeing that since we originally (in understanding 'Socrates is wise') grasped S('Socrates') by some non-descriptive method of cognitive access, in belief contexts we shift this 'grasping', as it were, from the expressive to the referential mode, and thus refer to S('Socrates') without denoting it by some mysterious new sense.[43]

III

This completes our clarification and 'improvement' of Frege's theory. I have asked you to follow me some way into the belly of the beast because only by so doing will it become apparent that (1) some of the thorniest problems raised for Frege (e.g. Thesis VII) can be handled smoothly, if we adjust (not give up) his theory, and (2) the resultant theory is (a) clearly Fregean (we have helped the theory, not hurt it—contrast with Russell's Paradox and Frege's logic and set theory), and (b) more powerful than ever. What remains is to sum up the virtues of the new, improved Fregean theory, and to remind ourselves of the consequent dangers of following Kripke down his alternative path.

The most striking virtue of our new and improved Fregean theory (which from now on I will simply call Fregean theory) is that it satisfies every one of Theses I–VII, while Kripke's new path (at least in the extreme versions of his followers) leads us (primarily) to just Thesis VII. Indeed, Thesis VII itself is often invoked as what demonstrates the unfeasibility of a distinctively Fregean theory (which I take to be one that fulfils I–VI). A clearer understanding of Frege's theory itself and the improvements made to it, above, should help keep us from such a temptation. Frege's theory, moreover, is well suited to help us resolve the three puzzles Russell said, in 'On Denoting', form a litmus test for any adequate account of denoting terms: (1) negative existentials, (2) failures of substitutivity in belief contexts, and (3) apparent violations of the principle of excluded middle when sentences contain vacuous names (e.g.

---

[43] To see how this development of Frege's theory can handle the hierarchy of iterated belief operators, see 'Frege, Perry, and Demonstratives'.

Santa is neither a good Mozart player nor a mediocre or inadequate Mozart player—since there is no Santa at all). It is obvious how Frege's theory provides insight into these conundrums: (1) we can have sense without reference;[44] (2) recall our discussion of Frege on belief contexts and 'indirect reference'; (3) just as we can have sense without reference for singular terms, we can have thought without truth-value—or, more accurately, without sentential reference (to 'facts'), and *hence* without truth-value—for sentences are themselves a kind of singular term, for Frege. Now Russell's opposition to senses prevented him from accepting these 'solutions' (and this is not the place to defend Frege from Russell's recent defenders on this point[45]).

Further, we should not lose sight of the fact that Frege uncovered for us the pure metaphysical hierarchy of senses (column [B] in Fig. 5.1). Our uncovering of column [A] should serve to highlight, not obscure, the importance and nature of [B].[46] Now it was not an easy task to discover the 'invisible' senses—as the contemporary opponents of Frege's (and Plato's) 'invisibles' show us, it is hard to appreciate Frege's discovery even after he has made it. Since (to simplify for a moment) sense, like light[47] is the invisible medium that reveals everything else, it took an extraordinary insight of self-reflection to turn our (intellectual) eyes back on to sense (light) itself; and who would we expect to do this if not a

---

[44] Evans (*The Varieties of Reference*, p. 22–30) argues that although Frege sometimes maintains this thesis, elsewhere (and more profoundly) he rejects it. But if we look at the passages in the *Posthumous Writings* (ed. H. Hermes *et al.*, Chicago, 1979) to which Evans alludes, we see that he has misunderstood what Frege means by a 'fictitious sense'. The sense of a non-denoting term in fiction, for Frege, is 'fictitious'—i.e. *appropriate to* fiction (i.e. a sense without reference). "William Tell", Frege says (p. 130), 'is a mock proper name, [but] we cannot deny it a sense.' Further, Frege adds that if such names turned out to refer, 'the thoughts [expressed using them] would strictly remain the same; they would only be transported from the realm of fiction to that of truth' (p. 191).

[45] See, e.g., S. Blackburn and A. Code, 'The Power of Russell's Critique of Frege: "On Denoting": pp. 48–50', *Analysis*, 38, March, 1978.

[46] We can see Wittgenstin as focusing on column [A], and trying to do without [B] (even in the philosophy of mathematics). Here we have a profound disagreement over which of the Paths to take. My sympathies, I confess, lie with Plato, Frege, and Gödel here—but obviously this is not the place to defend this choice.

[47] The difference between (Fregean) *sense* and *grasp* is usefully compared with that between *sight* and *touch*. For the hand cannot but leave its subjective impression on what it grasps, and hence, in trying to know it, distorts it, while the eye does not harm its object. Frege, like Plato, tried to elucidate this kind of purely 'visual', or contemplative, contact with reality (see 'The Thought', pp. 533–5). It is no accident, therefore, that Wittgenstein (cf. n. 46), who focused on *grasping* (i.e. on column [A]), was also suspicious of a Reality (like Plato's) that reveals itself to us in the way it 'really is'. (Note: Frege's (Plato's) 'contemplative grasping' is to be likened to physical *seeing*, and both distinguished from physical grasping.) I owe to Stanley Rosen ('Thought and Touch', *Phronesis*, 6:2 (1961), 127–37), which appears as ch. 8 in this volume, the idea of thus comparing sight and touch, and to Mike Byrd (in conversation) the felicitous likening of Fregean sense to light.

philosopher of language, who thinks not just about objects but about thought about objects, and hence about the medium of thought. (As C. S. Lewis said (about God): 'I know that God exists the way I know the sun does: not because I see it, but because I see everything else.') The heavy task that falls to us post-Fregeans is to illuminate column [A], non-descriptive grasping, to show how it differs from a mere blind, Kantian 'intuition'.

Having uncovered the realm of senses, Frege was able to solve both (1) his own problem of the cognitive advance, in mathematics, between knowing $23 = 23$, and learning $\sqrt{529} = 23$, and (2) Plato's problem, in the *Theaetetus*, of providing a mode of cognitive access to an object sufficient both (*a*) to show we had it (and not 'the remotest peasant in Asia') in mind to refer to, and (*b*) to show how we could still make *mistakes* about our referent. It is, I take it, obvious how this theory would accomplish this.

Finally, Frege's theory, *pace* Salmon and Burge, shows us how we can combine sense$_1$ (the 'conceptual presentation of the referent'), sense$_2$ (the 'semantic' determiner of the referent), and sense$_3$ (the information value of assertions about referents) into a single notion of sense (and thus avoid the noumenalization of semantics). First, we must revise sense$_1$, to accord with our improved version of Frege, to read: the method of cognitive access (descriptive or non-descriptive) that secures us our referents. It is clear, then, why $S_1 = S_2$. How about S_3? In *Frege's Puzzle*, Salmon goes to great pains to develop a notion of information content different from, and (he claims) incompatible with, Frege's. He presses into service Russell's 'singular propositions', ordered *n*-tuples of objects and properties. For Salmon, then, 'Socrates is wise' and 'Plato's teacher is wise' 'really' have the same information value—to wit, that that-man-Socrates is wise (and we can take that content to be, ⟨Socrates, S ('is wise')⟩. Now, I have nothing at all against this notion of information content. No doubt it is a useful definition, for some purposes. (Though it would not help *Frege* with his problem, to characterize the 'information' gained in the move from $23 = 23$ to: $\sqrt{529} = 23$).[48] What disturbs me is why Salmon thinks (*a*) this is the *right* notion of information content, and (*b*) Frege could not avail himself of this new notion as well.

---

[48] For Salmon the information content of both sentences would be: ⟨23(i.e. $\sqrt{529}$), S ('= 23'). It would not help to turn the sentences around, to get (*a*) '23 = 23', and (*b*) '23 = $\sqrt{529}$', and the different information contents, (*a*) ⟨23, S ('= 23')⟩, and (*b*) ⟨23, ('= $\sqrt{529}$')⟩. For someone who *doesn't* know that $23 = \sqrt{529}$ *does* already know content (*a*) (because he will accept '23 = 23'), and content (*b*) (because he would accept '$\sqrt{529} = \sqrt{529}$', which also has (*b*) as its content).

Let us take (b) first. Recall that, for Frege, 'Socrates is wise' is analysed thus: [see Fig. 5.3]

For Frege, 'is wise' refers to a function-in-extension (something *like* a set), which I write here as: [is wise] (to distinguish it from S('is wise'), which is what determines [is wise]). Now, it is easy to see from Fig. 5.3. that Frege can, from within his own theory, '*construct*' the Russellian proposition, ⟨Socrates, S('is wise')⟩[49], and so *use* it, as well as Salmon can, to theorize about this extended notion of 'information content'. Why didn't Frege? The answer is simple: (1) he was interested in his *own* puzzle (about mathematical knowledge), for which his definition is more useful, and (2) his interest was thus in *propositional* epistemic logic, not in *quantified* epistemic logic (belief *of* something that it is ∅) (nor, of course, in *either* propositional or quantified modal logic). Notice, further, that Frege can 'construct' (and use for any theoretical purposes that interest him) *all* the following 'propositions' (or 'thoughts'): (a) ⟨S('Socrates'), S('is wise')⟩, (b) ⟨Socrates, [is wise]⟩, (c) ⟨Socrates, S('is wise')⟩, and (d) ⟨S('Socrates'), [is wise]⟩. (No one, to my knowledge, has

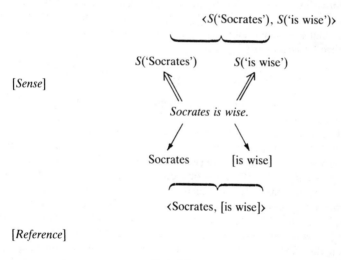

[Sense]

[Reference]

FIG . 5.3

---

[49] It is in fact a nice question just what corresponds, in Frege's system, to a Russellian proposition, and the suggestion in the text is not meant to settle this, but only to offer a plausible line of approach, for heuristic purposes.

yet found a use for (*d*)—but give them time.) And this brings us to our first worry about Salmon, (*a*) is Salmon's, or Frege's, the 'right' notion of 'information content' ('proposition', 'thought')?

On this question Salmon takes sides with Russell, against Frege (who writes, in a letter to Russell: '. . . Mont Blanc with its snowfields is not itself a component part of the thought that Mont Blanc is more than 4000 metres high.')[50] It is delightful to think of Frege's exasperation with Russell, who clung to his view that snowy Mont Blanc could find itself in the diaphanous realm of pure thought. In point of fact, however, what we have here is really a pseudo-question. Given the full picture revealed in Fig. 5.3, *all* the 'thoughts' we just characterized, (*a*)–(*d*), are intellectually sanitary. What remains is the relative interest of the uses to which we can put such 'thoughts'. Frege needed conception (*a*), the most fine grained, for his interest in 'mathematical information'; Salmon feels he needs the coarser notion, (*c*), for his purpose (of the 'information content' of everyday discourse). There is thus nothing to be gained by trying to resolve the pseudo-problem of what the 'correct' notion of information content (or 'thought') really is. And it follows, then, that for the notion of 'information content' that is the most fine grained, and that relates to Frege's problem, we can have $S_1 = S_2 = S_3$. (It should be clear by now, also, that if we use a different notion of information, this would also not disturb Frege's theory.)[51]

IV

The new and improved Frege, then, represents a path in semantics that it is dangerous to stray from. Many problems remain, of course, and the path will soon divide into alternative ways of thought on some of the deepest issues in philosophy. I have already mentioned some of these areas where, like Wittgenstein (and Kant—and Nietzsche) one might wish to challenge Frege. There is one dramatic feature of Frege's theory, however, that has so far not received sufficient attention. Before coming to this, I want to get out of the way two problems that, though serious, are not, I believe, fatal—the one epistemological, the other ontological. One might wonder how one could come to know the Platonic Fregean senses, given the causal theory of knowledge. This problem, of knowing (and

---

[50] G. Frege, *Philosophical and Mathematical Correspondence*, ed. B. McGuinness (Chicago, 1980), 163.

[51] What if S_1 represents our non-descriptive grasp of objects? What would then be the corresponding notion of information content? I have no room here to answer—but see 'Frege, Perry, and Demonstratives'.

referring to) Platonic entities was put into sharp relief by Paul Benacerraf, in 'Mathematical Truth'.[52] One might be tempted to respond by trying, like Penelope Maddy in 'Perception and Mathematical Intuition',[53] to defend Platonism by showing its compatibility with a causal epistemology. I am more inclined, however, to hold with Gödel, that '[the epistemic "given" of Platonistic mathematics] . . . may represent an aspect of objective reality, but, as opposed to the sensations, their presence in us may be due to another kind of relationship between us and reality'.[54] In any event, I have elsewhere written against the causal theory of knowledge itself,[55] and am not therefore overly impressed with this as an objection to the Platonism of Frege's.

A very interesting problem from pure ontology, however, has been raised by Mike Byrd[56] (building on ideas from William Rapaport). The idea here is to suggest a formal existence scheme for senses, and then to show that it runs into paradoxical difficulties via self-reference (à la Russell's Paradox, for sets). Without going into details (where I think his argument needs some tightening up) let us simply note that Byrd's existence principle holds, in effect, that every syntactically well-formed referring expression expresses a sense; it is then not too much work to cook up a 'Gödelian' term that says of its own sense that it is not self-predicable. The question that remains is what to make of this term, which cannot have an objective sense (since it will turn out to be neither self-predicable nor not). I am tempted to conclude, again with Gödel, that such antinomies in formalization cast no more ontological suspicion on the realm at hand than do the illusions of the senses on the realm of physical

---

[52] In P. Benacerraf and H. Putnam (eds.), *Philosophy of Mathematics*, (Cambridge, 2nd edn., 1983), 403–20.

[53] *The Philosophical Review*, 89:2 (1980), 163–96.

[54] 'What is Cantor's Continuum Problem?', pp. 470–85, p. 484.

[55] See 'Information Retrieval and Cognitive Accessibility', 'Lost Knowledge', and 'Knowledge and Relevant Alternatives'. This is not to say, of course, that the Platonist does not owe us a theory of knowledge—and I agree that on this point Platonism is still weak (as Plato himself confessed). For example, in his recent *Language and Other Abstract Objects* (Totowa, NJ, 1981), Jerrold Katz presents, I believe, a forceful case for Platonism in linguistics. But his bold attempt at a 'Kantian' epistemology for his ontology is not, I think, as successful (see also n. 59).

[56] 'Russell's Paradox, Sense, and Reference' (mimeo, Madison: University of Wisconsin, Dept. of Philosophy, 1983). Byrd's actual argument does not quite work, I believe, if applied (as he intends) to definite descriptions. But we can apply it to predicate expressions. In brief, then, Byrd says that a sense, s, 'presents its referent as falling under the concept $D(\xi)$; abbreviated, $E(s,D(\xi))$ ', and adds that this is the unique 'concept' s presents its referent as falling under. He then defines a predicate, R, as follows: $Rx =(T) ((E(x,T(\xi)) \supset Tx).$' Now consider our 'Gödel' predicate, $-Rx$. Predicates, for Frege, have sense and reference. Call the sense of $-Rx$, s. Now we ask: (1) Rs?, and (2) $-Rs$? Both assumptions, it turns out, lead to contradiction.

objects.[57] One must rather, as in the case of set theory, seek better and deeper principles for the entities at hand, guided not by a 'naïve' semantics but rather by ontological insight. (It's a hard job and requires clear 'vision', not tricks with language.)

But a doubt lingers here. This is all well and good, you may say, for sets, but senses were supposed to help Frege solve his puzzle about the cognitive value of identity statements, and in general to represent what it is about language itself that enables us to think and communicate. How can senses, then, be thus epistemically aloof? In answer to this, let me remind you first that although not *all* syntactically well-formed expressions will have a sense, those Frege considered in his puzzle (e.g. '$\sqrt{529} = 23$') clearly *do* express a sense. Next, note that it is a mistake to view Frege's senses as themselves the final clue to our mastery of language. As we saw earlier, for Frege there is only a loose fit between the structure of natural language and the order of senses. Linguistic competence represents (in part, at least, for our 'new' Frege) our ability to connect words with senses (and thus, with every kind of object). (Recall our earlier remarks on possible linguistic rules for 'today' and 'yesterday'.) Senses are not themselves linguistic rules; rather, we (somehow) learn to use linguistic rules to attach our words to senses (as well as, perhaps, to objects themselves). The kind of naïve linguistic reflection scheme of Byrd's argument represents a misconception of Frege's notion of how the world of sense maps on to the world of natural language. There is simply no guarantee that every syntactically well-formed expression of natural language expresses a sense. To learn how to 'make sense', then, with natural language, is a skill that goes beyond acquiring the rules of grammar—it means learning how to think. It is indeed true that Frege thought (like Leibniz) that he had, in his 'Begriffsschrift', gone beyond natural language and cooked up an ideal language-of-thought, where, so to speak, the words almost do the thinking for us.[58] But now that we know of Russell's Paradox, Tarski's results on truth, and Gödel's incompleteness results, we should no longer be tempted to equate 'entification' with 'formalization' (in a single system). The ideal of a single formal system, internally consistent and semantically 'complete', adequate even to the demands of arithmetic (never mind the realm of senses), is now known to

---

[57] See 'What is Cantor's Continuum Problem?', p. 484. 'The set-theoretical paradoxes are hardly any more troublesome for mathematics than deceptions of the senses are for physics.' Even if we can save set theory for Frege, however, I am sceptical of neo-Fregean attempts to use these sets (or, as with Maddy, proper classes) to define the natural numbers. See my 'Sets, Aggregates, and Numbers', *The Canadian Journal of Philosophy*, 5:4 (Dec. 1985), 581–91.

[58] See J. Van Heijenoort, 'Logic as Calculus and Logic as Language', *Boston Studies in the Philosophy of Science*, 3 (1967), 440–6.

be an illusion. But we should not read into Gödel's profound limitation theorems any hasty conclusions about either the ontological legitimacy or the epistemic accessibility of the relevant (abstract) domains (as Godel himself did not).[59] A language is an indispensable tool for thinking—but, given any reasonable (e.g. recursively axiomatizable rules) constraints on what a language is, no single language captures our ability to think, both with senses and about senses (or numbers, etc.).

If our reasoning has been sound, then neither the epistemic nor the formal–ontological objection to Frege is conclusive. One problem does remain, however. Time, I believe, represents for Frege (as for Plato) a most serious challenge. For Frege's theory of senses seems to presuppose that all (ultimate) truths are tenseless, and therefore that the so-called *A*-series of McTaggart (with the 'moving-*now*' of the temporal flux) must be an illusion. This feature of Frege's theory is, however, shared even by his opponents, like Kaplan and Perry (cf. their account of the semantics of 'now').[60] And we begin to appreciate the recalcitrance of the problem when we realize that even formal theories designed precisely to capture this feature of time (like Richmond Thomason's 'Indeterminist Time and Truth-Value Gaps)[61] do not really work (as I have argued elsewhere).[62] In fact, as far as I know, the solution is simply not at hand, at present. But the question is: is Frege committed to disregarding, in principle, the *A*-series?[63] Remember that we are dealing here with the 'new and improved' Frege, and recall that in the new Fregean picture of Fig. 5.1 there were

[59] See P. Benacerraf, 'Skolem and the Skeptic', *The Aristotelian Society*, suppl., 59 (July 1985), 85–116. He argues that the lesson of the Skolem Paradox is *not* that our 'access' to Cantor's 'absolutely non-denumerable' domain is forever limited by our confinement to the lens of a first-order formal system—through which we never get more than a relatively-non-denumerable multitude (denumerable from 'outside' the system itself). Rather, he suggests we have some alternative method of access (which, he admits, we as yet do not understand).

[60] For the argument, see 'Frege, Perry, and Demonstratives', pp. 744–5, and 'The Dead'. 36:3.   [61] *Theoria*, (1970), 264–81.

[62] 'On the Logic of Indeterminist Time', *The Journal of Philosophy*, 82:10 (Oct. 1985), 548–59.

[63] It would seem that Kaplan ('Demonstratives') and Perry ('Frege on Demonstratives', *Philosophical Review*, 86:4 (Oct. 1977), 474–97), which appears as ch. 3 in this volume, are committed, by their analysis of demonstratives like 'now', to 'spatializing' time, since on their account no basis can be found for singling out one time as privileged, as '*the* now'—rather, for them, each time is now-with-respect-to-itself. But the problem with their theory goes even deeper than this: to quote from my analysis in 'The Dead' (p. 99 n. 21),

'The Kaplan–Perry rule for "now", if put precisely, would be: "For all times *t* and speakers *s*, if *s* employs "now" correctly at *t*, he refers to *t*." Now a rule is no good unless you can use it, but, if you try to employ this rule, it becomes obvious that, in grasping it, you get a handle not on any particular time, but only on a universal conditional on times (and speakers). The problem is that to use the rule to get to a particular time you must *instantiate* the universal quantifier, but, to accomplish this instantiation, you must already have a particular time *t* in mind. But how do you get to have it in mind? By describing it (e.g., as Saturday, 10.00 A.M.)?

two columns representing our cognitive access to reality. Column [B] represented the timeless realm of the hierarchy of pure senses. But what about column [A]? This gave us an alternative mode of access, alternative in being 'non-descriptive'. But could it not also be alternative in not being tenseless? In naming it column [A] I have already suggested the answer: for all we know so far, it remains open that column [A] (of Fregean theory) can capture the elusive A-series of time, and thus represent a tensed access to a tensed reality. Only a detailed account of the nature of the [A]-column and of McTaggart's A-series will be able to settle this question. The path back to Frege, once again, has led us to the brink of a clearer view of reality.

(This is vigorously denied by Kaplan and Perry.) By taking t to be the present moment—i.e., now? (This is circular; it is the rule itself that was supposed to show how we use 'now' to get to a particular time.) It seems, rather, that Kaplan and Perry have mistaken a necessary constraint on a mode of designation for a particular use of 'now' (that if 'now' is used at t, the mode of designation should determine t) for the mode of designation itself. But *the now* has a more formidable opponent than this, in the person of Einstein and Relativity Theory. See Gödel's fascinating study, 'A Remark about the Relationship between Relativity Theory and Idealistic Philosophy', in P. A. Schilpp (ed.), *Albert Einsten—Philosopher–Scientist* (La Salla, Ill., 1949), 557–62), which appears as ch. 13 of this volume.

PART II

THE FIRST PERSON

6

THE FIRST PERSON

G.E.M. ANSCOMBE

Descartes and St Augustine share not only the argument *cogito, ergo sum*—in Augustine *si fallor, sum* (*De Civitate Dei*, book XI, 26)—but also the corollary argument claiming to prove that *the mind* (Augustine) or, as Descartes puts it, *this I*, is not any kind of body. 'I could suppose I had no body,' wrote Descartes, 'but not that I was not', and inferred that 'this I' is not a body. Augustine says 'The mind knows itself to think', and 'it knows its own substance': hence 'it is certain of being that alone, which alone it is certain of being' (*De Trinitate*, book X). Augustine is not here explicitly offering an argument in the first person, as Descartes is. The first-person character of Descartes's argument means that each person must administer it to himself in the first person; and the assent to St Augustine's various propositions will equally be made, if at all, by appropriating them in the first person. In these writers there is the assumption that when one says 'I' or 'the mind', one is naming something such that the knowledge of its existence, which is a knowledge of itself as thinking in all the various modes, determines what it is that is known to exist.

Saul Kripke has tried to reinstate Descartes's argument for his dualism. But he neglects its essentially first-person character, making it an argument about the non-identity of *Descartes* with his own body. Whatever else is said, it seems clear that the argument in Descartes depends on results of applying the method of doubt.[1] But by that method

---

This chapter appeared originally in S. Guttenplan (ed.), *Mind and Language: Wolfson College Lectures 1974* (Oxford: Clarendon Press, 1975), 45–64. © Oxford University Press 1975 and reprinted with their permission.

[1] *Principles of Philosophy*, i, bk. LX, contains Descartes's best statement, which is I think immune to the usual accusation of substitutional fallacy. 'Each of us conceives of himself as a conscious being, and can in thought exclude from himself any other substance, whether conscious or extended; so from this mere fact it is certain that each of us, so regarded, is really distinct from every other conscious substance and from every corporeal substance. And even if we supposed that God had conjoined some corporeal substance to such a conscious substance so closely that they could not be more clearly joined, and had thus compounded a unity out of the two, yet even so they remain really distinct' (*Philosophical Writings*, trans. G. E. M. Anscombe and P. T. Geach). Rendering Descartes's premiss here as 'I can conceive myself not to include or be my body', we come close to Kripke's version (but in the first person) 'Possibly I am not *A*', where '*A*' means my body. But why can I so conceive myself if not because I can doubt the existence of my body? But 'doubting' here does not mean merely reflecting that I am

Descartes must have doubted the existence of the man Descartes: at any rate of that figure in the world of his time, that Frenchman, born of such-and-such a stock and christened René; but also, even of the man—unless a man is not a sort of animal. *If*, then, the non-identity of himself with his own body follows from his starting-points, so equally does the non-identity of himself with the man Descartes. 'I am not Descartes' was just as sound a conclusion for him to draw as 'I am not a body.' To cast the argument in the third person, replacing 'I' by 'Descartes', is to miss this. Descartes would have accepted the conclusion. That mundane, practical, everyday sense in which it would have been correct for him to say 'I am Descartes' was of no relevance to him in these arguments. That which is named by 'I'—*that*, in *his* book, was not *Descartes*.

It may seem strange to say: 'The non-identity of himself with Descartes was as valid a conclusion as the other' and not treat this as already a *reductio ad absurdum*. For is that phrase not equivalent to 'the non-identity of *Descartes* with Descartes'?

No. It is not. For what is in question is not the ordinary reflexive pronoun, but a peculiar reflexive, which has to be explained in terms of 'I'. It is the reflexive called by grammarians the 'indirect reflexive' and there are languages (Greek, for example) in which there is a special form for it.[2]

'When John Smith spoke of James Robinson he was speaking of his brother, but he did not know this.' That's a possible situation. So similarly is 'When John Smith spoke of John Horatio Auberon Smith (named in a will perhaps) he was speaking of himself, but he did not know this.' If so, then 'speaking of' or 'referring to' oneself is compatible with not knowing that the object one speaks of is oneself.

Yet we are inclined to think that 'It's the word each one uses in speaking of himself' explains what 'I' names, or explains 'I' as a 'referring expression'. It cannot do so if 'He speaks of himself' is compatible with ignorance and we are using the reflexive pronoun, in both cases, in the ordinary way.

---

ignorant of the existence of my body though not of myself. So understood, the argument would indeed involve the substitutional fallacy. 'Doubting' means clearly understanding that the existence of my body is not guaranteed by something which is thoroughly understood, and is all I am sure of: the existence of myself. We see the importance of the premiss supplied by St Augustine, 'The mind knows its own substance.'

[2] ε, ον, οι. . See Thucydides 2. 13. The form is rare. Credit for discerning the indirect reflexive in English, which does not have a distinct form for it, belongs in the present day to H.-N. Castañeda in 'The Logic of Self-Knowledge', *Noûs*, 1 (1967), 9–22. But his presentation is excessively complicated and I believe it has not attracted enough attention to the substantive point.

Nor can we explain the matter, as we might suppose, by saying ' "I" is the word each one uses when he knowingly and intentionally speaks of himself.' For did not Smith knowingly and intentionally speak of Smith? Was not the person he intended to speak of—Smith? And so *was* not the person he intended to speak of—himself?

It may be said: 'Not in the relevant sense. We all know you can't substitute every designation of the object he intended to speak of and keep the statement about his intention true.' But that is not the answer unless the reflexive pronoun itself is a sufficient indication of the way the object is specified. And that is something the ordinary reflexive pronoun cannot be. Consider: 'Smith realizes (fails to realize) the identity of an object he calls "Smith" with himself.' If the reflexive pronoun there is the ordinary one, then it specifies for us who frame or hear the sentence an object, whose identity with the object he calls 'Smith' Smith does or doesn't realize: namely the object designated by our subject word 'Smith'. But that does not tell us what identity Smith himself realizes (or fails to realize). For, as Frege held, there is no path back from reference to sense; any object has many ways of being specified, and in this case, through the peculiarity of the construction, we have succeeded in specifying an object (by means of the subject of our sentence) without specifying any conception under which *Smith*'s mind is supposed to latch on to it. For we don't want to say 'Smith does not realize the identity of Smith with Smith.'

We only have to admit a failure of specification of the intended identity, if we persist in treating the reflexive in 'He doesn't realize the identity with himself' as the ordinary reflexive. In practice we have no difficulty at all. We know what we mean Smith doesn't realize. It is: 'I am Smith.' But if that is how we understand that reflexive, it is not the ordinary one. It is a special one which can be explained only in terms of the first person.

If that is right, the explanation of the word 'I' as 'the word which each of us uses to speak of himself' is hardly an explanation! At least, it is no explanation if that reflexive has in turn to be explained in terms of 'I'; and if it is the ordinary reflexive, we are back at square one. We seem to need a sense to be specified for this quasi-name 'I'. To repeat the Frege point: we have not got this sense just by being told which object a man will be speaking of, whether he knows it or not, when he says 'I'. Of course that phrase 'whether he knows it or not' seems highly absurd. His use of 'I' surely guarantees that he does know it! But we have a right to ask *what* he knows; if 'I' expresses a way its object is reached by him, what Frege called an 'Art des Gegebenseins', we want to know what that way is and how it comes about that the only object reached in that way by anyone is identical with himself.

To say all this is to treat 'I' as a sort of proper name. That is what gets us into this jam. Certainly 'I' functions syntactically like a name. However, it has been observed not to be a proper name. Now this observation may strike us as obvious enough in a trivial sense. After all, we do not call it a proper noun but a personal *pro*noun. It is at any rate not an ordinary proper name. It could not have a lot of the characteristic use of a proper name. For if it is such, it is one that everyone has, and, worse still, one that each person uses only to refer to that person that he himself is. So it is no use for introducing people to one another, or for calling to someone, or for summoning him. And while it might be used as a signature (like the signature of an aged and doddering parson that I heard of, on someone's marriage lines: Me, Vicar), one would be quite dependent on other clues to the identity of the signatory. If this were the only name anyone had, the situation would be worse than it is for a bank in a Welsh village. These inconveniences are avoided, of course, because there are other more various proper names which people have as well. So the observation that 'I' is not a proper name seems to reduce to the triviality that we perhaps would not *call* a word a proper name if everyone had it and used it only to speak of himself. But is even that true? After all, all Sikhs seem to be called 'Singh'. So the real difference lies in that one point that each one uses the name 'I' only to speak of himself. Is that a ground not to call it a proper name? Certainly to the eyes of our logicians it is a proper name. Are their eyes dim? Or is it really logically a proper name?

Let us ask: is it really true that 'I' is only not called a proper name because everyone uses it only to refer to himself? Let us construct a clear case of just such a name. Imagine a society in which everyone is labelled with two names. One appears on their backs and at the top of their chests, and these names, which their bearers cannot see, are various: '*B*' to '*Z*' let us say. The other '*A*', is stamped on the inside of their wrists, and is the same for everyone. In making reports on people's actions everyone uses the names on their chests or backs if he can see these names or is used to seeing them. Everyone also learns to respond to utterance of the name on his own chest and back in the sort of way and circumstances in which we tend to respond to utterance of our names. Reports on one's own actions, which one gives straight off from observation, are made using the name on the wrist. Such reports are made, not on the basis of observation alone, but also on that of inference and testimony or other information. *B*, for example, derives conclusions expressed by sentences with '*A*' as subject, from other people's statements using '*B*' as subject.

It may be asked: what is meant by 'reports on one's own actions'? Let us lay it down that this means, for example, reports issuing from the mouth of B on the actions of B. That is to say: reports from the mouth of B saying that A did such-and-such are prima facie verified by ascertaining that B did it and are decisively falsified by finding that he did not.

Thus for each person there is one person of whom he has characteristically limited and also characteristically privileged views: except in mirrors he never sees the whole person, and can only get rather special views of what he does see. Some of these are specially good, others specially bad. Of course, a man B may sometimes make a mistake through seeing the name 'A' on the wrist of another, and not realizing it is the wrist of a man whose other name is after all not inaccessible to B in the special way in which his own name ('B') is.

(It may help some people's imagination if we change the example: instead of these rather inhuman people, we suppose machines that are equipped with scanning devices are marked with signs in the same way as the people in my story were marked with their names, and are programmed to translate what appears on the screens of their scanners into reports.)

In my story we have a specification of a sign as a name, the same for everyone, but used by each only to speak of himself. How does it compare with 'I'? The first thing to note is that our description does not include self-consciousness on the part of the people who use the name 'A' as I have described it. They perhaps have no self-consciousness, though each one knows a lot about the object that he (in fact) is; and has a name, the same as everyone else has, which he uses in reports about the object that he (in fact) is.

This—that they have not self-consciousness—may, just for that reason, seem not to be true. B is conscious of, that is to say he observes, some of B's activities, that is to say his own. He uses the name 'A', as does everyone else, to refer to himself. So he is conscious of himself. So he has self-consciousness.

But when we speak of self-consciousness we don't mean that. We mean something manifested by the use of 'I' as opposed to 'A'.

Hence we must get to understand self-consciousness. Unsurprisingly, the term dates only from the seventeenth century and derives from philosophy. Getting into ordinary language, it alters, and by the nineteenth century acquires a sense which is pretty irrelevant to the philosophical notion: it comes to mean awkwardness from being troubled by the feeling of being an object of observation by other people. Such a change often happens to philosophical terms. But this one also gets into psychology and psychiatry, and here its sense is not so far removed from the philosophical one.

The first explanation of self-consciousness that may occur to someone, and what the form of the expression suggests, is this: it is consciousness of a self. A self will be something that some things either have or are. If a thing has it, it is something connected with the thing, in virtue of which the thing that has it is able to say, and mean, 'I'. It is what he calls 'I'. Being able to mean 'I' is thus explained as having the right sort of thing to call 'I'. The fanciful use of the word, if someone should put a placard 'I am only a waxwork' on a wax policeman, or in the label on the bottle in *Alice in Wonderland*, 'Drink me', is a pretence that the objects in question have (or are) selves. *The self* is not a Cartesian idea, but it may be tacked on to Cartesian Ego theory and is a more consequent development of it than Descartes's identification of 'this I' with his soul. If things are, rather than have, selves, then a self is something, for example a human being, in a special aspect, an aspect which he has as soon as he becomes a 'person'. 'I' will then be the name used by each one only for himself (this is a direct reflexive) and precisely in that aspect.

On these views one would explain 'self' in 'self-consciousness' either by explaining what sort of object that accompanying self was, or by explaining what the aspect was. Given such explanation, one might have that special 'way of being given' of an object which is associated with the name one uses in speaking of it.

Now all this is strictly nonsensical. It is blown up out of a misconstrual of the reflexive pronoun. That it is nonsense comes out also in the following fact: it would be a question what guaranteed that one got hold of the right self, that is, that the self a man called 'I' was always connected with him or was always the man himself. Alternatively, if one said that 'the self connected with a man' meant just the one he meant by 'I' at any time, whatever self that was, it would be by a mere favour of fate that it had anything else to do with him.

But 'self-consciousness' is not any such nonsense. It is something real, though as yet unexplained, which 'I'-users have and which would be lacking to '*A*'-users, if their use of '*A*' was an adequate tool for their consciousness of themselves.

The expression 'self-consciousness' can be respectably explained as 'consciousness that such-and-such holds of oneself'. Nor should we allow an argument running: since the occurrence of 'oneself' is just like the occurrence of 'himself' which left us perfectly well understanding what Smith failed to realize, the word 'self' must itself connote the desired 'way of being given' that is associated with 'I' as (logically speaking) a proper name. We must reject this argument because 'oneself' is here nothing but the indirect reflexive: that is to say, the reflexive of indirect speech.

Understanding indirect speech we know what the related direct speech is. That is all.

These considerations will lack appeal. The question was, what does 'I' stand for? If that question is asked, and 'I' is supposed to stand for its object as a proper name does, we need an account of a certain kind. The use of a name for an object is connected with a conception of that object. And so we are driven to look for something that, for each 'I'-user, will be the conception related to the supposed name 'I', as the conception of a city is to the names 'London' and 'Chicago', that of a river to 'Thames' and 'Nile', that of a man to 'John' and 'Pat'. Such a conception is requisite if 'I' is a name; and there is no conception that can claim to do the job except one suggested by 'self-consciousness'. That is why some philosophers have elaborated the notion of 'selves' (or 'persons' defined in terms of self-consciousness) and conducted investigations to see what such things may be. And just as we must be continuing our reference to the same city if we continue to use 'London' with the same reference, so we must each of us be continuing our reference to the same self (or 'person') if we continue to use 'I' with the same reference.

This led to an imaginative *tour de force* on the part of Locke: might not the thinking substance which thought the thought 'I did it'—the genuine thought of agent-memory—nevertheless be a different thinking substance from the one that could have had the thought 'I am doing it' when the act was done? Thus he detached the identity of the self or 'person' from the identity even of the thinking being which does the actual thinking of the I-thoughts.

Considerations about reflexive pronouns are certainly not going to dam up the flood of inquiries about 'the self' or 'selves', so long as 'I' is treated as a name and a correlative term is needed for its type of object. Nevertheless, these are embarrassing credentials for such inquiries. And a self *can* be thought of as what 'I' stands for, or indicates, without taking 'I' as a proper name. The reasons for considering it as a proper name were two: first, that to the logician's eye it is one, and second, that it seemed to be just like our '*A*' (which was clearly a proper name) except that it expressed 'self-consciousness'. So we tried to explain it as a proper name of a self. Now a lot of people who will have no objection to the talk of 'selves' will yet feel uneasy about calling 'I' a proper name of a self or anything else. I assume it was made clear that the different reference in each mouth was not an objection (there is no objection to calling '*A*' a proper name), and so there is some other reason. The reason, I think, is that, so understood, a repeated use of 'I' in connection with the same self would have to involve a reidentification of that self. For it is presumably always a use in the presence of its object! There is no objection to the topic of reidentification of selves—it is one of the main interests of the philosophers who write about selves—but this is not any part of the role of 'I'. The corresponding reidentification *was* involved in the use of '*A*', and that makes an additional difference between them.

So perhaps 'I' is not a name but rather another kind of expression indicating 'singular reference'. The logician's conception of the proper name after all only required *this* feature. There are expressions which logically and syntactically function as proper names without being names. Possibly definite descriptions do, and certainly some pronouns. 'I' is called a pronoun, so we will consider this first. Unluckily the category 'pronoun' tells us nothing, since a singular pronoun may even be a variable (as in 'If anyone says that, *he* is a fool')—and hence not any kind of singular designation of an object. The suggestion of the word 'pronoun' itself is not generally borne out by pronouns. Namely, that you get the same sense in a sentence if you replace the pronoun in it by a name, common or proper: what name in particular, it would be difficult to give a general rule for. Perhaps 'pronoun' seemed an apt name just for the personal pronouns and especially for 'I'. But the sense of the lie 'I am not E.A.' is hardly retained in 'E.A. is not E.A. .' So that suggestion is of little value.

Those singular pronouns called demonstratives ('this' and 'that') are a clear example of non-names which function logically as names. For in true propositions containing them they provide reference to a distinctly identifiable subject-term (an object) of which something is predicated. Perhaps, then, 'I' is a kind of demonstrative.

Assimilation to a demonstrative will not—as would at one time have been thought—do away with the demand for a conception of the object indicated. For, even though someone may say just 'this' or 'that', we need to know the answer to the question 'this *what*?' if we are to understand him; and he needs to know the answer if he is to be meaning anything.[3]

Thus a singular demonstrative, used correctly, does provide us with a proper logical subject so long as it does not lack a 'bearer' or 'referent', and so it conforms to the logician's requirement for a name. And the

---

[3] This point was not grasped in the days when people believed in pure ostensive definition without the grounds being prepared for it. Thus also in those days it was possible not to be so much impressed as we ought to be, by the fact that we can find no well-accounted-for term corresponding to 'I' as 'city' does to 'London'. It was possible to see that there was no 'sense' (in Frege's sense) for 'I' as a proper name, but still to think that for each one of us 'I' was the proper name of an 'object of acquaintance', a *this*. What *this* was could then be called 'a self', and the word 'self' would be felt to need no further justification. Thus, e.g. McTaggart. See *The Nature of Existence* (Cambridge, 1921–7), ii. 382, 386–7, 390–1, 394.

answer to the question 'this what?' might be taken to be 'this self', if it can be shown that there are selves and that they are apparently what is spoken of by all these people saying 'I'. Thus would these philosophical inquiries about selves have a certain excuse.

It used to be thought that a singular demonstrative, 'this' or 'that', if used correctly, could not lack a referent. But this is not so, as comes out if we consider the requirement for an answer to 'this what?'. Someone comes with a box and says 'This is all that is left of poor Jones.' The answer to 'this what?' is 'this parcel of ashes'; but unknown to the speaker the box is empty. What 'this' has to have, if used correctly, is something that it *latches on to* (as I will put it): in the example it is the box. In another example it might be an optical presentation. Thus I may ask 'What's that figure standing in front of the rock, a man or a post?' and there may be no such object at all; but there is an appearance, a stain perhaps, or other marking of the rock face, which my 'that' latches on to. The reference and what 'this' latches on to may coincide, as when I say 'this buzzing in my ears is dreadful', or, after listening to a speech, 'That was splendid!' But they do not have to coincide, and the referent is the object of which the predicate is predicated where 'this' or 'that' is a subject.

There is no other pronoun but a demonstrative to which 'I' could plausibly be assimilated as a singular term that provides a reference. Of course someone may say: 'Why assimilate it at all? Each thing is what it is and not another thing! So "I" is a pronoun all right, but it is merely the pronoun that it is.' But that is no good, because 'pronoun' is just a rag-bag category; one might as well say: 'It is the word that it is.' The problem is to describe its meaning. And, if its meaning involves the idea of reference, to see what 'reference' is here, and how accomplished. We are now supposing that it is not accomplished as it is for a regular proper name; then, if 'I' is not an abbreviation of a definite description, it must catch hold of its object in some other way—and what way is there but the demonstrative?

But there is a contrast between 'I' and the ordinary demonstrative. We saw that there may be reference-failure for 'this', in that one may mean 'this parcel of ashes' when there are no ashes. But 'I'—if it makes a reference, if, that is, its mode of meaning is that it is supposed to make a reference—is secure against reference-failure. Just thinking 'I . . .' guarantees not only the existence but the presence of its referent. It guarantees the existence *because* it guarantees the presence, which is presence to consciousness. But note that here 'presence to consciousness' means physical or real presence, not just that one is thinking of the thing. For if the thinking did not guarantee the presence, the existence of the referent could be doubted. For the same reason, if 'I' is a name it cannot be an empty name. I's existence is existence in the thinking of the thought expressed by 'I . . .' This of course is the point of *cogito*—and, I will show, of the corollary argument too.

Whether 'I' is a name or a demonstrative, there is the same need of a 'conception' through which it attaches to its object. Now what conception can be suggested, other than that of *thinking*, the thinking of the I-thought, which secures this guarantee against reference-failure? It may be very well to describe what selves are; but if I do not know that I am a self, then I cannot mean a self by 'I'.

To point this up, let me imagine a logician, for whom the syntactical character of 'I' as a proper name is quite sufficient to guarantee it as such, and for whom the truth of propositions with it as subject is therefore enough to guarantee the existence of the object it names. He, of course, grants all that I have pointed out about the indirect reflexive. It cannot perturb him, so long as the 'way of being given' is of no concern to him. To him it is clear that 'I', in my mouth, is just another name for E.A.. 'I' may have some curious characteristics; but they don't interest him. The reason is that 'I' is a name governed by the following rule: 'If X makes assertions with "I" as subject, then those assertions will be true if and only if the predicates used thus assertively are true of X.'[4] This will be why Kripke—and others discussing Descartes—make the transition from Descartes's 'I' to '*Descartes*'.

Now first, this offers too swift a refutation of Descartes. In order to infer straight away that Descartes was wrong, we only need the information that Descartes asserted 'I am not a body', together with the knowledge that he was a man; that is, an animal of a certain species; that is, a body living with a certain sort of life.

But there would and should come from Descartes's lips or pen a denial that, strictly speaking, *the man Descartes* made the assertion. The rule was sound enough. But the asserting subject must be the thinking subject. If you are a speaker who says 'I', you do not find out what is saying 'I'. You do not for example look to see what apparatus the noise comes out of and assume that that is the sayer; or frame the hypothesis of something connected with it that is the sayer. If that were in question, you could doubt whether anything *was* saying 'I'. As, indeed, you can doubt whether anything is saying it out loud. (And sometimes *that* doubt is correct.)

---

[4] My colleague Dr J. Altham has pointed out to me a difficulty about this rule about 'I'. How is one to extract the *predicate* for purposes of this rule in 'I think John loves me'? The rule needs supplementation: where 'I' or 'me' occurs within an oblique context, the predicate is to be specified by replacing 'I' or 'me' by the indirect reflexive pronoun.

Thus we need to press our logician about the 'guaranteed reference' of
'I'. In granting this, there are three degrees of it that he may assert.

1. He may say that of course the user of 'I' must exist, otherwise he
would not be using 'I'. As he *is* the referent, that is what 'guaranteed
reference' amounts to. In respect of such guaranteed reference, he may
add, there will be no difference between 'I' and '*A*'. But the question is,
why 'I' was said to *refer* to the 'I'-user? Our logician held that 'I' was
logically a proper name—a singular term whose role is to make a
reference—for two reasons: one, that 'I' has the same syntactical place as
such expressions, and the other, that it can be replaced *salva veritate* by a
(more ordinary) name of *X* when it occurs in subject position in assertions
made by *X*. In saying this, he no doubt thought himself committed to no
views on the sense of 'I' or what the 'I'-user means by 'I'. But his second
reason amounts to this: one who hears or reads a statement with 'I' as
subject needs to know whose statement it is if he wants to know of whom
the predicate holds if the statement is true. Now, this requirement could
be signalled by flashing a green light, say, in connection with the
predicate, or perhaps adding a terminal '-O' to it. (I apologize to anyone
who finds this suggestion altogether too fanciful, and beg him to suspend
disbelief.) What would make such a signal or suffix into a referring
expression? The essential argument cannot be an argument back from
syntax to reference, for such an argument would depend only on the form
of sentence and would be absurd. (For example, no one thinks that 'it is
raining' contains a referring expression, 'it'.) And so it seems that our
logician cannot disclaim concern with the sense of 'I', or at any rate with
what the 'I'-user must mean.

2. So the 'I'-user must intend to refer to something, if 'I' is a referring
expression. And now there are two different things for 'guaranteed
reference' to mean here. It may mean (*2a*) guaranteed existence of the
object meant by the user. That is to say, that object must exist, which he is
taking something to be when he uses the expression in connection with it.
Thus, if I suppose I know someone called '*X*' and I call something '*X*' with
the intention of referring to that person, a guarantee of reference in this
sense would be a guarantee that there is such a thing as *X*. The name '*A*'
which I invented would have this sort of guaranteed reference. The '*A*'-
user means to speak of a certain human being, one who falls under his
observation in a rather special way. That person is himself, and so, given
that he has grasped the use of '*A*', he cannot but be speaking of a real person.

If our logician takes this as an adequate account of the guaranteed
reference of 'I', then he will have to grant that there is a third sort of
'guaranteed reference', which 'I' does *not* have. Guaranteed reference for

that name 'X' in this further sense (2b) would entail a guarantee, not just that there is such a thing as X, but also that what I take to be X *is* X. We saw that the 'A'-user would not be immune to mistaken identification of someone else as 'A'. Will it also be so with 'I'?

The suggestion seems absurd. It seems clear that if 'I' is a 'referring expression' at all, it has both kinds of guaranteed reference. The object an 'I'-user means by it must exist so long as he is using 'I', nor can he take the wrong object to be the object he means by 'I'. (The bishop may take the lady's knee for his, but could he take the lady herself to be himself?)

Let us waive the question about the sense of 'I' and ask *only* how reference to the right object could be guaranteed. (This is appropriate, because people surely have here the idea of a sort of pure direct reference in which one simply first means and then refers to an object before one.) It seems, then, that this reference could only be sure-fire if the referent of 'I' were both freshly defined with each use of 'I', and also remained in view so long as something was being taken to be *I*. Even so there is an assumption that something else does not surreptitiously take its place. Perhaps we should say: such an assumption is extremely safe for 'I', and it would be altogether an excess of scepticism to doubt it! So we accept the assumption, and it seems to follow that what 'I' stands for must be a Cartesian Ego.

For, let us suppose that it is some other object. A plausible one would be *this body*. And now imagine that I get into a state of 'sensory deprivation'. Sight is cut off, and I am locally anaesthetized everywhere, perhaps floated in a tank of tepid water; I am unable to speak, or to touch any part of my body with any other. Now I tell myself 'I won't let this happen again!' If the object meant by 'I' is this body, this human being, then in these circumstances it won't be present to my senses; and how else can it be 'present to' me? But have I lost what I mean by 'I'? Is that not present to me? Am I reduced to, as it were, 'referring in absence'? I have not lost my 'self-consciousness'; nor can what I mean by 'I' be an object no longer present to me. This both seems right in itself, and will be required by the 'guaranteed reference' that we are considering.

Like considerations will operate for other suggestions. Nothing but a Cartesian Ego will serve. Or, rather, a stretch of one. People have sometimes queried how Descartes could conlude to his *RES cogitans*.[5] But this is to forget that Descartes declares its essence to be nothing but thinking. The thinking that thinks this thought—that is what is guaranteed by *cogito*.

Thus we discover that *if* 'I' is a referring expression, then Descartes was

[5] e.g. A. J. Ayer. See *Language, Truth and Logic* (2nd edn., London, 1946), 142.

right about what the referent was. His position has, however, the intolerable difficulty of requiring an identification of the same referent in different 'I'-thoughts. (This led Russell at one point to speak of 'short-term selves'.)

Our questions were a combined *reductio ad absurdum* of the idea of 'I' as a word whose role is to 'make a singular reference'. I mean the questions how one is guaranteed to get the object right, whether one may safely assume no unnoticed substitution, whether one could refer to oneself 'in absence', and so on. The suggestion of getting the object right collapses into absurdity when we work it out and try to describe how getting hold of the wrong object may be excluded.

How, even, could one justify the assumption, if it is an assumption, that there is just one thinking which is this thinking of this thought that I am thinking, just one thinker? How do I know that 'I' is not ten thinkers thinking in unison? Or perhaps not quite succeeding. That might account for the confusion of thought which I sometimes feel. Consider the reply 'Legion, for we are many', given by the possessed man in the gospel. Perhaps we should take that solemnly, not as a grammatical joke.[6] These considerations refute the 'definite description' account of 'I'. For the only serious candidate for such an account is 'The sayer of this', where 'sayer' implies 'thinker'.

Getting hold of the wrong object *is* excluded, and that makes us think that getting hold of the right object is guaranteed. But the reason is that there is no getting hold of an object at all. With names, or denoting expressions (in Russell's sense) there are two things to grasp: the kind of use, and what to apply them to from time to time. With 'I' there is only the use.

If this is too hard to believe, if 'I' *is* a 'referring expression', then Descartes was right. But now the troubles start. At first, it seems as if what 'I' stands for ought to be the clearest and certainest thing—what anyone thinking of his own thinking and his own awareness of anything is most evidently aware of. It is most certain because, as Augustine said, it is involved in the knowledge of all mental acts or states by the one who has them. They could not be doubted. But the *I*, the 'mind', the 'self', was their subject, not their object, and looking for it as an object resulted, some people thought, in total failure. It was not to be found. It was rather

---

[6] Ambrose Bierce has a pleasant entry under 'I' in the *Devil's Dictionary*: 'I is the first letter of the alphabet, the first word of the language, the first thought of the mind, the first object of the affections. In grammar it is a pronoun of the first person and singular number. Its plural is said to be *We*, but how there can be more than one myself is doubtless clearer to the grammarians than it is to the author of this incomparable dictionary. Conception of two myselves is difficult, but fine. The frank yet graceful use of 'I' distinguishes a good author from a bad; the latter carries it with the manner of a thief trying to cloak his loot.'

as it were an area of darkness out of which light shone on everything else. So some racked their brains over what this invisible subject and the 'thinking of *it*' could be; others thought there was no such thing, there were just all the objects, and hence that 'I', rather, was the name of the whole collection of perceptions. But that hardly fitted its grammar, and anyway—a problem which utterly stumped Hume—by what was *I* made into a unity? Others in effect treat selves as postulated objects for 'I' to be names of in different people's mouths. Yet others denied that the self was invisible, and claimed that there is a unique feeling of oneself which is indescribable but very, very important, especially in psychology, in clinical psychology, and psychiatry.

With that thought: 'The *I* was subject, not object, and hence invisible', we have an example of language itself being as it were possessed of an imagination, forcing its image upon us.

The dispute is self-perpetuating, endless, irresoluble, so long as we adhere to the initial assumption, made so far by all the parties to it: that 'I' is a referring expression. So long as that is the assumption you will get the deep division between those whose considerations show that they have not perceived the difficulty—for them 'I' is in principle no different from my '*A*'; and those who do—or would—perceive the difference and are led to rave in consequence.

And this is the solution: 'I' is neither a name nor another kind of expression whose logical role is to make a reference, *at all*.

Of course we must accept the rule 'If *X* asserts something with 'I' as subject, his assertion will be true if and only if what he asserts is true of *X*.' But if someone thinks that is a sufficient account of 'I', we must say 'No, it is not', for it does not make any difference between 'I' and '*A*'. The truth-condition of the whole sentence does not determine the meaning of the items within the sentence. Thus the rule does not justify the idea that 'I', coming out of *X*'s mouth, is another name for *X*. Or for anything else, such as an asserting subject who is speaking through *X*.

But the rule does mean that the question '*Whose* assertion?' is all important. And, for example, an interpreter might repeat the 'I' of his principal in his translations. Herein resides the conceivability of the following: someone stands before me and says, 'try to believe this: when I say "I", that does not mean this human being who is making the noise. I am someone else who has borrowed this human being to speak through him.' When I say 'conceivability' I don't mean that such a communication may be the truth, but only that our imagination makes something of the idea. (Mediums, possession.)

If I am right in my general thesis, there is an important consequence—

namely, that 'I am E.A.' is after all not an identity proposition. It is connected with an identity proposition, namely, 'This thing here is E.A.' But there is also the proposition 'I am this thing here.'

When a man does not know his identity, has, as we say, 'lost his memory', what he doesn't know is usually that *that* person he'd point to in pointing to himself (this is the direct reflexive) is, say, Smith, a man of such-and-such a background. He has neither lost the use of 'I', nor would he feel at a loss what to point to as his body, or as the person he is; nor would he point to an unexpected body, to a stone, a horse, or another man, say. The last two of these three points may seem to be part of the first of them; but, as we have seen, it is possible at least for the imagination to make a division. Note that when I use the word 'person' here, I use it in the sense in which it occurs in 'offences against the person'. At this point people will betray how deeply they are infected by dualism, they will say: 'You are using "person" in the sense of "body" '— and what *they* mean by 'body' is something that is still there when someone is dead. But that is to misunderstand 'offences against the person'. None such can be committed against a corpse. 'The person' is a living human body.

There is a real question: with what object is my consciousness of action, posture, and movement, and are my intentions connected in such fashion that *that* object must be standing up if I have the thought that I am standing up and my thought is true? And there is an answer to that: it is this object here.

'I am this thing here' is, then, a real proposition, but not a proposition of identity. It means: this thing here is the thing, the person (in the 'offences against the person' sense) of whose action *this* idea of action is an idea, of whose movements *these* ideas of movement are ideas, of whose posture *this* idea of posture is the idea. And also, of which *these* intended actions, if carried out, will be the actions.

I have from time to time such thoughts as 'I am sitting', 'I am writing', 'I am going to stay still', 'I twitched'. There is the question: in happenings, events, etc., concerning what object are these verified or falsified? The answer is ordinarily easy to give because I can observe, and can point to, my body; I can also feel one part of it with another. 'This body is my body' then means 'My idea that I am standing up is verified by this body, if it is standing up.' And so on. But observation does not show me which body is the one. Nothing shows me that.[7]

---

[7] Professor Føllesdal and Mr Guttenplan tell me that there is some likeness between what I say and what Spinoza says. I am grateful for the observation; but cannot say I understand Spinoza.

If I were in that condition of 'sensory deprivation', I could not have the thought 'this object', 'this body'—there would be nothing for 'this' to latch on to. But that is not to say I could not still have the ideas of actions, motion, etc. For these ideas are not extracts from sensory observation. If I do have them under sensory deprivation, I shall perhaps *believe* that there is such a body. But the possibility will perhaps strike me that there is none. That is, the possibility that there is then nothing that I am.

If 'I' were a name, it would have to be a name for something with this sort of connection with this body, not an extraordinary name for this body. Not a name for this body because sensory deprivation and even loss of consciousness of posture, etc., is not loss of *I*. (That, at least, is how one would have to put it, treating 'I' as a name.)

But 'I' is not a name: these 'I'-thoughts are examples of reflective consciousness of states, actions, motions, etc., not of an object I mean by 'I', but of this body. These 'I'-thoughts (allow me to pause and think some!) . . . are unmediated conceptions (knowledge or belief, true or false) of states, motions, etc., of this object here, about which I can find out (if I don't know it) that it is E.A., about which I did learn that it is a human being.

The 'I'-thoughts *now* that have *this* connection with E.A. are 'I'-thoughts on the part of the same human being as the 'I'-thoughts that had that connection twenty years ago. No problem of the continuity or reidentification of 'the *I*' can arise. There is no such thing. There is E.A., who, like other humans, has such thoughts as these. And who probably learned to have them through learning to say what she had done, was doing, etc.—an amazing feat of imitation.

Discontinuity of 'self-feeling', dissociation from the self-feeling or self-image one had before, although one still has memories—such a thing is of course possible. And so perhaps is a loss of self-feeling altogether. What this 'self-feeling' is is no doubt of psychological interest. The more normal state is the absence of such discontinuity, dissociation, and loss. That absence can therefore be called the possession of 'self-feeling': I record my suspicion that this is identifiable rather by consideration of the abnormal than the normal case.

Self-knowledge is knowledge of the object that one is, of the human animal that one is. 'Introspection' is but one contributory method. It is a rather doubtful one, as it may consist rather in the elaboration of a self-image than in noting facts about oneself.

If the principle of human rational life in E.A. is a soul (which perhaps can survive E.A., perhaps again animate E.A.) *that* is not the reference of

'I'. Nor is it what I am. I am E.A. and shall exist only as long as E.A. exists. But, to repeat, 'I am E.A.' is not an identity proposition.

It will have been noticeable that the I-thoughts I have been considering have been only those relating to actions, postures, movements, and intentions. Not, for example, such thoughts as 'I have a headache', 'I am thinking about thinking', 'I see a variety of colours', 'I hope, fear, love, envy, desire', and so on. My way is the opposite of Descartes's. These are the very propositions he would have considered, and the others were a difficulty for him. But what were most difficult for him are most easy for me.

Let me repeat what I said before. I have thoughts like 'I am standing', 'I jumped'. It is, I said, a significant question: 'In happenings, events, etc., concerning what object are these verified or falsified?'—and the answer was: 'this one'. The reason why I take only thoughts of actions, postures, movements, and intended actions is that only those thoughts both are unmediated, non-observational, and also are descriptions (e.g. 'standing') which are directly verifiable or falsifiable about the person of E.A. Anyone, including myself, can look and see whether that person is standing.

That question 'In happenings, events, etc., concerning what object are these verified or falsified?' could indeed be raised about the other, the Cartesianly preferred, thoughts. I should contend that the true answer would be 'if in any happenings, events, etc., then in ones concerning this object'—namely the person of E.A. But the description of the happenings, etc., would not be just the same as the description of the thought. I mean the thought 'I am standing' is verified by the fact that this person here is *standing*, falsified if she is not. This identity of description is entirely missing for, say, the thought 'I see a variety of colours.' Of course you may say, if you like, that this is verified if this person here sees a variety of colours, but the question is, what is it for it to be so verified? The Cartesianly preferred thoughts all have this same character, of being far removed in their descriptions from the descriptions of the proceedings, etc., of a person in which they may be verified. And also, there may not be any. And also, even when there are any, the thoughts are not thoughts of such proceedings, as the thought of standing is the thought of a posture. I cannot offer an investigation of these questions here. I only want to indicate why I go after the particular 'I'-thoughts that I do, in explaining the meaning of 'I am E.A.' This may suffice to show why I think the Cartesianly preferred thoughts are not the ones to investigate if one wants to understand 'I' philosophically.

Suppose—as is possible—that there were no distinct first-person expression, no pronoun 'I', not even any first-person inflection of verbs. Everyone uses his own name as we use 'I'. (Children sometimes do this.) Thus a man's own name takes the place of 'I' in this supposed language. What then? Won't his own name still be a name? Surely it will! He will be using what is syntactically *and* semantically a name. That is, it is semantically a name in other people's mouths. But it will not be so in his mouth, it will not signify like a name in his utterances.

If I used 'E.A.' like that, and had no first-person inflections of verbs and no such words as 'I', I should be in a difficulty to frame the proposition corresponding to my present proposition: 'I am E.A.' The nearest I could get would be, for example, 'E.A. is the object E.A.' That is, 'E.A. is the object referred to by people who identify something as E.A.'

There is a mistake that it is very easy to make here. It is that of supposing that the difference of self-consciousness, the difference I have tried to bring before your minds as that between 'I'-users and 'A'-users, is a private experience. That there is this asymmetry about 'I': for the hearer or reader it is in principle no different from 'A'; for the speaker or thinker, the 'I'-saying subject, it is different. Now this is not so: the difference between 'I'-users and 'A'-users would be perceptible to observers. To bring this out, consider the following story from William James. James, who insisted (rightly, if I am right) that consciousness is quite distinct from self-consciousness, reproduces an instructive letter from a friend:

We were driving . . . in a wagonette; the door flew open and X, alias 'Baldy', fell out on the road. We pulled up at once, and then he said, 'Did anyone fall out?' or 'Who fell out?'—I don't exactly remember the words. When told that Baldy fell out he said, 'Did Baldy fall out? Poor Baldy!'[8]

If we met people who were A-users and had no other way of speaking of themselves, we would notice it quite quickly, just as his companions noticed what was wrong with Baldy. It was not that he used his own name. That came afterwards. What instigated someone to give information to him in the form 'Baldy fell out' was, I suppose, that his behaviour already showed the lapse of self-consciousness, as James called it. He had just fallen out of the carriage, he was conscious, and he had the idea that someone had fallen out of the carriage—or he knew that someone had, but wondered who! That was the indication of how things were with him.

Even if they had spoken a language without the word 'I', even if they had had one without any first-person inflexion,[9] but everybody used his

---

[8] *Principles of Psychology*, II, (London, 1901), 273 n.
[9] In Latin we have 'ambulo' = 'I walk'. There is no subject-term. There is no need of one.

own name in his expressions of self-consciousness, even so, Baldy's conduct would have had just the same significance. It wasn't that he used 'Baldy' and not 'I' in what he said. It was that his thought of the happening, falling out of the carriage, was one for which he looked for a subject, his grasp of it one which required a subject. And that could be explained even if we didn't have 'I' or distinct first-person inflexions. He did not have what I call 'unmediated agent-or-patient conceptions of actions, happenings, and states'. These conceptions are subjectless. That is, they do not involve the connection of what is understood by a predicate with a distinctly conceived subject. The (deeply rooted) grammatical illusion of a subject is what generates all the errors which we have been considering.

7

DESCARTES'S *COGITO*

JERROLD J. KATZ

This chapter presents the interpretation of Descartes's *cogito, ergo sum* in my book *Cogitations* in a concise and accessible form.[1] The emphasis is on conveying the essentials of the argument that *cogito, ergo sum* is an analytic entailment, but I have taken the opportunity to improve the argument in a few small ways and extend it to the *cogito*-like reasoning in Descartes's *Second Meditation*. I will not here be able to give the justification for a number of the major claims on which my argument rests. Justification for them will be found in *Cogitations* and in works cited there. My aim here is to provide a philosophical explanation of how the *cogito* can both be the simple inference we find in Descartes's own presentation and yet be formally valid.

The conclusion of the *cogito* is presented as inferred from the premiss and as indubitable in virtue of the indubitability of the premiss and in virtue of following validly from it. This is surely correct, but in so far as the inference, as presented, has the logical form '*P*, therefore, *Q*', the question arises of how it can be valid. To account for the validity of the *cogito* many Cartesian scholars have treated Descartes's presentation as enthymematic. The inference is taken to have a suppressed premiss, some general principle like 'what thinks exists', and to be valid in virtue of its premisses and conclusion falling under a law of logic like *modus ponens*.[2]

The problem with trying to account for the validity of the *cogito* in this way is that an enthymematic interpretation conflicts with Descartes's own characterizations of the inference. In one place, for example, he characterizes the *cogito* as an inference in which one does

... not deduce existence from thought by a syllogism, but, by a simple act of mental vision, recognizes it as if it were a thing that is known *per se*.[3]

This chapter has been expanded by the author for this volume from his paper of the same title in *Pacific Philosophical Quarterly*, 68: 3, 4 (1987), 175–96. Reprinted by permission of Basil Blackwell.

[1] J. J. Katz, *Cogitations* (Oxford and New York, 1986).
[2] e.g. M. Wilson, *Descartes* (London, 1978), 54–61.
[3] *The Philosophical Works of Descartes*, ed. and trans. E. Haldane and G. R. T. Ross (Cambridge, 1969), ii. 38.

It is not easy to reconcile the enthymematic interpretation with such statements. Some Cartesian scholars have tried therefore to restrict the scope of Descartes's protest by distinguishing syllogistic inference from logical inference of a modern flavour. That, however, would ignore both the fact that the term 'syllogism' would have been used in Descartes's time to cover hypothetical forms like *modus ponens* and the fact that Descartes's explicit contrast of a syllogism with 'a simple act of mental vision' is most naturally seen as a protest against treating the *cogito* as a *complex* inference of any sort. Moreover, Descartes goes on to observe that invoking a further premiss would leave him with a principle for which he lacks the grounds on which to say it is 'known previously'.[4] Finally, in saying that the validity of the deduction is grasped in a simple intuition, Descartes seems to be setting the *cogito* apart from complex inferences where it is possible that

... I am always mistaken [as] when I add two and three or count the sides of a square,[5]

and to be classifying it with 'simple matters'. He writes:

... each individual can mentally have an intuition of the fact that he exists, and that he thinks; that the triangle is bounded by three lines only, the sphere by a single superficies, and so on. Facts of such a kind are far more numerous than many people think, disdaining as they do to direct their attention to simple matters.[6]

Other philosophers try to reconcile Descartes's statements with an enthymematic treatment by claiming that Descartes was confused, perhaps due to not having the resources of modern logical theory available to him. But the amount of confusion on Descartes's part that is required to sustain an enthymematic treatment of the *cogito* is too great to be plausible in the case of so clear and distinctive a mind as Descartes's. Either the *cogito* as Descartes intends it is a simple inference, as he himself claims, in which case the inference is of the form '*P*, therefore, *Q*' and it is invalid. In this case, Descartes must be pictured as unable to see the invalidity of the simplest invalid argument. Or, the *cogito* as he intends it is a complex inference, as logical theory requires for it to be valid, in which case the inference is nothing like what Descartes presents it as, insists on its being, and needs it to be. In this case, Descartes must be pictured as bungling the job of presenting the proper complex argument. This would be especially strange since he would have been familiar with the notion expressed in the *Port-Royal* definition of an enthymeme as

---

[4] *The Philosophical Works of Descartes.*
[5] Ibid. i. 147.
[6] Ibid. 7.

a syllogism which though complete in the mind is incomplete in expression.[7]

Why, then, wouldn't he provide an appropriate presentation? Be this as it may, in either case, the picture of Descartes in this connection looks nothing like our picture of him otherwise. This, then, is the Cartesian scholar's dilemma.

Cogitations proposes a radical solution to this dilemma. The dilemma exists, I submit, because of a general acceptance of the philosophy of language and logic which says that *every* formally valid inference is such in virtue of falling under laws of logic. There would be a way out of the dilemma if we reject this philosophy. In this spirit, let us turn things around and entertain the idea that some arguments are formally valid without the sanction of logic, and that the *cogito* is one. Now instead of the *cogito* having to be recast to fit with the prevailing philosophy of logic and language, the *cogito* is a counter-example.

To entertain this idea is not to challenge modern logic itself, which is a systematic treatment of inferences that do depend on derivations via laws of logic, but to challenge a philosophical theory. The idea may be fleshed out by viewing the 'simple matters' of which Descartes speaks in the above extract as matters of linguistic definition. This would be to suppose that the *cogito* is a form of inference whose validity rests solely on sense relations in the grammatical structure of the premiss and conclusion. That is to say, it belongs to a class of inferences whose truth-preserving character is a matter of language *per se*: it turns on nothing beyond the senses of the sentences 'I think' and 'I exist.'

The radicalness of my proposal thus has to do with the fact that it runs counter to one of the central tenets of twentieth-century Anglo-American philosophy, the view that logical structure and grammatical structure are very much bound up with one another. The proposal, in effect, draws a sharp line between logical and linguistic truth.[8] Hence, it challenges both the Quinean and the Carnapian positions. Each in its own way denies the possibility of a purely linguistic source of inferential validity. Quine argues that there is no genuine validity in the domain of linguistic meaning, while Carnap argues that the validity found there is, at bottom, logical validity.[9]

---

[7] A. Arnauld, *The Art of Thinking*, trans. J. Dickoff, and P. James, (Indianapolis, 1964), 228. My assumption is that the doctrines codified in the *Port-Royal Logic* were widely known in Descartes's time.

[8] A full treatment of the distinction between these 2 forms of symbolic truth appears in G. E. Smith and J. J. Katz, *Supposable Worlds* (Cambridge, Mass., forthcoming). This work was referred to in *Cogitations* and elsewhere under the working title 'Intensionally Admissible Models'.

[9] W. V. Quine, 'Two Dogmas of Empiricism', in *From a Logical Point of View* (New York, 1953, rev. 1961), 20–46; R. Carnap, 'Meaning Postulates', in *Meaning and Necessity* (Chicago, 1956), 222–9.

Indeed, the enthymematic interpretation of the *cogito* seems to be nothing more than a way of subsuming the inference under laws of logic where the 'missing premiss' is conceived of as a meaning postulate.

If I am to explain how the Cartesian scholar's dilemma can be solved, I must show how to defuse Quine's objections to a solution which uses linguistic meaning as a basis for validity and truth, and I must exhibit an alternative to Carnap's account of inferences which turn on properties of the extra-logical vocabulary and display some advantages of the alternative in the case at hand.

I will start with Quine. 'Two Dogmas of Empiricism' contains Quine's argument against meaning, truth by virtue of meaning, and validity by virtue of meaning.[10] The argument has the form of a proof by cases.[11] The cases are areas where we might reasonably expect to find some way to explain objectively the concepts of the theory of meaning, especially analyticity and synonymy. Those areas are definition, logical theory, and linguistics. The cases can be accepted as exhaustive: where else might one look for a paradigm on which to explain objectively concepts like analyticity and synonymy? Anyway, I will concede this point to Quine. Furthermore, I will also concede that he convincingly shows that no suitable paradigm can be found in either the area of definition (broadly construed) or the area of logical theory. The point where I want to challenge his argument is in the case of lingusitics. Here he shows that any attempt to provide substitition crteria for analyticity or synonymy is viciously circular, but the argument falsely assumes that substitution criteria are the only way to explain concepts in linguistics.[12] The assumption is false because there is also the possibility of a non-operationalist, theory construction paradigm of explanation. That form of explanation was, in fact, introduced into linguistics as part of Chomsky's theory of generative grammar.

On the theory construction paradigm, the explanation of analyticity or synonymy would take the familiar form of an axiomatic explanation in logic or mathematics. A set of axioms or rules explains a concept by relating it to other concepts in its family, and in virtue of the concept's systematic relations to the other concepts in its family, to a wide range of phenomena in the domain. Here, unlike the case of an operationalist

---

[10] *From a Logical Point of View*, pp. 20–37.

[11] This criticism of Quine's argument appears in *Cogitations*, pp. 27–32.

[12] Not only is there no other way mentioned in the argument, but Quine endorses substitution criteria as the official methodology of scientific linguistics; see 'The Problem of Meaning in Linguistics', in *From a Logical Point of View*, p. 56. Moreover, the logic of Quine's argument requires that either there be no other way or else that his way is the proper one for lingusitic concepts.

paradigm, there is no requirement to specify the concept to be explained in terms of concepts *outside* its family. There is no assumption that the understanding of a family of concepts must derive from some other family whose status is somehow taken as satisfactory at the outset. Hence, here there is no circularity when a concept is explained in terms of others in its immediate family. Since Quine's argument rests on there being no possibility of a non-circular explanation of semantic concepts in linguistics, to refute him it suffices to exhibit one overlooked explanatory paradigm that provides the possibility.[13]

Now, many philosophers have thought that Quine has not overlooked a theory construction paradigm because he considers and successfully criticizes Carnap's attempt to account for semantic facts within a system of meaning postulates. I agree with Quine that such systems

tell us that such and such statements, and only those, are the analytic statements of L_o. [But] here the difficulty is simply that the rules contain the word 'analytic', which we do not understand! We understand what expressions the rules attribute analyticity to, but we do not understand what the rules attribute to those expressions.[14]

The problem with Carnap's approach is that it brutely applies the method of recursive specification from logic to a case where the application of the method is not appropriate. The approach would be like accounting for the validity of the inference from 'All horses are animals' to 'All heads of horses are heads of animals' by the postulate 'S_1 S_2', where 'S_1' and 'S_2' stand for the premiss and conclusion, respectively, without first determining whether there is a level of quantificational structure to be taken into consideration. A criticism parallel to Quine's would apply to this account of the inference, since the failure to expose its quantificational structure leaves us with no basis for an explanation of its quantificational validity. In Carnap's case, there is no basis for an explanation of linguistic validity.

My alternative to Carnap's account of analyticity will expose the sense structure which Carnap fails to expose, and hence, will explain what is attributed to sentences marked *analytic*. But before considering such an alternative, we ought to look briefly at the source of Carnap's approach. His notion of analyticity is an explanation of Frege's notion of logical truth. As Frege expresses the notion:

[13] A full account of this criticism is found in J. J. Katz, 'The Refutation of Indeterminacy', *Journal of Philosophy*, 85: 5 (1988), 1–26.
[14] *From a Logical Point of View*, p. 33.

If, in [finding the proof of the proposition, and in following it up right back to the primitive truths], we come only on general logical laws and on definitions, then the truth is an analytic one.[15]

Carnap's explanation makes Frege's notion uniform by formulating the definitions as meaning postulates, that is, as principles that have the form and model-theoretic function of logical postulates. Thus, an inference like that from 'Mary is a sister' to 'Mary is a sibling' is an enthymematic inference which, fleshed out, takes the form of a premiss 'Mary is a sister', a meaning postulate 'For all x, if x is a sister, then x is a sibling', and an application of appropriate logical laws. The meaning postulates constrain the admissible models so that the conclusion is true on any model on which the premiss is.

Now, Frege's notion of analyticity was, in turn, based on Kant's. Frege says that he does

not, of course, mean to assign a new sense to [the terms 'analytic' and 'synthetic'], but only to state accurately what earlier writers, *Kant* in particular, have meant by them.[16]

Kant had *two* notions which he presented side by side. Frege collapsed them into one. One of Kant's notions was that

Analytical judgments express nothing in the predicate but what has already been actually thought in the concept of the subject.[17]

The other was that analytical judgments are ones that

I have only to extract from [the concept of the subject], in accordance with the principle of contradiction, the required predicate.[18]

Those two notions of analytic containment in Kant's writings seem to represent a confluence of the Lockean tradition of trifling propositions and the Leibnizian tradition of logical truth.

The difference between Kant's two notions of analytic containment is nicely brought out by Frege in his metaphors of 'beams in the house' and 'the plant in the seed'. In the former case, we have literal containment: the subject concept is a construction out of simpler concepts, one of which is the predicate concept. In the latter case, we do not have literal containment. Generally, the proposition that is the conclusion of a logical inference is not actually there as such in the premisses.

Now if there is such a difference between the two notions of analyticity,

[15] G. Frege, *The Foundations of Arithmetic* (Oxford, 1953), 3^e–5^e.
[16] Ibid. 3^e n. 1.
[17] I. Kant, *Prolegomena to Any Future Metaphysics*, ed. L. W. Beck (New York, 1951), 14.
[18] Ibid. 14.

we can begin to see how the philosophy of logic and language which claims that every valid inference depends on logical laws could be wrong. There could be a class of inferences which are valid because the meaning of the premiss contains, in the 'beams of the house' sense, the meaning of the conclusion, so that the truth conditions of the premiss include those of the conclusion. Here validty would rest not on logical laws that bridge the gap from premiss to conclusion, but on the fact that the meaning of the premiss is such that there is no gap to be bridged.

Frege clearly saw the difference between 'beams in the house' analyticity and 'plant in the seed' analyticity. He had positive reasons for taking the approach he took. He thought that the former notion is not viable apart from the latter. He had three criticisms of Kant's 'beams in the house' notion.[19] These he took to doom it. First, as defined, it is restricted to subject-predicate sentences; second, it is based on a psychological criterion for determining the components of a concept, and third, it is an extremely weak account of what it is for one concept to be a part of another. His criticisms may identify genuine shortcomings of Kant's definition of analyticity, but they do not suffice to justify rejecting the possibility of an independent 'beams in the house' species of analyticity. Frege gives no reason to suppose that the shortcomings of Kant's definition are essential rather than an accidental feature of Kant's formulation. Therefore, we may treat Frege's criticisms as possible objections to any alternative definition which must be satisfactorily answered at some point, and not as actual objections which block the search for a way of cashing the 'beams in the house' metaphor.

The natural place to begin our search for a way of explaining meaning containment is in linguistics with the very paradigm of theoretical explanation Quine ignored. We want a theoretical treatment of meaning containment that is in relevant respects like the treatment in generative syntax of the containment of the sentence 'John meets Mary' in the sentence 'John is eager to meet Mary'; that is, we want formal representations of sentence structure which expose enough sense structure to identify the inclusion of one sense in another.[20] But, of course, if such formal representations are to be adequate descriptions of the meaning of sentences, they must also enable us to define, on the basis of their formal features, the full range of semantic properties and relations, including, in

---

[19] *The Foundations of Arithmetic*, pp. 3ᶜ–4ᶜ, 99ᶜ–102ᶜ.

[20] Just as syntactic treatments of 'John is eager to meet Mary' represents 'John' as the subject of 'meet' in an underlying phrase marker, so we want semantic treatments of redundant expressions like 'free gift' to represent the sense of 'free' as a part of the sense of 'gift'.

addition to analyticity, synonymy, ambiguity, antonymy, and meaningfulness.

A formal definition of analyticity automatically avoids Frege's criticism of Kant for having a psychological criterion for analyticity. Instead of consulting introspection, we have an objective way of determining analyticity. We check the representation of the sentence to see if it has the formal property in the definiens of 'S is analytic'.

A system of semantic representations will have to have two fundamental properties: it has to be *compositional*, and it has to be *decompositional*. Compositionality is a familiar feature of language, perhaps best illustrated in cases where compositional meaning contrasts with idiomatic meaning, as in a sentence like 'Go fly a kite.'[21] We will say that a system is compositional in case assignment of semantic representations to the constituents of sentences reconstructs the way in which the senses of the constituents are a function of the senses of their syntactic parts and the syntactic relations.

Decompositionality is less familiar in discussions of language. It is the property Kant assumed in characterizing analytic judgements as those which add

nothing through the predicate to the concept of the subject, but merely break . . . it up into those constituent concepts that have all along been thought in it.[22]

We will say that a system of semantic representations is decompositional in case the representations formally distinguish the component senses and exhibit their constitutive relations. Decompositionality is not only a desired property in light of the philosophical aim of defining the 'beams in the house' notion of analyticity, it is also a desired property from a purely linguistic perspective. For unless semantic representations expose decompositional structure, we will fail to account for semantic phenomena. For example, without exposing component senses, we could not distinguish a redundant expression like 'naked nude' from a non-redundant one like 'naked nudist'.

I will now describe some of the features which make a formal representation decompositional. Syntactic representations like (1), called 'phrase markers', analyse the constituent structure of sentences. Correspondingly, we may use 'semantic markers' like (2) to analyse the sense structure. (2) may be thought of as expressing an Aristotelian conception of the sense of 'human'. The node labels in such representations stand for component senses, and the branches of the trees represent the constitutive

---

[21] See J. J. Katz, 'Compositionality, Idiomaticity, and Lexical Substitution', in *A Festschrift for Morris Halle* (New York, 1973), 357–76.

[22] I. Kant, *The Critique of Pure Reason*, trans. N. K. Smith (New York, 1929), 49.

(1)

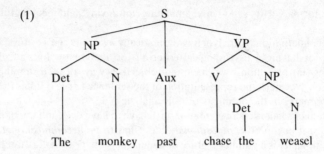

relations: the domination relation represents the forming of a subordinate concept from a superordinate concept by means of qualification.[23]

Generally, semantic markers represent superordination relations in the following manner. Suppose a sense is a complex concept c^* whose component concepts are $c_1 \ldots, c_n$. We could represent the superordination structure as (3). The entire semantic marker (3) represents the concept c^*. For example, the semantic marker (2) represents the Aristotelian concept of being human. The branches represent the component concepts of c^*. Thus, c_1 represents the major superordinate in (2), c_2 represents the next, and so on. Thus, for instance, c_3 is represented as a subordinate of c_2 and c_1. But c_1 is not a subordinate of anything, and c_n is not a superordinate of anything.

Now let us look at how the sense of the verb 'chase' in (1) could be represented so as to achieve both decompositionality and compositionality. We might represent the verb as (4). The decompositional structure in (4) makes a variety of predictions about the relations of 'chase' to other verbs. For example, the superordination marked by the branch ending in '(Physical)' distinguishes 'chase' from activity verbs like 'think', 'plan', and 'remember' and relates it to activity verbs like 'swim', 'run', and 'climb'. The superordination marked by '(Purpose)' distin-

(2)

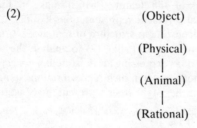

---

[23] See *Cogitations*, pp. 71–97.

(3)

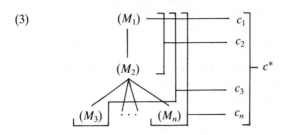

guishes 'chase' from activity verbs like 'meander' and 'wander' and also relates it to activity verbs like 'teach' and 'murder'. Or again, the superordination marked by '(Movement)' distinguishes 'chase' from activity verbs like 'scratch' and relates it to activity verbs like 'follow'.

The variables occurring in (4) function to express the predicate structure of the concepts out of which the sense of 'chase' is built and the concept 'chase' itself. They do this under the convention that a predicate is represented as having n argument places just in case the representation has exactly n distinct variables. Two occurrences of a variable are counted as occurrences of the same variable if and only if they have the same symbols above and below 'X'. Thus, (4) represents 'chase' as a two-place predicate.

The complex form of these variables is designed for the representation of compositionality. The meaning of (1) is a function of the meanings of the words 'the', 'monkey', 'chase', and 'weasel' plus the syntactic relations in which they stand to one another in (1). Thus, the meanings of (5) and (6) will be appropriately different from that of (1).

(4)

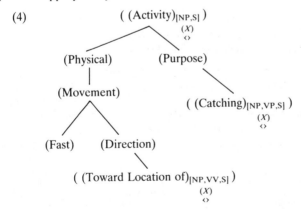

(5) The weasel chased the monkey.
(6) The cat chased the rat.

The syntactic symbols in brackets over the letter in a variable state which constituent in a sentence supplies the semantic representation to replace that variable when semantic rules derive the semantic representation of the sentence from the semantic representations of its constituents. The syntactic symbol '[NP, S]' is read as specifying the segment of a terminal string of a phrase marker which is first dominated by 'NP' and then dominated by 'S', namely, the subject, and the syntactic symbol '[NP, VP, S]' is read as specifying the segment of a terminal string which is first dominated by 'NP', then by 'VP', and finally by 'S', namely, the direct object.[24] Thus, in deriving a semantic representation for (1), the semantic representation of the subject, 'the monkey', replaces the variable with '[NP, S]' over it, and the semantic representation of the direct object, 'the weasel', replaces the variable with '[NP, VP, S]' over it.

The angles under the letter contain a restriction that blocks syntactically possible embeddings that must be thrown out on semantic grounds. Such a restriction is necessary to determine the number of senses of sentences correctly. Consider that an ordinary sentence has maybe fifteen or twenty words and each word is, on the average, about five or more ways ambiguous. Were there no mechanism to block syntactically permissible semantic combinations, there would be a combinatorial explosion that would imply that ordinary sentences of English are hundreds of ways ambiguous. Furthermore, semantic restrictions, when properly formulated, enable us to explain the deviance of (7), (8), and (9) as the absence of a (well-formed) sense.

(7) The null set chased the weasel.
(8) The throbbing pain chased the weasel.
(9) The circular definition chased the weasel.

The heavy parentheses that enclose some variables mark the argument place as referential. Absence of heavy parentheses marks a place as non-referential. Marking of argument places is necessary for an adequate account of compositionality. To be adequate, an account must explain how the semantic properties of sentences are fixed by the semantic properties of their constituents. A sentence like (1) entails that there is a

---

[24] This syntactic notation for grammatical relations like *subject-of* and *direct-object-of* are discussed more fully in N. Chomsky, *Aspects of the Theory of Syntax* (Cambridge, Mass., 1965), 64–74. My use of Chomsky's notation is entirely a matter of convenience. I could have used any other systematic treatment of grammatical relations for my purposes.

monkey and a weasel, while a sentence like (10) does not entail there is or will be a nuclear free world.

(10) Jane Fonda wants a nuclear free world.

The truth of (10) does not depend on the semantic properties of the object, as shown by the fact that the false sentence (11) has the very same verb phrase.

(11) Caspar Weinberger wanted a nuclear free world.

Lexical items of the language, which are the basis for compositional projection, must be represented so that, throughout the compositional projection, terms appearing in argument places in the senses of sentences are properly marked as referential or non-referential.

Given this brief account of semantic representation, we can return to the task of defining 'beams in the house' analyticity. In order to avoid Frege's criticism that Kant's definition is restricted to subject–predicate sentences, our definition must be constructed to cover sentences involving transitive verbs and complex grammatical forms of various sorts. Frege's way of avoiding his own criticism was to use logical truths as paradigmatic of non-subject-predicate analytic sentences. But it was just this step that took him to the 'plant in the seed' notion of analyticity. Hence, if we are to preserve the 'beams in the house' notion, we have to identify a different set of non-subject–predicate sentences as the paradigmatic cases. I submit that the natural counterparts of 'beams in the house' analytic sentences like 'Bachelors are unmarried' are sentences like (12), (13), and (14).

(12) John marries those whom he weds.
(13) Mary walks with those she strolls with.
(14) The library buys books from those who sell it books.

These sentences have the same redundant predication as the classical subject–predicate analytic sentences. Thus, the sense of 'stroll', being the concept of walking slowly and leisurely, makes the predication expressed in 'walks' redundant in the same way that the sense of 'bachelor', being the concept of an unmarried man, makes the predication expressed in 'unmarried' redundant.

The only difference between cases like (12)–(14) and classical subject–predicate analytic sentences is that, in (12)–(14), a term other than the subject is the source of the redundancy. Kant did not look at relational sentences, and as a consequence, defined analyticity too narrowly, reflecting what is only a special case of the property. But, taking relational sentences into account, we can define analyticity with sufficient generality to cover redundant predication due to the sense of any term in a proposition. (15) informally expresses this generalization. (12) is analytic by (15) because, in (12), the sense of 'those whom he weds' contains the sense of 'married' together with the sense of 'John' (the sense of (12) in question is the one where 'he' is anaphoric to 'John').

> (15) Let the sense of a sentence be taken as an n-place predicate, each of whose argument places is occupied by a term. Then, a sense of a sentence is analytic in case there is a term whose sense contains the sense of the predicate together with the senses of each of the other terms.

Quine rightly criticized Carnap's explication of analyticity for failing to provide an account of what property is attributed to sentences when they are specified as analytic. (15) expresses the property which is attributed to a sentence when it is marked as analytic. Hence Quine's criticism is inapplicable to our definition, since the definition specifies the property of redundant predication.

On the basis of our semantic markers representation, (15) can be formalized as (16).[25]

> (16) A sense of a sentence is analytic in case its semantic representation has the form $P_{T_1}, \ldots, T_n$ and some term T_i, $1 \leq i \leq n$, is of the form $P'_{t_1}, \ldots t_m$ and $P_{x_1}, \ldots, x_n$ is a same-rooted subtree of $P'_{x_1}, \ldots x_m$ and also each term $T_1, \ldots, T_{i-1}, T_{i+1}, \ldots, T_n$ is a same-rooted subtree of the corresponding term in $t_1, \ldots, t_m$.

We now come to Frege's third and final criticism of Kant's definition of analyticity. Let me present this criticism in Frege's own words. In the *Grundlagen*, Frege writes that Kant

seems to think of concepts as defined by giving a simple list of characteristics in no special order; but of all ways of forming concepts, that is one of the least fruitful.

Three things should be said. First, take the definition (16), in its intended application to semantic markers like (4). The concepts are not 'a simple list' whose items are given 'in no special order'. The superordination structure by itself shows that much. Second, the presentation of semantic markers in the above discussion is incomplete in a number of respects, e.g. the relations of sense opposition underlying antonymy have been left

---

[25] I should note that the definitions of 'analytic' and 'analytic entailment' given below are not intended as complete. Even the definitions in *Cogitations*, p. 93 and 111, which are more complete, are still not full definitions. An attempt at full definitions is presented in *Supposable Worlds*.

out. The representations are even less like lists when their presentation is complete. Third, although semantic marker representations are not as excessively fruitful as the apparatus from logic and mathematics with which Frege contrasts Kant's definitional apparatus, that is irrelevant. The aim is to define a certain property of sentences of natural language, analyticity. If the apparatus needed to define that property is weaker than the apparatus needed to define other properties, inside or outside of natural language, that does not make the definition inadequate. It may be an adequate definition of a weaker property.

Every analytic sentence has a corresponding analytic entailment. Thus, corresponding to (17) is (18).

(17) Bachelors are unmarried men.
(18) John is a bachelor.

     John is an unmarried man.

(16) can easily be converted into a definition of analytic entailment, namely (19).

(19) A sense s^1 analytically entails a sense s^2 in case the semantic representation of s^1 has the form $P^1_{x_1}, \ldots, x_n$ with the terms $T^1_1, \ldots, T^1_n$ occupying the argument places, and the semantic representation of s^2 has the form $P^2_{x_1}, \ldots, x_{n-k}$, $n > k \geqslant 0$, with the terms $T^2_1, \ldots, T^2_{n-k}$, and both $P^2_{x_1}, \ldots, x_{n-k}$ is a same-rooted subtree of $P^1_{x_1}, \ldots, x_n$, and each T^2_i is a same-rooted subtree of T^1_i.

(19) handles cases like (18), and also analytic entailment like (20), assuming a semantic representation for the verb 'follow' such as (21).

(20) The monkey chased the weasel.

     The monkey followed the weasel.

(21)

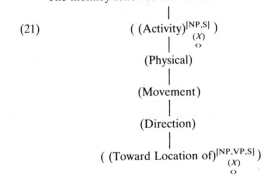

Thus far, I have said nothing directly about the same-rooted subtree relation in the definitions of analyticity and analytic entailment, relying on an intuitive understanding of path identity in labelled trees. Now, however, I must say something about the relation. For, although it is clear, on the one hand, that (22) is an analytic entailment, and on the other, that the semantic representation of 'wreck' would contain the information that both argument-places are referential, it is unclear how such information is to be used in marking (22) as analytic entailments.

> (22) John wrecked his new sports car.
> ―――――――――――――――――――――――
> John existed.
> A new sports car existed.

What is required is a semantic representation for 'exists' which brings existential sentences under the path identity relation in definitions (16) and (19).

Since the referential information necessary for marking existential entailments is already available in the semantic representation of the entailing sentence (in the representations of verbs like 'chase' or 'wreck'), the representation of 'exists' ought to make appropriate use of it. Given that we require the semantic representation of 'exists' to be identifiable with the parts of semantic representations marking existential information, and further that such information is marked with the notation of heavy parentheses, we can make appropriate use of available notation by representing the sense of 'exists' in the form (23).

> (23) (( ) $^{[NP, S]}_{x}$)

The syntactic categorization over the variable specifies its values as heavy semantic representations of the subject of 'exists'. The fact that the heavy parentheses are empty, i.e. do not enclose a semantic marker such as (2), expresses Kant's observation that existence is not a 'real predicate'. That is, existence is not a predicate which, in Kant's words, 'is added to the concept of the subject and enlarges it'.[26] The interpretation of an instance of (22) in which the variable is replaced by a semantic representation for the subject-term is essentially the same as the interpretation of a term in referential position, namely, that something in the world falls under the sense of the term.

All that remains now for (19) to handle analytic entailments with existential conclusions is to add (D) to the specification of the same-rooted subtree relation.

―――――――――

[26] *The Critique of Pure Reason*, p. 504.

(D) (( ) $_{(M_1)}$) is a same-rooted subtree of any semantic marker with a node that is labelled ((M_2) $_{(\,(M_3)\,)}$) just in case (M_1) is a same-rooted subtree of (M_3).

Allowing (M_1) to be a same-rooted subtree of (M_2) enables us to mark analytic entailments like (24).

> (24) A bachelor wrecked a sports car.
> ─────────────────────────────
> A man existed.
> A male existed.
> Someone unmarried existed.
> A car existed.
> A vehicle existed.
>
> .
> .
> .

We are now very close to accounting for the *cogito* as an analytic entailment. If the *cogito* can be subsumed under the definition of analytic entailment, it will be shown to be valid as it stands. It is valid because the containment of the conclusion of an analytic entailment in its premiss makes satisfaction of the conclusion one with satisfaction of the premiss. To put the point in a slightly different way, it is valid as it stands because 'beams in the house' containment of the conclusion leaves no inferential gap that needs to be bridged by laws of logic. The supposition that the *cogito* has the logical structure '*P*, therefore, *Q*', and hence, that there is a gap, is only an artefact of the prevailing philosophy of logic and language on which the only sanction for validity is logical law. The failure is a failure to look into the decompositional structure of senses of *P* and *Q*.

But for the *cogito* to be an analytic entailment, the first person pronoun must occur referentially in the premiss. The problem here is the famous one raised by Lichtenberg:

> (25) Shhh, the dean is thinking.

one may grant that the subject of (25) refers to a dean without granting that the subject of (26) refers to anyone, for one can hold that (26) is parallel in grammar to (27).

> (26) Shhh, I am thinking.

The claim, then, is that a sentence like (26) means just that there is some thinking taking place.

> (27) It is lightning.

The Lichtenberg claim has its contemporary advocates in Geach and Anscombe.[27] Geach thinks that Descartes holds that

> introspection can give the 'I' a special sense, which each of us can learn on his own account.[28]

Geach claims that Descartes commits the fallacy of taking every word to stand for something. Responding to this claim, Kenny points out that Descartes is not guilty of this fallacy: Descartes has an argument for the existence of something as the substance on which his thought depends. But Kenny leaves the matter at this. He makes no reply to Geach's other criticisms, in particular to Geach's claim that the 'I' of the *cogito* and other soliloquy uses has no sense.

There is a very straightforward reply to Geach, namely, neither introspection nor metaphysics is needed to 'give the "I" a special sense' because the pronoun has a sense in the language already. I do not know how to express the sense generally, but, in sentences like 'I dream of Jeanne with the light brown hair', it can be expressed as the concept of being the agent of the action expressed by the verb whose subject is the pronoun. Introspection may be needed to acquaint us with the referent of the sense of 'I' in soliloquy uses, and metaphysics may be needed to form a satisfactory conception of the self on the basis of such acquaintance, but neither seems needed to provide the sense.

Geach argues for there being no sense for 'I' in these cases by asking

> what is going to count as an allowable answer to the question 'What is this "I"?' or 'Who then am I?' These questions might have a good clear sense in certain circumstances—e.g. if Descartes had lost his memory and wanted to know who he was ('Who am I?' 'You are René Descartes'), or if he knew that somebody had said 'I'm in a muddle' but not that it was himself ('Who is this "I"—who said he was in a muddle?' 'You did'). The states of mind that would give the questions sense are queer and uncommon, but they do occur. But no such rare circumstance was involved in Descartes's actual meditation; in the actual conditions, it is simply that the questions 'Who am I?' 'Who is this "I"?' are deprived of any ordinary use and no new use has yet been specified.[29]

Geach's argument trades on the equation of meaning or sense with use: unless absence of 'ordinary use' is *ipso facto* absence of sense, nothing in what Geach says implies that 'I' stands in need of a sense. But before I show that this is the case, the identification of meaning with use needs to be undermined as a possible basis for Geach's conclusion.

The identification can be undermined by examples of sentences which

[27] P. T. Geach, *Mental Acts* (New York, 1957), 117–20. G. E. M. Anscombe, 'The First Person', in S. Guttenplan (ed.), *Mind and Language* (Oxford, 1975), 45–65, which is reprinted here as ch. 6. See also A. Kenny, *Descartes: A Study of His Philosophy* (New York, 1968), 59–60.   [28] Geach, *Mental Acts*, p. 117.   [29] Ibid. 118–19.

have a sense but no use. Examples are multiply centre-embedded sentences like (28), or a sentence formed by conjoining a trillion meaningful English sentences.

> (28) The girl who the boy who the children like recognized in the park danced a minuet.

Such monsters are clearly beyond the range of language use, but they are meaningful, as can be seen from the fact that they violate no semantic constraint. The sentence (28) has the same meaning as 'the children like the boy and the boy recognized the girl in the park and the girl danced a minuet'. The monstrously long sentence is the joint assertion of each of its trillion meaningful conjuncts. Use is under biological constraints, meaning is not.

Undermining the equation of meaning with use puts a chink in Geach's argument, even granting that the question 'Who am I?' and 'Who is this I?' have no use in the actual circumstances. For now it has to be shown that what stops these questions from having a use in Descartes's soliloquy, i.e. in the privacy of one's own subjectivity, is that 'I' stands in need of a sense outside the context of requests for historical identification. But, now, whether we can say that 'I' stands in such need depends on whether there is an alternative explanation of the deviance in the use that is consistent with 'I' having a sense. If there is such an alternative explanation, Geach's argument has no force.

The alternative explanation is that the use of 'I' is deviant in the subjective applications in question because it is part of an obviously pointless request for information. The questioner knows already that the questioner is he himself or she herself. The omni-presence of the agent in the asking as the referent of the 'I' in the question and the omni-absence of other possible referents from the subjectivity (which might cause misidentification) conspire to guarantee successful identification. The request for information expressed in these uses of 'Who am I?' and 'Who is this I?' is thus as pointless as asking 'Can I utter this utterance?'

Geach concludes by saying that

the use of 'I' in such soliloquies is derivative from, parasitic upon, its use in talking to others; when there are no others, 'I' is redundant and has no special reference; 'I am puzzled at this problem' really says no more than 'This problem *is* puzzling' (*demonstratio ad intellectum* again). Similarly 'I have (had) frightful pain' really says no more than 'That pain is (was) frightful'; the question *whose* pain it is does not arise if the remark is a soliloquy.[30]

First, note that Geach is wrong in saying that a first-person sentence like 'I

---

[30] *Mental Acts*, 120.

am very puzzled at this problem' 'really says no more than' a sentence like 'This problem *is* puzzling.' The first can be continued '. . . but the problem isn't really so puzzling; I must be pretty hungover today', while the second can be continued '. . . but I'll make short work of it because I've got an I.Q. of 200'. Second, note that, again, an alternative explanation is readily available: we can agree that 'the question *whose* pain . . . does not arise', but explain this fact pragmatically rather than semantically. The question would not arise in a soliloquy just as the question 'But do you believe it?' would not arise as a response to the frantic exclamation 'I've been robbed of my jewels'. It is pointless (to say the least) to ask the victim whether he or she believes the statement, and it is pointless to ask oneself on thinking 'That pain is frightful' whose pain it is. It is pointless because one knows that a pain that one feels is *ipso facto* one's own. Such a pragmatic explanation of the deviance of the question 'Whose pain is it?' shows that Geach would not be entitled to assume the absence of sense on the grounds that it explains the deviance of the question.

Geach's line of argument assumes also that subjective uses of 'I' derive from objective uses in a way that makes the sense and reference of a soliloquy use depend on the existence of an appropriate objective use. This assumption is only tenable if the meaning of a sentence is equated with its use. If the meaning of a sentence is thought of compositionally and the sense and reference of expression tokens are thought of as derivative from the sense and reference of expression types, then the sense and reference of 'I' in soliloquies does not depend on 'its use in talking to others'. Both uses of 'I', in talking to oneself and in talking to others, depend on the semantic structure of the language.

Anscombe has tried to show that Descartes's mistake was to take the first-person pronoun to be a referring expression. She has argued that 'I' is neither a pronoun nor a referring expression. To support the first of these conclusions, she says

you do not get the same sense in a sentence if you replace the pronoun in it by a name, common or proper.[31]

Surely, as the term itself suggests, pronouns function, in some sense, to replace nouns, but there is no reason to suppose that the test for pronounhood is that they do so *salva* sense. Anscombe is probably misled by the way traditional grammars base syntactic distinctions on semantic criteria. On a more modern approach, pronominal replacement requires only preserving syntactic well-formedness. Anscombe's argument that 'I'

---

[31] Anscombe, 'The First Person', p. 53.

is not a pronoun fails because her semantic criterion is neither the only nor the most plausible criterion for pronounhood.

Furthermore, Anscombe's remark

Unluckily the category 'pronoun' tells us nothing, since a singular pronoun may even be a variable (as in 'If anyone says that, *he* is a fool')—and hence not any kind of singular designation of an object.[32]

backfires. True enough, some singular pronouns have a generic use as a variable, as in her example. But 'I' contrasts with them in a way that shows that 'I' is a kind of singular designation. 'I' does not function as a variable in the parallel case, 'If anyone says that, *I* give up', but rather denotes the speaker. This is quite clear in 'If anyone breathes a word about it, I'm a dead duck.' Note also that sentences like 'If anyone says that (breathes a word about it, spills the beans), *he*'s a fool (a dead duck, finished around here)' are open to two readings, Anscombe's and also one on which 'he' refers to some contextually definite male (whose scandalous behaviour may be divulged). Note further that the use of an identifying proper name in apposition selects between these two readings in 'If anyone says that, *he*, Jack Jones, is a fool'. Of course, no such selection can occur in 'If anyone says that, I, Jerrold Katz, am a fool', since there is no reading on which the pronoun functions as a variable in the first place. Thus, Anscombe's case shows that 'I' does not function via an anaphoric link back to a quantified subject, but initiates reference on its own.

We turn now to Anscombe's argument that 'I' is not a referring expression. Her choice of cases is significant. As she herself says, the cases are

only those relating to actions, postures, movements, and intentions. Not, for example, such thoughts as 'have a head-ache', 'I am thinking about thinking', 'I see a variety of colours', ... My way is the opposite of Descartes's. These are the very propositions he would have considered, and the others were a difficulty for him. But what were most difficult for him are most easy for me.[33]

On Anscombe's view, the problem with Descartes's cases is that the 'identity of description' that can be given in objective situations to relate a first-person pronoun use to a description (e.g. 'the person E.A.') is 'entirely missing for, say, the thought "I see a variety of colours." ' Her point seems to be that, while 'the thought "I am standing" is verified by the fact that this person here is *standing*, falsified if she is not, the thought "I see a variety of colours" cannot be similarly verified because such thoughts are "far removed in their descriptions from the descriptions of the proceedings, etc., of a person in which they might be verified." ' My first objection to this line of argument is that, like Geach's, it

[32] Anscombe, 'The First Person'.   [33] Ibid. 63.

assumes that subjective uses of 'I' are derivative from objective ones, and, as we have seen, there is no reason to concede this. Indeed, there is no need even to accept the choice that Anscombe would force on us. Why do we have to proceed in what she calls 'Descartes's way' (taking the subjective cases as basic and the objective ones as derivative from them) or in her way (taking the objective cases as basic and the subjective ones as derivative from them)? It might be that neither case is basic, that both uses obtain their meaning from a common linguistic structure. This is to say that the meaning on which the reference of 'I' depends in both cases is the same. In sentences like 'I am thinking about thinking' and 'I am scratching my ear' the meaning of 'I' is 'agent of the action' and I am equally the agent of the action in thinking about thinking and in scratching my ear. If meaning is not equated with use, my report of these actions can be taken to express the meaning which the reporting sentences have in English.

My second objection is that Anscombe's argument could only convince the faithful, since the Cartesians clearly do not think that descriptions of the kind she has in mind play a role in verifying 'the very propositions he [Descartes] would have considered'. For Cartesians, a proposition like the one expressed by 'I see a variety of colours' is verified by the subjective fact that the agent of the mental act saw a variety of colours (and falsified if not). Descriptions of the kind Anscombe has in mind are unnecessary because we can make first-hand determinations of truth or falsehood on the basis of direct acquaintance with the subjective fact. Given the essential difference between subjective and objective facts, the Cartesian might well turn Anscombe's claim around and argue that what are most easy for them are most difficult for her. Hence, the Cartesian can claim a stand-off: there is a perfect parity of easy and difficult cases on both sides of the issue.

Anscombe seems to have taken steps to try to block such a Cartesian response by arguing that the occurrences of 'I' in the sentences in question are non-referring, and, hence, that there are no difficult cases for her. But her line of argument to establish non-reference is peculiar. The line of argument offers no grammatical reason to establish that the 'I' in these sentences is non-referring. Rather, she claims that taking 'I' to be referring is the first step down a slippery slope into a quagmire of 'self-perpetuating, endless, irresolvable' disputes. She argues as follows: if at all possible, we ought to avoid landing in such a quagmire; we can avoid doing so in the present case if 'I' is not taken to be a referring expression in the critical sentences; hence, we ought not to take it to be a referring expression in them. She says,

And this is the solution: 'I' is neither a name nor another kind of expression whose logical role is to make reference.[34]

Two comments about the argument: first, since it offers no grammatical reason for thinking 'I' is non-referring, there are no grammatical considerations that a rejoinder needs to overcome; second, her argument is what might be called a that-way-lies-madness warning, and as such, it is a sort of *reductio*. But, as a *reductio*, it is incomplete because it leaves open just the questions that a forceful *reductio* must close, namely, are there other ways of avoiding the undesirable situation?, are some of them preferable to the one advocated?, does the advocated way-out lead to its own quagmire?, is it as bad or worse?

With all these questions left open, the Cartesian can take a cynical view of Anscombe's quagmire: the 'self-perpetuating, endless, irresolvable' disputes are nothing more than philosophical business as usual and are not to be avoided by doing business on Anscombe's side of the street. The Cartesian can point out that each side in a philosophical controversy can make the same claim, that acceptance of its solution is a way of preventing the controversy from continuing. The materialist, idealist, and dualist can each claim to solve the mind–body problem in the narrow sense that general acceptance of their solution will put an end to the controversy. But, of course, putting an end to a controversy offers no assurance that the issue is properly resolved. Anscombe cannot even claim that her solution that 'I' does not refer stirs up no philosophical disputes and is trouble free. Her solution raises indefinitely many grammatical and philosophical problems: she herself presents one,[35] and I will present some of them now.

The problems are most naturally stated as arguments against the Lichtenberg view. The 'it' in (27) and in sentences like 'It's cold outside' or 'It's a long way to Tipperary', is what linguists call an 'expletive'. Expletives are dummy elements which occur in grammatical structures different from those in which the ordinary referential pronoun 'it' occurs. Accordingly, we can test the Lichtenberg view by comparing the behaviour of sentences with 'I' as subject with the behaviour of sentences with an expletive subject, or a genuinely referential subject. Take (29), for example.

(29) Bill is cold and it is cold.

The second clause of (29) can be read as saying either that some unspecified thing is cold or that it's cold out. But the ellipsed forms in (30) have only the referential reading.

---

[34] Anscombe, 'The First Person', 60.   [35] Ibid. 57–8; see *Cogitations*, p. 194 n. 18.

(30) Bill is cold and it is too.
      Bill is cold and so is it.

Ellipsed co-ordination only occurs when both subjects are referential or both are expletive. Now take (31). The ellipsed co-ordination shows that the subject of 'think' is referential.

(31) Virginia is thinking and I am too.
      Virginia is thinking and so am I.

For another grammatical example, note that a parenthetical qualification of the subject is possible in a referential case like (32), but not in an expletive one like (33).

(32) It is eager to feel cooler.

We can say (34) but not (35).

(33) It is easy to compose music.
(34) It, the polar bear you pointed out, is eager to feel cooler.
(35) It, the polar bear you pointed out, is easy to compose music.

The same possibility of parenthetical qualification exists in (36), as (37) shows.

(36) I am eager to feel cooler.
(37) I, the person you barred from the polar bear club, am eager to feel cooler.

Although these arguments count against the Lichtenberg view, they provide, in virtue of their being syntactic, only indirect evidence for the desired semantic analysis of 'I think.' Direct evidence for this semantic analysis would be given by cases where referentiality has to be assumed in order to account for semantic properties and relations. Referentiality must be assumed in the cse of (38) for us to account for the fact that (38) is contradictory when the pronoun is anaphoric to the noun 'Jones', e.g. when (38) is a continuation of the remark, 'No need to keep saying, "SHHH, Jones is thinking".——.'

(38) Sure, Jones is thinking, but he doesn't exist.

Another piece of direct evidence comes from comparing the two argument places of 'thinks'. We know that the recipient place of the predicate expressed by this verb is non-referential along with the recipient place of the predicates expressed by 'wants', 'hopes for', etc. Hence, there is nothing out of the ordinary about (39):

(39) Brentano often thinks about something non-existent.

But, switching the subject and object, we get (40), which is either a category mistake or contradictory.

(40) Something non-existent often thinks about Brentano.

Still other direct evidence comes from the redundancy of the clause 'who exists' in a sentence like (41) or (42).

(41) The politican who thought up such dirty tricks and who exists is even worse than Dick Nixon.
(42) The thinker of thoughts like those who is an existing thinker of such thoughts is surely Dick Nixon's equal.

As we see from the fact that the redundancy of an expression consists in the sense of its modifier being part of the sense of its head (e.g. 'naked nude'), the redundancy of sentences like (41) and (42) can only be accounted for if occupancy of the agent place within the sense of 'thinks' entails existence. Finally, there is the example of the slogan appearing on buttons worn by religious people: 'Who says God doesn't exist, I just talked to Him this morning.'

The use of the explanatory paradigm employed in these examples of direct evidence can be extended in two directions. The effect of doing so is to consolidate and strengthen the direct evidence for the *cogito* being an analytic entailment. One direction involves increasing the list of semantic properties and relations that are brought under the paradigm. The other direction involves increasing the generality of the principle about the referentiality of the agent place in question. The examples of analyticities and analytic entailments that have been shown to come under (*D*) already provide these extensions. These examples provide two more kinds of direct evidence for taking the occupancy of the agent place of 'thinks' to entail existence.

(43) Whatever thinks exists.

For, on this assumption, the semantic property of the sentence (44) and the semantic relation between the premiss sentences in (44*a*) and the corresponding conclusion sentences in (44*b*) are accounted for, and hence, along with the redundancy, semantic deviance, and contradictoriness, become direct evidence for the claim that the agent place in the sense of 'thinks' is referential.

(44) (*a*) I (he, she, they, Ronald Reagan . . .) is thinking.
(*b*) I (he, she, they, Ronald Reagan . . .) exists.

Having removed Lichtenberg's objection to the saying that the subject of

'I think' is referential, we have removed the last impediment to
accounting for the *cogito* as an analytic entailment. Thus we can claim to
have explained Descartes's inference in a way that both shows it to be
valid and also to be precisely the simple inference he thought it was.
Instead of having to be made to seem confused, Descartes emerges here as
an acutely perceptive philosopher who anticipated the distinction between
different kinds of formal truth and validity.

There are a number of questions about what has been accomplished in
showing the *cogito* to be an analytic entailment. I cannot go into all of
them, but two are particularly important. The first arises in the context of
the *petitio* criticisms which have long plagued the *cogito*: isn't the
argument circular since knowledge of the truth and certainty of 'I exist'
must already be available to know that 'I think' is true and certain? Now
my explanation of the *cogito* as an analytic entailment seems to make the
inference more vulnerable to the charge of circularity. Two aspects of the
explanation encourage the thought that I have made matters worse for
Descartes. First, on my explanation, the *cogito* is a purely explicative
inference. Second, on my explanation, there is no possibility of a defence
against the *petitio* criticism like that offered by Margaret Wilson,

this version of the *petitio* objection would cut against any valid deductive argument
whatsoever considered as a vehicle of inference.[36]

But, as an analytic entailment, the *cogito* is sharply separated from
logically valid deductive arguments generally. Only with the rejected
philosophy of logic, on which the *cogito* is a logical argument, is a defence
like Wilson's possible.

Yet the *petitio* is only apparent. For the criticism to hold, explicativity
must be equated with question begging. But they are very different things.
For one thing, explicativity is a purely grammatical matter, having to do
with the structure of senses, while question begging is, at least in part, a
pragmatic matter, having to do with what question is at issue in the
context, and with what standards are to be employed to judge arguments
addressing the point at issue.

Thus, we must look at the question at issue in the context where
Descartes introduces the *cogito*. In that context, the indubitability of 'I
think' is taken for granted and Descartes must argue for the indubitability
of 'I exist'. The standards are that the argument must be demon proof.
Now, the critic asks why Descartes must argue for the indubitability of the
'I exist' if he knows the 'I think' is indubitable and the sense of 'I think'
contains the sense of 'I exist'. The answer, I believe, is that it doesn't

[36] *Descartes*, p. 63.

follow from the fact that Descartes knows *explicitly* the indubitability of 'I think' and the fact that the sense of 'I think' contains the sense of 'I exist', that Descartes knows *explicitly* the indubitability of the 'I exist'. At best, it follows that Descartes knows it *tacitly*. The *cogito* is the vehicle by which he comes to have explicit knowledge of the sort that satisfies the standards. Therefore, the *cogito* begs no question because the question is how Descartes can establish explicit, demon proof knowledge of his existence.

There are two loose ends in my account. One is that some explanation is necessary for what blocks explicit knowledge of the 'I exist' prior to the inference. The other loose end is that some explanation is necessary for why the *cogito* meets the standard of being demon proof.

A decompositional theory of meaning is ideally suited to explaining what blocks explicit knowledge of 'I exist'. The theory's principal claim is that, over and above the familiar case of surface syntactic structure concealing logical form, there is the case of deep syntactic structure concealing semantic form. The claim of a decompositional semantic theory is that, typically, the syntactic simples of a language are semantically complex. Thus, what blocks Descartes from having explicit knowledge of his existence at the point where he knows explicitly what he is thinking is that the semantic structure of 'I think', in particular, the containment of the sense of 'I exist' in that structure, is masked by the syntactic simplicity of the verb 'I think'. The *existo* proposition is therefore not transparent on cursory inspection, and must be revealed by an intuition of analytic entailment. Hence, the absence of explicit knowledge of his existence prior to his act of intuition is another case of how grammatical form disguises inferential form.

Why is the *cogito* secure against the best efforts of the demon? A full answer would be quite long and complicated, but a short answer suggesting the basic reason for the special security of the *cogito* is feasible.[37] As Descartes observes, the demon can make trouble whenever an inference involves computation, that is, whenever operations are performed and information stored or retrieved. But, if the *cogito* is an analytic entailment rather than a logical inference, its conclusion is literally contained in the premiss. Hence, there is no computation, and no inferential gap requiring the application of laws of logic. Consequently, there is no foothold for the demon to use in trying to deceive Descartes.

The point may be sharpened by considering another famous deceiver of philosophical lore, Lewis Carroll's Tortoise.[38] Recall that, each time poor

---

[37] *Cogitations*, pp. 157–67, and *Supposable Worlds*.
[38] *Cogitations*, pp. 160–2.

Achilles writes down the premisses from which a desired mathematical conclusion follows and then proceeds to argue that if the Tortoise accepts the premisses written down, he must also accept the conclusion, the Tortoise, noting the application of the hypothetical, refuses to accept the conclusion until the hypothetical too is written down in Achilles's book. As will also be recalled, Achilles never gets to draw his desired conclusion, since each compliance creates a situation where a new piece of hypothetical reasoning is necessary. But, now, let us ring one change in this fable. Let us make the inference Achilles is trying to draw an analytic entailment rather than a logical implication. Let us take it to be the *cogito*. This change gives us a new fable, with a different, and for Achilles, happier ending:

'I'm to force you to accept the *existo*, am I? And your present position is that you accept the *cogitatio*, so that I may write the *cogitatio* down in my note-book?'
'Yes,' replied the Tortoise.
'In that case, force is unnecessary. For having written down the *cogitatio*, the *existo* is written down as well. Before when you asked what else I had written down in my notebook, I was in the embarrassing position of having nothing to report but memoranda of the battles in which I distinguished myself. But now I can say that I have the *existo* written down. Surely you won't balk at the fact that the *cogitatio* and the *existo* are written in markerese—which won't be invented for some two thousand years.'

The second important question to be considered was raised by Gareth Matthews.[39] He asks how the account of Descartes's *cogito, ergo sum* as an analytic entailment relates to the *cogito*-like reasoning in the meditations. Matthews observes that the term '*cogito*' is frequently used more broadly than I used it in *Cogitations*, to refer not only to the *cogito, ergo sum* but also to statements like (45).[40]

(45) *I am, I exist* is necessarily true each time I utter it or conceive it mentally.

I shall ignore the terminological question and try to answer Matthews's important question of how the two forms of Cartesian reasoning are related.

The first point to make about the relation is that, as Descartes's reply to Gassendi makes clear,[41] the verb 'think' is not unique in giving rise to

[39] G. Matthews, 'Thoughts on Jerrold Katz's *Cogitations*', Pacific American Philosophical Association meetings, San Francisco, symposium on Descartes, 26 Mar. 1987.
[40] Rightly or wrongly, in *Cogitations*, I took my cue from Frankfurt's remark that 'the passage [*The Philosophical Works of Descartes*, i. 150] consists of a number of different statements, and *none* of them is the *cogito*. The statement, *I think, therefore I am*, simply does not occur in the passage at all; and neither does any exactly equivalent statement. In fact, the *cogito* as such does not appear anywhere in the *Meditations* (H. Frankfurt, *Demons, Dreamers, and Madmen*, Indianapolis, 1970, 92).   [41] Ibid. ii. 137.

existential entailments: 'I exist' follows not only from 'I utter', 'I conceive', 'I am persuaded', etc., but also from 'I walk.' As I have argued in *Cogititations*,[42] the semantic fact is, roughly speaking, that action verbs generally have a sense in which the agent–place is referential. The second point to make is that, this being so, Descartes's remark in the *Second Meditation* '. . . if I persuaded myself of anything, I was' is essentially *cogito, ergo sum*. The third point is that Descartes's next remark '. . . if [a consummately powerful and crafty deceiver] deceives me, there is no doubt that I am' departs from the *cogito, ergo sum* by running the existential entailment off of a referential recipient-place. This is because the sense of 'deceive' is like that of 'murder' and unlike that of 'want' or 'imagine'.

(45), Descartes's 'final conclusion', differs even more from *cogito, ergo sum* than does 'if someone deceives me, I am'. In the case of (45), we no longer have two propositions one of which is said to follow from the other. Rather, we have a proposition or a sentence said to be necessarily true on every occasion when a certain condition is satisfied. (45) is thus like an instance of Tarski's schema (T) adjusted for modality and temporally restricted.

(T) 's' is true if, and only if, p.

The similarity may be highlighted by first writing (45) as (46)

(46) 'I exist at t' is true if, and only if, I exist at t.

and then noting that nothing significant changes if we replace the description of the truth-condition in (46) with another description that analytically entails the description in (46), as, for example, with (47).

(47) 'I exist at t' is true if, and only if, I utter something at t.

So, basically, the final conclusion is obtained from the fact that a sentence must be true when its truth-condition (in the Tarskian sense) is satisfied and the fact that a sentence's truth-condition must be satisfied when it is contained in a truth-condition that is satisfied.

[42] *Cogitations*, pp. 127–30.

PART III

THOUGHT AND TOUCH

8

THOUGHT AND TOUCH
A NOTE ON ARISTOTLE'S *DE ANIMA*

STANLEY ROSEN

Tangere enim et tangi, nisi corpus, nulla potest res.
Lucretius, i. 304

In the history of philosophy, it would be difficult to discover an effort to explain the nature of thought which does not make some fundamental analogy between the processes of thinking and sense-perception. This is as true in the case of 'metaphysicians', 'idealists', and 'mystics' as it is of 'materialists' or 'empiricists'.[1] Even where such an analogy is not explicitly made (if only to be subsequently revised in purely intellectual terms), it seems to be possible to infer it from the terms and concepts employed by whatever philosopher we may be considering. The capacity whereby 'thought thinks itself' without recourse to analogies, terms, and concepts drawn from sense-perception, seems to be restricted either to God or *noûs* (the god of the philosophers). Every human effort to transcend (whether partially or altogether) the body is conditioned, to one degree or another, by its corporeal beginning. This condition is exhibited in the fact that words or phrases employed both by philosophical and ordinary speech to designate the processes of thinking, are largely derived from the three senses of sight, hearing, and touch. We may notice two radical examples. (1) The man of faith *sees* manifestations or revelations of God; or he *hears* God's words, directly, or in the voices of prophets. (2) The man of *logic* is faithful to a procedure, the name of which is derived from *legein*: speech as the instrument of logic is related etymologically to 'collecting' or 'gathering together', the most obvious meaning of which is dependent upon the sense of touch. Thus Kant, for instance, in the *Critique of Pure Reason*, 'gathers together' the particulars made accessible through *Anschauung* and synthesizes them into wholes (and the relations

This chapter appeared originally in *Phronesis*, 6:2 (1961), 127–37. Used by permission.

[1] Whether 'metaphysics' means 'the things *after* the physical things' or 'the things *above* the physical things' (in other words, whether its origins are Greek or Christian), its subject-matter is only intelligible with reference to the physical or perceptible.

of wholes) by the interaction of *Anschauung* with the transcendental imagination. The Kantian 'gathering together', whereby the knowable world is 'made', would seem to be a mixture, or synthesis, of activities explicable primarily by seeing and touching. The categories must 'embrace' their schemata, they must 'touch' the particulars in order to subsume them, just as the particulars must be touched or embraced by the forms of space and time; on the other hand, the transcendental Ego must 'see' the particulars as they are grasped by the forms of perception, it must 'see' the subsumption or synthesis of particulars by categories, and it must 'see' the relationship between categories in the act of judgement.

Whatever the proper interpretation of Kant, it is fruitful to inquire whether one may generally differentiate philosophical analyses of thought according as they give precedence to one of the three senses of sight, hearing, or touch. One might then go on to determine the pervasive consequences of choosing one sense rather than another as of essential importance to an account of thinking. Among the great Greek philosophers, it seems at first glance that, in terms of this criterion, they divide into two camps; first, the empiricists, materialists, and scientists, for whom touch predominates, and the 'metaphysicians' (a word which must be enclosed in quotation marks when applied to the classical Greeks), for whom sight is of primary importance. Of course, any effort consistently to employ this initial distinction, without further qualifications, would soon lead to failure perhaps in every case. Is not geometry, for example, a mode of *theoria*, and so an analogue of sight? Granted that the atomists explain thought as a material (and so, in principle, *tangible*) process, do they not also differentiate atoms in terms of their shapes or forms (and so, in principle, of their *visual* properties)? The enterprise makes sense so long as we attempt to ascertain, not which sense is *exclusively* employed as the example from which thought is expounded, but which sense *predominates* (explicitly or implicitly). The demonstration of such a predominance, furthermore, must be complex and concrete in each individual case, and can seldom if ever be concluded merely through a superficial collection of the terms that each philosopher employs. To mention only one obvious difficulty, a philosopher may employ, at various places, *different* terms, now drawn from one sense, now from another. It would be careless, to say the least, to assume that the sense to which he refers most frequently is necessarily the one which plays the most fundamental role in his philosophy. We must in each case analyse thoroughly the total doctrine concerning thought, presented by the author, in order to find what we are looking for: which of the senses he tends to use as the paradigm for the structure and function of thinking, and the broader consequences of this tendency for his general conception of the structure of reality.

In the following remarks about Aristotle, no claim to such a complete analysis is made or intended. I hope to show just this much: the *De Anima*, which contains Aristotle's fullest account of the process of thinking (as distinct from the objects, or the results, of thought, or from the logical rules whereby that process is governed), rests fundamentally upon an analogy between thought and touch. Contrary to the impression given by the opening lines of the *Metaphysics*, Aristotle rejects the Platonic interpretation of thinking as a kind of seeing. This rejection is inseparable from Aristotle's conception of *ta onta*, the 'beings' or things about which one thinks, and it underlies Aristotle's critical revision of Plato's theory of *eidē*. By identifying the *eidos* or *idea* of a thing with its individual, finite form, Aristotle makes it possible for the mind, in thinking, to grasp the being or essence of a thing, and so he makes possible the *accomplishment*, and not just the pursuit, of wisdom or certitude, a step which he does not himself clearly or unambiguously take, but for which he at least lays the foundation.[2] I hope to show that the way in which Aristotle develops his account of thinking, although it is intended to refute the contention presented by Socrates in the Platonic dialogues that the *psychē* (i.e. fundamentally the noetic aspect of the *psychē*) cannot distinctly grasp itself, *actually supports that Socratic contention*. Indirectly, I believe one may suggest that, if the Aristotelian rejection of the importance given to sight by Plato and his own subsequent analogy between thought and touch, is inadequate, then so, too, is his rejection of the Platonic theory of *ideai*.[3] In any case the following remarks are offered as partial support of such claims. They do not pretend to exhaust the

[2] In the *Metaphysics*, Aristotle defines σοφία as αὐτὴν τῶν πρώτων ἀρχῶν καὶ αἰτιῶν εἶναι θεωρητικήν (982ᵇ8) and then proceeds to explain these principles and causes. On the other hand, he is unclear as to whether God alone is wise, or chiefly wise (983ᵃ10). See also 1028ᵇ3: the question τι το ον was, is, and always will be, baffling to us. The step toward wisdom is unambiguously extended in modern philosophy by Descartes, for example, whose clear and distinct ideas are more Aristotelian than Platonic, as the 'stuff', immanent in thought (and 'grasped' from the study of extension through the procedures of mathematical physics), from which the intelligible world is constructed. The initial Aristotelian step was completed, however, not by Descartes but by Hegel (at least such is Hegel's claim).

[3] For Aristotle, the form must also be somehow separate from the concrete thing, since *eidos* is generically *different* from matter, whereas all generated things, natural and artificial, are composites of matter and form. Ungenerated or eternal entities, as pure form, are virtually equivalent to *ideai* (it is hard to say that, for Aristotle, they possess intelligible forms). See *Metaphysics*, 1034ᵃ33 ff. The form is *prior* to the individual precisely *because* that which generates is capable of producing an individual, whose form is the same as that of its generator: the form of the individual exists prior to the individual itself (this is stated explicitly at 1034ᵇ11 ff.). In other words, actuality as *eidos* is prior to potentiality or matter (1049ᵇ4 ff.). See also 1050ᵃ15: ἔτι ἡ ὕλη ἔστι δυνάμει, ὅτι ἔλθοι ἂν εἰς τὸ εἶδος ὅταν δὲ γε ἐνεργείᾳ ἦ,

riches of the *De Anima*, let alone to do justice to the entire Aristotelian conception of thought.

One of the fundamental problems in philosophy is whether man *sees* or *touches*, reality as it is, or whether he *makes* the objects which he sees and touches, or decisively forms them in the process of perceiving them. But we can neither see clearly *nor* make well the things or beings (*ta onta*) of the world, and the world itself as the order of its things (*kosmos*), unless we see (or touch) the relationship between things seen–touched and made on the one hand, and that which see–touches and makes on the other. Even if seeing–touching *is* essentially making, there is a fundamental sense in which we must first *see* or *theorein* before we can *make* or do (*prattein*); we must first 'see' even in order to determine whether *theoria* is ultimately touching. And that which we must see, that within which our questions are illuminated, if not answered, is the *psychē*. Things and world emerge within the perspectives illuminated by the *psychē* because ἡ ψυχὴ τὰ ὄντα πώς ἐστιν.[4] *Somehow* the *psychē* is the things which are; somehow it must itself be seen and thought as it is: we must somehow grasp it directly as it itself grasps the things which are. We can grasp the *psychē* only if it can somehow grasp itself. The *psychē* can grasp itself only if it can somehow stand before itself as a visible (or tangible) *entity*. Entities are visible (or tangible) because they have delineated edges which distinguish them from other entities. Aristotle does not explain (as does Kant, for example) how the entity is *unified*, or transformed from a succession of multiplicities into a unity. Just as does Plato with his *ideai*, Aristotle begins with entities whose unity is already expressed by the delineation or definition which he calls a form (*eidos*).[5] The form renders

---

τότε ἐν τῷ εἴδει ἐστίν. For Aristotle, forms (except those of eternal unmoved movers) are general *qua* identical throughout a species, and particular *qua* actual only within perishable individuals.

[4] *De Anima*, 431[b]21.

[5] See *Metaphysics*, 1037[b]11: διὰ τί ποτε ἕν ἐστιν οὗ τὸν λόγον ὁρισμὸν εἶναι. . His answer seems to be (1037[b]25): ὁ γὰρ ὁρισμὸς λόγος τίς ἐστιν εἰς καὶ οὐσίας, ὥστε ἑνός τινος δεῖ αὐτὸν εἶναι λόγον. But this does not tell us *how* an individual *is* a unity. See also 1038[b]10 ff.: if an individual substance had parts, these parts would be prior to it. But substance is prior to everything else. On the other hand, a substance, as a form, or as a concrete unity of form and matter, *does* have 'elements'; otherwise, it would be absolutely One, and so ungraspable (cp. 1039[a]15 ff., 1040[b]16 ff.). The question remains: how do these 'elements' constitute a unity? For Aristotle, this is not a real question, since it means merely to ask, 'why is a thing itself?' (since τὸ ὂν and τὸ ἐν are the same): 1041[a]14. Or else, the answer is merely 'because it has such and such a form' (1041[b]9 ff.). Cp. also 1045[a]14 ff. and 1052[a] ff. In general, one may conjecture that, for Aristotle, to speak of a 'synthesis' of mutiplicities into unity is to suggest that reality, or Being, is not given as intelligible in itself (i.e. as distinguishable into forms), but that man somehow *makes* forms, and so reality itself. Kant is led to posit such syntheses because he rejects Aristotle's claim that the *psychē* becomes the form of the entity: for Kant, the form of the entity is a determination of the Ego.

the thing *actual* by bringing or grasping it from the potentiality of matter, and the actuality of a thing is its *logos*, i.e. its exposition or explanation: ἔτι τοῦ δυνάμει ὄντος λόγος ἡ ἐντελέχεια.[6] The bringing forward or setting up of the thing from potentiality to actuality in the grasp of its form is directly analogous to the way in which the *psyche* grasps the thing through the two functions of sensation (*aisthēsis*) and thought (*noēsis*):

ἀπαθὲς ἄρα δεῖ [sc. τὸ νοεῖν] εἶναι δεκτικὸν δὲ τοῦ εἴδους καὶ δυνάμει τοιοῦτον ἀλλὰ μὴ τοῦτο καὶ ὁμοίως ἔχειν, ὥσπερ τὸ αἰσθητικὸν πρὸς τὰ αἰσθητά, οὕτω τὸν νοῦν πρὸς τὰ νοητά.[7]

The *logos* of thinking results from the grasping by *noûs* of the *eidos* of the entity, just as the perception of a thing grasps its *eidos* in a material imprint, as the signet is imprinted on to wax.[8] The sense somehow becomes identical with the sensed; in sensation, the object is assimilated to the sensing *psyche* and is thus identical in quality with it.[9] So, too, the noetic *psyche* becomes identical in thinking with the thing thought: ὅλως δὲ ὁ νοῦς ἐστιν ὁ κατ' ἐνέργειαν τὰ πράγματα.[10]

This identification presumes the accessibility of *ta pragmata* or *ta onta* to the sensitive (aesthetic) and noetic modes of the *psyche* in the same sense that, in ordinary experience, things are accessible to our sight and touch. Aristotle makes precisely this assumption. Simple sensation and *noēsis* cannot err; error is always in the realm of synthesis.[11] The *psyche*, as aesthetic and noetic, is so formed as directly to grasp the things or *ousiai* in the world. That is, it grasps them as *objects* delineated by *forms*, it grasps them directly in their essential unity, their 'whatness', their τὸ τί ἦν εἶναι.[12] Thus Aristotle, in a passage of central importance, compares the mind (i.e. the noetic *psyche*) to the hand: καὶ γὰρ ἡ χεὶρ ὄργανόν ἐστιν ὀργάνων, καὶ ὁ νοῦς εἶδος εἰδῶν καὶ ἡ αἴσθησις εἶδος αἰσθητῶν.[13] By conceiving of thought as analogous to perception, Aristotle is led to define thinking by analogy from *touch*, the most fundamental of our senses, the sense which defines life itself.[14] It is the

---

[6] *De Anima*, 415ᵇ14.   [7] Ibid. 429ᵃ15.   [8] Ibid. 424ᵃ17.
[9] Ibid. 424ᵃ1 ff., 418ᵃ3.   [10] Ibid. 431ᵇ17; cp. 430ᵃ19, 431ᵇ26 ff., etc.
[11] Ibid. 418ᵃ15, 418ᵃ24, 430ᵃ26, 430ᵇ1, 430ᵇ28: these difficult passages can only be alluded to here. Consider 432ᵃ9: συμπλοκὴ γὰρ νοημάτων ἐστὶ τὸ ἀληθές ἢ ψεῦδος. It would seem then that an individual *noēma* cannot be either true or false: i.e. it is just given or *existent*. Cp. *Metaphysics*, 1010ᵇ1 ff., for a distinction between the *aisthēsis*, which cannot be false, and the *phantasia*, or impression of an *aisthēsis* (which is not the same as the latter). See also n. 5 above: for Aristotle, beings are accessible to man prior to synthesis, and are not 'made' by synthesis.   [12] *De Anima*, 430ᵇ28.   [13] Ibid. 432ᵃ1.
[14] Ibid. 435ᵇ16: ταύτῃ δὲ ὥρισται τὸ ζῷον· ἄνευ γὰρ ἁφῆς δέδεικται ὅτι ἀδύνατον εἶναι ζῷον.

character of the sense of *touch* which determines whether a man will have a good or bad mental nature.[15] Touch alone of all the senses perceives by immediate contact.[16] Despite the opening lines of the *Metaphysics*, then, it is not sight, but touch, which is the most philosophical of the senses, because touch is prior to, more general, and more intimately related to *ta pragmata* than sight.[17] 'Seeing' is just a kind of *touching*. We grasp the forms of the things which are, and thereby know them: touch is the differentiation of forms which is the necessary condition for knowing. Knowing is touching.

Just as the physical hand can touch only concrete individuals (formal delimitations of extension), so, too, with the mental 'hand'. In discussing the difference between *aisthēsis* and *epistēmē*, Aristotle says: τῶν καθ' ἕκαστον ἡ κατ' ἐνέργειαν αἴσθησις, ἡ δ' ἐπιστήμη τῶν καθόλου· ταῦτα δ' ἐν αὐτῇ πώς ἐστι τῇ ψυχῇ.[18] The universal is somehow (*pōs*) in the *psychē*: i.e. it is somehow grasped from the individual entities grasped somehow from potentiality by the actuality of their forms. We note in passing that Aristotle has now introduced three distinct (though analogous) and unexplained 'graspings' in his account of thought. The point here at issue is that the account of thought is inseparable from Aristotle's conception of Being itself, of the *way* in which things are. Things are touchable; i.e. they are discriminable through aesthetic–noetic touch, which is presumably, *qua* touching, an 'identification' in both the literal and figurative senses. Through touch, the *psychē* identifies things by becoming identical *with* them. The 'touch' which identifies the universal is derivative from the 'touch' which identifies *with* the particular. That is, Being is particular, ἐπεὶ δὲ οὐδὲ πρᾶγμα οὐθὲν ἔστι παρὰ τὰ μεγέθη, ὡς δοκεῖ, τὰ αἰσθητὰ κεχωρισμένον, . . .[19] That which *is*, is primarily an *ousia*,[20] i.e. an extended sensible object.[21] For this

[15] *De Anima*, 421ª20 ff.

[16] Ibid. 435ª17: ἡ δ' ἁφὴ τῷ αὐτῶν ἅπτεσθαί ἐστιν, διὸ καὶ τοὔνομα τοῦτο ἔχει.

[17] Cp. *Metaphysics*, 980ª21–7. The more revealing formulation is to be found at *Metaphyics*, 1072ᵇ20 ff: '*noûs* thinks itself through sharing the thing thought; for, touching and thinking it, it becomes the object, so that *nous* and *noēton* are the same.' The mind *grasps* rather than sees; thus the identity of mind and thing, which is not present in Plato. It is this identity which makes possible wisdom or certitude (and the further possibility of transforming reality). Touch perceives by immediate contact, whereas there is a distance between sight and thing seen. For Plato's view that philosophy begins with sight, see, among other passages, *Timaeus*, 47 A–B. One should also consider *Metaphysics*, 1063ª14, for the function of the heavens in regulating philosophical discourse: it may well be to repeat that my intention is not to claim that sight was of no importance for Aristotle; that would indeed be absurd.

[18] *De Anima*, 417ᵇ22.   [19] Ibid. 432ª3.   [20] Ibid. 415ᵇ12; cp. 410ª11.

[21] At *Metaphysics*, 985ᵇ25, he says that incorporeal beings exist. The subsequent discussion shows him to be thinking of mathematical objects. And from 1071ᵇ3 ff., we learn that *noûs* and the unmoved movers are immaterial substances (*ousiai*). Mathematical objects, however, are not *ousiai* (e.g. 100ᵇ2, 1076ª ff., 1080ª13 ff., 1087ª ff., etc.), whereas it is doubtful whether we

reason, thinking is impossible without sense-perception, and that which is thought *is* (primarily) that which is perceived: ἐν τοῖς εἴδεσι τοῖς αἰσθητοῖς τὰ νοητά ἐστι, τά τε ἐν ἀφαιρέσει λεγόμενα καὶ ὅσα τῶν αἰσθητῶν ἕξεις καὶ πάθη.[22] More strictly: not only is thinking dependent upon sensation, but when one actively thinks, one necessarily does so with an accompanying *image*: καὶ διὰ τοῦτο οὔτε μὴ αἰσθανόμενος μηθὲν οὐθὲν ἂν μάθοι οὐδὲ ξυνείη, ὅταν τε θεωρῇ, ἀνάγκη ἅμα φάντασμά τι θεωρεῖν.[23] In slightly different words: the *psychē* never thinks without an image, which serves *as if* it were a perception.[24]

If, then, the *psychē* is to grasp itself directly, it must be primarily *imaginable*: i.e. it must have an *eidos*, and therefore it must be perceptible. It must be material: an entity or *ousia*. As such, it must be *actual*, an *entelecheia* having a *logos* which expresses its τὸ τί ἦν εἶναι. But by Aristotle's own account, and despite his assurance that *nous* is thinkable in the same way that its objects are,[25] none of this is possible. The impossibility of grasping the *psychē* (i.e. the noetic mode, which is the crucial one) stems from the impossibility of touching its *eidos*. The *psychē* is unable to identify with its *eidos*, not because it already *is* its *eidos*, but because, except in a vague and metaphorical sense, *it has no eidos*. The non-eidetic character of the *psychē* may be specified as follows. Assuming that the *psychē* is the *eidos eidōm*, this *eidos* will depend in fact upon the power of the *psychē* to identify with, i.e. to *be*, each *eidos*; but Aristotle's exposition does not, as we shall see, allow us to accept this hypothesis. More fundamentally, however, it follows from Aristotle's account that *the psychē is not*, except when it is *not* itself.[26] Consider again the analogy between the mind and the hand. The hand, in grasping the object, may be said to *hold* it, not to *become* it. The hand 'discerns' the form of the held object precisely by retaining intact its own form, and so by continuing to exist independently of, delimited from, what it holds.

---

actually grasp the unmoved movers into thought. Furthermore, at *Metaphyics*, 1017^{b2}4, Aristotle so defines *ousia* as to apply to *eidos*: namely, an independent thing (τόδε); and *eidoi* are immaterial (generically different from matter: 1024^{b}10 ff.). But, at 1033^{b}20, in speaking of created things, he says unqualifiedly that an *eidos* is *not* a τόδε, but a τοιόνδε (i.e. 'of such a kind'—a characteristic). The definitive discussion of the kinds of *ousiai* occurs in Book 12 (1069^{a}30 ff.): these kinds are (1) sensible (*a*) eternal (heavenly bodies), (*b*) perishable (natural physical things); (2) immutable (insensible), i.e. the unmoved movers and *noûs*.

[22] *De Anima*, 432^{a}3 ff.   [23] Ibid.
[24] Ibid. 431^{a}14 ff., 431^{b}2. For the definition of *phantasia* as a movement ὑπὸ τῆς αἰσθήσεως τῆς κατ' ἐνέργειαν γιγνομένη, see 429^{a}1.   [25] Ibid. 430^{a}2 ff.
[26] Compare the Hegelian conception whereby man's mode of existence is 'not to be that which he is' and to become 'that which he is not'. But man (i.e. *psychē*) has as his form the sum of *becomings* which constitutes the actualization of *Geist*. See *Phenomenology of Mind* (Hamburg, 1969), 32.

In the case of thinking, the 'holding' or 'touching' of the *eidos* cannot be a unity. Aristotle says: οὐ γὰϱ ὁ λίθος ἐν τῇ ψυχῇ, ἀλλὰ τὸ εἶδος.[27] But if the *eidos* of the stone is being held in the mind in a way analogous to the holding of the stone in the hand, then the *eidos* cannot at the same time be in the stone. Mental grasping is exclusively *formal*: the stone incarnate is not in the mind. Mental grasping must then be an abstracting of the form from the stone, a taking away from the stone of its form, which is held in the mind (by hypothesis) as the hand holds the stone. If, however, the form and matter in the stone are sundered, then the stone is destroyed: the act of knowing is then identical with the act of destruction, which is absurd. To mention only one consequence, unnecessary though it may be, if knowing were destroying, then the same thing could not be known again, nor at once by several persons. It is clear that this alternative need not be pursued. If the form in the mind merely *imitates* (e.g. 'photographs') the form in the stone, then it is wrong, and even senseless, to say, as does Aristotle constantly, that mind and thing are formally identical in active knowing. If they *were* identical the stone *would* be in the mind; if they are not identical, then the mind has a form of its own (just as the hand does), which it *holds on to* while somehow 'holding' what it knows. This separate, enduring form would then be separately knowable, at least, if not directly to itself, then to another mind seeking to know it. But this is merely to admit that the mind cannot think or grasp itself because it is already itself. The consequences of Aristotle's account are radically more obscure. For Aristotle has in effect denied that the mind has a separate, enduring form of its own. That which has a form, *is* in actuality; it is not mind, however, but the individual man who persists actually as an *ousia*. The mind is not the man, it is not the body, it is not *a* body. It moves from potentiality into actuality by *somehow grasping another* individual form. Since it is actualized by the form of another, it is not actually itself a form. It comes from *nothing*, somehow through the instrumentality of the body (with which it is not identical), and becomes somehow something not itself. *It is not, except when it is not itself*.

What is it? It is somehow *ta pragmata*, *ta onta*.[28] The mind (and so the *psychē*) must be grasped from among *ta onta*: it must be abstracted from

---

[27] *De Anima*, 431[b]26.

[28] At *Metaphysics*, 1032[a]32, Aristotle says: 'ἀπὸ τέχνης δε γιγνεται οσων το ειδος εν τη ψυχη. If the form of a created thing is *in* the *psychē* then (1) it is separate from the thing made, in just the way which Aristotle blames Plato for maintaining; (2) in knowing or thinking some created *x*, the *psychē* does not grasp the form of *x*, but rather thinks itself *as* the other; i.e. it thinks an aspect of itself, but not itself as a single form. Is there, finally, a radical difference between thinking natural and artificial objects? Must we revise *De Anima*, 431[b]20, so that, in thinking *natural* things, the *psychē* is somehow *ta onta*, whereas, with respect to artificial things, *ta onta* are somehow the *psychē*?

the things which it sees. To see itself directly, it would have to be entirely other than it is. What *is* it? It *is* that which is other than it is. To see itself, it would have to be *that which is in itself*. It would have to be an *on* or *pragma*, an *ousia* in the primary sense of the term. Thus, the *psychē* is bound into the multiplicity of its objects; it is bound by multiplicity as well as unity. Its unlimited power of self-transformation[29] depends upon the *other*, just as the power to transform *itself* depends upon its unity (in some sense of the word). Self and other, the one and the many, unity and succession: these are the self-differentiation of the *psychē*. Not merely, then, does the *psychē* not think itself, *qua* itself, but it does not know *how* to think itself, and consequently, it does not know *whether* it ever thinks itself. For how could the *psychē*, which thinks by becoming an entity or determinate form, even know what it would be like to think pure or *indeterminate* form? Precisely then if the *psychē* is itself formally indeterminate, it cannot think itself, since to do so would be to determine the indeterminate.

I conclude that (1) Aristotle has not established his analogy between thinking and touching; (2) his treatment of the noetic *psychē* leads to the Platonic doctrine of the incapacity of the *psychē* to see itself directly. The indeterminability of the indeterminate leads to the question of how, if the *psychē* exists, we can conceive it as a finite single entity. Can the *psychē* see its finite existence in the recognition of other *psychai*? But in what sense can it have even an indirect recognition of another *psychē*? In no determinate sense, as we have already seen. Furthermore, the *psychē* cannot infer its finitude (i.e. its *form* or boundary) from the unlimited sequence of determinate stages in its career of 'being' *ta onta*. Neither can the *psychē* define itself by conceiving of its death or non-existence, for it cannot become the form of that which is not, and so which has no form.[30] There remains (within the boundaries of philosophy) just one more possibility; the *psychē* infers its finitude (its form) from the *indirect* evidence of the existence of other *psychai*. The multiplicity of finite

---

[29] *De Anima*, 429ᵃ18: παντα νοει [sc. ο νους] . . .

[30] Aristotle avoids deriving the *psychē* from 'nothing' in the Heideggerian sense, in so far as potentiality must inhere in a prior actuality. The definition of the *psychē* can only be derived, as we are now arguing, from a consideration of the actuality within which the *psychē* emerges. Nevertheless, in so far as the *psychē* has no form of its own, it remains even for Aristotle an ambiguous mixture of 'something' and 'nothing'. Cp. Plato, *Sophist*, 240 E 1 ff., for a discussion of the co-presence of Being and non-Being, in the structure of the Whole. Aristotle's *psychē* 'is' (potentially) *everything*, i.e. the form of the Whole. The Hegelian conception of *Geist* may be regarded as (by intention) the *completion*, or complete actualization of, Aristotle's *psychē*, which is itself a version of the Socratic–Platonic conception. Hegel reconciles the distinction between (living) finite *psychē* and world-soul or *nous* by the *Aufhebung* of the former into the latter. Compare Aristotle's doctrine of immortality as the absorption of the individual into the world-soul.

psychai constitutes a community or *polis*, a class of indirect traces (of the *psychē*) having a common structure which mirrors the structure of the *psychē*. And just as there is a multiplicity of citizens within the *polis*, so too is there a multiplicity of *poleis*. The multiplicity of citizens (or of *poleis*) is the public, i.e. visible, presentation of the invisible *psychai*. Man is a *zōion logon exon* because he is a *zōion politikon*. The structure of the city casts light on the functions and powers of the citizens, and vice versa. The city is the *psychē* writ large. Thus the Socratic conception of the philosophical significance of political experience: we wish to see the *psychē* because it is the place within which the conditions of visibility themselves become visible. But our eyesight is not keen enough to see the *psychē* itself; we cannot determine the indeterminable.[31] We turn therefore toward the city, within which the *psychē* becomes visible. The articulated structure of the city, the structure which both differentiates and integrates the possible modes of experience, is the mirror-image of the *psychē*. Thus the attempt to touch the *psychē* is transformed into an attempt to see it.

---

[31] See Xenophon, *Memorabilia*, 10.3 ff., where Socrates discusses with a painter how the *eidos* of the *psychē* as mirrored in the body may be imitated. But this one aspect of political existence, upon which both the states of the *psychē*, and the skills of the painter, depend. In other words, it would be short-sighted and misleading to think of art as the medium through which the *psychē* is imitated, without thinking of the political context of art.

9

MATHEMATICAL INTUITION

CHARLES PARSONS

In a much quoted passage, Gödel writes:

> But, despite their remoteness from sense-experience, we do have something like a perception of the objects of set theory, as is seen from the fact that the axioms force themselves upon us as being true. I don't see any reason why we should have less confidence in this kind of perception, i.e. in mathematical intuition, than in sense-perception.[1]

If we leave aside its specific reference to set theory, the passage is a classic expression of what might be called the philosophical conception of mathematical intuition. As I see it, the principal mark of this conception is an analogy between sense-perception as a cognitive relation to the physical world, and 'something like a perception' giving a similar relation to mathematical objects, and perhaps other abstract entities. If it is to be central to the philosophy of mathematics, it should play a role like that of sense-perception in our knowledge of the everyday world and of physics.

My aim in this paper is to begin a reasoned explication of this conception. I shall argue that something answering to it does in fact exist. However, this positive result is very limited in scope, and we shall already see some limitations of the conception. Unlike Gödel, I shall not focus on set theory, where the conception of intuition has special difficulties, which I have discussed elsewhere.[2] One is more likely to make progress by concentrating on the simplest case, such as elementary geometry or arithmetic. I shall concentrate on the latter, but look at it from a somewhat geometric point of view.

I

When Gödel speaks of something like a perception *of* the objects of set

[1] 'What is Cantor's continuum problem?', in P. Benacerraf and H. Putnam (eds.), *Philosophy of Mathematics: Selected Readings* (Englewood Cliffs, NJ, 1964), 271. This passage and others cited below are from a supplement added to this edn. of the paper, which first appeared in 1947.

[2] 'What is the Iterative Conception of Set?', in R. E. Butts and J. Hintikka (eds.), *Logic, Foundations of Mathematics, and Computability Theory* (Dordrecht, 1977), at 339–45.

theory, he expresses something central to the conception I am examining: mathematical intuition has a certain *de re* character; it involves a relation of a person to (presumably mathematical) *objects*. The vocabulary of sense-perception contains locutions expressing relations to physical objects or events: *a* sees *x*, *a* hears *x*, *a* smells *x*, *a* perceives *x*, etc. Just how literally this is to be carried over into the concept of mathematical intuition is one of the trickiest questions about it.

For some perceptual verbs, notably 'see' and 'perceive', we can contrast such object-relational uses with uses with sentence complements, which we can call propositional attitude uses. Which type of use is more fundamental has been controversial, but the *existence* of the object-relational uses is obvious. The matter is otherwise with mathematical intuition, and philosophers have not expressed themselves very clearly on the point. However, we can find both kinds of use in the philosophical literature.[3] To abbreviate reference to the object-relational or propositional attitude use of 'intuit', I shall talk of intuition *of* and intuition *that*.

We find some unclarity already in the above-cited passage of Gödel: that there is 'something like a perception of the objects of set theory' is, he says, 'seen from the fact that the axioms force themselves on us as being true'. Here he seems to conclude from the evident character of certain *statements*, which we might express as intuitions *that*, to the existence of intuitions *of*. The premiss may be disputed, but even if it is granted the *inference* seems to be a *non sequitur*. What Gödel says in the next paragraph by way of explanation (and probably qualification) is quite obscure.

Intuition *that* is of course a very traditional rationalistic theme. It might be taken to subsume almost any conception of the evidence or self-evidence of truths of reason, where this is taken not to be derived from habit, practice, or convention. Just for this reason, the analogy with perception does not enter the picture until it is used for an *account* of such rational evidence, or perhaps to mark clearly the distinction between a proposition's being genuinely evident and its merely seeming obviously true. At this point the analogy is likely to be developed in the direction of intuition *of*, simply because the presence of an object is so central to perception.

I suggest that we can find such a picture in Descartes, for whom *clear and distinct perception* is certainly mainly a propositional attitude.[4] Two

---

[3] The relevance of the distinction to mathematical intuition is pointed out by Mark Steiner in *Mathematical Knowledge* (Ithaca, NY, 1975), 131. Steiner maintains that no one would defend object-relational mathematical intuition. That seems to me clearly false.

[4] Descartes seems to rely on perception of in his explanations, e.g. the explanation of clarity in *Principles*, i. 40.

important philosophers of the past who seem more directly committed to intuition *of* where the objects involved may be mathematical are Kant and Husserl. In Kant, intuition as a propositional attitude plays no explicit role. By definition, an intuition is a singular representation, that is a representation of a single object.[5] When Kant in the *Critique of Pure Reason* says that it is through intuition that knowledge has 'immediate relation' to objects ($A19 = B33$), this immediacy seems to be a direct presence of the object to the mind, as in perception. At all events, intuition gives 'immediate evidence' to propositions of, for example, geometry.[6] Thus intuition that seems to be present in Kant, although his official use of 'intuition' is only for intuition of.

Husserl's discussions of 'categorial intuition' in the *Logische Unter-suchungen* and of 'intuition of essences' in the *Ideen* represent a sustained and interesting attempt to develop a theory of rational evidence based on an analogy with perception, in which the feature of perception as being of an object is central. Husserl understands rational evidence in general as intuition and undertakes to give a unified account of intuition of and intuition that.

Both Kant's and Husserl's conceptions have had some influence on discussions of the foundations of mathematics in this century. Kant's influence is more visible and pervasive. Hilbert's conception of the intuitive character of finitary mathematics is explicitly based on a Kantian conception of pure intuition, though perhaps more on Kant's theory of geometry than on his theory of arithmetic. Intuitionism also owes much to Kant, particularly to the notion of time as the form of inner sense. Husserl's ideas have not had nearly so much influence, but he did have an impact on Weyl and Gödel.[7]

---

[5] *Logic*, §1 (Academy edn., ix. 91).

[6] My interpretation of the immediacy of intuition in relation to *objects* is controversial. See my 'Kant's Philosophy of Arithmetic', in S. Morgenbesser, P. Suppes, and M. White (eds.), *Philosophy, Science and Method: Essays in Honor of Ernest Nagel* (New York, 1969), esp. 569–71, and J. Hintikka, 'Kantian Intuitions', *Inquiry*, 15 (1972), 341–5. However, I do not see how there could be controversy about the fact that according to Kant intuition (in particular a priori intuition) confers *evidence* that is immediate. *This* immediacy can surely not be reduced to singularity, as Hintikka proposes for the other dimension of immediacy.

[7] Concerning Hilbert, Gödel writes, 'What Hilbert means by "Anschauung" is substantially Kant's space–time intuition confined, however, to configurations of a finite number of discrete objects.' From n. (h) added to 'On an Extension of Finitary Mathematics Which Has Not Yet Been Used', unpubl. Engl. transl., emended by the author with some additional notes, of 'Ueber eine noch nicht benützte Erweiterung des finiten Standpunktes', *Dialectica*, 12 (1958), 280–7. As if to stress the difference with the notion of intuition in 'What is Cantor's Continuum Problem?' the term 'Anschauung' is translated as 'concrete intuition'. The aspect of intuitionism which was most original and may have proved most fruitful, seeing the meaning of a mathematical statement as constituted by what would be a proof of it, does not seem to owe its inspiration to Kant. In recent discussions of the foundations of intuitionism, the very concept of intuition seems to drop out.

II

The idea of 'something like a perception' of mathematical objects seems at first sight outrageous. If mathematical objects are given to us in a way similar to that in which physical objects are given to our senses, should it not be *obvious* that this is so? But the history of philosophical discussion about mathematics shows that it is not. Whatever mysteries and philosophical puzzles there may be about perception, it works to a large extent as a straightforward empirical concept. We can make a lot of assured judgements about when we perceive something, and confidence about the description of our experience can often survive doubt about what it is an experience of. Thus the proposition that I now *see* before me a typewriter with paper in it is one that I expect that no other philosopher, were he in this room now, would dispute except on the basis of sceptical arguments, and many of these would not touch weaker statements such as that it *looks* to me as if I see these things. There is a phenomenological datum here that is as close to being undisputed as anything is in philosophy.

It is hard to maintain that the case is the same for mathematical objects. Is it *obvious* that there is an experience of intuiting the number 7, or a triangle, or at least of its 'looking' as if I were intuiting 7 or a triangle? Are there any experiences we can appeal to here that are anywhere near as undisputed as my present experience of seeing my typewriter? If we don't know what to point to, isn't that already a serious disanalogy between sense-perception and whatever consciousness we have of mathematical objects?

This embarrassment is connected with an obvious disanalogy. In normal cases of perception, there is a physical action of the object perceived on our sense-organs. Our perception is as it were founded on this action, and there are serious philosophical reasons for holding that such a causal relation is a necessary condition for perceiving an object.[8] It would be implausible to suppose that in *mathematical* intuition there is a causal action of a mathematical object on us (presumably on the mind). Moreover, this is no part of the view of the upholders of mathematical intuition that I have mentioned, though it is sometimes included in popular conceptions of 'Platonism'.

---

[8] In attempting to develop an analogy between perception and knowledge of abstract objects, Husserl is helped by his phenomenological perspective. The causal foundation of perception is not part of the subject-matter of phenomenology, even in the form it takes in the *Logische Untersuchungen* (hereafter *LU*). Husserl does undertake to show that in categorial intuition there is something analogous to sensations in sense-perception. In my view, he lapses into obscurity in explaining this (*LU* vi, §56). I am not sure to what extent this can be cleared up.

At this point we find qualifications in accounts of mathematical intuition, which raise the question just how close an analogy with perception is intended. Gödel says that 'mathematical intuition need not be conceived of as a faculty giving an *immediate* knowledge of the objects concerned.'[9] Husserl is even prepared to call categorial intuition 'perception' (*Wahrnehmung*),[10] but he contrasts sense-perception as *schlicht*, in which the object is 'immediately given', with categorial intuition which is *founded* in other 'acts' such as ordinary perceptions and imaginings.[11]

Kant expresses puzzlement about how intuition can be a priori. In the *Prolegomena*, after introducing the notion of pure intuition, he writes (§8):

An intuition is such a representation as would immediately depend on the presence (*Gegenwart*) of the object. Hence it seems impossible to intuit spontaneously (*ursprünglich*) a priori because intuition would in that event have to take place without either a former or a present object to refer to, and in consequence could not be an intuition . . . But how can the intuition of an object precede the object itself?[12]

Here (and elsewhere) Kant does not explicitly express a view about intuition of *mathematical* objects. It is clear from the context that by 'object' he means *real* object, in practice physical object. So the question is how it is possible for a priori intuition to be 'of' physical objects that are not given a priori.

In §9 Kant claims that the puzzle is resolved by the fact that a priori intuition contains only the form of our sensibility. It is a nice question just what this does to the characterization of intuition that gives rise to the puzzle. Clearly, in the a priori case, the causal dependence of the intuition on the object has to go. Whether and how the *phenomenological* presence of an object is preserved is a further question, as is the question whether the object thus present is a physical or a purely mathematical object. The

---

[9] 'What is Cantor's Continuum Problem?', p. 271.   [10] *LU* vi, §45.

[11] Ibid., §46.

[12] Kant's puzzle is related to the dilemma about mathematical truth posed by Paul Benacerraf in 'Mathematical Truth', *Journal of Philosophy*, 70 (1973), 661–79: according to Benacerraf, our best theory of mathematical *truth* (Tarski's) involves postulating mathematical objects, while our best account of *knowledge* requires causal relations of the objects of knowledge to us; but mathematical objects are acausal. One can present Kant's problem as a similar dilemma: mathematical truth requires applicability to the physical world. But our best account of mathematical knowledge makes it rest on intuition, which requires the prior presence of the object. But this contradicts the a priori character of mathematics. This is of interest because it is a form of the dilemma that does not require that the semantics of mathematics involve mathematical objects (which it seems one might avoid by a modal interpretation of quantifiers). But of course it depends on other assumptions, in particular that mathematics is a priori.

former is not ruled out by the a priori character of pure intuition, since the 'presence' might be that characteristic of *imagination* rather than sense. In fact, a number of passages in Kant indicate that just that is his position.

We might find a difficulty for the idea of intuition of mathematical objects in what, following Leibniz, might be called their incompleteness. I do not need to go into this much, because it has been much discussed, not least by me.[13] The properties and relations of mathematical objects that play a role in mathematical reasoning are those determined by the basic relations of some system or structure to which all the objects involved belong, such as the natural numbers, Euclidean or some other space, a given group, field, or other such structure, or the universe of sets or some model thereof. It seems that the properties and relations of mathematical objects about which there is a 'fact of the matter' are either in some way expressible in terms of the basic relations of this structure or else are 'external relations' which are independent of the choice of a system of objects to realize the structure.

Consider for example the natural numbers, with o and the successor function S as giving the relevant structure (perhaps with other functions such as addition, if we give ourselves no second-order apparatus). Examples of the former type are number-theoretic properties such as being prime or being the sum of four squares. External relations include those arising in counting other objects, and such properties as being believed by me to be prime. Such relations will not in general be definable in the language of number theory, even higher order, but they are in general definable in terms of the basic relations and others that do not depend on the choice of a system of objects and relations to realize the structure.

Now the question is, how can mathematical intuition place objects 'before our minds' when these objects are not identifiable individually at all? For example, unless one is presupposing a structure including numbers and sets, it seems indeterminate whether the number 2 is identical to the one-element set $\{ \{ \Lambda \} \}$, the two-element set $\{ \Lambda, \{ \Lambda \} \}$, or neither.[14] How can this be if numbers and sets are objects of mathematical intuition? Can such intuition be a significant

---

[13] 'Frege's Theory of Number', in M. Black (ed.), *Philosophy in America* (London, 1965); 'Ontology and Mathematics', *Philosophical Review* 80 (1971), 151–76, at pp. 154–7; 'Quine on the Philosophy of Mathematics', in P. A. Schilpp (ed.), *The Philosophy of W.V. Quine* (La Salle, Ill., 1986). Among others see esp. P. Bernays, 'Mathematische Existenz und Widerspruchsfreiheit (1950), in *Abhandlungen zur Philosophie der Mathematik* (Darmstadt, 1976); and P. Benacerraf, 'What Numbers Could Not Be', *Philosophical Review*, 74 (1965), 47–73.

[14] The first follows from Zermelo's proposal for a set-theoretic construal of numbers, the second from von Neumann's, the third if set theory takes the natural numbers as individuals.

source of mathematical knowledge if it does not determine the answers to such simple questions?

One could press the matter further and urge the possibility of an interpretation of mathematics which dispenses with distinctively mathematical objects. One such possibility is a nominalistic reconstrual of such objects. Another, more promising as an approach to the whole of mathematics, is a modal interpretation of quantifiers in which, roughly, statements of the existence of a mathematical object satisfying some condition are rendered as statements of the *possible* existence of an object satisfying purely structural conditions.[15]

These difficulties are at bottom one. What is really essential to mathematical objects is the relations constituting the structure to which they belong. Accordingly, in the end there is no objective ground for preferring one realization over another as 'the' intended domain of objects, in particular for rejecting concrete (nominalistic) realizations if they are available. Moreover, actual, as opposed to merely possible, realization of a structure adds nothing mathematically relevant. Both these points need *some* qualification, first because often actually given realizations of a structure presuppose some more comprehensive structure, such as the natural numbers or sets, and because in discussions of potential totalities, something like a distinction between actual and potential existence can be made. However, the exactly right way to put these points need not concern us here.

III

I propose to show that there is at least a limited application of the notion of mathematical intuition *of* which is able to meet these objections. First, let us review briefly the reasons why one might introduce the concept. Intuition *that* becomes a persuasive idea when one reflects on the obviousness of elementary truths of mathematics. Two alternative views have had influential advocates in this century: conventionalism, the view that as least some mathematical propositions are true by convention, and a form of empiricism according to which mathematics is continuous with science, and the axioms of mathematics have a status similar to that of high-level theoretical hypotheses. Both these views have unattractive

---

[15] H. Putnam, 'Mathematics Without Foundations', *Journal of Philosophy*, 84 (1967), 5–22; my 'Ontology and Mathematics', pp. 158–64; C. Chihara, *Ontology and the Vicious Circle Principle* (Ithaca, NY, 1973), 191. Applied to arithmetic and other more elementary parts of mathematics, the modal interpretation of quantifiers may serve to defuse scruples about abstract objects. In 'Quine on the Philosophy of Mathematics', I argue that this is not the case for higher set theory.

features. Conventionalism has been much criticized, and I need not repeat the criticisms here.

The empiricist view, even in the subtle and complex form it takes in the work of Professor Quine, seems subject to the objection that it leaves unaccounted for precisely the *obviousness* of elementary mathematics (and perhaps also of logic). It seeks to meet the difficulties of early empiricist views of mathematics by assimilating mathematics to the theoretical part of science. But there are great differences: first, the 'topic-neutrality' of logic, which receives considerable recognition in Quine's writings, although he insists that it depends on a specification of the logical constants that is at bottom arbitrary; second, the very close connection of mathematics and logic, where the potential field of application of mathematics is as wide as that of logic, in spite of the fact that the existence of mathematical objects makes mathematics not strictly topic-neutral; third, the existence of very general principles that are universally regarded as obvious, where on an empiricist view one would expect them to be bold hypotheses, about which a prudent scientist would maintain reserve, keeping in mind that experience might not bear them out; fourth, the fact that differences about logic and elementary mathematics, such as the issues raised by intuitionism, are naturally explained as differenecs about *meaning*. Quine recognizes this by the role that logic plays in his theory of translation, but the obviousness of logic is an unexamined premiss of that theory.

Some version of the pre-Quinean view of logic as true by virtue of meaning may be the most promising way of addressing the difficulties of the Quinean view of *logic*. There is no a priori reason why the conception of intuition we are examining should play a role in working out such a view. In the case of arithmetic, the situation is different because unlike logic, it has ontological commitments. That a structure such as the natural numbers should exist, or at least should be *possible* in some mathematically relevant way, is hard to make out as true by virtue of the meanings of arithmetical or other expressions.

Just at this point, the idea of intuition *of* suggests itself. We are taking as a gross fact about arithmetic, that a considerable body of arithmetical truths is known to us in some more direct way than is the case for the knowledge we acquire by empirical reasoning. And this knowledge takes the form of truths about certain objects—the natural numbers. What is more natural than the hypothesis that we have direct knowledge of these truths because the objects they are about are given to us in some direct way? The model we offer of this givenness is the manner in which a physical body is given to us in perception.

IV

As applied to the natural numbers, this picture is oversimplified. However, I propose to meet the difficulties by a strategy suggested by Kant's conception of pure intuition as giving the *form* of empirical intuition and by Husserl's thesis that categorial intuition is *founded* on sensible intuition. The quasi-perceptual manner in which mathematical objects can be given to us is in a certain way exemplified by situations of *ordinary* perception *or imagination* of realizations (sometimes partial) of the structures involved.

Elsewhere I presented an account of arithmetical intuition.[16] However, the presentation was tied to a modal interpretation of quantifiers, and the idea was intended to have greater generality. The following exposition is intended to make some other aspects of the earlier account more explicit.

It is well to follow Hilbert and to begin by considering the 'syntax' of a 'language' with a single basic symbol '|' (stroke), whose well-formed expressions are just arbitrary strings containing just this symbol, i.e. |, ||, |||, . . . This sequence of strings is isomorphic to the natural numbers, if one takes '|' as o and the operation of adding one more '|' on the right as the successor operation. This yields an interpretation of arithmetic as a kind of geometry of strings of strokes. At first sight the interpretation leaves out the concept of *number*, that is, the role of natural numbers as cardinals and ordinals.

Ordinary perception of a string of strokes would have to be perception of a *token*, but we naturally think of such symbols as types. Beginning with the notion of a token being *a* stroke, we can recast the explanation of the stroke-language in such a way that types are not presupposed as objects. Two strings are 'of the same type' if they *can* be placed side by side so that strokes correspond one-to-one.[17] The use of 'can' in the criterion for sameness of type may be non-essential; someone, such as an actualist nominalist, could argue that some other type of empirical test is sufficient, or he might appeal to an inductive definition: two strings are of the same type if they are both single strokes, or if the strings consisting of all but the rightmost stroke in each are of the same type. However, shortly we shall face a much stronger temptation to use modality.

That one can go this far (and indeed much farther) in doing syntax nominalistically is not news. What is less widely appreciated is that we have here the basis of an explanation of types, which first of all makes them no more mysterious than other objects, in spite of their 'abstract-

---

[16] 'Ontology and Mathematics', § 111.
[17] Ibid. 159–60, to which I refer the reader for details.

ness', and secondly makes it quite reasonable to say that they are *given* in a way analogous to that in which middle-sized physical objects are given. Indeed ordinary language recognizes this, in that we speak of hearing or seeing *words* and *sentences*, where what is clearly meant are types.

Of course a perception of a string of stroke-tokens is not by itself an 'intuition' of a stroke-string type. One has to approach it with the *concept* of a type, first of all to have the capacity to recognize other tokens as of the same type or not. Something more than the mere capacity is involved, which might be described as seeing something *as* the type. But this much is present in ordinary perception as well. One can of course see an object without recognizing it as this or that, but when it does occur such recognition is part of normal perception, and when one sees an object one at least recognizes it under *some* description that permits reidentification.

One might object that in the case of ordinary perception, the *Auffassung* as an object, even of a particular kind, is entirely spontaneous and natural, whereas what I want to call 'intuiting' a symbol-type is a conscious exercise of a conceptual apparatus which may be quite artificial. I agree that this may be true in this case and is certainly true in some. However, in some cases, taking what is given as a type is quite spontaneous and natural. The most obvious is the understanding of natural language: the hearer is without reflection ready to reidentify the type (in the linguistic, not the acoustic sense). Typically, the hearer of an utterance has a more explicit conception of *what was uttered* (e.g. what words) than he has of an objective identification of the *event* of the utterance.[18] I believe that the same is true of some other kinds of universals, such as sense-qualities and shapes.[19] Indeed, in all these cases it seems not to violate ordinary language to talk of perception of the universal *as an object*, where an instance of it is present. This is not just an overblown way of talking of perceiving an instance *as an instance* (e.g. seeing something red *as* being red), because the identification of the

---

[18] Of course when we talk of what was uttered, and even more of what was *said*, this is often best understood in a way that invites regimentation in terms of *propositions*. One might then offer a similar argument for the claim that propositions are objects of intuition. However, such considerations cannot get us past the well-known doubts about the objectivity of propositions. A response to an auditory stimulus can count as intuition of a *sentence* because we can attribute to the hearer a reasonably sharp concept of *same sentence*.

[19] Such a view is not necessarily incompatible with all versions of nominalism. The British empiricists sometimes understood sense-qualities as universals, but admitted them as 'simple ideas' rather than 'abstract ideas'. Similarly the *qualia* admitted by Nelson Goodman in *The Structure of Appearance* (Cambridge, Mass., 1951) are universals. Neither on the empiricist's view, nor Goodman's, nor on the view I suggest should sense-qualities be understood as a kind of *attribute* in the sense of something denoted by a nominalized predicate.

universal can be firmer and more explicit than the identification of the object that is an instance of it.

These observations should begin to dispel the widespread impression that mathematical intuition is a 'special' faculty, which perhaps comes into play only in doing pure mathematics. At least one type of essentially mathematical intuition, of symbol- and expression-types, is perfectly ordinary and recognized as such by ordinary language. If a positive account of mathematical intuition is to get anywhere, it has to make clear, as its advocates intended, that mathematical intuition is not an isolated epistemological concept, to be applied only to pure mathematics, but must be so closely related to the concepts by which we describe perception and our knowledge of the physical world that the 'faculty' involved will be seen to be at work when one is not consciously doing mathematics.

V

The preceding discussion indicates that we should be careful in talking, with Husserl, of 'intuition' of a type as founded on perception of a token. In ordinary cases there will be perception in the full sense, which requires physical presence and action on the senses. Ordinary talk of hearing *words* normally carries this implication. In many cases the token will be pushed into the background by the type, but that does not make the former not an object of perception. However, even in normal cases the background and further experience that are necessary to the perception's being of something physically *real* are irrelevant to its being of the *form* given by the type. In most cases, physical reality is important not for taking in the type, but for further considerations: what is likely to be of interest about the words is that they were spoken by a speaker at a certain time, or stand written in a certain book.

Perceptions and imaginings, as founding such intuitions, play a paradigmatic role. It is through this that intuition of a type can give rise to propositional knowledge about the type, i.e. intuition *that*. A simple case is singular propositions about types, such as that ||| is the successor of ||. We see this to be true on the basis of a single intuition, but of course in its implications for tokens it is a general proposition. Let a be the token of ||| above; let b be the token of || above; the statement implies that if c and d are respectively of the same type as a and b, then c consists of a part of the same type as b, and one additional stroke on the right. We can of course buttress the statement that ||| is the successor of || by considering arbitrary tokens of the relevant types and verifying the above consequence. But we have to verify it in the same way, by instances that we take as paradigmatic. This situation is not peculiar to our artificial framework. The same is true of calculations done on paper and of formal proofs, such as the deductions done in elementary logic courses.

A more problematic situation arises when we consider general propositions about *types*, which have in their scope indefinitely many *different* types. It is this which prompts us to follow Husserl in saying that sometimes *imagination* of the token can found intuition of the type. Consider for example the assertion that each string of strokes *can* be extended by one more. This is the weakest expression of the idea that our 'language' is potentially infinite. But we cannot convince ourselves of it by perception or by the kind of mathematical intuition we have talked about so far, founded on actual perception. But if we imagine any string of strokes, it is immediately apparent that a new stroke can be added. One might imagine the string as a *Gestalt*, present all at once: then since it is a figure with a surrounding ground, there is space for an additional stroke. However, this may not be the right way to look at the matter, since the imagination of an *arbitrary* string in this way will have to leave inexplicit its articulation into single strokes. Alternatively, we can think of the string as constructed step by step, so that the essential element is now succession in *time*, and what is then evident is that at any stage one can take another step.

Either way, one has to imagine *an arbitrary string of strokes*. We have a problem akin to that of Locke's general triangle. If one imagines a string in a specific way, one will imagine a string with a specific number of strokes, and therefore not a perfectly arbitrary string. There seems to be a choice between imagining *vaguely*, that is imagining a string of strokes without imagining its internal structure clearly enough so that one is imagining a string of n strokes for some particular n, or taking as paradigm a string (which now might be perceived rather than imagined) of a particular number of strokes, in which case one must be able to see the irrelevance of this internal structure, so that in fact it plays the same role as the vague imagining.

We naturally think of perception as at least sometimes uncorrupted by thinking, in that without conscious thinking one can take in some aspect of the environment and respond to it, and one can take a stance toward one's perceptions that is largely non-committal with respect to the judgements we would ordinarily be prepared to make. However that may be, it is clear that the kind of *Gedankenexperimente* I have been describing can be taken as intuitive verifications of such statements as that any string of strokes can be extended only if one carries them out on the basis of specific concepts, such as that of a string of strokes. If that were not so, they would not confer any generality.

Brouwer may have been trying to meet this difficulty, in a special case of this sort, with his concept of two-one-ness, according to which the activity of consciousness brings about 'the falling apart of a life-moment into two qualitatively distinct things', of which the moment then present retains the structure of the original, so that the resulting 'temporal two-ity' can be taken as a term of a new two-ity, giving rise to temporal three-ity.[20] Thus the process can always give rise to a new moment, which for Brouwer is the foundation for the infinity of the natural numbers. One has something similar in the figure-ground structure of perception, which was appealed to above. However, in all versions we think of whatever step it is as one that *can be iterated indefinitely*. In a sense this is given by the fact that after the step of 'adding one more' one has essentially the same structure. But a concept such as that of a *string* of strokes involves the notion of such iteration. To spell that out, we are led into the circle of ideas surrounding mathematical induction. Although the view has been attributed to Brouwer that 'iteration' is the fundamental intuition of mathematics, my view is that the particular concept of intuition I am explicating runs out at this point, and it is only in a weaker and less clear sense that mathematical induction is a deliverance of intuition.

Although the concept of a string of strokes involves iteration, the proposition that every such string can be extended is not an inductive conclusion. A proof of it by induction would be circular. Such a proof would be called for only if we really needed the fact that every string of strokes can be obtained by iterated application of the operation of adding one more. In fact, I think the matter is thus: we have a structure of perception, a 'form of intuition' if you will, which has the essential feature of Brouwer's two-one-ness, that however the idea of 'adding one more' is interpreted, we still have an instance of the same structure. But to see the *possibility* of adding one more, it is only the general structure that we use, and not the specific fact that what we have before us was obtained by iterated additions of one more. This is shown by the fact that in the same sense in which a new stroke can be added to any string of strokes, it can be added to any bounded geometric configuration.

VI

It should be clear that we do not acquire in this way any reason to believe

[20] L. E. J. Brouwer, *Collected Works*, i, ed. A. Heyting (Amsterdam, 1975), 417 (from 1929). Cf. p. 17 (from 1907), p. 480 (1948), and p. 510 (1952).

it *physically possible* to extend any string of strokes. At most the structure of space and time is at stake here, and physical possibility requires something more, whatever makes the difference between the space of pure geometry and the physical universe, consisting at least of space containing matter. Actually we require less than the space of pure geometry, since even if we do hold to the spatiality of the strokes (which perhaps we can avoid), only very crude properties of space are appealed to, in particular not its metric properties.

We can call the possibility in question *mathematical possibility*; this expresses the fact that we are not thinking of the capabilities of the human organism, and it may even be extraneous to think of this 'construction' as an act of the *mind*. The latter construal agrees with the viewpoint of Kant and Brouwer. It is very tempting if we want to say that any string of strokes is *perceptible* or *imaginable*. (It is preferable to reserve these words for tokens, but then one can speak of the *intuitability* of the type.) The idea is that no matter how many times the operation of constructing one more stroke in imagination has been repeated, 'we' can still construct one more. However, I think there is really a hidden assumption that there is no constraint on what 'we' can perceive beyond the open temporality of these experiences, and some very gross aspects of spatial structure. Kant and Brouwer thought these were contributions of our minds to the way we experience the world. Kant of course thought that we could not know these things a priori unless our minds had contributed them. I am not persuaded by this, and in any case I do not want my argument to rest on the notion of a priori knowledge. If we express the *content* of the proposition in a way as independent as possible of the description of the insight, then it is just that for an arbitrary string of strokes, it is possible that there should be one that extends it by one stroke.

The nominalist seems to demand both more and less than we do. He may try to get on without even the potential infinity of a sequence like that of stroke-string-types, but then he will have to do without the infinity of the natural numbers. His position is really the embarrassing one that Russell found himself in about the axiom of infinity. He can treat it as an hypothesis to whose truth he is not committed, but then mathematics allows the possibility that where we have proved by ordinary mathematical means a proposition B, we are not entitled to reject its negation, since, where A is the relevant axiom of infinity, if A is false both $A \rightarrow B$ and $A \rightarrow \sim B$ are true.

Alternatively, he may accept as an empirical hypothesis some proposition entailing the existence in space and time of a ω-sequence such as a sequence of tokens of stroke-strings, each one extending the previous one.[21] Since he is talking about physical existence, he is making a stronger claim than we do, which mathematics does not need. (He could be a traditional empiricist and discern such a sequence in some phenomenal field, but on empiricist grounds this seems very questionable, and it has the same mathematically irrelevant strength.) Such an hypothesis clearly has a theoretical character, and it might even be rejected if physics were to evolve in such a way that space–time came to be understood as both finite and discrete. Any reason we have for believing it depends on the historically given physics, constructed in tandem with an arithmetic with an infinity of numbers.

A third position which might be called nominalistic is one alluded to above: one continues to hold that in strict usage one should talk only of tokens; the relation *same type* is available but is understood as just a useful equivalence relation, not the foundation of identity of types; and one meets the problem of the potential infinity of types by a modal interpretation of quantifiers.[22] Earlier I gave some reasons for denying this view the title of nominalist,[23] but although I still hold to them I would now say that the question whether it *is* nominalist is in the end terminological. So long as we stay short of set theory and other impredicative mathematics, and the modality involved is mathematical possibility, the position is not importantly different from my own. However, the latter qualification is important. If the modal theory of tokens is understood as a theory of physical tokens, and the modality is physical, then I think the view faces the same difficulties as the actualist forms of nominalism.

VII

I now turn to the question whether our conception of an intuition of types faces serious objections because of the timelessness, acausality, or incompleteness of types as abstract entities. Stroke-string-types and other

---

[21] This is e.g. entailed by the position of Hartry Field's interesting *Science without Numbers* (Princeton, 1980). His main project is to interpret physics in an extension of synthetic geometry, in which the variables range over points and regions of space–time, which he asserts to be physical. A model of arithmetic can certainly be constructed in his theory.

[22] Chihara, *Ontology and the Vicious Circle Principle*, p. 191; 'Ontology and Mathematics', pp. 160–2. In the latter, the last 2 lines of p. 160 are ambiguous. One way of taking it would be to say that '$\exists xFx$', where the variable 'ranges over natural numbers', is *true if and only if* we can construct a perceptible inscription which can be put into the empty place of an inscription of 'Fa' so that a truth results. Properly, this should be recast as a necessary statement about inscriptions. The truth-condition has a substitutional character, and then the resulting interpretation as a language of arithmetic is substitutional; inscriptions and construction thereof are talked of only in the metalanguage. Other readings are possible that make the quantifier range over inscriptions.   [23] Ibid. 162–4.

such expressions are minimally abstract, since they are types of tokens which are concrete. Our intuitions of them are founded on sense-experience or on imaginings which imagine their objects as in space and time, even if not at any particular location. The timelessness of types is simply universality: since they can be instantiated anywhere, they are understood as located nowhere. Because the existence of a type depends on the possibility of a token, they cannot be understood as mereological sums. The *problem* about the timelessness of types is really epistemological: how can we know truths about types by a certain kind of perception of tokens, which are then valid for *any* tokens of the types involved. In my remarks above, I have done little more than try to make clear that we *do* have such knowledge. More explanation should be given, though some experience tends to show that explanations of such matters are always in the end question-begging. Observe, however, that the problem is not created by an ontology of types. On the nominalistic views I have mentioned, there is also a question about knowledge of the general truths about tokens that are the nominalistic versions of the truths about types.

It might be questioned whether types are acausal after all; for example, I might say, 'His words made me furious.' Suppose he said, 'You have no right to call yourself a philosopher.' But in fact we do not think of the *sentence* as making me furious (and not just because of the indexicality of this particular example). Nor do we attribute the effect to the proposition expressed, although that might be more plausible in this case. It is much more natural to attribute the effect to the event of his saying the words, or his expressing that proposition, on the occasion on which he did. This preserves the acausality of the sentence, but its relation to causality is like its relation to space and time. Its tokens are caught up in the causal nexus, and indeed affect our senses. Once we see the relation between intuition of types and ordinary perception, I think this difficulty rather dissolves. However, an objector may be thinking of Benacerraf's dilemma (n. 12). To deal with this requires a longer story than I can tell now.

About incompleteness, one might first think that the closeness to the concrete of such abstract objects as strings of strokes would make them *not* incomplete. For example, it would be simply false that $|||$ is identical with an object given in some other way, say the number 3. $|||$ has some properties 3 lacks, such as that it is composed of strokes. Another problem is cognitive relations, including *de re* propositional attitudes; if I see on a blackboard the formula ' $Vx \, (x \neq o \rightarrow \exists y \, (x = Sy) \,)$ ', I do not see the number that corresponds to it under some arithmetization of the syntax of first-order arithmetic.

I suggest the following explanation. What is basic to the concept of type gives identity and difference relations only to other types in the same system of symbols. (Two inscriptions may be of the same type with respect to one symbolism and not with respect to another.) Since this is a distinctive feature of what types *are*, common sense tends to treat the types of a given symbolism as *sui generis*, so that none is identical with anything given in some other way. In one sense this resolves the incompleteness, since it determines all predicates (at least from the point of view of classical logic), but in a negative way: all atomic predicates except those from the structure and those expressing the basic facts about its instantiation, are false. But this inclination of common sense does not correspond to a feature of the nature of things, at least not to one that cannot be overridden when it comes to the regimentation of language.

However, this kind of consideration does show a significant disanalogy between this kind of mathematical intuition and ordinary perception. *What is intuited* depends on the concept brought to the situation by the subject. In some cases, such as natural language, the concepts involved may be innate or develop more or less spontaneously and unreflectively. In the more characteristically mathematical cases of geometric figures and the sort of artificial symbolism we have been discussing, this is not so. Therefore we do not have the scope that we have with ordinary perception for identifying the object of intuition independently of the subject's conceptual resources. If someone feels heat, and heat is the motion of molecules, then he feels something that is the motion of molecules. If we are using 'feel' in an object-relational way, he feels the motion of those molecules, even if he has no conception of molecules. But no one could intuit a stroke-string-type unless he saw it *as* a type constructed from strokes, and this requires that he have the concept of stroke. If, in regimenting our theory, we identify ||| with the number 3, then perhaps we can say that he is intuiting 3, although he may have no idea that that is what he is doing. But we can only say that because he has *some* identifying concept. There is probably an ordinary concept of perception for which this holds as well, but it does not obviously hold for the most ordinary object-relational uses of 'see', 'hear', and perhaps 'feel'.[24]

---

[24] In the case of natural language, we classify types according to the language, and not according to the conceptual apparatus of the perceiver. If I say to someone who has never heard English, 'Where is the American Embassy?', he hears that sentence of English, even though he does not recognize it as such and is not able to recognize an utterance of the same sentence by someone with a different accent. This case is analogous to the role of natural kinds in the description of what someone sees.

VII

Our investigation so far has reached a significant positive result. It is quite permissible to say that types of perceptible tokens are objects of intuition, where the concept of intuition involved is strongly analogous to that of perception. Moreover, we can represent some propositions about these objects as known intuitively.

This result is of very limited scope. Even though they form a model of arithmetic, from a mathematical point of view strings of strokes are rather special objects. The perception-like character of what we call intuition of types may be thought to be due to the closeness to perception of the objects involved. Perhaps our concept of mathematical intuition will not carry us beyond elementary syntax and maybe traditional geometry. Are we prepared to say, for example, that the *natural numbers* are objects of intuition?

I have to deal with this question more briefly than I would like. Our discussion so far suggests a moderate position: intuition gives objects which form a model of arithmetic, and this model is as good as any both for the foundations of arithmetic and for applications. But it may not be right to say that *the* natural numbers are objects of intuition, since intuition does not give a unique sequence to be 'the' natural numbers, and the concept of number does not rule out as the 'intended model' objects that are not objects of intuition.

However, we should try to come to terms with the higher-order aspects of the concepts of cardinal and ordinal number. I shall restrict myself to cardinal number. The formulation of a statement of number requires an operation on predicates, either a numerical quantifier like 'there are n xs such that Fx' or a term-forming operation like 'the number of xs such that Fx'. This point, however, imposes no constraint at all on what kind of objects the natural numbers are. We should resist the temptation to identify the numbers with the numerical quantifiers themselves (as 'second-level concepts' or the like) as well as the subtler temptation, to which Frege succumbed, to try to find an object that represents the numerical quantifier in an especially intrinsic way.

A more serious matter is that apparently the truth-conditions for statements of number must incorporate the Fregean criterion for sameness of number: the number of Fs is the same as the number of Gs if and only if *there is a one-to-one correspondence of the Fs and the Gs*.

We might seek to accommodate this in a way which makes numbers objects of intuition by understanding numbers as a kind of generalized types, in which the tokens are numeral-tokens serving as counters.[25] The

[25] 'Frege's Theory of Number', p. 201. Cf. 'Ontology and Mathematics', p. 160.

relation playing the role of sameness of type is that of 'representing the same number'. Since what is involved in this relation is what is involved in *counting*, observe that verifying by counting that there are *n* *x*s such that *Fx* involves exhibiting a one-to-one correspondence between the *F*s and a sequence of *n* 'counters'—standardly numerals. If the predicate '*F*' is simple enough and the objects are objects of perception, 'there are *n* *F*s' can be verified by perception. We do not have to take it as *saying* that there *is* such a correspondence between the *F*s and the counters. But it does in some way imply it, and in order to establish the elements of number we do have to reason about such correspondences.

For arithmetic, however, the correspondences we need are finite. I will assume that *finite sets* of objects of intuition are themselves objects of intuition. Space does not permit defending that assumption here. What I want to observe is that from it follows what is needed to justify the claim that the natural numbers, considered as 'numbering' objects of intuition, are objects of intuition. Two numerals *a* and *b*, perhaps from different notation systems, represent the same number if there is a one–one correspondence of the numerals up to *a* and those up to *b*. Our assumption implies that this does not involve reference except to objects of intuition.

However, this approach would suggest that arithmetic, as applied to objects *in general*, belongs to set theory. We could still say in this context that finite numbers are objects of intuition, on the ground that for the constitution of numbers as objects this full generality is not needed. However, the general principles of cardinal and ordinal number, applied to arbitrary sets, even arbitrary (possibly not hereditarily) finite sets, will not be intuitive knowledge unless sets in general are objects of intuition. I have not tried to argue that they are.

Before we end this paper, we must say something about mathematical induction, which arises already for strings of strokes. I have not said much about our understanding of what an arbitrary string of strokes, or an arbitrary natural number, is. However, this understanding should surely yield the relevant induction principle. What bearing does this have on our remarks on intuition?

Let us concentrate on the more intuitive case of strings of strokes. In such a case, the conclusion of an inference by induction is a general statement about objects of intuition. It does not follow that it is therefore intuitive knowledge. There is a temptation to call our understanding of the general notion of a string of strokes an intuition, because it is clear and seems to make inductive inference evident.[26] However, this would have to

---

[26] For the natural numbers, Dummett makes such a suggestion, in order to criticize it, in 'Platonism', in *Truth and other Enigmas* (London, 1978).

be a different, and in this context potentially confusing, sense of 'intuition', since what is involved is the understanding of a general term; this does not give any *object*.[27]

Because of the essential way in which this understanding is used, I am inclined to deny that even very simple inductive conclusions are intuitive knowledge. Gödel, however, in discussing a distinction between intuitive and abstract evidence, uses another criterion.[28] His line is drawn where one begins to refer to what he calls 'abstract objects', by which he means statements and proofs.[29] I do not deny that this is also an important distinction. Moreover, I do not claim to have shown that his terminology is inappropriate. More needs to be said about the epistemological aspects of the concept of intuition, even the very limited concept that I have developed, than I have said in this chapter.

---

[27] Of course there are strings of strokes which as a practical matter can never be intuited, and it is only by means of the general notion of a string of strokes that we conceive such objects. But the thought of 10^{100} strokes, however clear, is not an intuition of them.

[28] 'Ueber eine noch nicht benüzte Erweiterung des finiten Standpunktes', pp. 280–2. In the trans. referred to in n. 7 above, 'anschauliche Erkenntnis' (p. 281) is trans. 'immediate concrete knowledge'.

[29] In my view, what is really essential is semantic reflection. See 'Ontology and Mathematics', pp. 165–7.

10

FORM AND CONTENT

MICHAEL FRIEDMAN

The appearance of Moritz Schlick's *Philosophical Papers* is an event to be welcomed by all students of twentieth-century philosophy of science and, indeed, by students of twentieth-century philosophy generally. Together they comprise the entire corpus of Schlick's published writings (and some previously unpublished writings) on epistemology, metaphysics, and philosophy of science with the exception of his magnum opus, *General Theory of Knowledge* (first edition: 1918, second edition: 1925, English translation by A. Blumberg: 1974). Only Schlick's ethical writings fail to be represented exhaustively (and judging from some that are included, e.g. 'On the Meaning of Life', *PP* ii. 112–29, this circumstance may not be cause for regret). Particularly noteworthy are translations of some of Schlick's best and most important, yet previously untranslated, papers (I have in mind especially 'The Philosophical Significance of the Principle of Relativity (1915), *PP* i. 153–89, and 'Experience, Cognition, Metaphysics (1926), *PP* ii. 99–111) and the inclusion of Henry Brose's 1920 translation of *Space and Time in Contemporary Physics* (1917), *PP* i. 207–69, which has long been out of print. As a whole, we are presented with a fascinating, if somewhat chaotic, picture of analytic philosophy in the making.

It must be admitted that Schlick's work has serious limitations, especially so for a twentieth-century thinker. His grasp of modern logic is imperfect at best (although he is acquainted with, and explicitly refers to, Russell's *Principles of Mathematics* (1903), he devotes a considerable amount of energy in *General Theory of Knowledge* (§14) to arguing that all rigorous inferences in mathematics and science can be expressed as sequences of syllogisms in the mood Barbara). His understanding of the logicist tradition of Frege, Russell, and early Wittgenstein is even worse (he is hopelessly confused about the crucial question of mathematical induction—*PP* i. 84–5—and propounds the disastrous conception, later popularized by Ayer, that all arithmetical propositions are in themselves

This chapter appeared originally as 'Critical Notice: Moritz Schlick, *Philosophical Papers*', in *Philosophy of Science*, 50 (1983), 498–514. Copyright © 1983 by the Philosophy of Science Association. Used by permission.

tautological, whether or not arithmetic is somehow a part of logic—*PP* ii. 344–5). Moreover, Schlick never developed the habit of formulating philosophical views and arguments with what we would call logical precision: he often reads more like a pre-analytic philosopher than a contemporary of Russell and Carnap.[1]

Despite these limitations, however, Schlick's contribution is invaluable. For he has both a wide-ranging synthetic sense and a remarkable ability to get to the heart of a matter. He clearly perceives the broad outlines of the philosophical, physical, and mathematical currents whose convergence resulted in the development of logical positivism, and he struggles honestly, acutely, and courageously—if not always coherently—with the intellectual stresses and strains produced by this convergence. And, in this connection, the fact that he is to some extent a pre-analytic philosopher is not a defect but a virtue. Reading Schlick yields an improved appreciation of the continuities between analytic philosophy and its immediate ancestors which, under the spell of logical positivism's revolutionary rhetoric, we are all too liable to forget.

According to one popular picture, logical positivism began as an empiricist or verificationist movement in the tradition of Hume, Mach, and Russell's external world programme. (See Schlick's own presentation of this picture in 'The Vienna School and Traditional Philosophy' (1937), *PP* ii. 495.) Add the 'meaning-theoretic' orientation of Wittgenstein's *Tractatus*, and the verifiability theory of meaning is the result. However, if one reads the early (pre-1930) works of the positivists themselves, a very different and, I think, much more interesting picture emerges. The verificationism of the positivists did not develop along a direct line from Hume and Mach via Russell and Wittgenstein. At least equally important is an evolution from German neo-Kantianism and neo-idealism via Hilbert and Einstein.[2] Schlick's writings on relativity theory provide a striking illustration of this evolution.

[1] It is instructive to compare Carnap, Reichenbach, and Schlick in this regard. Reichenbach appears to have had a much better understanding of logic than did Schlick, and he does attempt to formulate his views and arguments with 'logical precision'. Nevertheless, Reichenbach does not really put modern logic to work in his philosophizing; even more so than Schlick, his primary technical orientation is towards physics. Only Carnap is able to grapple technically *and* philosophically with both modern logic and modern physics, and this is undoubtedly a central reason for his pre-eminence.

[2] The neo-Kantian and neo-idealist influence on the early positivists has been widely neglected—again, largely because of positivism's own anti-Kantian rhetoric. To get an initial appreciation of this influence, one has only to list some of the authors referred to by the 2 great works of the period: Schlick's *General Theory of Knowledge* and Carnap's *Aufbau* (1928). Names such as Cassirer, Driesch, B. Erdman, Külpe, Natorp, Schuppe, Vaihinger, and Wundt predominate. (As Alberto Coffa has emphasized to me, Schlick's own initiation into neo-Kantianism probably came from Helmholtz via Planck, who was the adviser of Schlick's Ph.D. dissertation.)

The essential background against which Schlick's work on relativity theory develops is the philosophical view expressed in *General Theory of Knowledge*.[3] That view diverges from stereotypical positivism or empiricism in two important respects. First, the conception of knowledge is explicitly 'holistic'. Knowledge is essentially a *system* of interconnected judgements whose concepts get their meaning from their mutual relationships within this system (§§3–9). Knowledge or cognition (*erkennen*) is to be sharply distinguished from acquaintance (*kennen*) or experience (*erleben*) of the immediately given (§12). Direct confrontation with the given cannot yield knowledge; rather, knowledge always involves subsumption under concepts and, since concepts have meaning only in a *system* of judgements, always goes beyond the immediately given. Thus, for Schlick, unlike Russell, '*knowledge* by acquaintance' is an impossible contradiction. The paradigm of knowledge is not provided by Russellian sense-datum judgements but, for example, by Maxwell's equations—for these maximize the unified interconnectedness of our system of judgements (§11).

Second, Schlick militantly opposes the positivism of Mach and the phenomenalism of Russell's external world programme (§26). Science deals with real unobservable entities (Schlick goes so far as to call them 'transcendent' entities and 'things-in-themselves') which cannot be understood as mere logical constructions from sense-data (Mach's 'elements'). To think otherwise is to confuse knowledge and acquaintance, concepts (*Begriffe*) and images (*Vorstellungen*). While unobservable entities (atoms, electrons, the electro-magnetic field) are not intuitable or even picturable, this does not prevent them from being conceptualizable and knowable. Knowledge and conceptualization do not require experience (*erleben*) or intuitive representation (*vorstellen*), but only a relation of *co-ordination* (*Zuordnung*) or *designation* (*Bezeichnung*) between concepts and objects (§10). Hence, while we cannot experience, intuit, or picture the entities of modern science, we *can* catch them in the net of our concepts—and this is all that knowledge or cognition requires. Of course,

---

[3] I do not want to mislead the reader by calling *General Theory of Knowledge* the 'background' to Schlick's work on relativity. After all, the former was published in 1918, while the 2 major works on relativity appeared in 1915 and 1917 respectively. Nevertheless, *General Theory of Knowledge* reads like a pre-relativistic piece of philosophy. It is striking that there are very few explicit references to Einstein, and, in addition, it seems quite clear that the paradigm of a physical theory is late 19th cent. Maxwellian electrodynamics. Warren Goldfarb has suggested to me that Schlick had indeed incorporated relativity into his philosophy in *General Theory of Knowledge*, but he kept its influence veiled in order to 'soften up' and avoid shocking his philosophical audience. I confess that this suggestion seems implausible to me in view of the militant anti-Machian stance of Schlick's book; I think it is more likely that he had simply done most of the thinking and writing for the book before he grappled philosophically with Einstein's new theories. But these are matters for further scholarship to decide.

the net of our concepts must ultimately come in contact with experience or the given (in a way that Schlick never succeeds in making entirely clear), but this minimal empiricism would not be questioned by Kant, say, nor by contemporary, 'scientific realists'.

In other words, Schlick is not a positivist or strict empiricist in 1918, but a neo-Kantian or 'critical' realist[4]—his viewpoint is perhaps best described as a form of 'structural realism'.[5] Why did Schlick (and therefore logical positivism generally) move away from this view? An answer emerges from Schlick's writings on relativity theory. Briefly, developments in modern mathematics and modern physics make a Kantian solution to the question of theory choice untenable. We are left with the problem of theoretical underdetermination in all its sharpness, and a 'conventionalist' or verificationist solution becomes overwhelmingly tempting. Moreover, the development of Einstein's general theory of relativity appears to realize such a 'conventionalist' solution completely: Machian empiricism appears victorious.

Recall the Kantian conception of scientific cognition. On the one hand, we have pure intuition, the a priori forms of space and time, in which all mathematical reasoning takes place via a process of 'construction'. On the other hand, we have the empirical or phenomenal world, which is nothing but a distribution of matter (content) within the forms provided a priori by pure intuition. So we know a priori that the empirical world is subject to all the laws of pure mathematics and, since it must also conform to the unity of consciousness, to the continuity and conservation principles expressed in the Analogies of Experience as well. In particular, we know a priori: (1) space–time is Euclidean–Newtonian, (2) Galilean kinematics, (3) the law of inertia, (4) $F = ma$, (5) any two pieces of matter (point-masses) are related by forces of attraction and repulsion (this last follows from the definition of matter developed in *Metaphysical Foundations of Natural Science* (1786)). The only task left to a posteriori or empirical cognition, then, is a determination of the actual magnitudes of the forces specified in (5). For example, we apply (1)–(5) to the observed (Keplerian) orbits of the planets to 'deduce from the phenomena' Newton's formula for gravitational force, which we then 'make general by

---

[4] I do not want to mislead the reader by calling Schlick a 'neo-Kantian'. Schlick always rejected the synthetic a priori and Kant's theory of space and time. Yet Schlick's theory of *judgement* and *cognition* was Kantian (and anti-empiricist) in its 'holism' and 'formalism'. Schlick's view results from accepting a Kantian (or neo-Kantian) conception of judgement and cognition while rejecting Kant's doctrine of pure intuition.

[5] As such, the view of *General Theory of Knowledge* has close affinities with Russell's *Analysis of Matter* (1927), which also rejects phenomenalism in favour of 'structural correspondence'. One can get a partial sense of Schlick's view of this period from *PP* i. 201–5.

induction'. The point is that no theoretical underdetermination infects this process. There is only the ordinary inductive uncertainty that can always be corrected by future observations. For Kant, scientific cognition has—in principle, anyway—a unique and determinate outcome.

But developments in mathematics and physics upset this Kantian synthesis from all sides. Nineteenth-century foundational work, especially Weierstrass's 'rigorization' of analysis (1872) and Hilbert's *Foundations of Geometry* (1899), upsets Kant's conception of mathematical reasoning: 'rigorous' inference has no need for intuition and proceeds purely conceptually.[6] So pure mathematics has nothing in particular to do with space and time. By the same token, Einsten's work on special relativity (1905) upsets Kant's conception of physical reasoning. In particular, (1)–(5) are no longer 'fixed points', but can themselves be revised in the course of scientific inquiry. And, if there are no such 'fixed points', cognition no longer has—even in principle—a determinate outcome: theoretical underdetermination is the result.

Schlick begins to wrestle with these problems in 'The Philosophical Significance of the Principle of Relativity' (1915). In my opinion this is one of his very finest papers: it is clear, penetrating, accurate, and balanced; even today, I know of no better philosophical introduction to special relativity. We are fortunate that it is now easily accessible to the English-speaking student. The aim of the paper is to examine the impact of Einstein's new theory on the two prevailing philosophical systems of the day: the neo-Kantianism of Cassirer, Natorp, and the Marburg school and the positivism of Mach and Petzoldt (*PP* ii. 153–5). As we shall see, neither system comes out unscathed; neither is able to assimilate fully the new physical discoveries.

After giving an extremely clear account of what he calls the principle of relativity—that all inertial frames are physically indistinguishable and no (uniform rectilinear) motion relative to the ether can be detected— Schlick goes on to point out that this *principle*, which is indeed a well-confirmed empirical law, does not yet amount to the *theory* of relativity (*PP* i. 159–62). For there are two different ways of accommodating the empirical facts. We can, with Lorentz and Fitzgerald, maintain that (uniform rectilinear) motion relative to the ether exists, but remains undetectable because of compensatory contractions and retardations—

---

[6] Although Schlick, for one, is far from clear about this, these 19th-cent. foundational developments require, for the first time, complicated patterns of *polyadic* reasoning (as is evident in the Cauchy–Bolzano–Weierstrass treatment of continuity, convergence, etc., and in Weierstrass's distinction between pointwise and uniform properties). It is no accident that Frege's work follows closely on the heels of that of Weierstrass. For Kant, on the other hand, logic is essentially *monadic* or syllogistic: Kantian 'concepts' are monadic concepts.

thereby retaining Euclidean–Newtonian space–time and Galilean kinematics. Alternatively, we can, with Einstein, maintain that (uniform rectilinear) motion relative to the ether does not exist, and that indistinguishable reference frames are fully equivalent as well—thereby abandoning Euclidean—Newtonian space–time and Galilean kinematics. We have a choice here because the two theories are empirically equivalent: they are equally consistent with all experiential data (*PP* i. 164).

On a Kantian conception there is of course no choice here. Our spatio-temporal intuition has a determinate and objective structure, and so Euclidean–Newtonian space–time and Galilean kinematics are 'fixed points' as above. Therefore, only the Lorentz–Fitzgerald theory is a live option. For Schlick, on the other hand, spatio-temporal intuition has a merely 'subjective' and 'psychological' character (*PP* i. 162–3), and no such a priori considerations can rule out Einstein's theory. Moreover, Einstein's theory has important methodological advantages over the Lorentz–Fitzgerald theory. In particular, it possesses the kind of greater *simplicity* that has always moved scientists to prefer one theory over another—as in the choice of Copernican over Ptolemaic astronomy, for example (*PP* i. 164, 170–1). Unfortunately, however, there is no way to justify our methodological preference for the simpler theory: we cannot argue that simpler theories come closer to the truth (*PP* i. 169–70).

Schlick has obviously got himself into a quandary here. At times he flirts with a 'conventionalist' or verificationist solution. Thus, with a nod to Poincaré, we can maintain that two empirically equivalent theories are equally correct as well: there is no need for a choice between them (*PP* i. 167–9). Yet, since Schlick is a convinced Einsteinian, he cannot remain satisfied with this way out. He proceeds to argue that perhaps simpler theories are closer to reality after all, since they contain fewer '*arbitrary* elements' (*PP* i. 171–2). By the end of the paper, he is prepared to assert that the ether hypothesis is senseless and devoid of all 'physical meaning' (*PP* i. 185). With respect to the *real* case of empirically equivalent theories that the development of relativity theory itself supplies, then, Schlick is not ultimately willing to opt for strict empiricism. He does not want to say that empirically equivalent theories are necessarily equally correct.

Moreover, as Schlick makes amply clear, relativity theory itself retains important elements of unobservable, theoretical structure. Although Einstein's theory does have fewer unobservable elements than the Lorentz–Fitzgerald ether theory, it does not eliminate such elements completely. In particular, while it is true that relativity theory eliminates absolute rest and velocity, it does not eliminate *absolute acceleration and rotation*. So the kind of limitless relativity of motion maintained by Mach on empiricist grounds does not find expression in Einstein's theory (*PP* i. 179–84). Furthermore, even if relativity theory were to realize Mach's ideas, this could only be based on actual empirical findings (like the empirical findings that in fact support the special or restricted principle of relativity). A purely philosophical commitment to strict empiricism is quite insufficient (*PP* i. 183).

So things stood in 1915. In 1916, however, Einstein brought years of work on a relativistic theory of gravitation to successful completion with the publication of 'The Foundation of the General Theory of Relativity'. Sections §§1–3 of that paper make far-reaching philosophical claims on behalf of the new theory. In particular, Einstein claims finally to realize the thoroughgoing relativity of motion envisioned by Mach (hence the name of the new theory) and to remove from space and time 'the last vestige of physical objectivity'. The only spatio-temporal features left invariant under the *arbitrary* substitutions allowed by the principle of general covariance are space–time *coincidences*: meetings of material particles, matching of endpoints of rigid rods, coincidences between the hands of a clock and points on the dial, and so on. It follows that only such 'observable' events are physically real. Abstract theoretical structures— assignments of 'absolute' motion, attributions of a particular metrical geometry, etc.—can be arbitrarily transformed at will and are therefore only conventionally chosen aids for facilitating the description of the totality of space–time coincidences.

In *Space and Time in Contemporary Physics* (1917), *PP* i. 207–69, Schlick embraces these new ideas with easily understandable enthusiasm. Einstein's construction of an actual physical theory satisfying the principle of general covariance offers intoxicating relief from the sceptical problem of theoretical underdetermination. In particular, we are able to follow Poincaré in regarding empirically equivalent metrical geometries as equally correct (*PP* i. 223–33) and to follow Leibniz and Mach in regarding *all* motion as essentially relative (*PP* i. 233–43). We are left with a view that comes very close indeed to verificationism or strict empiricism:

The adjustment and reading of all measuring instruments of whatsoever variety— whether they be provided with pointers or scales, angular-diversions, water-levels, mercury columns, or any other means—are always accomplished by observing space–time coincidences of two or more points. This is also true above all of apparatus used to measure time, familiarly termed *clocks*. Such coincidences are, therefore, strictly speaking, alone capable of being observed; and the whole of physics may be regarded as a quintessence of laws, according to which the occurrence of space–time coincidences takes place. Everything else in our world-picture which *cannot* be reduced to such coincidences is devoid of physical reality, and may just as well be replaced by something else. All world pictures which lead to the same laws for these point-coincidences are, from the point of view of physics, in every way equivalent. (*PP* i. 241)

Thus, the development of physical theory itself appears to make Machian positivism a much more viable position.[7]

Nevertheless, Schlick still draws back from a thoroughgoing positivism (after all, it is 1917, and *General Theory of Knowledge* is just being completed). Only space–time coincidences are real or objective, but not all space–time coincidences are literally observable. Real physical coincidences include such point-events as the collision of two elementary particles or the electromagnetic field strength taking on a particular value. Such point-events are not strictly observable, but they are 'measurable', and this is all that is required for physical reality (*PP* i. 264–6). The view we end up with appears to go something like this. Some pieces of theoretical structure—assignments of 'absolute' motion, attributions of a particular metrical geometry—are given a positivist or 'conventionalist' interpretation. Other pieces of theoretical structure—atoms and electrons, the electromagnetic field—are given a 'realist' interpretation. However, since Schlick provides no principled reasons for making this kind of distinction, his view is intrinsically unstable. Accordingly, his post-1917 writings take on an increasingly verificationist tone.

In his important critical study of Cassirer's work on relativity, 'Critical or Empiricist Interpretation of Modern Physics?' (1921), *PP* i. 322–4, Schlick has nothing but praise for Mach (*PP* i. 330–1). He even prefigures the principle of verifiability: '*differences in reality may be assumed only*

---

[7] It is now more or less generally known that this positivistic interpretation of general relativity is completely untenable. General covariance implies neither a generalized relativity of motion nor a 'conventionalist' conception of physical space (or space–time) as 'metrically amorphous'. As a matter of fact, *any* space–time—including the space–times of Newtonian physics and special relativity—can be given a generally covariant description. What distinguishes general relativity is the use of a *non-flat* (non-Euclidean) space–time of variable, mass-energy dependent curvature. General relativistic space–time has a perfectly determinate and objective (although variable) metrical structure, and absolute acceleration and rotation have much the same status as they do in special relativity: Machian relativity is not realized. Furthermore, these (essentially mathematical) facts were established in Schlick's own time via the work of Kretschmann (1917) and Weyl (1918). (The final clarification was provided by Cartan's great papers of 1923–4, which showed, in particular, how *Newtonian* gravitation theory also makes use of a non-flat space–time structure.) Yet the philosophical pressures leading toward a 'conventionalist' misunderstanding of general relativity were quite irresistible (even to Einstein himself), and the notion of covariance is remarkably subtle and elusive. As a result, verificationist misinterpretations of general relativity have persisted almost to the present day.

where there are differences that can, in principle, be experienced' (*PP*
i. 330) and declares:

if the principle is recognized and evaluated in its true significance, it can, I believe,
be elevated to the supreme principle of all empirical philosophy, to the ultimate
guideline which must govern our attitude to every question of detail, and whose
ruthless application to all special problems is an exceedingly fruitful procedure. If
this view is correct, the connection of relativity theory with empiricist theory of
knowledge would then be seen as an intimate, strictly factual, and not merely
external or contingent one. (*PP* i. 331)

(Of course Schlick's principle is not the principle of verifiability itself: it is
a methodological principle, not a principle about meaning.) Finally, in a
popular lecture from 1922, 'The Theory of Relativity in Philosophy', (*PP*
i. 343–53), Schlick enunciates the principle, itself derived from Einstein's
1916 paper, that '*only something really observable should be introduced as
a ground of explanation in science*' (*PP* i. 345). (Note that this principle is
much stronger than the above principle from 1921.) He again sings Mach's
praises (*PP* i. 347), and, when he criticizes 'positivism', he now means
only the 'subjectivist' and 'relativist' views of Petzoldt (*PP* i. 347–8). We
here stand on the very threshold of logical empiricism.[8]

Schlick's life-long struggle with the form–content distinction is of
particular interest. His starting-point is Hilbert's *Foundations of Geometry*
and the notion of axiomatic or *implicit* definition (*General Theory of
Knowledge*, §7). According to the conception Schlick derives from
Hilbert, the primitive terms of geometry require no intuitive meaning or
content. All we need to know about these primitives for the purposes of
pure geometry are their mutual logical relationships set up explicitly in the
axioms. Points, lines, and planes are *any* system of objects whatsoever that

---

[8] It appears that Schlick's work on relativity was instrumental in 'converting' the other early
positivists to strict empiricism. Thus, Reichenbach's early work, *The Theory of Relativity and A
Priori Knowledge* (1920; trans. M. Reichenbach, Berkeley, 1960), takes an explicitly anti-
empiricist and neo-Kantian line. In marked contrast to the well-known views of *The Philosophy
of Space and Time* (1928; trans. M. Reichenbach and J. Freund, New York, 1957), he argues
that, although the choices of co-ordinate system and rest system are indeed arbitrary or
conventional, the choice of a *metric* is not. Accordingly, he rejects Poincaré's 'conventionalism'
(see the first footnote to Reichenbach's book). Schlick criticizes Reichenbach in the above-
mentioned article on Cassirer (*PP* i. 333), and by 1922 Reichenbach has capitulated:
'conventionalism' is correct and Poincaré is vindicated (see Reichenbach, *Selected Writings,
1909–1953*, ed. M. Reichenbach and R. S. Cohen ii. 34–5, 38–9, 44). Similarly, although it
would certainly be incorrect to describe Carnap's position in *Der Raum* (*Kantstudien*, 56
(1922)) as empiricist (his central conclusion is also neo-Kantian: *n*-dimensional *topology* is an a
priori condition of the possibility of experience), he does present a very clear and rigorous
defence of 'conventionalism' with respect to *metrical* structure that is directly inspired by
Schlick's account of the significance of general covariance in *Space and Time in Contemporary
Physics* (trans. H. L. Brose, Oxford, 1920) (see *Der Raum*, p. 83).

satisfy these axioms. Hence, pure geometry is intrinsically 'uninterpreted' and has nothing at all to do with intuitive space.[9] Schlick generalizes this picture to all concepts and all of science. The meaning of all concepts is ultimately determined by their mutual logical relationships within a system of scientific judgements, not by the intuitive content we may happen to associate with them. To think otherwise is to confuse concepts (*Begriffe*) with images (*Vorstellungen*).[10]

In other words, concepts generally are individuated by their *logical forms*, by their logical 'places' within a deductive system.[11] Nevertheless, scientific, as opposed to purely mathematical concepts have *content* as well: they designate (*bezeichnen*) real 'qualities' in nature, which, if our system of judgements is true, have the same formal properties as the corresponding concepts—that is, the real 'qualities' satisfy our (initially 'uninterpreted') judgements. But the point Schlick is most concerned to stress remains this: Knowledge or cognition (*erkennen*) relates only to such *formal* properties; *content* is never itself an object of knowledge but only (at most) of experience (*erleben*) and acquaintance (*kennen*). So the fact that some particular real 'quality' is unintuitable (like the electromagnetic field intensity, for example) presents no obstacle whatsoever to its knowability: all that is required is a grasp of its purely formal properties (*General Theory of Knowledge*, §§9, 12, 26).

There is no doubt that this kind of view suffers from overwhelming difficulties and verges on incoherence, for the relationship between form and content, concepts and reality, is left hopelessly obscure. Schlick makes the point himself with characteristic honesty and acuteness:

in implicit definition we have found a tool that makes possible completely determinate concepts and therefore rigorously exact thought. However, we require

---

[9] Such a conception of pure geometry would make no sense at all to Kant, for whom even geometrical *reasoning* requires the a priori manifolds supplied by pure intuition. Geometrical thinking is necessarily spatial in the intuitive sense, and 'uninterpreted *geometry*' is a contradiction in terms.

[10] Similar views are very much in evidence throughout the period. I have in mind esp. C. I. Lewis's *Mind and the World Order* (1929) and Russell's *Introduction to Mathematical Philosophy* (London, 1919) and *Analysis of Matter* (New York, 1927). Carnap's *Aufbau* (Berlin, 1928) presents the logically most sophisticated version. (For Russell and Carnap see W. Demopoulos and M. Friedman, 'The Concept of Structure in Russell's *Analysis of Matter*', in C. W. Savage and C. A. Anderson (eds.), *Rereading Russell: Essays on Bertrand Russell's Metaphysics and Epistemology* (Minneapolis, 1988).

[11] Again, such a view only begins to make clear sense in the context of modern *polyadic* logic. Monadic concepts correspond to unstructured sets whose only formal property is their cardinality. Polyadic concepts, on the other hand, can have infinitely many distinct formal properties: transitivity, reflexivity, connectedness, *n*-dimensionality, and so on. In Russell's terminology from *Introduction to Mathematical Philosophy* and *The Analysis of Matter*, only polyadic concepts have 'relation-numbers'. See also Carnap's *Aufbau* §§11–16.

for this purpose a radical separation between concepts and intuition, thought and reality. To be sure, we place the two spheres one upon the other, but they appear to be absolutely unconnected, the bridges between them are demolished (*General Theory of Knowledge*, §7)

Schlick is perfectly correct. The Kantian bridge between thought and reality—namely, pure intuition—has indeed been demolished. Hence, if we persist in a 'holistic' and 'formalistic' account of knowledge and judgement, we are driven towards idealism and the coherence theory of truth. In particular, we will have a hard time distinguishing physical or empirical knowledge from pure mathematics, on the one hand, and from arbitrary coherent systems of metaphysics or myth, on the other. Either way it will be difficult to maintain the Kantian commitment to mathematical physics as a paradigm of knowledge.[12] To Schlick, of course, the coherence theory of truth is anathema. So, as we shall see, he is continually tempted to renounce his 'holistic' conception of meaning in favour of an 'atomistic' empiricist conception which views the intuitively given as the ultimate repository of meaning after all.

Schlick returns to the form–content distinction in his classical paper, 'Experience, Cognition, Metaphysics' (1926), *PP* ii. 99–111. In the meantime he has moved to Vienna (1922) and read the *Tractatus* and drafts of Carnap's *Aufbau*. He again articulates the distinction between experience (*erleben*) and cognition (*erkennen*). Cognition relates always to purely formal or 'structural' features that are expressed in logical relationships or 'implicit definitions'. Experience, on the other hand, involves content: the actual 'qualitative' features of things, such as the redness of a red surface. Moreover, he makes the rather startling claim that all traditional metaphysics is based on a confusion of form and content, knowledge and intuition: metaphysics is the self-contradictory search for 'intuitive knowledge' (*PP* ii. 107–11). So far the basic ideas are familiar from *General Theory of Knowledge*. But there are also several important novelties.

First, form is not only said to be the sole object of knowledge, it is also all that is *communicable*. Form is what can be expressed in language; content is essentially private and incommunicable. Not only does content elude our cognition, it forever eludes our expression as well. Hence, logical form, and logical form alone, is the basis for intersubjective

[12] This is precisely the path taken by the 'logical idealism' of Cassirer and the Marburg school. Cassirer is perfectly happy to throw away the autonomous role played by Kant's pure intuition, and equally happy to dethrone mathematical physics from its position of pre-eminence. All coherent 'symbolic forms'—mathematics, physics, art, religion, myth, etc.—are equally respectable and, in particular, have their own characteristic standards of 'objectivity'. We can no longer equate the objective with the results of natural science. See e.g. *Substance and Function and Einstein's Theory of Relativity*, Chicago, 1923.

communication (*PP* ii. 99–102). Of course this view, which is a natural extension of the views in *General Theory of Knowledge*, immediately makes the form–content distinction itself unstatable. This is why there is no such distinction in the *Tractatus*, for example: the substance of the world (= the totality of objects) is both form *and* content (2.025).

Second, Schlick has abandoned the realism of *General Theory of Knowledge*. In fact, he articulates the characteristic claim of later logical positivism that the difference between realism and strict empiricism cannot itself be expressed or stated. It makes no difference at all whether the objects of physics are viewed as logical constructions from experience or as 'independent realities'. All that matters is that there are objects with such-and-such statable formal properties (*PP* ii. 103–4). Note that Schlick here simply assumes, without argument, that the objects of physics *can* be conceived as logical constructions from experience. Perhaps it is because he has meanwhile become convinced that they *must* be so conceived. In any case, the net effect of these two moves is clear. The form–content distinction now coincides (as it does for Carnap in the *Aufbau*) with the inter-subjective–private distinction: content is always internal and experienceable. In *General Theory of Knowledge*, by contrast, content includes both internal, intuitable 'qualities' and external, unintuitable 'qualities'. So in 1926 the gulf between form and content, thought and reality, has at least been diminished.

By 1929 the remaining gulf has somehow magically disappeared, and the transformation is complete. Schlick is now the militant prophet of logical positivism. He expounds the verifiability theory of meaning (apparently for the first time in 1930: see *PP* ii. 156–7) and begins to give the following, characteristically 'atomistic' and empiricist, argument for it: all explanations of meaning typically consist in defining some words in terms of other words; but this process cannot continue indefinitely or move continually in a circle; therefore, we must eventually attach words directly to experience in acts of ostention, and all meaning ultimately resides in the given. Thus, in 1930: 'if, say, I state the meaning of my words by elucidatory propositions and definitions, and thus by means of new words, we have again to ask for the meanings of these other words, and so on. This process cannot continue indefinitely, and always terminates at last in mere factual indications, in demonstrations of what is meant' (*PP* ii. 157–9). And in 1931: 'All of our definitions must end by some demonstration, by some activity. There may be certain words at the meaning of which one may arrive by certain mental activities just as I can arrive at the signification of a word which denotes colour by showing the colour itself' (*PP* ii. 220).

Schlick articulates his new position most clearly and explicitly in 'Positivism and Realism' (1932), *PP* ii. 259–84. There he gives the following argument:

But when do I understand a proposition? When I know the meaning of the words that occur in it? This can be explained by definitions. But in the definitions new words occur, whose meaning I also have to know in turn. The business of defining cannot go on indefinitely, so eventually we come to words whose meaning cannot again be described in a proposition; it has to be pointed out directly; the meaning of the word must ultimately be *shown*, it has to be given. This takes place through an act of pointing or showing, and what is shown must be given, since otherwise it cannot be pointed out by me . . . The *meaning* of every proposition is ultimately determined by the given alone, and by absolutely nothing else. (*PP* ii. 264)

Here, the 'holistic' conception of meaning of *General Theory of Knowledge* and 'Experience, Cognition, Metaphysics' has been turned completely on its head.

By now the contradiction has become too explicit to ignore. So Schlick takes up the problem again in 'Form and Content', *PP* ii. 284–369, written in the same year. He again claims (now obviously under the influence of the *Tractatus*) that logical form or structure is the basis for expression and communication. The content of the given is not itself expressible; rather, when we appear to communicate about the given, we are only expressing *its* structural properties (e.g. the logical structure of 'colour space'). In marked contrast to the above passage from 'Positivism and Realism', he says: 'understanding and meaning are quite independent of Content and have nothing whatever to do with it' (*PP* ii. 298). To be sure, he also defends the verifiability theory of meaning, and even gives the familiar 'regress of definitions' argument for it (*PP* ii. 310–11). But he now realizes that this argument must be seriously qualified in the context of the 'structuralism' of the logical form conception. The passage is worth quoting in full:

The chief reason why it was so generally believed that all real knowledge must in some way culminate in immediate acquaintance or intuition lies in the fact that they seem to indicate the points where we must look for the ultimate meaning of all our words and symbols. A definition gives the meaning of a term by means of other words, these can again be defined by means of still other words, and so on, until we arrive at terms that no longer admit of verbal definition; the meaning of these must be given by direct acquaintance: one can learn the meaning of 'joy' or 'green' only by being joyful or seeing green. Thus the final understanding and interpretation of a proposition seems to be reached only in those acts of intuition—is it not through them, therefore, that the real knowledge which the proposition expresses is ultimately attained?

The considerations in our first lecture have taught us already to what extent these remarks are true. We saw that our ordinary verbal language must be supplemented by pointing to objects and presenting them in order to make our words and sentences a useful means of communication, but we saw at the same time that in this way *we were only explaining our language of words by a language of gestures*, and that it would be a mistake to think that by this method our words were really linked to the content which intuition is supposed to provide for us. We showed that the meaning of our words was contained entirely in the *structure* of the intuitive content. So it is not true that the latter (the inexpressible greenness of green), which only intuition can furnish, actually enters into the understanding of knowledge. It cannot possibly do so. (*PP* ii. 321–2; first emphasis added)

'Holism' has returned with a vengeance.

Yet Schlick is still not prepared to jettison 'content' completely, although at times he comes very close to doing this (see e.g. *PP* ii. 306–7). Why not? Because, unless our symbols have content as well as form, we are unable to distinguish applied sciences such as mathematical physics from 'uninterpreted' deductive systems such as pure geometry:

if we are to have a science of some domain of reality instead of a mere hypothetical–deductive system, then our symbols must stand for real content; for if they stood for mere structure, we should again in the end be left without meaning, for again there would be the possibility of many different interpretations. But actual science deals with reality, which is unique, and not with possibilities only, of which there are many.

If this is the right answer it must appear difficult to reconcile with our former insight that content never enters into our propositions and that all expression is done solely by means of pure structure. (*PP* ii. 331).

Such a reconciliation is difficult indeed! Here is Schlick's solution:

the empty frame of a hypothetical–deductive system does have to be filled with content in order to become a science containing real knowledge, and this is done by observation (experience). But every observer fills in his own content. We cannot say that all the observers have the same content, and we cannot say that they have not—not because we are ignorant, but because there would be no sense in either assertion. (*PP* ii. 334)

Plainly, Schlick has now reached the end of his rope.[13] How can

---

[13] Schlick is again ill-served by his poor understanding of the logicist tradition, especially as represented by Wittgenstein's *Tractatus*. From such a logicist point of view the problem cannot even be set up. For, to formulate Schlick's problem we must take a *metalinguistic* stance towards the language of physics and regard the primitive terms of that language as uninterpreted *schematic letters*. But neither of these steps makes sense on a strict logicist conception. First, there is no distinction between object language and metalanguage. There is only one language: the single linguistic framework in which all our concepts and judgements are ultimately related. Second, there are no uninterpreted schematic letters. All symbols are either variables or constants (primitive or defined), and there is no room for a *choice* of interpretation. The interpretation of variables, for example, is fixed once and for all by their logical forms: first-level variables range over *all* individuals, second-level variables range over *all* functions of individuals, and so on. Similarly, there is no problem of distinguishing natural science (synthetic propositions) from pure mathematics (analytic propositions). On a logicist conception, pure mathematics is part of the logical framework of language itself, and so cannot

subjective, private, and inexpressible content possibly help ground an intersubjective, public science?

After 1932 Schlick's intellectual creativity is attenuated considerably, and I will leave it to the reader to trace the twists and turns of thought in his final essays. (Essays 16, 18, and 19 of vol. ii are especially interesting and revealing: Schlick gets into quite a quarrel with some of the younger positivists—Carnap, Neurath, and Hempel—over the status of 'protocol-sentences' and their relation to 'experience'.) Instead, I would like to conclude with some general remarks about the significance of Schlick's work for our understanding of logical positivism and the broader philosophical context within which it develops. For it seems to me that careful attention to the actual history of logical positivism forces us to revise drastically our contemporary assessment of that movement, especially our contemporary picture of the relationship between 'empiricism' and the new logic.

The standard picture of positivism goes something like this. Inspired by Hume, Mach, and Russell's external world programme, the positivists adopted the concerns, problems, and ambitions of traditional empiricism more or less unchanged. Starting from a naïve and 'atomistic' conception of experience, observation, and the given, the problem was to show how the theoretical structures of physics could be grounded in or constructed from the given. Here modern logic supplied powerful new tools—the theory of relations and set theory—for carrying out this traditional project. These new tools were deployed with great ingenuity and resourcefulness—especially in Carnap's *Aufbau*—but, in the end, the dream of classical empiricism could not be realized: the objects of physics could not be defined or constructed from experience or the given. Hence, logical positivism is a failed philosophical movement, but its 'logicization'

possibly be confused with non-logical propositions. Empirical science is just the totality of non-logical (non-tautologous) truths. (Of course this conception of empirical science has nothing in particular to do with 'experience' in the traditional sense, nor does it supply any kind of justification for mathematical physics as it now is or may become. Wittgenstein, for one, is quite sanguine about this: see *Tractatus*, 6.363–72). Hence, if Schlick had really understood the *Tractatus*, he would never have become so hopelessly entangled with the form–content distinction. Nevertheless, we are fortunate that Schlick did misunderstand Wittgenstein, for *our* conception of logic is in many ways closer to Schlick's 'Hilbertian' conception than to the logicist tradition (hence our contemporary problems about 'inscrutability of reference' and 'ontological relativity'). It would be wrong, however, simply to equate our conception of logic with Schlick's 'Hilbertian' view. For our conception is the result of an evolution *within* the logicist tradition that took its present form only in the synthesis wrought by Gödel in 1930. See the excellent account in W. D. Goldfarb, 'Logic in the Twenties', *Journal of Symbolic Logic*, 44 (1979), 351–68. I am also indebted to Thomas Ricketts for very helpful conversations about these matters.

of empiricism makes it a significant failure: it supplies a precise *proof* that strict empiricism cannot succeed.

Our reflections on Schlick and his philosophical context have shown, I hope, that this standard contemporary assessment is completely inadequate. The early positivists did not simply appropriate the new logic as a tool or technique for solving previously given philosophical problems. Rather, this logic was itself the source of radically new problems and a radically transformed philosophical situation. In particular, the new logic made it possible to implement precisely an essentially Kantian 'holistic' and 'formalistic' theory of judgement and meaning, while at the same time dispensing with Kant's pure intuition and the synthetic a priori. In rejecting the synthetic a priori the early positivists were indeed in agreement with traditional empiricism, but their 'holistic' theory of judgement was a point of sharp disagreement. Our cognitive relation to experience or the given could not be understood on an 'atomistic' paradigm, for *all* judgement—including perceptual judgement—makes sense only in the context of a total *system* of judgements (cf. *General Theory of Knowledge*, §§10, 11). In other words, what we now call the 'theory-ladenness' of observation was actually a commonplace of early positivism (as well as of neo-Kantianism generally).

Yet the very factors that moved early positivism towards traditional empiricism and away from Kant—the rejection of pure intuition and the synthetic a priori—also made a genuine empiricist position impossible. Without pure intuition, the 'formal' or 'structural' basis for objective judgement—the infinitely rich set of logical forms of Frege's new logic—now has no particular connection with experience or the empirical world: objective judgement has no need for 'content' in the Kantian sense. In this respect, it became much more difficult for the positivists to maintain a commitment to empiricism and empirical science than it was for Kant. It is clear, in any case, that empiricism cannot simply be combined with the new logic (as Russell attempted to do in his 'logical atomism', for example); rather, the two stand in a kind of 'dialectical opposition'.

I believe that this 'dialectical opposition'—exemplified so clearly and painfully in Schlick's struggles with the form–content distinction—animates both logical positivism and the analytic tradition as a whole. In Frege and the early Wittgenstein—thinkers whose primary concern is with mathematics and logic—the formal element predominates completely, and concern for empirical knowledge and epistemology in the traditional sense shrinks to the point of vanishing. In Schlick and Carnap—thinkers with an equal concern for physics and empirical science—the two elements are brought together with clearly evident resulting strains and tensions. (These tensions perhaps emerge most starkly and precisely in §§153–5 of the *Aufbau*, where Carnap is forced to argue that the notion of a 'natural' or 'experienceable' relation is itself a primitive concept of logic!) I believe that the 'dialectical opposition' between logic and experience, form and content, also informs Carnap's later work and the post-positivist philosophies of Quine and the later Wittgenstein. But these stories will have to wait for another day.

PART IV

REALITY AND THE PRESENT

11

OMNISCIENCE AND IMMUTABILITY

NORMAN KRETZMANN

It is generally recognized that omniscience and immutability are necessary characteristics of an absolutely perfect being. The fact that they are also incompatible characteristics seems to have gone unnoticed.

In the main body of this paper I will present first an argument that turns on the incompatibility of omniscience and immutability and, second, several objections to the argument with my replies to the objections.

(1) A perfect being is not subject to change.[1]
(2) A perfect being knows everything.[2]
(3) A being that knows everything always knows what time it is.[3]
(4) A being that always knows what time it is is subject to change.[4]
(5) A perfect being is subject to change.
(6) A perfect being is not a perfect being.

This chapter appeared originally in the *Journal of Philosophy*, 63: 14 (July 1966), 409–21. Reprinted by permission.

[1] This principle of immutability is regularly supported by 1 of 2 arguments. (*a*) From supreme excellence: a perfect being is a supremely excellent being; thus any change in such a being would constitute corruption, deterioration, loss of perfection. (See Plato, *Republic*, 2. 381 B.) (*b*) From complete actualization: a perfect being is a being whose capacities for development are all fully realized. A being subject to change, however, is in that respect and to that extent a being with an unrealized capacity for development, a being merely potential and not fully actualized, a being in a state of process and not complete; hence not perfect. (See Aristotle, *Metaphysics*, 12. 9, 1074^{b}26.) The principle of immutability is a thesis of orthodox Christian theology, drawn from Greek philosophy and having among its credentials such biblical passages as Malachi 3: 6 and James 1: 17. (See Aquinas, *Summa Theologica*, i, q. 9, art. 1.)

[2] Being incapable of knowing all there is to know or being capable of knowing all there is to know and knowing less than that are conditions evidently incompatible with absolute perfection. Hence (2), which seems even more familiar and less problematic than (1).

[3] Part of what is meant by premiss (3) is, of course, that a being that knows everything always knows what time it is in every time zone on every planet in every galaxy; but it is not quite in that horological sense that its knowledge of what time it is is most plainly relevant to considerations of omniscience and immutability. The relevant sense can be brought out more easily in the consideration of objections against the argument.

[4] Adopting 'it is now t_n' as a convenient standard form for propositions as to what time it is, we may say of a being that always knows what time it is that the state of its knowledge changes incessantly with respect to propositions of the form 'it is now t_n'. For such a being knows that it is now t_1 (and that it is not now t_2), and then it knows that it is now t_2 (and that it is not now t_1). To say of any being that it knows something different from what it used to know is to say that it has changed; hence (4).

Finally, therefore,

(7) There is no perfect being.[5]

In discussing this argument with others[6] I have come across various objections against one or another of its premisses. Considering such objections here helps to clarify the line taken in the argument and provides an opportunity to anticipate and turn aside several natural criticisms of that line.

Because premisses (1) and (2) present the widely accepted principles of immutability and omniscience, objections against them are not so much criticisms of the line taken in the argument as they are attempts to modify the concept of a perfect being in the light of the argument. And since premiss (3) gives every impression of being an instance of a logical truth, premiss (4) is apparently the one most vulnerable to attacks that are genuinely attacks on the argument. The first four of the following seven objections are all directed against premiss (4), although Objection D raises a question relevant to premiss (3) as well.

Objection A It must be granted that a being that always knows what time it is knows something that is changing—say, the state of the universe. But change in the object of knowledge does not entail change in the knower.

The denial that a change in the object necessitates a change in the knower depends on imprecise characterizations of the object. For example, I know that the Chrysler Building in Manhattan is 1,046 feet tall. If it is said that the Chrysler Building is the object of my knowledge, then of course many changes in it—in its tenants or in its heating system, for example—do not necessitate changes in the state of my knowledge. If, however, it is more precisely said that the object of my knowledge is the

---

[5] [If] $(x) (Px \supset \sim Cx)$; [2f] $(x) (Px \supset (p) (p \equiv Kxp))$ [K: . . . knows that . . .]; [3f] $(x ((p) (p \equiv Kxp) \supset (p) (Tp \supset (p \equiv Kxp))$ [T: . . . is of the form 'it is now t_n']; [4f] $(x) ((p) (Tp \supset (p \equiv Kxp)) \supset Cx$]; [5f] $(x) (Px \supset Cx)$ [entailed by 2f, 3f, 4f]; [6f] $(x) (Px \supset \sim Px)$ [entailed by 1f, 5f]; [7f] $(x) \sim Px$ [equivalent to 6f]. The formalization [3f] is an instance of a logical truth; nevertheless, premiss (3) is not one of the established principles in philosophical or theological discussions of the nature of a perfect being. Not only is it not explicitly affirmed, but it seems often to be implicitly denied. The circumstance may arouse a suspicion that the formalization [3f] is inaccurate or question-begging. Any such suspicion will, I think, be dissipated in the course of considering the objections to the argument, but it may be helpful in the meantime to point out that the validity of the argument does not depend on this formalization. It is of course possible to adopt less detailed formalizations that would not disclose the special logical status of premiss (3) and would nevertheless exhibit the validity of the argument. For example, [2f'] (x) $(Px \supset Ox)$; [3f'] $(x) (Ox \supset Nx)$ together with a similarly imprecise formalization of premiss (4) would serve that purpose.

[6] I am indebted esp. to Miss Marilyn McCord and to Professors H. N. Castañeda, H. G. Frankfurt, C. Ginet, G. B. Matthews, G. Nakhnikian, W. L. Rowe, S. Shoemaker, and W. Wainwright.

height of the Chrysler Building, then of course a change in the object of my knowledge does necessitate a change in me. If a 40-foot television antenna is extended from the present tip of the tower, either I will cease to know the height of the Chrysler Building or I will give up believing that its height is 1,046 feet and begin believing that its height is 1,086 feet. In the case of always knowing what time it is, if we are to speak of an object of knowledge at all it must be characterized not as the state of the universe (which might also be said to be the object of, for example, a cosmologist's knowledge), but as the *changing* of that state. To know the changing of anything is to know first that *p* and then that not-*p* (for some particular instance of *p*), and a knower that knows first one proposition and then another is a knower that changes.

Objection B   The beliefs of a being that always knows what time it is are subject to change, but a change in a being's beliefs need not constitute a change in the being itself. If last year Jones believed the Platonic epistles to be genuine and this year he believes them to be spurious, then Jones has changed his mind; and that sort of change in beliefs may be considered a change in Jones. But if last year Jones believed that it was 1965 and this year he believes that it is 1966, he has not changed his mind, he has merely taken account of a calendar change; and that sort of change in beliefs should not be considered a change in Jones. The change in beliefs entailed by always knowing what time it is is that taking-account sort of change rather than a change of mind, the sort of change in beliefs that might reasonably be said to have been at least in part initiated by the believer and that might therefore be reasonably attributed to him.

It seems clear, first of all, that the sort of change in beliefs entailed by knowing the changing of anything is the taking-account sort of change rather than a change of mind. But once that much has been allowed, Objection B seems to consist in no more than an expression of disappointment in the *magnitude* of the change necessitated by always knowing what time it is. The entailed change in beliefs is not, it is true, sufficiently radical to qualify as a change of character or of attitude, but it is no less incompatible with immutability for all that. If Jones had been immutable from December 1965 to January 1966 he could no more have taken account of the calendar change than he could have changed his mind.

It may be worth noting that just such small-scale, taking-account changes in beliefs have sometimes been recognized by adherents of the principle of immutability as incompatible with immutability. Ockham, for example, argues at length against the possibility of a change in the state of

God's foreknowledge just because God's changelessness could not be preserved through such a change. In Question Five of his *Tractatus de praedestinatione et de praescientia Dei et de futuris contingentibus*, Ockham maintains that "if 'God know that *A*' (where *A* is a future contingent proposition) and 'God does not know that *A*' *could* be true successively, it *would* follow that God was unchangeable", and the principle on which Ockham bases that claim is in no way restricted to future contingents. (As an adherent of the principle of immutability Ockham of course proceeds to deny that God could first know that *A* and then not know that *A*, but his reasons for doing so involve considerations peculiar to future contingent propositions and need not concern us here.)[7]

Objection C For an omniscient being always to know what time it is is to know the state of the universe at every instant, but it is possible for an omniscient being to know the state of the universe at every instant all at once rather than successively. Consequently it is possible for an omniscient being always to know what time it is without being subject to change.

The superficial flaw in this objection is the ambiguity of the phrase 'to know the state of the universe at every instant', but the ambiguity is likely to be overlooked because the phrase is evidently an allusion to a familiar, widely accepted account of omniscience, according to which omniscience regarding contingent events is nothing more nor less than knowledge of the entire scheme of contingent events from beginning to end at once. I see no reason for quarrelling here with the ascription of such knowledge to an omniscient being; but the underlying flaw in Objection C is the drastic *incompleteness* of this account of omniscience regarding contingent events.

The kind of knowledge ascribed to an omniscient being in this account is sometimes characterized as 'seeing all time at a glance', which suggests that if one sees the entire scheme of contingent events from beginning to end at once one sees all there is to see of time. The totality of contingent events, we are to suppose, may be known either simultaneously or successively, and an omniscient being will of course know it not

---

[7] The most interesting historical example of this sort that I have seen was called to my attention by Professor Hugh Chandler after I had submitted this paper for publication. It is Problem XIII in the *Tahāfut al Falāsifah* of al-Ghazali (d. *c.1111*): '*Refutation of their* [i.e. the philosophers', but principally Avicenna's] DOCTRINE THAT GOD (MAY HE BE EXALTED ABOVE WHAT THEY SAY) DOES NOT KNOW THE PARTICULARS WHICH ARE DIVISIBLE IN ACCORDANCE WITH THE DIVISION OF TIME INTO "WILL BE", "WAS", AND "IS" ' (trans. S. A. Kamali (Lahore, 1963), 153–62). This work was not known to medieval Christian philosophers', see E. Gilson, *History of Christian Philosophy in the Middle Ages* (New York, 1955), 216.

successively but simultaneously. In his *Summa Contra Gentiles* (I, ch. 55, 6–9) Aquinas presents a concise version of what seems to be the standard exposition of this claim.

the intellect of one considering *successively* many things cannot have only one operation. For since operations differ according to their objects, the operation by which the first is considered must be different from the operation by which the second is considered. But the divine intellect has only one operation, namely, the divine essence, as we have proved. Therefore God considers all that he knows not successively, but *together*. Moreover, succession cannot be understood without time nor time without motion . . . But there can be no motion in God, as may be inferred from what we have said. There is, therefore, no succession in the divine consideration . . . Every intellect, furthermore, that understands one thing after another is at one time *potentially* understanding and at another time *actually* understanding. For while it understands the first thing actually it understands the second thing potentially. But the divine intellect is never potentially but always actually understanding. Therefore it does not understand things successively but rather understands them together.

On this view an omniscient being's knowledge of contingent events is the knowledge that event *e* occurs at time *t* (for every true instance of that form). Thus an omniscient being knows that my birth occurs at t_n, that my writing these words occurs at t_{n+x}, that my death occurs at t_{n+x+y}. This omniscient being also knows what events occur simultaneously with each of those events—knows, for example, that while I am writing these words my desk calendar lies open at the page bearing the date 'Friday, 4 March 1966', and the watch on my wrist shows 10:15. Moreover, since an omniscient being by any account knows all necessary truths, including the truths of arithmetic, this omniscient being knows how much time elapses between my birth and my writing these words and between my writing these words and my death. But I *am* writing these words just *now*, and on this view of omniscience an omniscient being is incapable of knowing that that is what I am now doing, and for all this omniscient being knows I might just as well be dead or as yet unborn. That is what knowing everything amounts to if knowing 'everything' does not include always knowing what time it is. Alternatively, that is what knowing the state of the universe at every instant comes to if that phrase is interpreted in the way required by the claim that it is possible to have that sort of knowledge all at once.

According to this familiar account of omniscience, the knowledge an omniscient being has of the entire scheme of contingent events is in many relevant respects exactly like the knowledge you might have of a movie you had written, directed, produced, starred in, and seen a thousand times. You would know its every scene in flawless detail, and you would have the length of each scene and the sequence of scenes perfectly in mind. You would know, too, that a clock pictured in the first scene shows the time to be 3:45, and that a clock pictured in the fourth scene shows 4:30, and so on. Suppose, however, that your movie is being shown in a distant theatre today. You know the movie immeasurably better than do the people in the theatre who are now seeing it for the first time, but they know one big thing about it you don't know, namely, what is now going on on the screen.

Thus the familiar account of omniscience regarding contingent events is drastically incomplete. An omniscient being must know not only the entire scheme of contingent events from beginning to end at once, but also *at what stage of realization that scheme now is*. It is in this sense of knowing what time it is that it is essential to claim in premiss (3) that a being that knows everything always knows what time it is, and it is in this sense that always knowing what time it is entails incessant change in the knower, as is claimed in premiss (4).

In orthodox Christianity the prevalence of the incomplete account of omniscience regarding contingent events effectively obscures the incompatibility of omniscience and immutability. Aquinas, for example, is not content with proving merely that 'it is impossible for God to change in any way'. He goes on in the *Summa Theologica* (I, q. 14, art. 15) to argue that 'since God's knowledge is his substance, as is clear from the foregoing, just as his substance is altogether immutable, as was shown above, so *his knowledge likewise must be altogether invariable*'. What Aquinas, Ockham, and others *have* recognized is that God's knowledge cannot be variable if God is to remain immutable. What has *not* been seen is that God's knowledge cannot be altogether invariable if it is to be perfect, if it is to be genuine omniscience.

Objection D A perfect being transcends space and time. Such a thing is therefore not subject to change, whether as a consequence of knowing what time it is or for any other reason.

The importance of this objection lies in its introduction of the pervasive, mysterious doctrine of the transcendence of space and time, a doctrine often cited by orthodox Christians as if it were both consistent with their theology and explanatory of the notion that God sees all time at a glance. It seems to me to be neither.

In *Proslogium*, chapters 19 and 20, Anselm apostrophizes the being transcendent of space and time as follows:

Thou wast not, then, yesterday, nor wilt thou be tomorrow; but yesterday and today and tomorrow thou art; or, rather, neither yesterday nor today nor tomorrow thou art, but simply *thou art, outside all time*. For yesterday and today and tomorrow have no existence except in time, but thou, although nothing exists without thee, nevertheless dost not exist in space or time, but all things exist in thee. For nothing contains thee, but thou containest all.

For present purposes the spatial aspect of this doctrine may be ignored. What is meant by the claim that an entity transcends time? The number 2 might, I suppose, be said to transcend time in the sense that it does not age, that it is no older now than it was a hundred years ago. I see no reason to quarrel with the doctrine that a perfect being transcends time in *that* sense, since under that interpretation the doctrine is no more than a gloss on the principle of immutability. But under that interpretation the doctrine begs the question of premiss (4) rather than providing a basis for objecting to it.

Only one other interpretation of the doctrine of the transcendence of time suggests itself, and that is that from a God's-eye point of view there is no time, that the passage of time is a universal human illusion. (Whatever else may be said of this interpretation, it surely cannot be considered compatible with such essential theses of Christian doctrine as the Incarnation and the Resurrection.) Under this interpretation the doctrine of the transcendence of time does have a devastating effect on the argument, since it implies either that there are no true propositions of the form 'it is now t_n' or that there is exactly one (eternally) true proposition of that form. Thus under this interpretation premiss (3) either is vacuous or has a single trivializing instance, and premiss (4) is false. But this interpretation preserves the immutability of a perfect being by imposing immutability on everything else, and that is surely an inconceivably high price to pay, in the view of Christians and non-Christians alike.

The remaining three objections are directed against premisses (1) and (2) and may, therefore, be considered not so much criticisms of the argument as attempts to revise the principle of immutability or the principle of omniscience in the light of the argument. Objections E and F have to do with premiss (2), Objection G with premiss (1).

Objection E Since a perfect being transcends time it is logically impossible that a perfect being know what time it is and hence logically impossible that such a being know everything. But it is no limitation on a perfect being that it cannot do what is logically impossible. Therefore, its not knowing absolutely everything (in virtue of not knowing what time it is) does not impair its perfection.

Objections E and F are attempts to hedge on omniscience as philosophers and theologians have long since learned to hedge on omnipotence. In Objection E this attempt depends on directly invoking one of the standard limitations on omnipotence, but the attempt does not succeed. Perhaps the easiest way of pointing up its failure is to produce analogous inferences of the same form, such as this: since I am a human being and a human being is a mortal rational animal, it is logically impossible that I should live forever; therefore it is no limitation on me that I must die—or this: since I am a creature of limited power, it is logically impossible that I am capable of doing whatever is logically possible; therefore it is no limitation on me that I cannot do whatever is logically possible. What is wrong with all these inferences is that the crucial limitation is introduced in the initial description of the being in question, after which it does of course make sense to deny that mere consequences of the limiting description are to be introduced as if they constituted additional limitations. It is not an *additional* limitation on a legless man that he cannot walk, or on a mortal being that it must die, or on a creature of limited power that it cannot do whatever it might choose to do. No more is it an *additional* limitation on a being that is *incapable* of knowing what time it is that it *does not* know what time it is. But any claim to perfection that might have been made on behalf of such a being had already been vitiated in the admission that its transcendence of time renders it incapable of omniscience.

Objection F   Just as in explicating the concept of omnipotence we have been forced to abandon the naïve formula 'a perfect being can do anything' and replace it with 'a perfect being can do anything the doing of which does not impair its perfection', so the argument suggests that the naïve formula 'a perfect being knows everything' must be revised to read 'a perfect being knows everything the knowing of which does not impair its perfection'. Thus, since the argument does show that knowing what time it is impairs the perfection of the knower, it cannot be a part of the newly explicated omniscience to know what time it is.

Even if Objection F could be sustained, this particular grasping of the nettle would surely impress many as just too painful to bear, for in deciding whether or not to try to evade the conclusion of the argument in this way it is important to remember that in the context of the argument 'knowing what time it is' means knowing *what is going on*. Objection F at best thus provides an exceptionally costly defence of absolute perfection, emptying it of much of its content in order to preserve it; for under the newly explicated notion of omniscience Objection F commits one to the view that it is impossible for a *perfect, omniscient* being to know what is going on.

Objection F attempts to draw an analogy between an explication of omnipotence and a proposed explication of omniscience, borrowing strength from the fact that in the case of omnipotence such an explication has long since been recognized as a necessary condition of the coherence of the notion. In evaluating this attempt it is helpful to note that there are at least three types of provisos that may be inserted into formulas of omnipotence for that purpose. The first is relevant to omnipotence generally, the second specifically to eternal omnipotence, and the third specifically to eternal omnipotence as one perfect characteristic of a being possessed of certain other perfect characteristics. (For present purposes it is convenient to say simply that the third is relevant specifically to eternal omnipotence as one aspect of an absolutely perfect being.) These three types of proviso may be exemplified in the following three formulas of omnipotence:

1. A being that is omnipotent (regardless of its other characteristics) can do anything provided that (*a*) the description of what is to be done does not involve a logical inconsistency.
2. A being that is eternally omnipotent (regardless of its other characteristics) can do anything provided that (*a*) . . . and (*b*) the doing of it does not constitute or produce a limitation on its power.
3. A being that is absolutely perfect (and hence eternally omnipotent) can do anything provided that (*a*) . . . and (*b*) . . . and (*c*) the doing of it does not constitute a violation of some aspect of its perfection other than its power.

Provisos of type (*c*) only are at issue in Objection F, no doubt because provisos of types (*a*) and (*b*) have no effective role to play in the explication of omniscience. No being knows anything that *is not* the case; *a fortiori* no omniscient being knows anything that *cannot be* the case. So much for type (*a*). As for type (*b*), since certain things the description of which involves no logical inconsistency would if done incapacitate the doer—committing suicide, for example, or creating another omnipotent being—there is good reason for such a proviso in the explication of eternal omnipotence. It might likewise be claimed that an omniscient being knows everything except things that would if known limit the being's *capacity for knowledge*, the formal justification for this claim being just the same as that for the corresponding omnipotence-claim. The significant difference between these two claims is that the omniscience-claim is evidently vacuous. There is no reason to suspect that there *are* things that would if known limit the knower's capacity for knowledge. More directly to the point at issue in the argument, there is no reason whatever to think that knowing what is going on is a kind of knowing that limits the knower's capacity for knowledge. Thus although a type (*b*) proviso is needed in the explication of eternal omnipotence in order to preserve the coherence of the notion of eternal omnipotence, no such proviso need be inserted into the formula of omniscience in order to preserve the coherence of that notion.

The putative analogy in Objection F presupposes that a proviso of type (*c*) will preserve omniscience as it preserves omnipotence in such a (Cartesian) argument as the following. It is impossible for an absolutely perfect being to lie, for although such a being, as omnipotent, has the power to lie, the exercise of that power would violate the perfect goodness of the being. To say that it is impossible for an absolutely perfect being to lie is not to say that it lacks the power to lie but rather that its absolute perfection in another aspect—perfect goodness—necessitates its refraining from the exercise of that power. Whether or not this line of argument succeeds in doing what it is designed to do, it seems clear that there is no genuine analogue for it in the case of omniscience. Consider the following candidate. It is impossible for an absolutely perfect being to know what is going on, for although such a being, as omniscient, has the power to know what is going on, the exercise of that power would violate the immutability of the being. To say that it is impossible for an absolutely perfect being to know what is going on is not to say that it lacks the power to know what is going on but rather that its absolute perfection in another aspect—immutability—necessitates its refraining from the exercise of that power. A being that has the power to do something that it refrains from doing may not thereby even jeopardize its omnipotence. All the same, a being that has the power to know something that it refrains from knowing does thereby forfeit its omniscience. Omniscience is not the *power to know* everything; it is the *condition of knowing* everything, and that condition cannot be preserved through even a single instance of omitting to exercise the power to know everything.

Therefore, whatever strength Objection F seems to derive from its appeal to the putative analogy between omnipotence and omniscience in this respect is illusory, and this attempted evasion of the argument's conclusion reduces to an arbitrary decision to sacrifice omniscience to immutability.

Objection G The traditional view of philosophers and theologians that absolute perfection entails absolute immutability is mistaken, founded on the misconception that in a perfect being any change would have to be for the worse. In particular the kind of change entailed by always knowing what time it is is a kind of change that surely cannot be construed as deterioration, even when it is ascribed to an absolutely perfect being. No doubt an absolutely perfect being must be immutable in most and perhaps in all other respects, but the argument shows that absolute perfection *entails* mutability in at least this one respect.

Objection G proceeds on the assumption that immutability is ascribed to a perfect being for only one reason—namely, that all change in such a being must constitute deterioration. There is, however, a second reason, as has been indicated at several points in the discussion so far—namely, that any change in a 'perfect' being must indicate that the being was in some respect not in the requisite state of completion, actualization, fixity. The aspect of absolute completion is no less essential an ingredient in the concept of absolute perfection than is the aspect of absolute excellence. Moreover, those such as Aquinas and Ockham who argue against the mutability of a perfect being's *knowledge* would surely agree that the change they are intent on ruling out would not constitute *deterioration*, since they regularly base their arguments on the inadmissibility of *process* in an absolutely perfect being.

An absolutely perfect being may be described as a being possessing all logically compossible perfections. Thus if the argument had shown that omniscience and immutability were logically incompossible, it would have called for no more than adjustment in the concept of absolute perfection, an adjustment of the sort proposed in Objection G. The proposition 'things change' is, however, not necessarily but only contingently true. If as a matter of fact nothing else ever did change, an omniscient being could of course remain immutable. In Objection G, however, an absolutely perfect being has been confused with a being possessing all *really* compossible perfections, the best of all *really* possible beings. Perhaps, as the objection implies, the most *nearly* absolutely perfect being in the circumstances that happen to prevail *would* be mutable in the respect necessitated by always knowing what time it is. But that is of no consequence to the argument, which may be taken as showing that the prevailing circumstances do not admit of the existence of an absolutely perfect being.

This concluding section of the chapter is in the nature of an appendix. It might be subtitled 'Omniscience and Theism'; for it may be shown that the doctrine that God knows everything is incompatible also with theism, the doctrine of a personal God distinct from other persons.[8]

[8] The following argument was suggested to me by certain observations made by Professor Hector Castañeda in a paper entitled 'He', presented at the Wayne State University philosophy colloquium in the autumn of 1964.

Consider these two statements.

S_1 Jones knows that he is in a hospital.
S_2 Jones knows that Jones is in a hospital.

S_1 and S_2 are logically independent. It may be that Jones is an amnesia case. He knows perfectly well that he is in a hospital, and after reading the morning papers he knows that Jones is in a hospital. An omniscient being surely must know all that Jones knows. Anyone can know what S_2 describes Jones as knowing, but no one other than Jones can know what S_1 describes Jones as knowing. (A case in point: anyone could have proved that Descartes existed, but that is not what Descartes proved in the *cogito*, and what he proved in the *cogito* could not have been proved by anyone else.) The kind of knowledge S_1 ascribes to Jones is, moreover, the kind of knowledge characteristic of every self-conscious entity, of every person. Every person knows certain propositions that no *other* person *can* know. Therefore, if God is omniscient, theism is false; and if theism is true, God is not omniscient.

It may fairly be said of God, as it once was said of William Whewell, that 'omniscience [is] his foible'.

12

TIME, REALITY, AND RELATIVITY

LAWRENCE SKLAR

There is a doctrine, venerable and very familiar, that that which does not exist in the present does not, properly speaking, exist at all. Alternatively there is the equally ancient and equally intuitive view that only the past and present have determinate reality and that the future has no such being, or at least no such determinate being.

For the moment I do not wish to explore the fundamental questions to which these doctrines give rise: 'Why do they have the intuitive appeal they do?', 'Can any good reasons whatever be given to support them?', 'In the final analysis could they possibly be correct?' Rather I want to take a look at what purports to be a simple and conclusive refutation of all such doctrines. For, it has been claimed, 'science' refutes the asymmetric treatment of the present and non-present once and for all. While this argument too has been 'floating around' for some time, it has fairly recently appeared in the literature, once in a version replete with infelicities of expression and formulation (talking about determinism of the future when it is the question of determinate reality which is at issue)[1] and the other time framed with greater philosophical sophistication.[2] But in both cases the argument is fundamentally the same.

Consider an observer at a place–time. According to the doctrine in question, events in his future (say) are not determinately real. But according to relativity there is going to be another observer, coincident with the first, and hence certainly real to him, since immediately present to him. Now many of the events future to the first observer will be present to the second, so long as the two observers are in relative motion. Indeed, for any future event (relative to the first observer and space-like separated from him) there will be a second observer such that that event is present to the second observer when the second observer is coincident with the first.

This chapter appeared originally in R. Healey (ed.), *Reduction, Time and Reality* (Cambridge: Cambridge University Press, 1981), 129–42. Reprinted by permission of Cambridge University Press.

[1] C. Rietdijk, 'A Rigorous Proof of Determinism derived from the Special Theory of Relativity', *Philosophy of Science*, 33 (1966), 341–4.

[2] H. Putnam, 'Time and Physical Geometry', *Journal of Philosophy*, 64 (1967), 240–7.

So the 'future' event will be real, relative to the second observer. But surely 'being real' is a transitive notion. If the event is real to the second observer who is real to the first, it must be real to the first observer, contradicting our original claim that events future to an observer lack reality for him.

Once we have accepted the principle of transitivity of reality then we can go further. For even events in my future light cone will be present, hence real, for some observer who is present, hence real, for an observer in motion with respect to me but coincident to me and, hence, real for me. So even events in my absolute future must be declared to have determinate reality.

Now obviously the whole argument rests upon the fundamental assumption of the transitivity of 'reality to'. Given the relativization of simultaneity to a reference frame in relativity, anyone who wishes to relate determinate reality to temporal presence must also relativize having reality to a state of motion of an observer. And given the non-transivity of simultaneity in relativity across observers in differing reference frames, we could also easily find our way out of this argument by simply denying that 'having reality for' is a transitive relation. Now Putnam calls the transitivity of 'reality for' the principle of their being 'No Privileged Observers', and, surely, we would like all observers to have equal rights to a legitimate world-description.[3] But why one would think that such a doctrine of 'No Privileged Observers' would lead one immediately to affirm the transitivity of 'reality for', given that one has already relativized such previously non-relative notions as that of simultaneity, is beyond me.

But simply blocking the argument against the traditional doctrine in this way is of very little interest. For example, we still are at a loss as to what specific doctrine about reality we should adopt in the relativistic case. Should we simply relativize the old doctrine taking, as before, the present to be the real and simply denying the transitivity of 'reality for'? Or should we adopt some alternative, more radical, view? To decide requires that we look a little more closely into the metaphysical presuppositions which underlie the relativistic space–time picture itself. What I want to do here, rather than pay attention only to the problem as so far narrowly construed, is to explore the more general issue suggested by Putnam in the concluding remarks to his paper:

I conclude that the problem of reality and determinateness of future events is now solved. Moreover, it is solved by physics and not by philosophy . . . Indeed, I do not believe that there are any longer any *philosophical* problems about Time; there

---

[3] 'Time and Physical Geometry', 241.

is only the physical problem of determining the exact physical geometry of the four-dimensional continuum that we inhabit.[4]

I think that such a naïve view is as wrong as can be. Just as a computer is only as good as its programmer ('Garbage in, garbage out'), one can extract only so much metaphysics from a physical theory as one puts in. While our total world-view must, of course, be consistent with our best available scientific theories, it is a great mistake to read off a metaphysics superficially from the theory's overt appearance, and an even graver mistake to neglect the fact that metaphysical presuppositions have gone into the formulation of the theory, as it is usually framed, in the first place.

I

The original Einstein papers on special relativity are founded, as is well known, on a verificationist critique of earlier theories. Referring to the observational facts, generalizable as the null-results of the generalized round-trip experiments, he argues for the necessity of finding an 'operational' meaning to apply to simultaneity for events at a distance and for the impossibility of doing this in any way which allows us an empirical determination of the one-way velocity of light. From then on the moves are all well known which invoke the 'radar' method for establishing simultaneity, this resting upon the conventional stipulation of the uniformity of the velocity of light in all directions. Nothing in the way of newly predicted phenomena, such as those predicted by the mechanics designed to preserve the old conservation rules relative to the newly adopted space–time picture, changes the fundamental point—that quantities are to be introduced into one's theory only in so far as they are empirically determinable or conventionally definable from empirically determinable quantities.

Of course, even within the relativistic context it is easy to forget the verificationist arguments which initiated the theory in the first place, and to forget the distinction within the foundations of the theory between the genuinely factual elements and the merely conventional choices which go into the relativistic space–time picture. Hence the necessity for frequently reintroducing the claim of conventionality and the difficulty of seeing it through to its full consequences even for those who espouse it. Thus we have the Reichenbach–Grünbaum argument to the effect that in picking ε equal to ½ in the familiar 'radar' definition of simultaneity, a merely conventional element has been introduced, corresponding to picking the

[4] Ibid. 247.

velocity of outgoing and returning light as equal. But it then takes some effort to see that even the choice of a linear relationship on the time of emission and reception of a light signal to define the point simultaneous with the light's being reflected at a distant point is itself undetermined by the facts. Thus the very choice of a flat space–time for the space–time appropriate to special relativity is easily argued to be as much a 'mere conventional choice' as is that of the equal velocities of light in opposite directions.

Now it might be argued that Einstein's verificationism was a misfortune, to be encountered not with a rejection of special relativity, but with an acceptance of the theory now to be understood on better epistemological grounds. There is precedent for an attitude of this kind. Einstein was led to general relativity both by an attempt to satisfy Mach's requirements for an explanation of inertial forces and by the belief that covariance of equations represented a generalization of the relativity principle underlying special relativity. Most would now take the theory itself to be our best available current theory of gravitation, but would deny its conformity with Machian requirements and would deny the legitimacy of identifying covariance with a relativity principle of any kind. Even the principle of equivalence, another 'background principle' to general relativity, is questionable in a way the theory is not.

But I do not think a position of this kind will work in the present case. I can see no way of rejecting the older ether-compensatory theories, originally invoked to explain the Michelson–Morley results, without invoking a verificationist critique of some kind or other. And I know of no way to defend the move to a relativized notion of simultaneity, so essential for special relativity, without first offering a critique, in the same vein as Einstein's, of the pre-relativistic absolutist notion, and then continuing to observe that even the relativistic replacement for this old notion is itself, in so far as it outruns the 'hard data' of experiment, infested with a high degree of conventionality.

II

Once adopt a verificationist stance of any kind and certain fundamental questions arise. First of all there is the question of just what properties and relations are going to be taken as epistemically available by 'direct inspection'.

Obviously one such relation is that of coincidence between events. Without taking this as epistemically available to us, the whole project of providing an 'operational definition' for simultaneity for distant events is blocked at the start. For we must be able to synchronize clocks at a point (determine the emission and reception time of the light beam, etc.) and this amounts to a determination of spatio-temporal coincidence. It is less frequently noted that another fundamental notion is taken as primitive in the definition as well. This is the notion of continuity along a causal (time-like or light-like) path. The definition requires the use of the times of emission and reception of a reflected light beam. But how could these be determined unless there were available to us some method of determining that the light beam whose later reception time is determined is the very same light beam whose emission time was earlier recorded and whose reflection at the distant point coincided with the event at a distance which is to be identified as simultaneous with some local event? And if, as seems the only plausible move to make in this case, we take identity of the beam through time (or genidentity of the set of events making up the beam) to be constituted by the spatio-temporal continuity of the beam (and what else would serve in its place?), this presupposes that a determination of such continuity is epistemically available to us.

Now there are many absolutely crucial questions to be asked here. Can any coherent sense be made of the claim that our spatio-temporal knowledge is exhausted by reference to data formalizable in the two notions of coincidence and causal continuity? Can an intersubjective physical theory be formulated in terms of such 'immediately accessible' concepts at all? To what extent is the restriction of epistemic accessibility to such a limited class of notions in any sense a commitment to a denial of 'reality' to those features of the world whose description outruns the capacity of the meagre basis to which we have limited ourselves? We will return to some of these questions shortly when we ask ourselves what the consequences are for a doctrine of the 'irreality of the past and future' of such an epistemic foundation for relativity.

For the moment, however, I want to digress a little to show how in a slightly different, but closely related, context the natural choice of these two concepts as primitive once more suggests itself.

Even more primitive as a feature of our space–time than metric features, like simultaneity, is its topology. Both the Minkowski space–time of special relativity and the pseudo-Riemannian space–time of general relativity have determinate topologies—the usual manifold topologies. To what extent are these topologies empirically determinable and to what extent, once again, are they merely conventionally stipulated? A natural suggestion has been to look for the source of our epistemic access to topology in the causal structure among the events in the space–time.

What we soon discover is this. In Minkowski space–time there is, indeed, a topology definable solely in terms of the causal connectivity among events, the Alexandrov topology, which is provably equivalent to the ordinary manifold topology. Furthermore, the Alexandrov topology is 'natural' enough that one might be inclined to the view that what we really meant all along by the topological structure of the space–time was that which the Alexandrov topology gives us. Essentially, it identifies the basis of open sets of the topology with sets of events time-like accessible from a pair of events, i.e. an open set in the basis is the common region of the interior of a forward light cone from one event and the interior of the backward light cone from another.

When we go to the general relativistic picture, it is plain that there are pathological space–times which are such that the Alexandrov topology and the manifold topology will not even be extensionally equivalent. Only if the space–times are what is called strongly causal will the two topologies coincide. Indeed, it is easy to show that no topology defined in terms of causal connectibility in any way will be generally adequate even to capture extensionally the usual manifold topology of the space–time.

A recent result of Malament's does show us, however, that if one assumes the space–time to have some manifold topology or other, then the topology along the causal paths (time-like and light-like paths) does completely determine the topology of the space–time, in the sense that any one-to-one mapping from one space–time to another which preserves continuity along causal paths will be, relative to the assumption that both space–times have the usual manifold topology, a homeomorphism.[5]

But why assume the space–times have a manifold topology of the usual sort? Are there any other topologies which one can imagine which will differ from the manifold topologies but which will agree with them regarding the structure of continuity along causal paths? There are. For example, the topology which takes the maximum number of sets as open sets (the finest topology on the space–time) compatible with the continuity structure along causal paths will agree with the usual manifold topology along these paths and yet be non-homeomorphic to the manifold topology.

Now why are any of these mathematical results of any philosophical interest? Clearly the usual epistemic presuppositions are being made: in order to attribute a structure to the world we must indicate how that structure can be empirically determined by us. The full topological structure of space–time is not the sort of thing open to any kind of direct

[5] D. Malament, 'The Class of Continuous Timelike Curves Determines the Topology of Spacetime', *Journal of Mathematical Physics*, 18 (1399–404).

or immediate epistemic access. But the continuity structure along causal (light-like or time-like) world-lines is. Hence the topological structure of the world is determined only to the extent that it is fixed by the continuity structure of the causal world-lines. And why would one think continuity along causal world-lines open to us? Only, I think, because of the implicit claim that they can be 'lived along' by observers who, in their traversal of the world-lines, could directly determine the continuity or discontinuity of a set of points.[6]

III

Let us now return to our original question: to what extent is the old doctrine of the unreality of the past and future undermined by the adoption of a relativistic space–time picture of the world? Alternatively, can a metaphysics be constructed which retains the old 'intuition' and which is compatible with the new space–time view? And if the latter is the truth, what modifications in the old view must we make in order to retain this compatibility? And how plausible, given the original standpoint of the 'irrealist' metaphysics, are these modifications going to be?

Now one obvious way to reconcile irrealism with relativity is simply to drop the principle of the transitivity of 'reality for', and retain the original doctrine in the form most similar to its original version, that is, taking as real for an observer all and only those events which are temporally present to him. Of course we must now relativize 'reality for' so that it is just as non-transitive across observers in mutual motion with respect to one another as is simultaneity, but there doesn't seem to be anything very objectionable a priori about this. Making this move certainly doesn't seem to be positing any observer as 'privileged', as Putnam alleges when he calls the principle of transitivity of reality the principle that There are No Privileged Observers. For, just as with simultaneity in special relativity, all inertial observers are on a par and none are singled out as in any way 'privileged'.

But there does seem to be *something* wrong with this approach. The source of our scepticism about it lies, I think, in the strong pressures towards a conventionalist, and, hence, in a sense, irrealist, theory with regard to simultaneity for distant events. If the totality of our epistemic access to the theory is contained in the facts about coincidence and continuity along causal paths, can we reasonably take a realistic attitude toward relations not totally reducible in terms of these notions at all? Of

[6] L. Sklar, 'What might be Right about the Causal Theory of Time', *Synthèse*, 35 (1977), 155–71.

course we can *call* two space-like separated events simultaneous or not, picking the relativistic definition for distant simultaneity or some other. We can speak of light as having an isotropically distributed velocity, or not, again choosing either the standard relativistic convention or some other. But if any one of these accounts, framed in superficially inconsistent terms, can explain equally well all the hard data of experience, why should we take the accounts as differing at all in the real features they attribute to the world? We are easily led to the (standard) conventionalist claim that there is no fact of the matter at all about the equality of the velocity of light in all directions, and no fact of the matter at all about which distant events are 'really' simultaneous with a given event.

If we now associate the real (for an observer) with the simultaneous for him, we must, accepting the conventionality of simultaneity, accept as well a conventionalist theory of 'reality for'. It is then merely a matter of arbitary stipulation that one distant event rather than another is taken as real for an observer. Now there is nothing inconsistent or otherwise formally objectionable about such a relativized notion of 'reality for', but it does seem to take the metaphysical heart out of the old claim that the present had genuine reality and the past and future lacked it. For what counts as the present is only a matter of arbitrary choice, and so then is what is taken as real. At this point one can easily see why one would adopt, instead, the line standardly taken by proponents of relativistic space–time and declare all events, past, present, and future, equally real. For the distinction among them, being reduced to a mere conventional way of speaking, seems far too fragile to bear any real metaphysical weight.

IV

But there is an alternative. It is a radical one and one we will hesitate to take when we see the position into which we are being forced. It is, however, not only consistent with the relativistic space–time picture, but an option well in keeping, from at least one point of view, with at least some of the original motivations underlying the irrealist view about past and future.

Given an observer at a time, what, from the relativistic point of view, should we cast into the domain of unreality? Certainly all the contents of his absolute past and future, that is everything contained in either his forward or backward light cones.

But what about the contents of the world outside of both light cones altogether? The first alternative we looked at discriminated among these events, taking those simultaneous (in the relativistic sense) with the observer at the instant to be real and discarding the remainder as unreal. But such a discrimination seems all too arbitrary. The obvious alternatives are to count everything space-like separated from the observer as real or to count it all as unreal for him. And surely of these two alternatives it is the latter which best suits the initial motivation behind the irrealist viewpoint as originally construed.

Not that the former option has no plausibility. After all we do sometimes speak of the region outside the light cones as the region of the 'absolutely simultaneous', and if reality is to be identified with temporal presentness this does suggest that all which is now 'absolutely present' should be counted in the domain of reality. I don't think there is any way in which one could 'refute' this option. We are, after all, revising the older theory of the reality of only the present to fit the new world picture and, without some further constraints on our choices, I suppose the options are up to us.

None the less this view certainly seems peculiar. Having dismissed as unreal things whose only deficiency is the fact that causal signals from them have taken time to arrive at us now, or that causal signals from us will take some time to arrive at them, it seems very suspicious indeed to promote into the domain of the fully real those things causally inaccessible to us (now) altogether.

But just what were some of the motivations behind the original intuition of the irreality of all but the present? Perhaps if we get some grip on them we will have some guidance in our attempt to rework the theory to fit these changed circumstances.

1. One source of the old intuition is plainly the fact that our natural language is tensed. We speak of things now as existing but of the past only as having existed and of the future only as going to exist. But, of course, we can't look here for an explanation of the intuition of unreality, except possibly in a weak psychological sense. For the claim of the irrealist is that this natural way of speaking is not a mere trivial artefact of ordinary language but reflective of some deep metaphysical distinction between the elsewhen and the now. What we would like is some interesting distinction between past and future and the present which simultaneously explains the felt metaphysical distinction and its representation by means of tense distinctions in ordinary language.

2. There is the resort to irrealism which holds that an irrealist view of the future is necessary to avoid fatalism. This connects the alleged irreality of the future with an alleged present absence of truth-values for future

tensed statements. The claim is made that this absence of truth-values for future tensed statements allows us to avoid the disturbing conclusion that what will be is already the case, and, in the sense that statements about it already have a truth-value, is somehow fated. It allows us to avoid thinking that the future is as beyond our capabilities of changing as are facts about the past.

From this standpoint we obviously want events in the forward light cone to be unreal. From this perspective we will, contrary to the general time–irrealist point of view, want events in the backward light cone to be real, as sentences about them presumably have, now, determinate truth-value. But what are we to do with events outside either light cone?

By our previous argument from the arbitrariness of distant simultaneity, we will probably not want to discriminate among the events at space-like separation some we take to be real and some unreal. So our only option would be to take all of them as either real or all as not real. Given that irreality, from this motivational standpoint, was invoked in order to prevent there already being a fact of the matter which, now, determined the truth or falsehood of future tensed assertions, there seems to be little to constrain our choice of reality or unreality for those events which are now absent from both our causal past and our causal future.

Suppose we take all events at space-like separation to be unreal. We will, of course, have to suffer some consequences which, from the 'ordinary language' point of view are rather peculiar. For example there will be events which are now such that they will be in my real past at some future time, but which will never have a present reality to me at all.[7] But we expect that a move to a relativistic picture will force some violence on our ways of speaking and this is no refutation of adopting this way of thinking about things. Nor, from this point of view (the sole aim of which is to prevent the over-abundant reality of our to-be-experienced future) do I see any reason why we couldn't adopt the other alternative of simply taking all space-like separated events as now real. Of course both these options will have the virtue (if it is one) that two coincident observers, no matter what their relative motion, will, at an instant, attribute reality and irreality to the same regions of space–time.

3. The irrealism which we are primarily interested in is not, however, that which attributes reality to past and present and denies it only to the future, but rather that which takes the real to be only that which is present. What is the motivation behind this view, over and above the, possibly merely artefactual, special role of tensed discourse in our natural language?

[7] Putnam, 'Time and Physical Geometry', p. 246.

At least one motivation for the view is to be found in the 'epistemic remoteness' of past and future. This ties in the familiar intuition about the irreality of past and future with such familiar verificationist themes as the claim that all propositions about past and future are, unlike those about the present (or, at least, about present immediate experience) 'inferential' in nature. And it ties it in with the further move, so familiar with radical verificationist programmes, either to reduce statements about past and future to statements about present evidence or, alternatively, to adopt some kind of 'criterion' theory of the meaning of statements about past and future, taking their meaning to be fixed by their relation, in terms of warranted assertability, to statements about present experience which are exhaustive of the body of evidential statements for them. From the latter point of view it is fairly clear what the assertion of irreality to past and future amounts to (denial of bivalence to past and future tensed statements, etc.) and from the former it is at least clear why a radical asymmetry of some sort is being maintained between, on the one hand, present tensed statements and, on the other, those tensed past or future.

I certainly do not intend to examine either of these familiar verificationist claims, either in general or in their particular application to statements about past and future. Rather, I want only to explore what the impact of relativistic space–time thinking ought to be on the programmes. Let me also say here that to the objection that it is not these verificationist themes which really underlie our intuitions about the asymmetry of reality in question, I have no reply. I think the objection may be correct, but I am at a loss to imagine what other source to the asymmetry there might be (over and above, of course, the mere fact of asymmetric grammatical forms in our particular natural language).

Now looking at the asymmetry as presently motivated the first thing to say, once again, is that there is nothing in the relativistic picture to force the asymmetrist to give up his position. But how shall he frame it so as to fit the new space–time picture? Once again he could simply relativize everything to the state of motion of an observer, using the relativized simultaneity notion to demarcate present from past and future. But, as usual, this is subject to the objection of arbitrariness and, in addition, from the point of view of our present, epistemic, motivation for the asymmetrical standpoint we have a far more plausible option to take.

If the past and future are to be declared unreal due to their 'epistemic distance' from us, what attitude are we to take towards events at space-like separation from us? The answer is clear. For events at space-like separation from us are now (although they may not be in the future) totally immune from epistemic contact by us. That is the very fact which in special relativity leads us to the doctrine of conventionality of simultaneity in the first place, and in the context of general relativity leads to the notion of event and particle horizons, deterministic but unpredictable space–times, etc.

So surely in this case the option is fixed for us. If we are to take the past and future as unreal due to their epistemic distance from us, surely we are to declare everything outside the light cone as unreal as well.[8]

What is the most interesting here is this: even from the pre-relativistic point of view, it isn't the least bit clear why we should have ever treated the elsewhere differently than the elsewhen. At least it isn't clear until we have some backing for the intuition of unreality of past and future which doesn't rest upon the mere fact of epistemic distance. For even from the pre-relativistic point of view, events spatially separated from us seem to be as epistemically distant as those in the past or future. Why, even in the pre-relativistic situation, would anyone have wanted to deny reality to the past and yet affirm it of the spatially distant? From the relativistic point of view it seems clear that we are forced (not, of course, by logical consistency but only by plausibility of conceptual structure), if we are going to take an irrealist line as motivated by facts of epistemic distance at all, certainly to deny reality as fervently to the spatially distant as we do to past and future. What relativity does, with the invocation of space–time to replace space through time, is not to force us in any way (Putnam, Rietdijk, and others to the contrary) to reject our irrealist position, but only to symmetrize it in a natural way to include spatial separation on a par with temporal separation.

V

From the point of view we have been adopting, the doctrine of the irreality of past and future, taken as having a motivation in their epistemic distance, now seems clearer. We first reduce 'reality' to the lived experience of the observer; that is, we first fall, following a well-known verificationist path, into solipsism. Then seeing that our own future experiences and past experiences are as remote *now* from us as the

---

[8] There is also the position that the past, being now forever epistemically inaccessible to us, is unreal, but that the present and the future are real as both are, now, open to present or future inspection. From the point of view I have been proposing I think it evident what the relativistic revision of this doctrine ought to be. Surely the regions outside the light cone are to be lumped with the past into the domain of irreality, leaving only the future light cone and the present event-point in the realm of reality.

spatially distant, the non-immediately sensed, etc., we fall from solipsism into solipsism of the present moment. Reality has now been reduced to a point!

Now obviously we do not want to go along this path. Where to block it is an interesting question. One can challenge the basic tenets of verificationism either with regard to its theory of knowledge or with regard to its semantic theory. One could certainly try to break the connection between the facts of epistemic distance, even if it is acknowledged to exist, and 'irreality'.

But what role does relativity theory play in all of this? One thing is certain. Acceptance of relativity cannot force one into the acceptance or rejection of any of the traditional metaphysical views about the reality of past and future. It can lead one to see more clearly than one did previously that by parity of reasoning one ought to treat spatial separation on a par with temporal. By forcing one in addition to say some things which seem peculiar in ordinary language it might lead one to move towards one position or another on grounds one didn't have before. But one who wishes to stick by an irrealist position, and is willing to pay the price, is certainly able to do so, all the while accepting the scientific reasonableness of Minkowski space–time.

Much more interesting is the relationship between relativity and verificationism in general. Certainly the original arguments in favour of the relativistic viewpoint are rife with verificationist presuppositions about meaning, etc. And despite Einstein's later disavowal of the verificationist point of view, no one to my knowledge has provided an adequate account of the foundations of relativity which isn't verificationist in essence.

That one would want to do so seems fairly clear. Let me illustrate with just one problem. On the basis of verificationist principles one takes the attribution of distant simultaneity, of the isotropy of the velocity of light, etc., to be mere conventional decisions. On similar grounds, as we have seen, one can plausibly argue that the very adoption of the standard manifold topology for space–time is merely conventional, any other topology saving the continuity structure along causal paths serving to 'save the phenomena' equally well.

But now consider the problem of so-called indistinguishable space–times. These are space–times which are counted as distinct by general relativity (they are by no means isometric to one another), yet which are such that no single observer can tell, even given a complete infinite lifetime, which of the space–times he inhabits. This could only be determined by a 'super-observer' who had access to the collected information of all the observers of the ordinary sort. Is it merely a matter of convention which of a number of indistinguishable space–times an observer inhabits?[9]

Clearly, if one takes saving the phenomena as the sole task for which a theory is to be responsible, and a choice among theories which save the same phenomena to be a matter of mere convention, the answer depends on what one takes the phenomena to be saved to be. The pressure which drives us, verificationistically, to take the phenomena to be everything which is epistemically accessible to observers in general can also drive us to take them to be everything which is accessible only to one observer, oneself. This is, naturally, just the familiar slide from a phenomenalistic to a solipsistic position. Worse yet, should we not, given the epistemic inaccessibility *now* of past and future, take the phenomena to be rather the data of the one observer at the present moment, leading to a whole new range of indistinguishable space–times? Whereas before we counted as indistinguishable those space–times which appeared the same to any world-line in them, we now take them to be those which appear the same to single world-points. Surely verificationism has gone too far at this point.

But what I don't know is either how to formulate a coherent underpinning for relativity which isn't verificationist to begin with, or how, once begun, to find a natural stopping-point for verificationist claims of underdetermination and conventionality.

[9] C. Glymour, 'Topology, Cosmology and Convention', *Synthèse*, 24 (1972), 195–218; id., 'Indistinguishable Space–times and the Fundamental Group', in J. Earman, C. Glymour, and J. Stachel, (eds.), *Foundations of Space–Time Theories* (Minneapolis, 1977); D. Malament, 'Observationally Indistinguishable Space–times: Comments on Glymour's Paper', in Earman, Glymour, and Stachel (eds.), *Foundations of Space–Time Theories*.

13

A REMARK ABOUT THE RELATIONSHIP BETWEEN RELATIVITY THEORY AND IDEALISTIC PHILOSOPHY

KURT GÖDEL

One of the most interesting aspects of relativity theory for the philosophical-minded consists in the fact that it gave new and surprising insights into the nature of time, of that mysterious and seemingly self-contradictory[1] being which, on the other hand, seems to form the basis of the world's and our own existence. The very starting-point of special relativity theory consists in the discovery of a new and very astonishing property of time, namely the relativity of simultaneity, which to a large extent implies[2] that of succession. The assertion that the events A and B are simultaneous (and, for a large class of pairs of events, also the assertion that A happened before B) loses its objective meaning, in so far as another observer, with the same claim to correctness, can assert that A and B are not simultaneous (or that B happened before A).

Following up the consequences of this strange state of affairs one is led to conclusions about the nature of time which are very far reaching indeed. In short, it seems that one obtains an unequivocal proof for the view of those philosophers who, like Parmenides, Kant, and the modern idealists, deny the objectivity of change and consider change as an illusion or an appearance due to our special mode of perception.[3] The argument runs as follows: change becomes possible only through the lapse of time.

This chapter appeared originally in P. A. Schilpp (ed.), *Albert Einstein–Philosopher-Scientist*, vol. vii of The Library of Living Philosophers (La Salle, Ill.: Open Court, 1949), 557–62. Reprinted by permission of the publisher, Open Court Publishing Company, La Salle, Illinois.

[1] Cf. e.g. J. M. E. McTaggart, 'The Unreality of Time', *Mind*, 17 (1908).

[2] At least if it is required that any 2 point events are either simultaneous or one succeeds the other, i.e. that temporal succession defines a complete linear ordering of all point events. There exists an absolute partial ordering.

[3] Kant (in *The Critique of Pure Reason*, 2nd edn. (1787), 54) expresses this view in the following words: 'those affections which we represent to ourselves as changes, in beings with other forms of cognition, would give rise to a perception in which the idea of time, and therefore also of change, would not occur at all.' This formulation agrees so well with the situation subsisting in relativity theory, that one is almost tempted to add: such as e.g. a perception of the inclination relative to each other of the world-lines of matter in Minkowski space.

The existence of an objective lapse of time,[4] however, means (or, at least, is equivalent to the fact) that reality consists of an infinity of layers of the 'now' which come into existence successively. But, if simultaneity is something relative in the sense just explained, reality cannot be split up into such layers in an objectively determined way. Each observer has his own set of 'nows', and none of these various systems of layers can claim the prerogative of representing the objective lapse of time.[5]

This inference has been pointed out by some, although by surprisingly few, philosophical writers, but it has not remained unchallenged. And actually to the argument in the form just presented it can be objected that the complete equivalence of all observers moving with different (but uniform) velocities, which is the essential point in it, subsists only in the abstract space–time scheme of special relativity theory and in certain empty worlds of general relativity theory. The existence of matter, however, as well as the particular kind of curvature of space–time produced by it, largely destroy the equivalence of different observers[6] and

---

[4] One may take the standpoint that the idea of an objective lapse of time (whose essence is that only the present really exists) is meaningless. But this is no way out of the dilemma; for by this very opinion one would take the idealistic viewpoint as to the idea of change, exactly as those philosophers who consider it as self-contradictory. For in both views one denies that an objective lapse of time is a possible state of affairs, *a fortiori* that it exists in reality, and it makes very little difference in this context, whether our idea of it is regarded as meaningless or as self-contradictory. Of course for those who take either one of these two viewpoints the argument from relativity theory given below is unnecessary, but even for them it should be of interest that perhaps there exists a second proof for the unreality of change based on entirely different grounds, in view of the fact that the assertion to be proved runs so completely counter to common sense. A particularly clear discussion of the subject independent of relativity theory is to be found in P. Mongré, *Das Chaos in kosmischer Auslese* (1898; reissued Baden-Baden, 1976).

[5] It may be objected that this argument only shows that the lapse of time is something relative, which does not exclude that it is something objective; whereas idealists maintain that it is something merely imagined. A relative lapse of time, however, if any meaning at all can be given to this phrase, would certainly be something entirely different from the lapse of time in the ordinary sense, which means a change in the existing. The concept of existence, however, cannot be relativized without destroying its meaning completely. It may furthermore be objected that the argument under consideration only shows that time lapses in different ways for different observers, whereas the lapse of time itself may nevertheless be an intrinsic (absolute) property of time or of reality. A lapse of time, however, which is not a lapse in some definite way seems to me as absurd as a coloured object which has no definite colours. But even if such a thing were conceivable, it would again be something totally different from the intuitive idea of the lapse of time, to which the idealistic assertion refers.

[6] Of course, according to relativity theory all observers are equivalent in so far as the laws of motion and interaction for matter and field are the same for all of them. But this does not exclude that the structure of the world (i.e. the actual arrangement of matter, motion, and field) may offer quite different aspects to different observers, and that it may offer a more 'natural' aspect to some of them and a distorted one to others. The observer, incidentally, plays no essential role in these considerations. The main point, of course, is that the world itself has certain distinguished directions, which directly define certain distinguished local times.

distinguish some of them conspicuously from the rest, namely those which follow in their motion the mean motion of matter.[7] Now in all cosmological solutions of the gravitational equations (i.e. in all possible universes) known at present the local times of all *these* observers fit together into one world-time, so that apparently it becomes possible to consider this time as the 'true' one, which lapses objectively, whereas the discrepancies of the measuring results of other observers from this time may be conceived as due to the influence which a motion relative to the mean state of motion of matter has on the measuring processes and physical processes in general.

From this state of affairs, in view of the fact that some of the known cosmological solutions seem to represent our world correctly, James Jeans has concluded[8] that there is no reason to abandon the intuitive idea of an absolute time lapsing objectively. I do not think that the situation justifies this conclusion and am basing my opinion chiefly[9] on the following facts and considerations.

There exist cosmological solutions of another kind[10] than those known at present, to which the aforementioned procedure of defining an absolute time is not applicable, because the local times of the special observers used above cannot be fitted together into one world-time. Nor can any other procedure which would accomplish this purpose exist for them, i.e. these worlds possess such properties of symmetry, that for each possible concept of simultaneity and succession there exist others which cannot be

---

[7] The value of the mean motion of matter may depend essentially on the size of the regions over which the mean is taken. What may be called the 'true mean motion' is obtained by taking regions so large, that a further increase in their size does not any longer change essentially the value obtained. In our world this is the case for regions including many galactic systems. Of course a true mean motion in this sense need not necessarily exist.

[8] Cf. 'Man and the Universe', the Halley Stewart Lecture, in *Scientific Progress* (London, 1935), 22–3.

[9] Another circumstance invalidating Jeans's argument is that the procedure described above gives only an approximate definition of an absolute time. No doubt it is possible to refine the procedure so as to obtain a precise definition, but perhaps only by introducing more or less arbitrary elements (such as e.g. the size of the regions or the weight function to be used in the computation of the mean motion of matter). It is doubtful whether there exists a precise definition which has so great merits, that there would be sufficient reason to consider exactly the time thus obtained as the true one.

[10] The most conspicuous physical property distinguishing these solutions from those known at present is that the compass of inertia in them everywhere rotates relative to matter, which in our world would mean that it rotates relative to the totality of galactic systems. These worlds, therefore, can fittingly be called 'rotating universes'. In the subsequent considerations I have in mind a particular kind of rotating universes which have the additional properties of being static and spatially homogeneous, and a cosmological constant $< o$. For the mathematical representation of these solutions, cf. my paper, 'An Example of a New Type of Cosmological Solution of Einstein's Field Equations of Gravitation', *Review of Modern Physics*, 21 (1949), 447–50.

distinguished from it by any intrinsic properties, but only by reference to individual objects, such as, for example, a particular galactic system.

Consequently, the inference drawn above as to the non-objectivity of change doubtless applies at least in these worlds. Moreover it turns out that temporal conditions in these universes (at least in those referred to in the end of n. 10) show other surprising features, strengthening further the idealistic viewpoint. Namely, by making a round trip on a rocket ship in a sufficiently wide curve, it is possible in these worlds to travel into any region of the past, present, and future, and back again, exactly as it is possible in other worlds to travel to distant parts of space.

This state of affairs seems to imply an absurdity. For it enables one, for example, to travel into the near past of those places where he has himself lived. There he would find a person who would be himself at some earlier period of his life. Now he could do something to this person which, by his memory, he knows has not happened to him. This and similar contradictions, however, in order to prove the impossibility of the worlds under consideration, presuppose the actual feasibility of the journey into one's own past. But the velocities which would be necessary in order to complete the voyage in a reasonable length of time[11] are far beyond everything that can be expected ever to become a practical possibility. Therefore it cannot be excluded a priori, on the ground of the argument given, that the space–time structure of the real world is of the type described.

As to the conclusions which could be drawn from the state of affairs explained for the question being considered in this paper, the decisive point is this: that for *every* possible definition of a world-time one could travel into regions of the universe which are passed according to that definition.[12] This again shows that to assume an objective lapse of time would lose every justification in these worlds. For, in whatever way one may assume time to be lapsing, there will always exist possible observers to whose experienced lapse of time no objective lapse corresponds (in particular also possible observers whose whole existence objectively would be simultaneous). But, if the experience of the lapse of time can

---

[11] Basing the calculation of a mean density of matter equal to that observed in our world, and assuming one were able to transform matter completely into energy the weight of the 'fuel' of the rocket ship, in order to complete the voyage in t years (as measured by the traveller), would have to be of the order of magnitude of $10^{22}/t^2$ times the weight of the ship (if stopping, too, is effected by recoil). This estimate applies to $t \ll 10^9$. Irrespective of the value of t, the velocity of the ship must be at least $1/\sqrt{2}$ of the velocity of light.

[12] For this purpose incomparably smaller velocities would be sufficient. Under the assumptions made in 11 the weight of the fuel would have to be at most of the same order of magnitude as the weight of the ship.

exist without an objective lapse of time, no reason can be given why an objective lapse of time should be assumed at all.

It might, however, be asked: of what use is it if such conditions prevail in certain *possible* worlds? Does that mean anything for the question interesting us whether in *our* world there exists an objective lapse of time? I think it does. For, (1) our world, it is true, can hardly be represented by the particular kind of rotating solutions referred to above (because these solutions are static and, therefore, yield no red-shift for distant objects); there exist however also *expanding* rotating solutions. In such universes an absolute time also might fail to exist,[13] and it is not impossible that our world is a universe of this kind. (2) The mere compatibility with the laws of nature[14] of worlds in which there is no distinguished absolute time, and, therefore, no objective lapse of time can exist, throws some light on the meaning of time also in those worlds in which an absolute time *can* be defined. For, if someone asserts that this absolute time is lapsing, he accepts as a consequence that, whether or not an objective lapse of time exists (i.e. whether or not a time in the ordinary sense of the word exists), depends on the particular way in which matter and its motion are arranged in the world. This is not a straightforward contradiction; nevertheless, a philosophical view leading to such consequences can hardly be considered as satisfactory.

[13] At least if it required that successive experiences of one observer should never be simultaneous in the absolute time, or (which is equivalent) that the absolute time should agree in direction with the times of all possible observers. Without this requirement an absolute time always exists in an expanding (and homogeneous) world. Whenever I speak of an 'absolute' time, this of course is to be understood with the restriction explained in n. 9, which also applies to other possible definitions of an absolute time.

[14] The solution considered above only proves the compatibility with the general form of the field equations in which the value of the cosmological constant is left open; this value, however, which at present is not known with certainty, evidently forms part of the laws of nature. But other rotating solutions might make the result independent of the value of the cosmological constant (or rather of its vanishing or non-vanishing and of its sign, since its numerical value is of no consequence for this problem). At any rate these questions would first have to be answered in an unfavourable sense, before one could evidently think of drawing a conclusion like that of Jeans mentioned above. Note added 2 Sept. 1949: I have found in the meantime that for *every* value of the cosmological constant there do exist solutions, in which there is no world-time satisfying the requirement of n. 13. K.G.

NOTES ON THE CONTRIBUTORS

G. E. M. ANSCOMBE was Professor of Philosophy, Cambridge University until her retirement in 1986.

GARETH EVANS was Wilde Reader in Mental Philosophy, Oxford University.

MICHAEL FRIEDMAN is Professor of Philosophy, University of Illinois, Chicago.

KURT GÖDEL was Professor, The Institute for Advanced Study, Princeton.

DAVID KAPLAN is Professor of Philosophy, University of California, Los Angeles.

JERROLD J. KATZ is Distinguished Professor of Philosophy, The Graduate School, City University of New York.

NORMAN KRETZMANN is Susan Linn Sage Professor of Philosophy, Cornell University.

CHARLES PARSONS is Professor of Philosophy, Harvard University.

JOHN PERRY is Professor of Philosophy, Stanford University.

STANLEY ROSEN is Evan Pugh Professor of Philosophy, Pennsylvania State University.

LAWRENCE SKLAR is Professor of Philosophy, University of Michigan.

PALLE YOURGRAU is Assistant Professor of Philosophy, Brandeis University.

SELECT BIBLIOGRAPHY

1. GENERAL

ADAMS, R., 'Theories of Actuality', *Noûs*, 8 (1974), 211–31.
—— 'Primitive Thisness and Primitive Identity', *Journal of Philosophy*, 76 (1979), 5–26.
—— 'Actualism and Thisness', *Synthèse*, 49 (1981), 3–42.
BOER, S., and LYCAN, W., 'Knowing Who', *Philosophical Studies*, 28 (1975).
BURGE, T., 'Belief *De Re*', *Journal of Philosophy*, 75 (1978), 338–62.
—— '*Sinning* Against Frege', *Philosophical Review*, 88 (1979), 398–432.
BUTTERFIELD, J., 'Spatial and Temporal Parts', *Philosophical Quarterly*, 35: 138, (1985), 32–44.
CASTAÑEDA, H.-N., ' "He": A Study in the Logic of Self-Consciousness', *Ratio*, 8 (1966), 130–57.
—— 'Indicators and Quasi-Indicators', *American Philosophical Quarterly*, 4 (1967), 85–100.
—— 'Omniscience and Indexical Reference', 64: 7 (Apr. 1967), 203–10.
CHISHOLM, R., *The First Person: An Essay on Reference and Intentionality* (Minneapolis: University of Minnesota Press, 1981).
DAVIES, M., 'Actuality and Context Dependence I', *Analysis* (1983), 123–8.
DONNELLAN, K., 'Reference and Definite Descriptions', *Philosophical Review*, 75 (1966), 281–304.
DUMMETT, M., 'A Defense of McTaggart's Argument for the Unreality of Time', *Philosophical Review*, 69 (1960), 497–504.
—— 'Indexicality and *Oratio Obliqua*' in *The Interpretation of Frege's Philosophy*, (Cambridge, Mass., Harvard University Press, 1981.
EVANS, G., 'Does Tense Logic Rest on a Mistake', in *Collected Papers* (Oxford: Clarendon Press, 1985).
—— *The Varieties of Reference*, ed. J. McDowell (Oxford: Clarendon Press, 1982).
FITZGERALD, P., 'Stump and Kretzman on Time and Eternity', *Journal of Philosophy*, 82 (1985), 260–9.
FODOR, J., 'Methodological Solipsism Considered as a Research Strategy in Cognitive Psychology', *Journal of Behavioural and Brain Sciences*, 3 (1980), 63–73.
FORBES, G., 'Actuality and Context Dependence II', *Analysis* (1983), 128–33.
—— 'Frege and Indexicals', *Philosophical Review*, (1988).
FREGE, G., 'The Thought', in P. F. Strawson (ed.), *Philosophical Logic*, Oxford Readings in Philosophy (Oxford: Oxford University Press, 1967).
GALE, R., *The Language of Time* (London: Routledge and Kegan Paul, 1968).
—— ' "Here" and "Now" ', *The Monist*, 53 (1969), 396–409.
GEACH, P. T., *Mental Acts* (New York: Humanities Press, 1957), esp. 117–19.
HACKER, P. M. S., 'Frege and the Private Language Argument', *Idealistic Studies*, 2 (1972), 265–81.
KAPLAN, D., 'Quantifying In', in D. Davidson and G. Harman (eds.), *Words and Objections* (Dordrecht: Reidel, 1969), 206–42.

KAPLAN, D., 'On the Logic of Demonstratives', *The Journal of Philosophical Logic*, 8 (1979) 81–98; reprinted in N. Salmon and S. Soames (eds.) *Propositions and Attitudes* (New York: Oxford University Press, 1988).

—— 'Demonstratives', in J. Almog *et al.* (eds.), *Themes from Kaplan* (New York: Oxford University Press, 1989).

KENNY, A., 'The First Person', in C. Diamond and J. Teichman (eds.), *Intention and Intentionality: Essays in Honor of G. E. M. Anscombe* (New York: Cornell University Press, 1979), 3–13.

KIM, J., 'Critical Notice: Roderick Chisholm, *The First Person*', *Philosophy and Phenomenological Research*, 5: 46 (Mar. 1986), 483–507.

KRETZMANN, N., and STUMP, E., 'Eternity', *Journal of Philosophy*, 78: 8 (Aug. 1981), 429–58.

—— 'Atemporal Duration: A Reply to Fitzgerald' *Journal of Philosophy*, 84: 4 (Apr. 1987), 214–19.

KRIPKE, S., 'Speaker's Reference and Semantic Reference', in P. S. French *et al.* (eds.), *Contemporary Perspectives in the Philosophy of Language* (Minneapolis: University of Minnesota Press, 1979).

LEWIS, D., 'Anselm and Actuality', *Noûs*, 4 (1970), 175–88.

—— 'Attitudes *De Dicto* and *De Se*', *Philosophical Review*, 88 (1979) 513–43.

—— *On the Plurality of Worlds* (Oxford: Basil Blackwell, 1986).

LOAR, B., 'The Semantics of Singular Terms', *Philosophical Studies*, 30 (1976), 353–78.

LYCAN, W., and BOER, S., 'Knowing Who', *Philosophical Studies*, 28 (1975).

McDOWELL, J., '*De Re* Senses', *Philosophical Quarterly*, 34: 136 (July 1984), special issue: *Frege*, 283–94.

McGINN, C., 'The Mechanism of Reference', *Synthèse*, 49 (1981), 157–86.

—— 'The Structure of Content', in A. Woodfield (ed.), *Thought and Object* (Oxford: Clarendon Press, 1982), 207–58.

—— *The Subjective View* (Oxford: Clarendon Press, 1983).

MALCOLM, N., 'Whether "I" is a Referring Expression', in C. Diamond and J. Teichman (eds.), *Intention and Intentionality: Essays in Honor of G. E. M. Anscombe* (New York: Cornell University Press, 1979) 15–24.

MELLOR, D. H. *Real Time* (Cambridge: Cambridge University Press, 1981).

MOHANTY, J. N., 'Husserl, Frege and the Overcoming of Psychologism', in K. K. Cho (ed.), *Philosophy and Science in Phenomenological Perspective* (Dordrecht: Martinus Nijhoff, 1984), 143–52.

NAGEL, T., 'Subjective and Objective', in *Mortal Questions* (Cambridge: Cambridge University Press, 1979).

—— *The View From Nowhere* (New York: Oxford University Press, 1986).

PARSONS, C., 'Intuition in Constructive Mathematics', in J. Butterfield (ed.), *Language, Mind, and Logic* (Cambridge: Cambridge University Press, 1986), 211–29.

PARSONS, T., 'Frege's Hierarchies of Indirect Senses and the Paradox of Analysis', *Midwest Studies in Philosophy*, vi, ed. H. Wettstein *et al.* (Minneapolis: University of Minnesota Press, 1981).

PEACOCKE, C., 'Demonstrative Thought and Psychological Explanation', *Synthèse*, 49 (1981), 187–217.

PERRY, J., 'The Problem of the Essential Indexical', *Noûs*, 13 (1979), 3–21; reprinted in N. Salmon and S. Soames (eds.) *Propositions and Attitudes* (New York: Oxford University Press, 1988.

PUTNAM, H., 'Time and Physical Geometry', *Journal of Philosophy*, 64 (1967), 240–7.

—— 'The Meaning of "Meaning" ', in *Mind, Language, and Reality* (Cambridge: Cambridge University Press, 1975), 215–71.

QUINE, W. V. 'Identity, Ostension, and Hypostesis', in *From A Logical Point of View* (New York: Harper and Row, 1963), 65–79.

—— 'Quantifiers and Propositional Attitudes', *Journal of Philosophy*, 53 (1956), 177–87.

ROSEN, S., *The Quarrel Between Philosophy and Poetry* (New York: Routledge and Kegan Paul, 1988).

SAINSBURY, M., *Bertrand Russell* (London: Routledge and Kegan Paul, 1985).

—— 'Critical Notice: Gareth Evans, *The Varieties of Reference*', *Mind*, 94: 373 (1985), 120–42.

SCHIFFER, S., 'The Basis of Reference', *Erkenntnis*, 13 (1978), 171–206.

—— 'Indexicals and the Theory of Reference', *Synthèse*, 49 (1981), 43–100.

SHOEMAKER, S., *Self-Knowledge and Self-Identity* (Ithaca, NY: Cornell University Press, 1963).

SORABJI, R., *Time, Creation, and the Continuum* (Ithaca, NY: Cornell University Press, 1983).

SOSA, E., 'Propositional Attitudes *De Dicto* and *De Re*', *Journal of Philosophy*, 67 (1970), 883–96.

STALNAKER, R., 'Possible Worlds', *Noûs*, 10 (1976), 65–75.

—— 'Indexical Belief', *Synthèse*, 49 (1981), 129–51.

STEIN, H., 'On Einstein–Minkowski Space–Time', *Journal of Philosophy*, 65, I, (1968), 5–23.

STRAWSON, P., *Individuals* (New York: Doubleday, 1963).

STUMP, E., and KRETZMANN, N., 'Eternity', *Journal of Philosophy*, 78: 8 (Aug. 1981), 429–58.

—— 'Atemporal Duration: A Reply to Fitzgerald', *Journal of Philosophy*, 84: 4 (Apr. 1987), 214–19.

TAIT, W., 'Wittgenstein and the "Skeptical Paradoxes" ', *Journal of Philosophy*, 83: 9 (Sept. 1986), 475–88.

—— 'Truth and Proof: The Platonism of Mathematics', *Synthèse*, 69 (1986), 341–70.

VAN INWAGEN, P., 'Indexicality and Actuality', *Philosophical Review*, 89, (1980), 403–26.

WANG, H., 'Gödel and Wittgenstein', in *Logic, Philosophy of Science, and Epistemology*, Proceedings of the 11th International Wittgenstein Symposium, Aug. 1986 (Vienna: Hölder-Pickler-Tempsky, 1987).

—— *Reflections on Kurt Gödel* (Cambridge, Mass.: MIT Press, 1987).

WETTSTEIN, H., 'Demonstrative Reference and Definite Descriptions', *Philosophical Studies*, 40 (1981), 241–57.

—— 'How to Bridge the Gap Between Meaning and Reference', *Synthèse*, 58 (1984), 63–84.

WIGGINS, D., 'The Individuation of Things and Places', *Proceedings of the Aristotelian Society*, 38 (1963), 307–35.

YOURGRAU, P., 'On the Logic of Indeterminist Time', *Journal of Philosophy*, 82:10 (Oct. 1985), 548–59.

—— 'On Time and Actuality: The Dilemma of Privileged Position', *The British Journal for the Philosophy of Science*, 37 (1986), 405–17.

—Review Essay: Heo Wang, *Reflections on Kurt Gödel*, forthcoming, *Philosophy and Phenomenological Research*.

2. RECENT COLLECTIONS ON FREGE

Studies on Frege, i, ii, iii, ed. M. Schirn (Stuttgart: Frommann, 1976).
Philosophical Quarterly, 34: 136 (July 1984), special issue: Frege.
Frege Synthesized, ed. L. Hasparanta and J. Hintikka (Dordrecht: Reidel, 1986).
Notre Dame Journal of Formal Logic, 28: 1 (Jan. 1987), special issue: Frege.

3. RECENT COLLECTIONS ON REFERENCE AND BELIEF

Reference, Truth, and Reality, ed. M. Platts (London: Routledge and Kegan Paul, 1980).
Thought and Object, ed. A. Woodfield (Oxford: Clarendon Press, 1982).
Subject, Thought, and Context, ed. P. Pettit and J. McDowell (Oxford: Clarendon Press, 1986).
Belief, ed. R. J. Bogdan (Oxford: Clarendon Press, 1986).

INDEX OF NAMES

Agnew, Spiro 30
Alexandrov, P. 252
Almog, J. 7, 34
Altham, J. 144
Anderson, C. A. 224
Anscombe, G. E. M. 4, 94, 135–53, 170, 172–5
Anselm, St 240–1
Aquinas, Thomas 235, 239, 240, 245
Aristotle 3–4, 5, 16, 107, 161–2, 185–94, 235
Arnauld, A. 156
Audi, R. 104
Augustine, St 135, 136
Avicenna 238
Ayer, A. J. 146, 215

Barwise, J. 121
Beck, L. W. 159
Benacerraf, Paul 129, 131, 195, 199, 200, 210
Bernays, P. 200
Bierce, Ambrose 147
Black, M. 22, 50, 77, 200
Blackburn, S. 125
Blumberg, A. 215
Bouveresse, J. 71, 117
Brentano, Franz 98
Brose, Henry 215, 223
Brouwer, L. E. J. 207, 208
Burge, Tyler 98, 100, 126
Burks, A. W. 57
Butterfield, J. 6
Butts, R. E. 195
Byrd, Mike 99, 112, 125, 129, 130

Cantor, Georg 131, 197
Carnap, Rudolf 14, 30, 37, 48, 156–9, 166, 216, 223–6, 229–30
Carroll, Lewis 179–80
Cartan, E. 222
Cassirer, E. 219, 222, 223, 225
Castaneda, H.-N. 7, 61, 67, 88, 136, 236, 245
Caton, C. 11
Chandler, Hugh 238
Chihara, C. 201, 209
Chomsky, Noam 157, 164
Church, A. 40, 121
Code, A. 125
Coffa, Alberto 216
Cohen, R. S. 223
Cole, Peter 11
Copernicus 52, 220

Davidson, D. 74, 78, 92, 103
Demopoulos, W. 224
Descartes, René 4–5, 93, 99, 112, 114, 135–6, 140, 144, 146–7, 151, 154–81, 187, 196, 246
Dickoff, J. 156
Donnellan, Keith S. 7, 11, 12–13, 22, 25, 29–30, 99, 108, 111
Dretske, F. 104, 110, 113
Dummett, Michael 50, 58, 72–3, 74, 76, 78, 84, 118, 213

Earman, J. 260
Einstein, Albert 2, 3, 5, 217–22, 225, 249–50, 263
Euclid 220, 222
Evans, Gareth 8, 71–96, 97, 103, 105–6, 111, 115, 117, 118, 125

Feigl, H. 22, 23
Field, Hartry 112, 209
Fitzgerald, P. 219, 220
Fodor, J. 98
Follesdal, Dagfinn 60, 149
Fonda, Jane 166
Frankfurt, H. G. 180, 236
Frege, Gottlob 2, 3, 6–7, 8, 22, 23, 39–43, 45, 50–70, 71–93, 97, 100, 102, 103, 105, 112, 116–32, 137, 142, 158–60, 161, 165–67, 200, 215, 219, 230
Freud, Sigmund 99
Freund, J. 223
Friedman, Michael 5, 108, 215–31

Galileo 220
Gassendi, P. 180
Geach, P. 22, 50, 77, 109, 135, 170–2, 173–4
Gilson, E. 238
Ginet, C. 236
Glymour, C. 260
Gödel, Kurt 2–3, 6, 8, 119, 121, 125, 129, 131, 132, 195–6, 197, 199, 214, 229, 261–5
Goldfarb, Warren 217, 229
Goodman, Nelson 204
Grünbaum, A. 249
Guenther, F. 74
Guenther–Reutter, M. 74
Guttenplan, S. 94, 135, 149, 170

Haldane, E. 154
Harman, G. 78, 103
Healey, R. 247

Hegel, Georg 105, 187, 191, 193
Heidegger, Martin 193
Heimson 62, 68
Helmholtz, H. 216
Hempel, C. 229
Hermes, H. 77, 125
Heyting, A. 207
Hilbert, David 197, 203, 216, 219, 223, 229
Hintikka, J. 11, 12–13, 45, 92, 195, 197
Hume, David 62–3, 66, 68, 93, 94, 95, 96, 148, 216, 229
Husserl, Edmund 197, 198, 203, 205, 206

James, P. 156
James, William 152–3
Jeans, James 263, 265
Jesus 116

Kamali, S. A. 238
Kambartel, F. 77
Kant, Immanuel 3, 6, 93, 98, 100–2, 106, 113, 128, 159–61, 165–68, 185–6, 188, 197, 199–200, 203, 208, 216, 218–20, 223–5, 230, 261
Kaplan, David 7, 11–32, 34–49, 67, 71–2, 80, 84, 87, 92, 96, 103, 106, 115, 116, 125, 127, 131–2
Katz, Jerrold J. 1, 4–5, 129, 154–81
Kaulbach, F. 77
Kenny, A. 170
Kepler, Johann 218
Klemke, E. D. 50, 98
Kretschmann, E. 222
Kretzmann, Norman 3–4, 235–46
Kripke, Saul 38, 47, 78, 99, 102, 103, 105–6, 109–13, 114, 116, 118, 124, 135, 144

Leibniz, Gottfried 101, 102, 130, 159, 200, 221
Lewis, C. I. 224
Lewis, C. S. 126
Lewis, David 2
Lichtenberg, G. C. 173, 175, 176, 177–8
Lincoln, Abraham 116
Linsky, L. 11, 106
Locke, John 141, 206
Loewer, B. 98
Long, Peter 77, 78
Lorentz, H. 219, 220
Lucretius 185

McCord, Marilyn 236
McDowell, John 71, 74, 75, 103, 104
McGinn, Colin 4, 98, 99
McGuinness, B. 128
Mach, Ernst 216–19, 221–3, 229, 250

McTaggart, J. M. E. 131, 132, 142, 261
Maddy, Penelope 129, 130
Malament, D. 2, 252, 260
Marx, Karl 99
Matthews, Gareth 180, 236
Maxwell, J. 217
Mellor, D. H. 3
Michelson, A. A. 250
Minkowski, H. 251, 252, 259, 261
Mohr, R. D. 119
Mongré, P. 262
Montague, R. 27
Moore, G. E. 94
Moravcsik, J. 11
Morgenbesser, S. 197
Morley, S. G. 250
Morris, T. V. 3
Moses 109–10
Mulder, H. L. 107

Nagel, Thomas 4
Nakhnikian, G. 236
Natorp, P. 219
Neumann, Johann von 200
Neurath, O. 229
Newton, Isaac 218, 220, 222
Nietzsche, Friedrich 100, 128

Ockham, William of 237–9, 240, 245

Parmenides 2, 3, 261
Parret, H. 71, 117
Parsons, Charles 6, 195–214
Peacocke, C. 98
Perry, John 3, 7, 8, 23, 34, 41, 43, 50–72, 79–81, 88–96, 121, 131–2
Petzoldt, J. 219, 223
Planck, Max 216
Plato 2, 4, 5, 100, 104, 106, 107, 109, 113, 114, 117, 120, 122, 123, 125, 126, 129, 131, 187, 188, 192, 193, 235
Poincaré, Jules 221, 223
Ptolemy 220
Putnam, H. 41, 99, 100–2, 195, 201, 247, 248, 253, 256, 258

Quine, W. V. 22, 25–6, 48, 113, 156–8, 160, 166, 200–2, 231
Quinton, A. M. 50
Quinton, M. 50

Rapaport, William 129
Reichenbach, H. 216, 223, 249
Reichenbach, M. 223
Ricketts, Thomas 229
Riemann, B. 251

Rietdijk, C. 247, 258
Rosen, Stanley 5, 100, 125, 185–94
Ross, G. R. T. 154
Rowe, W. L. 236
Russell, Bertrand 5–6, 13–18, 75, 78, 103, 106, 107, 119–22, 124, 125, 127–9, 140, 147, 208, 215–18, 224, 229

Sainsbury, Mark 5
Salmon, Nathan 11, 34, 100, 102, 103, 122–3, 126–7, 128
Savage, C. W. 224
Schilpp, P. A. 132, 200, 261
Schlick, Moritz 5, 107, 108, 215–31
Schröder, E. 77
Schwartz, S. 97, 108
Scott, Dana 49
Sellars, W. 22
Sharvy, R. 107
Shoemaker, S. 236
Sklar, Lawrence 3, 102, 247–60
Smith, G. E. 156
Smith, N. K. 161
Soames, S. 11, 34
Socrates 189, 194
Spinoza, Baruch 149
Stachet, J. 260
Stalnaker, R. 105
Stein, H. 2
Steiner, Mark 196
Stoothoff, R. H. 50
Strawson, P. 38, 50, 100, 102, 118
Stump, Eleanor 3
Suppes, P. 11, 197

Tait, W. 6, 100
Tarski, Alfred 130
Thomason, Richmond 131
Thucydides 136

Van Heijenoort, J. 130
Van Inwagen, P. 105
Velde-Schlick, B. F. B. van de 107

Wainwright, W. 236
Wang, Hao 6
Weierstrass, K. 219
Weinberger, Caspar 165
Wettstein, Howard 34, 98
Weyl, Hermann 101, 197, 222
Whewell, William 246
White, M. 197
White, Roger 77, 78
Wilson, Margaret 154, 178
Wittgenstein, Ludwig 4, 5, 6, 8, 93, 94, 104, 105, 107, 109–10, 113–14, 121, 125, 128, 215, 216, 228, 230, 231
Woodfield, A. 98

Xenophon 194

Yourgrau, Palle 2, 97–132

Zermelo, E. 202

Index compiled by Peva Keane